ENGLISH BOOKS & READERS
II
1558 to 1603

I have thought it worth my poore labour, to take some paynes heerin, (though that the more learned sort would not willingly imploy their labour in the same,) to gather a Catalogue in such sort as I can, of the Bookes Printed in our owne tongue; which I doe hope will be delightsome to all English men that be learned, or desirous of learning: for hereby they may know even in their studies, what Bookes are eyther by our own Countrymen written, or translated out of any other language, that those which desire to set foorth more Bookes for the benefit of their Countrey, may see what is already extant upon any argument.

A. MAUNSELL, *The Seconde Parte of the Catalogue of English Printed Bookes (1595)*

ENGLISH BOOKS & READERS 1558 to 1603

BEING A STUDY IN
THE HISTORY OF THE BOOK TRADE
IN THE REIGN OF ELIZABETH I

BY

H. S. BENNETT

*Fellow of the British Academy and formerly Reader in English in the
University of Cambridge*

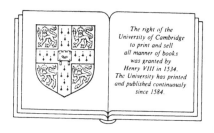

CAMBRIDGE UNIVERSITY PRESS

Cambridge
New York   Port Chester
Melbourne   Sydney

CAMBRIDGE UNIVERSITY PRESS
Cambridge, New York, Melbourne, Madrid, Cape Town, Singapore,
São Paulo, Delhi, Dubai, Tokyo

Cambridge University Press
The Edinburgh Building, Cambridge CB2 8RU, UK

Published in the United States of America by Cambridge University Press, New York

www.cambridge.org
Information on this title: www.cambridge.org/9780521379892

© Cambridge University Press 1965

This publication is in copyright. Subject to statutory exception
and to the provisions of relevant collective licensing agreements,
no reproduction of any part may take place without the written
permission of Cambridge University Press.

First published 1965
First paperback edition 1989
Re-issued in this digitally printed version 2009

A catalogue record for this publication is available from the British Library

Library of Congress Catalogue Card Number: 52-12000

ISBN 978-0-521-37988-5 paperback (volume 1)
ISBN 978-0-521-37989-2 paperback (volume 2)
ISBN 978-0-521-37990-8 paperback (volume 3)
ISBN 978-0-521-37991-5 paperback (3 volume set)

Cambridge University Press has no responsibility for the persistence or
accuracy of URLs for external or third-party internet websites referred to in
this publication, and does not guarantee that any content on such websites is,
or will remain, accurate or appropriate.

TO
JOHN U. NEF
PROFESSOR OF ECONOMIC HISTORY AND
CHAIRMAN OF THE COMMITTEE ON SOCIAL THOUGHT
IN THE UNIVERSITY OF CHICAGO

PREFACE

'I wish that all that I have written heretofore were by me revised, and that I might have license and leysure to runne them over againe, thereby to make them a little more substantiall if my habilitie served thereto.' So wrote Edward Hake in 1579, and his words must often have been echoed by many a writer as he came to the end of his work and looked back over the years of research and preparation that had gone to its making. What was once dark and confused is now seen in clearer perspective, and he realizes that a better arrangement of his material and a different emphasis here and there would have brought out his argument more clearly. 'But at my back I alwaies hear | Times winged chariot hurrying near', and what might have seemed possible and even prudent for a first book does not have the same cogency for a last.

This volume follows fairly closely the pattern of my earlier work which dealt with the provision of books from the time of Caxton until the death of Mary. In this volume, which covers the reign of Elizabeth I only, my object has been to survey the printed output of her reign in the hope that it would provide a conspectus of the kind of matters that interested people at that time. It does not attempt to be all inclusive, but at the same time it shows the many ways in which the printers and booksellers tried to serve the reading public. To take but one example: the massive output of books concerning religion in its many phases is only dealt with selectively. Many kinds of religious literature are no more than mentioned, but a few outstanding categories are examined in detail in order that the reader may appreciate the way in which supply and demand worked. To this end much attention has been paid to what can be learned from the prefaces and other matter with which the authors and printers introduce their books, since it is here that we see most clearly what were the reasons and the hopes and

PREFACE

fears that animated writers, and encouraged printers to put these books on the market.

It is obvious that a book of this nature depends very largely on the labours of others who have assembled the materials of various kinds and in various ways which have made it possible for us to realize what was the exact contribution made by authors and printers in that age. First in importance there is the *Short-title Catalogue* (*STC*), edited by A. W. Pollard and G. R. Redgrave for the Bibliographical Society in 1926, from which the titles and authors of most books written in the period 1558–1603 can be found. A revised edition of this is in active preparation by Professor William A. Jackson and Dr F. S. Ferguson which will contain many hundreds of additional titles, but even without these the general lines of the picture are clear enough.[1] Next in importance there is the re-arrangement of the alphabetical items of the *STC* in chronological sequence, so that it is possible to see what was the output of books in any given year. This most useful work we owe to the enterprise of the Research Department of the Huntington Library of San Marino, California, and in 1941 Professor William A. Jackson was permitted to have the items copied on to cards, a number of which he made available for use in England. Thirdly there is another arrangement of the *STC* by Dr Paul G. Morrison of the University of Chicago, in which the items were placed under the names of their respective printers, publishers and booksellers in alphabetical order.[2] With these three aids it is now possible to arrange the books of the period in several different ways, and it would be impossible to overestimate the value of these three works to all students of our early printed books. Without them this book could not have been written.

[1] Shortly before his death in October 1964 Professor Jackson wrote saying that 'the new edition would average more than 30% of additions for the whole period 1475–1640 with I estimate at least ten per cent of new titles'.

[2] Paul G. Morrison, *Index of Printers, Publishers and Booksellers* (Bibliographical Society of the University of Virginia, Charlottesville, Virginia, 1950).

PREFACE

Great libraries are, of course, an indispensable part of any research such as this, and it is a pleasure to record my thanks and obligations to such institutions, both here and in the United States. Those two noble institutions, the Huntington Library and the Folger Library at Washington, D.C., honoured me by making it possible for me to work for considerable periods in their great collections, and it would be difficult to exaggerate the stimulus that was provided by them and by the kindness and expert help given in many ways by their staffs. In England my main sources of information have been found in the library of the British Museum and in the Cambridge University Library, and to my many friends in both I am deeply indebted, the more so since the nature of my inquiries put heavy strains on their time and patience.

In the many quotations that I have made from the books of the period certain liberties have been taken. I have endeavoured to retain the spelling of the originals, although the vagaries of the compositor have sometimes, I fear, escaped me. Capitalization and punctuation have often been modified to suit the needs of present-day readers; *i* and *u* have replaced *j* and *v* in accordance with modern usage, while occasionally an overlong paragraph has been broken up for the ease of reading.

According to the conventions which are to be used in the new edition of the *STC* items not recorded in the first edition are interpolated by means of the decimal system, and if an item precedes one that is already in the *STC* it is given a decimal addition to the preceding number.

H.S.B.

CAMBRIDGE
NOVEMBER 1964

CONTENTS

Preface		*page* vii
Introduction		xiii
Chapter I	The inception of a book	1
II	Patronage	30
III	The regulation of the book trade	56
IV	Translations and translators	87
V	The variety of books	112
VI	Printers and booksellers	259
Bibliography		301
Index		306

INTRODUCTION

Although there have been many books dealing with 'Elizabethan literature', few of them have been concerned with anything more than those writings in verse or prose of an imaginative, philosophical, or religious nature that are still read by students and lovers of English letters. While it is true that such works comprised a large proportion of the total output of the presses it leaves unnoticed a far larger body of writings dealing with such matters as technical affairs, history or geography, everyday sports and pastimes, agriculture, medicine and so on. The object of this present work is to make a survey of the whole of the printed matter (other than ephemera, such as proclamations, lottery tickets, etc.) in the hope of showing the many ways in which the printer put at the disposal of readers a wealth of matter touching almost every side of their daily life, both intellectual and practical.

Such a survey, of course, is not primarily concerned with the literary value of the works that were produced. No attempt is therefore made to emphasize the high literary quality of some writers in this period—their wine needs no bush. For this study it is the number and variety of the works printed that is important. It is from these things that we are able to form some impression of the literacy of the age, and also of the way in which men's minds were working.

A brief summary of the many kinds of reading matter which the printers put out in Elizabeth's reign will serve to indicate the nature of the problem, and we may well begin by looking at the religious works, since these made the largest demands on the printers. As would be expected, the Bible, the New Testament and the Prayer Book kept a number of printers busy, while ancillary aids to devotion, such as commentaries on various books of the Bible, devotional works, catechisms and books of private prayer helped the devout to understand and follow the

INTRODUCTION

teaching that their ministers and others put before them. The sermon was a powerful weapon of the Protestants, and the number of these printed was very great. Outstanding continental, as well as English, preachers great and small were laid under contribution, and single sermons could be bought for a few pence, while for the well-to-do there were also the folio volumes, some of them containing over one hundred sermons. These sermons in their various forms were among the commonest features on the booksellers' stalls, and I think that it may be said with confidence that over two thousand sermons were put into print during this period, many of them being reprinted again and again. Another less agreeable feature of the religious output of this age was the spate of controversial works that never ceased to make their impassioned appeals to the various religious bodies all struggling for a hearing and all eager to display the faults, weaknesses, heresies and other failings of their opponents.

For the more sober minded there were also a number of works from which they could obtain guidance in their quest for the good life. 'The prudent workes of auncient Cato', it was hoped, would not merely 'stirre men... to like wisedome and knowledge', but would also 'instructe them in diverse factes of worldely pollicies whereby thei maie avoide daiely dangers'.[1] These words are the clue to much literature of this kind. The Elizabethans saw in the classical authors the theory and practice of 'how to live', and many moral treatises of the ancients were translated to this end. The study of history was also encouraged, since, as Professor L. B. Campbell writes, 'History... was increasingly consulted for its political precedents, not only in the law courts but also in everyday life. Nations and rulers and subjects might, it was believed, perceive in history the path of political virtue that led to national peace and prosperity.'[2]

[1] *STC* 4854, *Preceptes of Cato* (1553), sig. L2.
[2] 'Elizabethan Historical Patterns', *Huntington Library Quarterly* (1938), vol. I, p. 137.

INTRODUCTION

The learned professions other than the clergy were also catered for by the printers. The lawyers found ready to hand volumes of the *Statutes of the Realm*, or could conveniently consult the decisions of the courts from the time of Edward III by turning to one of the many *Year Books* that were constantly being printed by Richard Tottell. A whole series of books helped them to get their pleadings in the correct form, or instructed them in the many precedents of which they had to take notice if they were to get an hearing. Then again, the local magistrate was helped by little books advising him how to hold a court, or setting out the duties of constables and other minor officials.

Medical books of all kinds were constantly being printed and many of them were meant for the layman, some to be used 'in time of necessity when no learned Phisican is at hand'. Many of these cheap little books had an enormous circulation and were reprinted again and again. They were often little more than books of receipts, or of simple remedies which could be made from herbs and flowers, or they gave their readers a few simple rules of hygiene and diet. The endemic nature of the plague naturally produced a constant supply of books telling the goodman what steps to take should the fearful disease come upon his family.

Information and instruction were not confined to these matters. Indeed, the second half of the century saw a marked increase in the number of books giving information on a great variety of things. The old-fashioned encyclopaedias were not so much in use, though the great medieval encyclopaedia of Bartholomew was reprinted with very few additions by Stephen Batman in 1582. Most men found it more convenient to ask for a small book dealing with the subject in which they were interested, so that they could study at leisure, for example, such subjects as how to keep bees or silkworms, how to carve and serve at table, or how to make dyes and paints. Cookery books helped the housewife, while almanacs and prognostications contained much useful information, not only on the dates

INTRODUCTION

of various events, but also on how to judge the weather, or when it was a suitable time for blood letting and so on. Small books instructed the countryman in the arts of grafting and planting; he could read how to go about the various rural occupations throughout the year, while his betters could improve their knowledge of hunting, hawking, and horsemanship, or of how to swim or shoot at the butts.

Other helps to learning were also plentiful. There were books on arithmetic and geometry, the use of the spheres, the compass and the astrolabe. Manuals of seamanship were at hand for those trading in home waters and further afield. Books were forthcoming which taught men how to keep accounts, how to write letters for all kinds of emergencies, how to sing and play musical instruments, how to cultivate the memory and how to acquire a foreign language. No man could well complain in Elizabethan England that knowledge was hidden from him. Once he had learned to read, the way was open, and much that had hitherto been available in a foreign tongue only was given an English dress, for the translator was very much in evidence throughout the reign and both famous and little known authors were 'englished'. Men were eager to read for themselves the great works of antiquity, while books from French, German, Spanish and other tongues found a ready market, so that something like twenty per cent of the total publications of the reign were translations and, while many of them were of passing interest, others have remained as literary masterpieces.

Though travel was reserved for the few, the printing press opened up the way to Cathay, the North-west Passage, the Spanish Main, and many other places that intrepid English seamen and travellers had reached. Men could travel in imagination with these voyagers, fight with them, experience the ardours of the passage round the Horn or the Cape, suffer the pangs of hunger and exhaustion as they read of the adventures of those many men whose pens were so active, and who while on their journeys or on their return recorded for their country-

INTRODUCTION

men what they had done and suffered in the name of the Queen. As one writer put it, men believed that their 'countrymen would be no less earnest and desirous to learne and enquire, than attentive to knowe and heare of al our travelles, troubles, toyles and daungers, as of our late adventures and good successes'. Hakluyt's *Voyages* remain as an imperishable monument to this passion for overseas adventure, in which Hakluyt reproduced much that had already appeared in print as well as much that he collected from seamen and others who had written down their adventures, but had not hitherto attempted to put them into print.

Nor did events nearer home go unrecorded. For instance, men were anxious to hear of the fortunes of those embarking on the Northern Rebellion of 1569–70, and many ballads and pamphlets enlightened them, as did others in the stirring days of the summer of 1588 when the Armada made its abortive attempt. The Wars of Religion in France and the Low Countries called forth a host of pieces, large and small, in which the varying fortunes of the contending parties were reported, often by eyewitnesses of the events, and in any case by reports written soon after the happenings they recorded had taken place. Often, sent by one friend to another, they had little literary form or grace, but had to make up for these shortcomings by their obvious immediacy and straightforward reporting. They formed an important part of the stock in trade of the booksellers who knew that their clientele would expect to find on the stalls 'hot news' constantly available.

News of another kind was also much in demand, and the ballad writers and the cheap pamphleteers poured out a supply of pieces in which were set forth such things as monstrous births, strange creatures, or unusual happenings which could only be attributed to supernatural powers. The doings of those possessed, the evil practices of witches and their exposure and punishment made popular reading. Then again, there was a steady output of works dealing with the apprehension, trial and execution of traitors and other enemies of the State, and little

INTRODUCTION

was spared the reader in setting forth the gory details of the final moments of such men. Sometimes it was only a crude woodcut and a few shambling verses which told the story, but at others the printer had got hold of a well put together account of a trial, which showed that the writer had been present at the events he narrated and at times had had access to documentary materials in writing his story.

It goes without saying that the Elizabethans did not spend all their time in the pursuit of salvation, or of knowledge, or of health. From time to time pleasure was their object, and they turned to song and dance, to revels and plays, to poetry and romance, to realistic fiction and improving stories. The printers welcomed this and hastened to supply what was wanted. We have only to turn to the variety of works that they produced to see this. Anthologies, long and short poems, sonnet sequences, translations of some of the great classical works, long romantic stories such as the *Arcadia* or *Euphues*, a whole series of the great Spanish chivalric romances—these and many more filled the leisure hours of the more educated classes, while the others were entertained by ballads and verses of little literary merit, but sufficing to hold an audience of 'the children from play, and the old men from the chimney corner'. Towards the end of the century, the racy vivid writings of Greene, Nashe and others fired the imaginations of those that read them, and were carried along by the verve and homely realism of the narrative. At the same time, the growing interest in the drama was reflected in the number of printed copies of the plays that appeared on the market, and by the way in which many of them were reprinted a number of times.

Here indeed was God's plenty, and in the chapters that follow an attempt is made to show how the printers, booksellers and their allies each played their part in making this very diverse mass of reading matter readily available to the Elizabethan reading public.

CHAPTER I

THE INCEPTION OF A BOOK

When we consider the vast output by scholars and others concerning the age of Shakespeare, it is surprising to find how little we know about the actual conditions which were the necessary accompaniment of the printing and publication of the works which have given such lustre to the Elizabethan age. It is true that bibliographers and others have unravelled many of the secrets of the day-to-day practices of the printing house, and have been able to assemble the names and publications of a great many printers and publishers of that time.[1] But this is to be at the far end of the assembly line so to speak, and to view the product at the moment of its appearance on the stalls of the booksellers. What led up to this? What were the many preliminaries that had to be gone through before this? Printers were not in business for the sake of their health, but in order to earn a living, just as were their neighbours whose stalls displayed clothes or utensils for daily use. And in order to live it was necessary for them to know what response there was likely to be for the wares that they had printed and now exposed for sale. Even with all the resources of modern sales research and technique, no publisher can be sure before publication whether or no a work will sell well enough to make a profit or even to make ends meet. When printing was still in its infancy, the problem was much more acute, for it was well nigh impossible to gauge the public taste with any certainty, except for a limited kind of book, and the publisher had to take the risk of being left with much of the edition on his hands or, if he was specially cautious and lucky, he might get others to underwrite part or all of the expenses of publication.

[1] See the Bibliography at p. 301 *s.v.* Allison and Rogers, Arber, Blagden, Greg, Greg and Boswell, Herbert, Plomer, Pollard and Redgrave.

All Elizabethan printers were aware of these risks, and did what they could to keep them within bounds. Some, for instance, had established themselves as reliable printers of necessary text-books such as the elementary grammars which all grammar-school boys needed, while others printed the essential books that students and practitioners of the law were obliged to have. The most fortunate were lucky enough to hold a patent from the Sovereign which enabled them and no one else to print a certain class of book, such as almanacs and prognostications, and so on.[1] But for the most part, they had to rely on their knowledge of the trade, that is on the demand for this or that class of book and on the size and reliability of the reading public.

To speak of the reading public is to speak of a body about which we are very imperfectly informed. The output of books during the reign of Elizabeth makes it clear that reading was no longer the prerogative of a few, but at the same time we cannot estimate with any accuracy what percentage of the population could read. The detailed evidence is slender and contradictory, some writers leading us to think that a great proportion of people could read, while others suggest it was a minority. Since the art of printing was still confined almost exclusively to London, it was wellnigh impossible for the printers to estimate what demand there might be for their wares in the provinces, and it is possible that it was left to the middleman who travelled to the various fairs and markets up and down the country to take the risk of having a number of books left on his hands. But it may well be that such men went out on their rounds on the understanding that they could return to the printer such books as remained unsold at the end of their tour. I do not know.

In any case, the nature and extent of the reading public remained in doubt. We may imagine that some help was obtained from prospective customers as they turned over the books on the stalls, and asked for what they could not see

See pp. 64–8.

displayed and whether it was available in print. English printers on the whole were slow in printing editions of works in foreign languages, but did at times put forth translations as the result of inquiries which evidently convinced them that the book was a fair business risk. We may take it that then, as now, the printer's list at any given time represents the combined results of his own endeavours to find saleable wares, the urgent representations of men whose opinions he trusted, the works of authors who were willing to contribute toward the costs of publication and so on.

We can, I believe, get a little closer to the day-to-day operations of these people than has been done before by looking at what both authors and printers prefixed to the text concerning the reasons that caused them to put any given book into print, and while we may not always be able to accept their evidence as the whole (or at times, even as part) of the truth, in many cases there is no reason to disbelieve what they say.

'Never in any age were books more sought for and better esteemed...than in this our flourishing age',[1] we are told by a contemporary, so that as a result they are 'more in number than the leisure of any man of calling will permitte him to reade, or the strength of any ordinary memorie can be able to beare away'.[2] Some men, however, did not take this non-committal view of the output. They disliked both the number and the nature of the books which they saw around them. They were the wrong sort of books, they said, and the bad kept out the good. This point of view is forcibly expressed in the following outburst:

We live in a printing age, wherein there is no man either so vainely, or factiously, or filthily disposed, but there are crept out of all sorts unauthorized authors, to fill and fit his humor, and if a man's devotion

---

[1] *STC* 21744, F. Sansovino, *The quintesence of Wit* (1590), trans. R. Hitchcock, sig. A 2.

[2] *STC* 7539, S. Egerton, *A lecture preached...at the Blacke-friers, 1589* (1603), sig. A 3ᵛ. See also, *STC* 25405 (1578), sig. A 3; 13797 (1567), sig. A 2; 13524 (1577), sig. A 3ᵛ.

serve him not to goe to the Church of God, he neede but repayre to a Stationers shop and reade a sermon of the divels: I loath to speake it, [yet] every red-nosed rimester is an author, every drunken mans dreame is a booke, and he whose talent of little wit is hardly worth a farthing, yet layeth about him so outragiously, as if all Helicon had run through his pen, in a word, scarce can a cat looke out of a gutter, but out starts a halfpenny Chronicler, and presently *A propper new ballet of a strange sight is* endited. What publishing of frivolous and scurrilous Prognostications? as if Will Sommers were againe revived: what counterfeiting and cogging of prodigious and fabulous monsters? as if they labored to exceede the Poet in his Metamorphosis; what lascivious, unhonest, and amorous discourses...& yet they shame not to subscribe, 'by a Graduate of Cambridge, in Artibus Magister,' as if men should judge of the fruites of Art by the ragges and parings of wit.[1]

This rhetorical outburst must be considerably discounted, no doubt, but a factual survey of the nature and quality of the output shows that it was indeed 'a printing age', and that to escape into print was not very difficult, so eager were the printers and their associates to provide the public with reading matter. We have only to turn and look at the entries made by the printers in the *Stationers' Register* to see how they were on the *qui vive* to exploit every turn of the national fortunes, or to try for a quick profit out of some disaster, traveller's tale, or startling adventure overseas. More sober printers showed greater restraint and were more careful in entering a book in the *Register* as a preliminary to publication, but even so, desire often outran performance and many of the works never came to fruition.[2] The hopes of the printers, however, remain on record, and are a valuable indication of the activity that there was in the world of books. So much was this so that one man speaks of himself as being 'infected with the common contagion of our time, whiche maketh us small smatters (*sic*) in good letters like unto Aesopes Ape, ambitiously to bring

[1] *STC* 24913, R. W., *Martine Mar-Sixtus* (1591), sig. A3ᵛ. See also *STC* 10572 (1577), sig. ¶4.
[2] See p. 62.

abroade, and shewe unto all men the deformed broode of our witlesse braines'.[1]

A good example may be seen in the work of Austin Saker entitled *Narbonus. The Laberynth of Libertie. Very pleasant for young Gentlemen to peruse and passing profitable for them to prosecute.* Despite this, in his preface he writes:

> I stood marvailing, Gentlemen, after the writing of this troublesome trashe, and the finishing of this tedious travaile...I thought my booke might as well lie in a shop as other ballads which stand at sale: yet he that puts anything in print to the end to have it praised is like him that comes into a Church to have his bravery noted.[2]

Although there was a demand for printed matter of every description, a number of writers hesitated before venturing into print.[3] This arose in part from a feeling that it was indecorous for the work to be open to the criticism of every Tom, Dick, and Harry, or to the onslaughts of those whose scholarship or private interests caused them to look with disfavour on newcomers into their preserves. To protect themselves against such possible enemies men had created a number of defences. They dedicated their works to influential patrons in the hope that they might thus be protected from attack, and at the same time they stressed their limitations as writers and asked for the reader's indulgence. Both these conventions have a long history, going back to the manuscript period of writing, but the advent of printing had greatly increased the number of writers and had encouraged them to think that a protector was wellnigh a necessity. How much this was a sincerely felt belief it is hard to know, but the majority of writers played for safety and dedicated their work to a patron, even though in some cases they had to confess that he was a stranger to them.

In addressing his patron, or in an address to the reader, the writer frequently indulges in every variety of self-abasement.

---

[1] *STC* 3091 J. Bishop, *Beautifull Blossomes* (1577), sig. ¶ 2ᵛ.
[2] *STC* 21593 (1580), sig. A 4.
[3] For a discussion of this topic, see 'The Stigma of Print', by J. W. Saunders, in *Essays in Criticism*, vol. 1 (1951), pp. 139 ff.

Authors beg to 'shroude my simplicitie under the flag of thy protection', or confess to 'lacke such eloquence and learning as is to be required', or plead guilty to the 'baseness of the form of writing'.[1] 'Methinks the lady doth protest too much', and it may not be unreasonable to assume that much of this self-denigration meant very little, and was inserted by many authors more because custom demanded it, than as an expression of any deeply felt conviction of unworthiness.

When we turn to consider both the volume and the degree of hostile criticism that the average author had to face, the position suggested by many authors appears to be even more unreal. Nothing is more common than to find authors appealing for protection against the attacks of 'lewd and viperous carpers', or against the 'biting furies of snuffling detractors', well-known enemies of the writer, known as the sons of Zoilus or of Momus. Bishop Bale, with his characteristic vigour, describes one such as:

this cruell carper and malicious quarreller [who] leaveth no mans worke unrebuked, ministre it never so muche godlynesse. But lyke as rust, mothes, maggottes, cankers, catterpillers, with other vyle vermine corrupt all that is to the use of man, so doth this enemye, destroye both name and worke, only for the avancement of his owne preciouse person.[2]

These 'malignant, ready, backbiters' with their 'sharpe morosities and biting cavils, every Momus being ready to deface the good intention of the writer, so that he will make of a sillible a worde, of a worde a sentence, and of each sentence misconstrue sence', were held up as the enemies of the ordinary writer, so that as Ludowick Lloyd asserts:

Greater is the attempt of any simple booke writer to hazarde himselfe to present peril to encounter with divers men with a pen in his hande than the valiaunt Perithus with Cerebus, or...jollie

---

[1] For fuller treatment see chapter II.
[2] *STC* 1299, *The Ymage of both Churches* (1550), sig. a2ᵛ.

champiouns with swordes drawne, for that they fought with one apiece, and that before their faces, and the simple writer [fights] with themselves, and they behinde his backe slaunder him.[1]

These are but few of the many passages that might be quoted to show the outlook which many authors at this time appeared to hold concerning the perils they faced: nevertheless, however bitter were the alleged attacks of the Zoili, they certainly at times got as good as they gave from their victims, who vied one with the other in seeking epithets and abuse which they felt suitable to describe their opponents. In a vigorous outburst Francis Sabie declares that:

If squint eyed Zoylus, or splay-footed Momus shall carpe, or find fault, let them not, like angrie dogs, also beslaver with their jawes the stone cast at them; I meane teare in sunder my faultlesse Papers, but rather have accesse unto mee their Author who will straightwayes fetch forth an olde rust-eaten halberd, which saw no sun these seven yeares, wherewith I will either massacre their deformed limmes, or (if they speake mee faire) garde them safely to Coldharbour colledge, where they may have one whole monthes leysure to studie their backbiting arte.[2]

Other writers, such as John Weever in his *Faunus and Melliflora* (1600), took a more light-hearted view of the enemy when he wrote:

> Methinks I heare some foule-mouthed Momus say,
> What have we here, a shepheards roundelay?
> More love tricks yet? Will this geare never end?
> But slight lascivious toyes must still be pend?
> Content thee Momus, thou hast lost thy sight,
> For this is neither vaine, obscene, nor slight.[3]

---

[1] *STC* 16624, *The Pilgrimage of Princes* [1573], sig. **2.
[2] *STC* 21536, F. Sabie, *Flora's fortune* (1595), sig. A 2ᵛ.
[3] *STC* 25225 (1600), sig. A 4. And see the advice of William Cuningham to Thomas Gale, *STC* 11529 (1563), sig. A 4. 'Touching the malevolent detractors, it either needeth not, or helpeth not, to stand of them in dread. Apes will ever have apishe properties....'

These may be merely jocular flourishes, but the same cannot be said of Alexander Neville's verses, written as a warning to the enemies of his friend Barnaby Googe, which run as follows:

But as for those crabsnowted bestes, those ragyng feends of Hell.
Whose vile, malicious, hatefull mindes, with boylyng Rancour swell.
Which puse with Pryde, enflamed with spight, and drownd in deape disdain:
Lyke *Momus* monstrous broode outright even of a jelows Brayn,
With curious, canckard, carping mouthes, most famous dedes disfame,
Defacing those whose labours great, deserve immortall fame.
Such crabfaced, cankerd, carlish chuffs within whose hatefull brestes,
Such Malice bydes, suche Rancour broyles, such endles Envy rests
Esteem thou not. No prejudice to thee: nor yet oprest
Thy famous wrytynges are by them. Thou lyvest and ever shalt.
Not all the slaundryng tonges alive, may purchase blame or fault
Unto thy name (O worthy *Googe*). No tyme, no fyrye flame
Not all the furies frettyng Force, thy doynges may dysfame
Let them in broyle of burning spight, continuall Toyle sustayne
Let them fele scourging Plags of mind Let ever duryng payne,
Spred through their poisoned vaines, with payse of dedly waight:
    Let Care
Oppresse theyr vyle infected Harts with stynging Malyce fraight.[1]

How serious really was this critical opposition? Was it anything like as dangerous as was a hostile notice in the *Quarterly* or the *Edinburgh Review* in the early nineteenth century, or an adverse review today in *The Times Literary Supplement*, or by 'The Critics', or by any widely circulated paper or review? Can it be doubted that these can do much more harm to a writer's reputation than could the most violent outburst of any such of the Zoili as Bale speaks of? Professor C. H. Conley

[1] *STC* 12048, B. Googe, *Eglogs, Epytaphes, and Sonettes* (1563), ed. Arber, 1871, pp. 21–2.

has argued that vested interests, whether secular or religious, motivated the attack on certain kinds of writing. In his view it was:

The Zoilists, who were traditionalists with respect to all matters intellectual, cultural, ecclesiastical, moral, and political, and as such favored Papal and Spanish aspirations, condemned the work of translation altogether, attempted to destroy the value of translated works by means of pedantry, attacked *belles lettres*, and appealed to prejudice and passion.[1]

These enemies of the writer, I suspect, were nothing like so numerous nor so powerful as has been generally believed. Of course, if a man wrote a work of religious or political controversy, or one of propaganda, his opponents not unnaturally attacked him. When he deliberately indulged in scurrilous attacks on his fellow writers, as did such men as Churchyard, Nashe, Harvey and a number of others, a biting rejoinder was expected and was part of the game. All this, however, left a large field of activity open to writers of many kinds of literature which scarcely invited attack, and, if such attacks did occur, where are they to be found in print? They are very few and far between, whereas the vigorous replies which were allegedly invited by the unbridled outbursts occasioned by personal spite, or professional or doctrinal hatred, survive in plenty. However much a man's work may have been traduced *viva voce*, it seems that few were to be found who felt that such things as a sonnet sequence, a tale of romance, or any straightforward literary performance were worth the trouble and expense of an attack in print. As in modern times, literary and other coteries had their shibboleths, their likes and dislikes: some still clung to the old ways whether in theology, medicine, learning, or merely the correct way in which to compose a sonnet. Those who adventured from these accustomed ways no doubt risked censure, and it was obviously safer to follow the

[1] C. H. Conley, *The First English Translators of the Classics* (New Haven, 1927), p. 123.

conventions, and in deference to the presiding deities of literature and learning it was best to make the hallowed protestations of literary unworthiness, or to ask for the protection of some patron, or to write a placatory address to the reader. Among such devices, the references to Momus and Zoilus take their place, and should not be taken too seriously. When all is said and done, despite all these pleas, men never ceased to write, and if we ask why this was so, the reasons were as various as they are today. Some wrote for pleasure, some for gain. Men wrote to instruct, to controvert, to amuse. The divine, the lawyer, the scholar—all wished to communicate their learning; the traveller to tell of what he had seen and done; the teller of tales 'to shorten the lives of the long winter's nights that lie watching in the dark for us'.

At times we can see this the more clearly, since some authors tell us a little of the reasons which led them to write and then to send their work to the printer. Of course, it must be borne in mind that since most of the evidence comes from the authors themselves, it cannot be taken as more than an *ex parte* statement. Nevertheless, while a man is not upon oath in an introductory letter, or in an address to the reader, we need not go to the other extreme and disbelieve everything he says and reject his evidence altogether. Take, for example, the account that William Baldwin gives to his friend John Young of how *Beware the Cat* came to be written:

I have penned for your maisterships pleasure one of the stories which M. Stremer tolde the last Christmas, and which you would so faine have herd reported by M. Ferers himselfe, and although I be unable to pen or to speak the same so pleasantly as he coulde, yet have I so neerly used bothe the order and words of him that spake them, which is not the least vertue of a reporter, that I dout not but that he and M. Willet shal in the reading think they hear M. Stremer speak, and he himself in the like action shal dout whether he speaketh or readeth. I have devided his oration into three parts, and set the argument before them and an Instruction after them with such notes as might be gathered therof, so making it look like and intituled *Beware the Cat*. But because I dout whether M. Stremer wil be contented that other men plowe with his oxen (I mean penne suche thinges as he speaketh) which perhaps he would rather doo himself, to have, as he deserveth, the glory of bothe. Therefore I besech you to learne his mind herein. And if he agre it pas in such sort, yet that he peruse it before the prynting, and amend it if in any point I have mistaken him. I pray you likewise to ask M. Ferers his judgement heerin and shew him that [...M. Stremer's] translation out of the Arabique which he sent me from Margate, shal be imprinted as soon as I may conveniently. And if I shal perceive by your triall that M. Stremer allow my endeavours in this kinde, I wil heer after pen out such things of the rest of our Christmas communications as shal be to his great glory, and no lesse pleasure to all them that desire such kindes of knowledge....

Then comes 'The Argument', which reads as follows:

It chaunced that at Christemas last, I was at Court with Maister Ferrers then maister of the Kings majesties pastimes, about setting foorth of certain Interludes, which for the Kings recreation we had devised and were in learning. In which time among many other exercises among ourselves we used nightly at our lodging to talke of sundry things for the furtherance of such offices, wherein eche man as then served. For which purpose it pleased Maister Ferrers to make me his bedfellowe, and upon a pallet cast upon the rushes in his owne Chamber to lodge Maister Willet and Maister Stremer, the one his Astronomer, the other his Divine. And among many other things to long to rehearce it hapned on a night (which I think was the twenty eight of December) after that M. Ferrers was come from the Court and in bed; there fel a controversie between Maister Stremer (who with M. Willet had already slept their first sleep) and mee that was newly come to bed, the effect whereof was whether Birds and beasts had reason; the occasion therof was this, I had heard that the Kings Players were learning a play of Esops Crowe, wherein the most part of the actors were birds, the device whereof I discommended, saying it was not Comicall to make either speechless thinges to speake; or brutish things to commen reasonably. And although to a tale it be sufferable to immagin and tell of some thing by them spoken or reasonably doon (which kinde Esope laudably used) yet it was uncomly (said I) and without example of any authour to bring them in lively parsonages to speake, doo, reason, and allege authorities out of authors. M. Stremer, my Lordes Divine, being more divine in this point than I was ware of, held the contrary parte, afferming that beastes and foules have reason, and that as much as men, yea and in some points more. M. Ferrers himself and his Astronomer waked with our talke and harkoned to us, but would take parte on neither side. And when M. Stremer had for proofe of his assertion declared thinges of Elephants that walked upon cords; Hedghogs that knew alwaies what wether would come; Foxes or Dogges that after they had been all night abrode killing Geese and Sheep, would come home in the morning and put their necks into their collers...and an hundred things more which I denyed to come of reason and to be but naturall, kindely, actions, alledging for my proof authoritie of moste grave and learned Philosophers. Wel, quoth Maister Stremer, I knowe what I knowe, and I speak not onely what by hearsay of some Philosophers I knowe, but what I myself have proved. Why, quoth I then, have you proofe of beasts and foweles reason? Yea, quoth he, I have herd them and understand them bothe to speak and reason as wel as I hear and understand you. At this M. Ferrers laughed, but I remembring what I had red in Albertus Woorks, thought there might be somewhat more than I did knowe; wherefore I asked him what beasts or fowles he had heard, and where and when. At this hee paused awhile, and at last said: 'If that I thought you would be content to hear me, and without interruption, til I have done to marke what I say, I woulde tel you such a story of one peece of myne owne experimenting, as should bothe make you wunder and put you out of dout concerning this matter; but that I promise you afore if I do tel it, that as soon as any man curiously interrupteth mee I will leave of and not speak one woord more.' When we had promised quietly to heare, he turning himselfe so in his bed as we might best heare him, said as followeth....[1]

Another example of what seems to be a genuine account of how a work came to be written is given in a letter written by Arthur Hall to his patron Sir T. Cecil. Hall writes:

About two or three yeres past (good Knight) ransacking divers olde and asidecast Papers of small moment, I found some fragments of

[1] *STC* 1245 (1584), sig. A3–A5.

THE 'ILIAD' TRANSLATED

Homers *Iliades* translated out of Frenche verse into Englishe metre at such time as I groped thereat, being a Scholer with you in my Lord, your fathers house; which when I had considered and founde of as small reckoning as the rest they were stored up with, which was in truth none at all, I was about to bequeth them to the fire, but being either better or worse advised, for in your allowing or disallowing of this my proceeding consisteth the same, I took them again in hand and not onely as my leasure and capacitie did serve me, somwhat corrected my first translation, which God knows needes even now much mending and therefore in liklihood verie roughly hewed at the first; but also proceeded to finish up tenne whole Bookes. The which having performed this yeere I have till nowe rested . . in such disquiet of mind, by means of some practise of my contraries (I must say undeserved by me) such vexation in Lawe and carefull turmoyle to preserve somewhat to my poore house, in a manner overthrown by my ungoverned youth that I was fully persuaded I coulde not go thorowe well with my desire, being so harried in other wayes, for yourself best knowes, that to a Poet there is no greater poyson than vexation of sprite. Againe when I considered the ripe wittes of this age . . . these persons whose books I am not worthe to carrie, when I minded, I wished I had been otherwise occupied, I condemned my travaile; I scratched my head as men doe, when they are greatly barred of their willes. But when I lighted on M. Thomas Phaer's Virgilian *Englishe*, quoth I, 'What have I done? Am I become senselesse to travaile, to be laughed at, to presume, and to be scorned and to put forth myselfe, and not to be received'; for I was so abashed looking at M. Phaers *Heroical* Vergill, and my *Satirical* Homer, as I cried out, envying Virgils prosperitie, who gathered of Homer that he had fallen into the oddest mans hands that ever England bred. And I lamented poore blind Homers case, who gathered of nobody, to fall to me poore blinde foole, poorly and blindly to learne him to talke our mother tongue. These steppes laide before me, and considered, made me for a while cast my papers behinde mee. But as it is a propertie of everie man soone to finde a reason to will him proceede with his owne humour, be it never so unreasonably grounded, in like case fell it with me, for these were my arguments against these sound persuasions, objected to staie me. First I remembered that about 18 or 19 yeeres past, walking with M. Richard [*sic*] Aschame, a verrie good Grecian, and a familiar acquaintaunce of Homer, and reciting upon occasion of talke betweene us, certaine verses Englished by me of the said author, he animated me much with great entreatie to goe forward with my begun enterprise, The like did also about that time M. Jasper Heywood.... Thirdly, forasmuch as I did assure myselfe that you, to whom I have so long vowed my labour, would regard my good will more than the worthinesse of my translation, which if you doe, I have with a most contented mind, made holiday. And wholly presuming therof, it hath made me blind Bayard, as bold as ever blind jade was.[1]

Both these examples have an air of verisimilitude about them. We know that George Ferrers was the Master of the King's pastimes in 1551 and 1552, and that William Baldwin was his assistant. Furthermore, Baldwin's insistence that his manuscript should be shown to Stremmer before it was printed, and his further reference to Stremmer's translation sent him from Margate for publication, suggest that we are dealing with something that really happened, and not with a tale made up for the occasion. Similarly, the detailed account given by Hall bears the stamp of truth with its mention of Ascham, 'a verrie good Grecian, and a familiar acquaintaunce of Homer', and still more by his allusions to his difficulties occasioned by his 'ungoverned youth', and his ingenuous account of how he sought about for reasons to justify doing that which he longed to do: 'I scratched my head, as men do when they are greatly barred of their willes.' All these things encourage us to think that we are reading the truth about the reasons that led Hall to publish.

While few writers give their reasons as fully as these two, many tell us something about the reasons which have led them to the printer. A number preface their work by saying that it was undertaken and is now printed because of the entreaties of their friends. It is obviously impossible to check the truth of such statements, which necessarily arouse suspicions, since they are so easily made and so difficult to confute. When, therefore, we are told that 'divers gentlemen of worship', or 'the importu-

---

[1] *STC* 13631, *Ten books of Homers Iliades translated out of the French* (1581), sig. A 3, A 4.

nities of a friend', or 'some well wishers', have prevailed upon the author, we may or may not accept what they say as true. Some writers, however, give us details which may incline us to believe them, as when one tells us that he was 'constrained by some friends to break off a work of some greater importance and larger discourse, to undertake the translation of this brief and pithie treatise', and having done so he felt that it was necessary to print it, since the manuscript 'being but one could not well satisfy so many'.[1] Another strengthens his case by saying that he has translated the work at 'the special request of G. Churchey, Fellow of Lions [sic] Inne',[2] while another prints to satisfy the demands of three friends 'namely my cousine Hontwood, my uncle Mantel and learned Maister Bale'.[3]

Not only friends but patrons were obviously responsible for many writings. For example, Professor Conley notes that translators were especially encouraged by such means. He writes:

The third book of Hoby's *Courtier* was translated in 1551 at the desire of the Marchioness of Northampton... Bury's *Isocrates* (1557) was performed at the desire of his uncle, Sir William Chester, Lord Mayor of London in 1560; and Golding's *Trogus* was executed in fulfilment of a promise made to his brother-in-law... Underdown translated Ovid's *Ibis* (1569) at the request of Lord Buckhurst; and Sadler, *Vegetius* (1572) at the request of Sir Edmund Blundell. Besides, Heywood, Neville, and Hoby, like Studley, were urged to do their work by friends to whom they could 'not well deny anything that frendshyps ryght may seeme justly to requyre'. Finally, Cecil was directly responsible for Golding's translating Caesar and for Wilson's translating Demosthenes.[4]

[1] *STC* 842, R. Ashley, *A comparison of the English and Spanish Nation* (1589), sig. A 4.
[2] *STC* 7268, J. Dubravius, *A new booke of good husbandry* (1599), sig. A 2.
[3] *STC* 19148 (1560), M. Palingenius, *The first thre bokes of the Zodyake of lyfe*. Trans. B. Googe, sig. A 2.
[4] Conley, *The First English Translators of the Classics*, p. 38. For examples of the importance attached by writers to patronage, see the detailed evidence collected by Dr Eleanor Rosenberg in *Leicester: Patron of Letters* (New York, 1955).

The fact that a work had been asked for did not necessarily imply to the author that it would ultimately be printed. A good example of this was the translation of the famous chronicles of Philippe de Commines. These were translated about 1566 by Thomas Danett, who then presented his work to the Earl of Leicester and to Lord Burghley. Some years later, at the request of Sir Christopher Hatton, he 'perused it anew and enlarged it with such notes and pedigrees as seemed necessary'. Then, after Sir Christopher's death, certain gentlemen into whose hands the book had happened to come,

> tooke so great pleasure and delight therein, that they determined to put it to the presse, supposing it a great dishonor to our nation, that so woorthy an historie being extant in all languages almost in Christendome, should be suppressed in ours. Notwithstanding their resolution, they forbare of curtesie to put in execution till their purpose should be made knowen to me. And albeit that I alleaged many reasons why in my conceit bookes of this nature, treating of Princes secrets were unfit to be published to the vulgare sort...yet none of my reasons could prevaile, but they continued in their former determination...So that would I nould I to the presse the booke must go.[1]

So at last, in 1596, some thirty years after Danett first made his translation (and still against his will) the work was published.

As another example of a work never originally intended for the press we may take Richard Bancroft's *Daungerous Positions* (1593). The author tells us that when he was asked

> to sette down by way of an historicall narration, what he had observed touching certain positions holden, and some enterprises atchieved or undertaken, for recommending, and bringing the *Presbiteriall Discipline* into this Iland of *Brittaine*, under pretence of reformation...he found the worke to grow farre greater upon him, then at the first, he did imagine. Insomuch as although in the beginning hee verily

---

[1] *STC* 5602 (1596), sig. A2. For other examples of delay in publication, *STC* 6324 (21 years); 21413 (3 or 4 years); 10868 (8 years); 17518 (at least 9 years); 12403 ('4 years and more').

UNWILLING PUBLICATION

supposed, that hee might easily have contrived his matter into a few sheetes of paper: so that as many coppies, as were to be disposed, might easily and in very short time have beene written foorth: yet by the necessarie length of the Discourse, as it fell out... he was constrayned...to procure for the better dispatch, that some few copies might bee printed.[1]

In 1573 Thomas Bedingfield's translation of Girolamo Cardano's book, entitled *Cardanus Comforte*, was published as the title-page says 'by the commaundement of the right honourable the Earle of Oxenford'. In his dedication to the Earl, the author relates that his patron, 'unawares to me founde some parte of this worke, and willed me in any wyse to proceede therein. My meaning was not to have imparted my travayle to any, but your honour hath power to countermaund myne intention.' Then in a letter to Bedingfield the Earl writes:

After I had perused youre letters...findinge in them your request farre differing from the desert of your labour, I could not chose but greatly doubt whether it were better for me to yelde you your desyre, or execute myne owne intention towardes the publishinge of youre Booke.... But when I had thoroughlye considered in my mynde of sondrye and divers argumentes, whether it were best to obeye myne affections or the merites of your studyes, at the length I determined it better to denye your unlawfull request than to graunte or condiscende to the concealment of so worthy a worke. Whereby as you have bene profited in the translatynge, so many may reape knowledge by the reading of the same....[2]

What the Earl of Oxford gave as a reason for printing Bedingfield's book was similar to what was commonly advanced by authors, and especially by translators. Edward Hellows, the translator of Guevara's *Familiar Epistles*, tells his readers that since he has often read the book to his great delight and pleasure, but much more to his profit, he has translated it, because 'I thought it mete and right and also my duty'

[1] *STC* 1344 (1593), sig. A 2.   [2] *STC* 4607, sig. A 2, A 3.

to make it available in English.[1] William Fulwood enlarges on this a little when he says that he has translated *The Castel of Memorie* (1562), by W. Gratarolus, 'chiefly and especially for the common utilitie and profyte of my native countrye, the advancement and benefyte whereof every man is bound both by nature and conscience to studie...to the uttermost of hys power'.[2] Similarly other men have made their translations they say to 'doe great good to this land',[3] or 'to pleasure my country'.[4] This insistence on the writer's duty to his country arose from the widely held belief immortalized in Donne's words: 'No man is an *Iland*, intire of it selfe; every man is a peece of the *Continent*, a part of the *maine*', so that it followed that if he wished not to 'bee adjudged and imputed...an inprofitable lumpe of clay'[5] he should put his talents at the service of his fellow men. So thought Samuel Gardiner who wrote his *Cognizance of a true Christian* (1597) animated by 'my dutie to my dere sovereigne, whose loyall subject I am', and 'the love of my countrie whose unfaigned friend I am'.[6]

While considerations such as these were in the minds of some authors, others were more concerned for themselves. Among the many reasons given by writers in justification of their works, none was more common than the plea that they wrote 'to eschew idleness'. Men were brought up to think of idleness, as did the author of *The Institucion of a Gentleman* (1555), who declared that 'idlenes is the Mistres of wanton appetites, and the portres of Lustes gates'.[7] Some such view was in the mind of Thomas Newton when he made his translation of Cicero's *The worthye booke of Old Age* (1569): 'The

---

[1] *STC* 12432 (1574), sig. A3ᵛ.
[2] *STC* 12191, sig. A6.
[3] *STC* 11037, A. Fleming, *A bright burning beacon* (1580), sig. A3.
[4] *STC* 11798, C. Gesner, *The newe jewell of health* (1576), sig. A2ᵛ For other examples, see *STC* 14275, sig. B2; *STC* 16624 [1573], sig. **2; *STC*, 18815 (1563), sig. A3.
[5] *STC* 19894, *Phisicke for the soule in the agonie of death*, tr. H. Thorne (1568), sig. A5.
[6] *STC* 11573, sig. A5ᵛ.   [7] *STC* 14104, sig. K3.

work was begonne and ended by me this last yere, having a quiet time of vacation among my frendes in Cheshyre, thereby to exclude and avoyde the lothsome and horrible Monster Idlenesse, which holye Ambrose aptly called the Pillowe or Cussyon of Sathan.'[1] It was the fear of being accused of this vice that kept Richard Robinson, one of the Earl of Shrewsbury's household, steadily at work throughout the night, 'in such time as my turn came to serve in watche of the Scottische Queen... to the end that it might the better appear that I used not altogether to sleepe'.[2]

'My meaning was not to have imparted my travaile to any', wrote Thomas Bedingfield, and there can be little doubt that such was the intention of a number of men when first they wrote. What sometimes happened can be seen from what Joshua Sylvester tells us of his translation of the work of Saluste du Bartas, entitled *The first day of the worldes creation*. This Sylvester made to please himself, and it might have been 'smothered from the world... had not some of my dere friends weaned it from my hands... promising it light and life, if not with me, without me'. Sylvester was unhappy about this, and arranged that only 'The first day' should be printed, leaving the question of any further publication of the story of the other days until he was sure that greater men than himself, such as Sidney, Spenser or Daniel, had no intention of translating any of the work.[3]

Another example may be taken from Alexander Neville's experience in translating the *Oedipus* of Seneca:

I minded nothing lesse when first I travayled in the translation of the present Tragedy than that at any time thus rudely transformed he shoulde come into the Printer's hands, for I to no other ende removed him from his naturall and lofty style to our corrupt

---

[1] *STC* 5294, sig. ‡2.
[2] *STC* 21120, *The rewarde of Wickednesse* [1574], sig. A 2ᵛ. Among other examples, see *STC* 4268 (1595), sig. A 3; 24061 [1570], sig. F 5; 5532 (1571), sig. A 2; 21536 (1595), sig. A 2ᵛ.
[3] *STC* 21658 (1595), sig. A 2.

and base, or as all men assyne it, most barbarous language, but onely to satisfy the instant requestes of a fewe of my familiar frendes.[1]

Unfortunately for him, they 'wrested it to another effect, and by this meanes [they have] blowen it abroade by over rashe and unadvised printyng'.

While many of the above statements seem to be genuine we have to move with caution. In 1579 J.C., styling himself a gentleman writing from Gray's Inn, put into print the work of 'a student at Cambridge', entitled *A poore Knight, his Pallace of Private Pleasures*, which the author had sent to him for the delectation of himself and his brother. 'Let mee therefore, gentle J.C. intreate you to kepe these close, lest they come to the handes of them which may from the publishing of them bee right moved with mee', and asked him not to show it to anyone else, and he added: 'In case anyone sees it, I withhold my name.' It looks as if J.C. overcame any scruples that this appeal might have aroused in him, for in publishing the work he writes:

The feare of ignomynie and shamefull reproach hath caused the Author of these posies to witholde his name from the same, whom for this time I have thought not much amisse to collour and set forth in the name of the poore Knight, and I do duly protest unto thee that without my great intreaty, these fewe posies had not yet come unto thy hand.[2]

---

[1] *STC* 22225 (1563), sig. A 3, A 4. For further examples, see *STC* 11096 (1578), sig. Ss 3, a translation from Florio, which the author deprecates seeing in print, since it was originally done 'to pleasure a private friend of myne, not thinking it should have come to light, for if that I had, I woulde have taken more heede'; *STC* 23413 (1581), sig. A 2, 'the which this three or four years I have kept in secret, being doubtfull (although emboldened by diverse of my friends) to publish this my travaile'; *STC* 11900 (1585), sig. *2, wherein N.W., writing from Oxford on 20 November 1584, urges Samuel Daniel to print his translation of Giovio's book about emblems and devices, and to dedicate it to the Queen's Champion, Sir E. Dimmock: *STC* 24631 [1572], a translation by J. Sadler of Vegetius, was made 'for his patron's private use and readinge', but his patron 'did afterwarde purpose to cause the said work to be printed'.

[2] *STC* 4283, sig. O 1^v, A 2.

Do both the author and his friend protest a little too much, or can we accept as the truth all that they say?

When we turn to the protestations of a professional author we have to be even more on our guard. For example, in his *Terrors of the Night* (1594), Thomas Nashe writes:

A long time since hath it beene suppressed by mee, untill the urgent importunitie of a kind frend of mine (to whome I was sundrie waies beholding) wrested a Coppie from me. That Coppie progressed from one scriveners shop to another, and at length grew so common that it was readie to bee hung out for one of their signes, like a paire of indentures. Whereupon I thought it as good for mee to reape the frute of my owne labours as to let some unskilfull pen-man or Noverint-maker startch his ruffe and new spade his beard with the benefite he made of them.[1]

We may well hesitate before accepting this *au pied de la lettre*.

Whether men wrote to amuse themselves or to please others within their intimate circle, they could never be sure that their work would remain private. Abraham Fraunce tells us that what was prepared 'for one or two, was afterward by the meanes of a few, made common to manie, and so pitifully disfigured by the barbarous handling of unskilfull pen men that he [i.e. the hero, Amyntas] was like to have come abroad so unlike himselfe as that his own Phillis would never have taken him for Amyntas'. As a result, the author felt bound 'to repair his ragged attire' and to send the work to the press.[2] So did Thomas Lodge, who tells his friends of the Inns of Court that he has had to print that which was 'whollie predistinate to your friendship', because others had made it 'to hazard an apprenticeship in Paules'.[3]

One more example must be quoted, because it sets out in such detail the steps by which a work was put into print with-

[1] *STC* 18379, sig. A 2.
[2] *STC* 23692, Tasso, T., *The lamentations of Amyntas* (1587), tr. A. Fraunce, sig. ¶ 2.
[3] *STC* 16674, *Scillaes metamorphosis: enterlaced with the unfortunate love of Glaucus* (1589), sig. *2. For other examples, see *STC* 1381 (1598), sig. *6; 19618 (1594), sig. A 2; 17227 (1601), sig. A 2; 22225 (1563), sig. A 3.

out the author's knowledge. The circumstances were as follows. In June 1566 Sir Humphrey Gilbert wrote a private letter to his brother telling him of his discovery of a new passage to Cathay, and a copy of his letter lay in Sir Humphrey's study until it was seen there ten years later by George Gascoigne when he visited him in Limehouse. Gascoigne borrowed it for two or three dayes to reade and to peruse. And hee verie friendly granted my request.... And to be plaine, when I had at good leasure perused it, and therewithall conferred [sic] his allegations by the Tables of Ortelius, and by sundrie other Cosmographicall Mappes and Charts, I seemed in my simple judgement not onely to like it singularly, but also thought it very meete to give it out in publike. Whereupon I have (as you see) caused my friendes great travaile, and mine owne greater presumption to be registred in print.

He goes on to excuse this outrage by the following extraordinary series of justifications:

1. First it is but a Pamphlet and no large discourse, and therefore the more to be borne withall: since the faults (if any be) shall be the fewer because the volume is not great.

2. Also it was ment by the autour but as a private letter unto his Brother, for his better satisfaction, and therefore his imperfections therein (if any were) are to be pardoned, since it is very likely that if he had ment to publish the same, he would with greater heede have observed and perused the worke in everie parte.

3. Againe, it commeth forth without his consent. So that he had neither warning nor time to examine, nor yet to amende anie thing that were worthie misliking.

4. Furthermore it treateth of a matter whereof no man hath heretofore written particularly, nor shewed ani approved reason for the same. So that not only his travaile and paine are very commendable... but also the worke is not to be thought bareine, although it doe not fully proove so much as may be expected.[1]

Worse things could happen. Some were audacious enough to send a work to the printer, even though the author was close

[1] *STC* 11881, Sir H. Gilbert, *A discourse of a discoverie for a new passage to Cataia* (1576). sig. ¶¶ 1ᵛ, 2ᵛ.

at hand and had expressed his unwillingness to see his book printed. The history of the publication in 1588 of *Musica Transalpina* illustrates this very well. Nicholas Yonge tells us that 'I had the hap to find in the hands of some of my good friends, certaine Italian Madrigales translated...by a Gentleman for his private delight'. Yonge went to him and got from him the remainder of his collection, which he was then asked to print. When he consulted their owner, however, he found him unwilling to give his permission for their publication, since 'those trifles being but an idle man's exercise, of an idle subject, written onely for private recreation, would blush to be seene otherwise then by twilight, much more to be brought into the common view of all men'. Yonge kept them for a long time, but when he heard that they were in wide circulation and likely to be printed, 'I went ahead, without his permission (he being neither privy or present)'.[1]

Yonge evidently paid little or no attention to the author's wishes here, nor, to take another example, did the two men responsible for sending to the press Robert Tofte's *Laura* (1597). One of them, Valentine Sims, the printer, writes: 'Only in this I must confesse we are both to blame, that whereas he having promised to keepe private the originall, and I the copie, secret, we both have consented to send it abroad, as common.' His fellow, one R.B., makes matters no better when he adds a note at the end of the book, headed: 'A frends just excuse about the booke and author, in his absence', which runs as follows:

Without the Authors knowledge, as is before said by the Printer, this poeme is made thus publiquely knowen: which (with my best indeavour) the Gentleman himselfe (suspecting what is now prooved too true) at my comming up, earnestly intreated mee to prevent. But I came at the last sheetes printing, and finde more than thirtie sonnets not his, intermixt with his. Helpt it cannot be, but by the wel judging Reader, who will with lesse paine distinguish between them than I on this sodaine possibly can.[2]

[1] *STC* 26094, sig. A2.   [2] *STC* 24097, sig. K1ᵛ.

Despite all these excuses, however, there is a dedication initialled R.T. (i.e. Robert Tofte), so perhaps the author made the best of a bad matter, or this may be but another example of a publisher's ruse to attract the reader.

It has been suggested that this was in the mind of Richard Jones when he wrote in a preface to an edition of Nicholas Breton's poems, entitled *Brittons Bowre of Delights* (1591), as follows:

I present you here in the Authors absence with sundrie fine Devices and rare conceytes in english verse...I am (onely) the Printer of these chiefly to pleasure you, and partly to profit myselfe if they proove to your good liking: otherwise, my hope is frustrate, my labour lost, and all my cost is cast away.[1]

When the next year Breton published at Oxford *The Pilgrimage to Paradise* he denounced this edition with some vigour:

Gentlemen, there has beene of late printed in London by one Richarde Joanes, a printer, a booke of English verses entituled *Bretons bower of delights*. I protest it was donne altogetheur without my concent or knowledge, and many thinges of other mens mingled with a few of mine, for except *Amoris Lachrimae*, an epitaphe upon Sir Phillip Sydney and one or two other toies, which I know not how he unhappily came by, I have no part with any of them, and so I beseech yee assuredly beleeve.[2]

Two years later, however, Jones published another work by Breton, *The Arbour of Amorous Devices*, and reprinted both of them in 1597, so that it looks as if Breton was not very serious in his disclaimer.

Doubts have also been thrown on the truthfulness of an address to the reader by William Ponsonby, the publisher of Edmund Spenser's *Complaints* (1591), who writes:

Since my late setting foorth of the *Faerie Queen*, finding that it hath found a favourable passage amongst you, I have sithence endeavoured by all good meanes...to get into my handes such

---

[1] *STC* 3633, sig. x2.   [2] *STC* 3683, sig. ¶3

smale Poemes of the same Authors as I heard were disperst abroad in sundrie hands, and not easie to bee come by, by himselfe; some of them having bene diverselie imbeziled and purloyned from him since his departure over Sea. Of the which I have by good meanes gathered togeather these fewe parcels present, which I have caused to bee imprinted altogeather.[1]

Professor W. L. Renwick has made a careful examination of the circumstances that went to the making of this volume, and gives convincing reasons for his belief that the volume was assembled by the joint efforts of the poet and the publisher.[2]

Since men were so cavalier in their treatment of an author's work, even when he was close at hand, it is not surprising to find a number of books which assert that the work was printed in the author's absence (and presumably without his knowledge). The truth or otherwise of such statements is very difficult to assess, but a genuine case of this kind seems to have been Thomas Blenerhasset's *The Seconde part of the Mirrour for Magistrates* (1578). In his prefatory address 'to the friendly Reader', Richard Webster, whose name appears as the printer, says that the author is overseas and 'wyl marvele at his return, to fynde thys imprinted. For his intent was but to profite and pleasure one private man, as by his Epistle may appear. But I finding a booke alredy in print, entitled *The first and third part of the Mirrour for Magistrates*, I was moved diversely of divers men, by printing this latter worke, to make perfit the former booke'.[3] This would appear to be borne out from Blenerhasset's letter to a friend in which he says that 'the most part of these my Princes dyd pleade their causes unto me, even in the Sea, a place in fayth, not meete to penne Tragedies. And as for bookes I was altogether destitute.' He therefore entreats his friend to take 'the fruites of these my idle houres, sent unto you with a good wyll, and according unto the trust reposed in you, keepe these trifles from the view of all men, and

---

[1] *STC* 23078, sig. A2.
[2] *Complaints*, ed. by W. L. Renwick (1928), p. 180.
[3] *STC* 3131, sig. *2.

as you promysed, let them not raunge out of your private Study'.[1] Whether the copy came to the hands of the printer 'by chance' as he asserts, or whether the author's friend played him false, we have no means of knowing.

One of the most obvious sources of the supply of books has yet to be mentioned—that which resulted from the efforts of the printers and the book-sellers. Then, as now, they could not rely solely on books being brought to them by those who wished to see them in print, but they had to seek about for saleable wares. Some of them, it is true, like Richard Jugge, or Robert Crowley, or John Day, were animated by moral or religious motives, which impelled them to print a number of such works. We can see the printers approaching writers, as did 'Lucas Harrison and George Bishop, Stationers, men well minded towards godlinesse and true religion', who invited Arthur Golding to translate *A postill, or exposition of the Gospels...written by Nicholas Heminge, a preacher of the Gospel of the Universitie of Hafnie* [1569]. This Golding was willing to do, the two stationers 'taking uppon them too imprint this Woorke at their proper charges'.[2]

Similarly, *Newes out of Powles Churchyarde*, a work 'wherein is reprooved excessive and unlawfull seeking after riches and the evil spending of the same', by Edward Hake, was reprinted in 1579, because as Hake tells us:

It pleaseth the Printer, (Gentle Reader) after twelve yeeres scilence to hale againe into the lighte, this my litle booke of Englishe Satyrs, which else mighte have soonge unto itselfe, *Ecce nunc in pulvere dormio*: what his gaine shalbe, I knowe not: and I am perswaded, that gaine is not the onely, no nor the chiefest ende hee respecteth.[3]

The book had been originally entered (and probably first printed) by Henry Denham, a 'man well minded towards

---

[1] *STC* 3131, sig. *3ᵛ.
[2] *STC* 13061 [1569], sig. *3. And see p. 107.
[3] *STC* 12606, sig. A3.

religion', who some time before 1579 had commissioned Thomas Rogers to make a new translation of one of the most popular of all devotional works, *The Imitation of Christ*. This he did because he wished to see the book purged of all Catholic doctrine and thus made suitable for Protestant readers. In his second epistle, Rogers thus describes Denham's part in the affair: 'This... was taken in hand at the motion of the Printer hereof; whose zeale to set forth good bookes for the advancement of virtue, and care to publish them as they ought to be, would some printers folowe.'[1]

It is hardly to be expected that the majority of printers and booksellers would follow this advice very closely. After all, theirs was a trade and for many of them that meant the necessity to produce and sell books that would appeal to the public. If at the same time they were 'good books for the advancement of vertue', so much the better, and many prefaces bear witness to the desire of the writer and bookseller that this should be so. But both parties were on the look-out for books that they thought would appeal to the public, and it is clear that they followed up suggestions and took the initiative where necessary, as may be seen in the dedicatory epistle which John Wolfe, the printer, wrote to his patron in sending him a book of discoveries recently made in the Indies. He writes:

About a twelvemonth agoe, a learned Gentleman brought unto mee the Voyages and Navigation of John Huyghen van Linschoten unto the *Indies*, written in the *Dutche* tongue, which he wished might be translated into our language, because hee thought it would be not onely delightfull, but also very commodious for our *English Nation*. Upon this commendation and opinion, I procured the Translation thereof accordingly, and so thought good to publish the same in Print, to the ende it might bee made common and knowen to everybody.[2]

---

[1] *STC* 23973 (1580), quoted from L. B. Wright, *Middle-Class Culture in Elizabethan England* (Chapel Hill, N.C., 1935), p. 231. And see *STC* 11800 [1559] and 14018 (1560), both printed by J. Day. Also *STC* 21135 (1582), by R. Jones and 23076 (1595) for W. Ponsonby.

[2] *STC* 15691, J. H. van Linschoten, *Discours of voyages into ye Easte & West Indies*, tr. W. Phillip (1598), sig. A1ᵛ.

In a later 'Letter to the Reader' Wolfe tells him that the 'learned Gentleman' was none other than 'R. Hackluyt, a man that laboureth greatly to advance the English name and Nation'.[1]

A good example of a printer taking the initiative may be seen in the desire of Christopher Barker to put into print foreign works on hunting and other field sports. To this end, he tells us 'I had with some charge caused [*The Noble Arte of Venerie or Hunting*] to be collected and translated out of sundry good authorities, and thought it could not but generally delight all Noblemen and Gentlemen of the Realm'. His statement is amplified by the translator, George Turberville, who says that the printer has well recompensed him for his work, and then goes on to emphasize that the printer 'to his great costs hath sought out as muche as is written and extant in any language concerning the noble Artes of Venerie and Falconrie, and to gratifie the Nobilitie and Gentlemen of this land, hath disbursed great summes for the copies, translations, pictures and impressions of the same'.[2] Turberville translated for him '*The Booke of Faulconrie or Hawking*... collected out of sundry Authors as well Italian as French', and both works were put on sale at the same time, 1575.[3]

Some books, however, caused the printer (or whoever was responsible for their publication) to proceed with caution, even though they had bought the copy. Such was the case with John Proctor, who had the work of Richard Robinson, entitled *A Golden Mirrour. Conteining certaine Pithie and figurative Visions prognosticating good fortune to England and all true English Subjectes* (1589). Proctor's dedicatory letter explains his reasons for delay as follows:

About two yeares past I chaunced to have offered me this present Treatise, whiche though I then accepted and gave money for; yet,

---

[1] *Ibid.* sig. A3ᵛ. For another example see *STC* 19838 (1598), sig. A2, where W. Ponsonby causes a translation to be made, after a friend has read the French version and advised him.
[2] *STC* 24328, sig. A1, A2.   [3] *STC* 24324, sig. A2ᵛ. See also p. 195.

dreading least I might be over rashe in committyng it to the Printer, especially before I had fully seene into the end and purpose of the writer...yet nowe after long deliberation I finding the same both pleasaunt and profitable, have adventured the charge of printing it.[1]

It will thus be seen that even after he had bought the work Proctor considered carefully the risks, both political and financial, that he was taking in putting the book into print, but in the end came down in favour of publication.

What conclusions can we draw from a survey of evidence such as this, which may be taken as a fair sample of what was alleged by Elizabethan writers, printers and publishers? First, as we should expect, the appearance of a book on the stalls in Pauls was brought about by a series of circumstances which were as various then as they are now. I have attempted to set out some of the reasons which were given by writers and others at the time, and on the whole I believe that these may be taken at their face value for the most part. For the most part—since there are many cases in which convention and not actuality seem to have been uppermost in the mind of the writer. Hence the variety of pleas, such as the request of a friend, or the pressure of relatives, or the desire to please a patron, or one who might be of use to the author. Some of these pleas are undoubtedly genuine; the only difficulty is to distinguish the true from the false.

As we have seen, the matter was not made the easier by the widespread convention which argued that to expose oneself to print was to invite the censure of a number of critics who were all agog to tear to pieces the work of those daring enough to give them the opportunity. I have given reasons for thinking that this was in fact more a convention than reality; it did, however, encourage men to shelter behind others, so that dedication after dedication states that the author relies on the rank or the fame of his patron to make the critics think twice before attacking.[2]

[1] *STC* 21119, sig. A 2.   [2] See also chapter II, pp. 30 ff.

CHAPTER II

PATRONAGE

The sixteenth-century author who wished to publish his book generally found himself with two cares. The first was to find someone who would print what he had written and the second was to find a patron whose name could figure in the forefront of his work. Before the age of printing a patron had usually been deeply involved in the production of most works of literature since they had been written at his request by someone in his service, or by someone who looked to him for the recompense of his labours. This was necessary, since few could afford the labour or pay for the materials, or face the uneconomic loss of time entailed, unless he was first assured of a market for his wares. Without such support a would-be writer had first to be assured that his bread and butter was forthcoming from somewhere or other. It might be from a monastic order in whose ranks he was enrolled, or from the revenues of a secular living that he enjoyed, or from some employment that assured him a living. Otherwise, unless he had a private income, to write meant to starve.

With the coming of printing the chances that a man could get what he had written published increased, but did little to make it possible for him to live by his pen. What it did do was to encourage men to seek to persuade some influential or wealthy person to take an interest in their writings. This is what Caxton did when he got the support of royalty, the aristocracy, or rich London merchants, before venturing into print with some of his publications. Out of his 77 original works he was assured of financial support for 23 of them, and of course this carried with it the favour and recommendation of his guarantors.

Where Caxton led, others followed, and during the first

half of the sixteenth century we see that a great many books were printed, as we are told, at the wish or command of eminent persons, and that this was sometimes done at their expense. Given the importance attached to rank and position in those days, it was but natural that the name of such a person at the head of the book should give it a sort of warranty that might persuade men to buy it. Other benefits also, in the shape of money or other gifts, might have come to the author, depending on the circumstances of each case.

This state of affairs continued to exist throughout the century, and there are no grounds for the belief that patronage was on the decline and was moribund as the most influential writer on this subject has asserted.[1] A far more informed view is put forward by Dr Eleanor Rosenberg who points out that it is

because of our modern habit of emphasising 'pure literature' at the expense of 'utilitarian writings' that we have been so ready to harbor misconceptions regarding the nature and extent of Elizabethan patronage.... In our preoccupation with creative and imaginative forms, we have attempted to assess the Elizabethan patronage system without taking into account the great bulk of informational and didactic literature to which both common reader and noble lord gave generous support.[2]

The recent publication of Professor Franklin B. Williams's *Index of Dedications*[3] confirms this opinion, for we have only to look down the four hundred odd columns of names of dedicatees that he records to see how impossible it is to sustain the view put forward by Miss Sheavyn. Nor would the Elizabethan readers have supported her. They expected to find in the forefront of most books the name of a patron, and beneath it a letter which in various ways emphasized the importance and the

---

[1] Phoebe Sheavyn, *The Literary Profession in the Elizabethan Age* (Manchester, 1909), pp. 7, 38.
[2] E. Rosenberg, *Leicester: Patron of Letters* (New York, 1955), p. 16.
[3] Franklin B. Williams, Jr., *Index of Dedications and Commendatory Verses in English Books before 1641*, the Bibliographical Society (1962). This indispensable work by Professor Franklin Williams must form the basis for any future study of patronage in this period.

function of a patron as the writer understood them. Sometimes this is quite explicit, as when George Wither tells Sir William Cecil and Sir Walter Mildmay that

it is a usuall manner...for all those that goe about to publish any work or writing of theirs, to dedicate it to some one or other, eyther to be a Testimony to the World, of their mutuall love and friendshippe, or else to witnesse their dutifulnesse or thankfulnes for benefites receyved, or else that under the protection, defence and favour of authority, their works may the better passe, and be the safelier guarded and defended against all busie reprehenders.[1]

Even fuller and more explicit is Miles Mosse's statement of the matter when he writes dedicating his book to the Archbishop of Canterbury as follows:

The inscription and dedication of bookes, to men of note and regarde in their time, either for religion, or vertue, or learning, or authoritie: is well knowne to your Grace...for continuance to be very ancient, and for use to be exceeding profitable.

Auncient it is, as appeareth by the writings of the Fathers...so it is also exceeding profitable. For first, the sacred memorie of worthie men, is by the continuance of the bookes that are dedicated unto them, preserved...from the ruine of time....Secondly, this cannot but cheare up and encourage men of vertue and of godlines to persever and to growe olde in goodnes, when they see that their persons are regarded of men that now live, and their names are like...to bee registred, and recorded to the generations to come....

Thirdly, by the learning and authoritie of those to whome bookes are dedicated, the bookes themselves are protected from the causelesse censures of the ignorant, and the biting teeth of the Carper. Hesiode fayned that Momus was begotten, or brought forth of the night, for that, (as I suppose) he walketh in darknes, & stingeth in silence as a serpent in the grasse....

These and some other respects have caused me to resolve, to commend this my poore labour, and endevour unto the defense and protection of some worthie personage: yea though I knew right well, that the trueth is great and prevaileth of it selfe, and God the author of truth is all sufficientlie able to defend it.[2]

[1] *STC* 25888, *An A.B.C. for laye-men* (1585), sig. 2.
[2] *STC* 18207, *The arraignment and conviction of usurie* (1595), sig. A 2, A 3ᵛ.

REASONS FOR PATRONAGE

Many harped on the mutual benefits arising from the practice of patronage, which (in theory at least) protected the author while the patron was remembered or 'commended to posteritie'. Both parties were said to benefit: the writers were protected and perhaps rewarded, while on the other hand the patrons would 'have their names extolled and their virtues eternised'.

Reasons such as these are constantly to be found in dedicatory epistles to men of authority and others; indeed, the frequency with which they appear has made them suspect, and it is tempting very often to believe that there is more convention than sincerity in what they have to say. At this distance of time it is impossible to gauge the degree of sincerity in every case, but, as we shall see, the dedication often convinces us that it conveys the writer's feelings. Occasionally this is made clear by a man coming out in the open and, disregarding the conventions, giving the reasons for his dedication, despite the fact that he is fully aware of the stereotype. Such was John Bridges, Vicar of Herne, who in 1592 wrote: 'Sundry menne have sundry meanings in dedycating their studyes and traveyles to such men of honor as you are. Some seeke their friendshippe and good will, some augmentation of living, some authoritie to commende and sette forth their workes and labour, some one thing, some another.'[1] So far nothing could be more in keeping with the commonly accepted tradition. But from this point Bridges is intent to set down the special reasons that have motivated him in dedicating his work to the Earl of Bedford. 'I have herein beene ledde', he writes with none of these considerations. For your Honors benevolence and friendship, I long sithence well founde and prooved, which gave me the best part of that exhibition, whereby I lyved in Italie three or foure yeares togither, and whereby also I lyve at this daye the better:

[1] See, for example, *STC* 25331, J. Wheeler, *A Treatise of Commerce* (1601), sig. A 2, 'I am not ignorant also, that it is the manner of writers, to fill up the greatest parte of their Prefaces with the praises and commendations of those to whom they dedicate their travailes'.

I meane the experience and knowledge which I learned in that space.... Mine onely intent in this simple labour of mine was, to shewe my selfe some maner of wayes not unmindefull of your Lordshippes liberalitie so longe agone bestowed upon me, nor of that great humanitye which the same used about a nine yeres past, twice in one Lent at the Court being then in White Hall, towarde so poore a man as I, preventing my bashfull nature and slackenesse of speach towarde my superiors, with such curteous affabilitie, that among the manifolde experiments which I had eftsoones before seene in you, of a noble and gentle nature, I judged this not one of the least.... And for proofe that I never forgat your honors good will and friendship, I could shewe you the three bookes of Machiavelles discourses translated by me out of Italian into Englishe, more than fourtene yeares past, which I thought to have presented unto your Honour, but was stayed therefrom, partly because I hearde the worke inveighed against at Paules crosse, as a treatise unworthy to come abroade into mennes handes, and partly for that I hoped still to have some other matter more plausible and acceptable to gyve unto the same.[1]

It has been too easily assumed that dedications were solely or mainly made in the hope of a reward, generally of money. The professional men of letters at the end of the century have certainly given colour to the view, but it is a one-sided one. However much such men hoped for place or money, for many others this was not in the forefront of the picture. As Bridges says, 'some one thing, some another'. Protection against unfriendly critics; support for causes and opinions held in common by both patron and author; gratitude for past favours and aid—any or all of these animated men in penning dedications. The writers of the vast mass of religious literature naturally turned to the great leaders of their causes such as Leicester and the Bedfords, while Drake, Howard of Effingham, or Essex were obvious possibilities for those with books on naval, maritime or military subjects.

[1] *STC* 25013, R. Walther, *An hundred, threescore and fiftene Homelyes or Sermons, uppon the Actes...translated by J. Bridges* (1572), sig. A2.

FLATTERY OF PATRONS

In addition to these inducements, it may well be, as Dr Eleanor Rosenberg has argued,

> that the writers themselves were more interested in obtaining preferments as the rewards of their labors than in gifts of money or other forms of direct support. Once appointed to a clerical or governmental post, a writer might utilize his leisure and security for further literary endeavor—and perhaps obtain further advancement as a result. Since composition was seldom merely an end in itself, an author would naturally... seek a patron reputedly devoted to the subject dear to his heart.[1]

Whatever considerations may have swayed individual writers, it is true that a stereotyped pattern was evolved which was followed by many. Some thought it necessary to begin with 'a grae-headed Apopthegm, or some straightened sentence out of Tully',[2] or by an allusion to some event or personage of classical times, such as the overworked allusion to the great king Artaxerxes who, after receiving the rich gifts of the great, did not disdain the 'cup of troubled water' which was all the poor man had to offer to him.[3] Many sought to 'glorifie the parties whom they have chosen to be patrons of their workes' by making use of 'many strained wordes and far sought for phrases',[4] particularly when they were addressing the Queen. Thus Gervase Markham begins his dedication of *The Poem of Poems* [1596] with the words: 'Bound to your eternall service, divinest of all virgin cretures.... Daine then, deare flower of deare virginitie, with gracious aspect to smile upon mine infant Muses devotion, &c.[5]

Lesser mortals were also extravagantly flattered, as when the Countess of Kildare is told that 'if thou be pleased, then all are satisfied',[6] and so we might go on noting the extent to which flattery is applied, according to the particular circum-

---
[1] Rosenberg, *Leicester: Patron of Letters*, p. xviii.
[2] *STC* 5624, sig. A2.
[3] *STC* 18670, sig. A3. Cf. *STC* 12562, 13974, 18943, 21535, 24857.
[4] *STC* 20977, sig. A2. See also *STC* 572, 5647, 12908, 14927, 19809, etc.
[5] *STC* 17386, sig. A2.   [6] *STC* 20167, sig. A2.

stances. Not all, however, could bring themselves to pour out the flattery that some thought necessary. We may take as the spokesman of such Ulpian Fulwell who, in addressing Sir William Cecil, tells him that:

I have not the gifte of flowing eloquence, neyther can I enterlace my phrase with Italian termes, nor powder my style with Frenche Englishe or Inkhorne Rhethoricke, neyther cowche my matter under a cloake of curious inventions, to fede the daintie eares of delicate yonkers. And as I cannot, so if I could, I woulde not.[1]

Flattery or no flattery, the common motive put forward by authors is the protection that they can expect, once a powerful patron has accepted their work. 'Shrouded under the shadow of your wings',[2] as one poetically puts it, or more prosaically, 'taking your name for a patron and defender against the biting furies of snuffling detractors and momish affections of biting Zoilus', writers felt that they had a 'shielde and defence... from the bitter tauntes and biting scoffs of cruel reprehension'.[3] Fortified by such protection the author felt that his work 'may creepe along to the behoofe of my Countrey and the better be fenced and fortified against the encountering and wilful reprehension of shameless tongues'.[4] 'I am not the first,' writes John Northbrooke, that 'venemous tongues (tipped with the Metal of infamy and slaunder) have torne to pieces and uncharitably abused', and he asks Sir John Young to be his 'strong bulwarke against the fuming threates and belching wayes of sundrie sycophantes' and other detractors.[5] It would seem from these and other examples that patrons were sought for by many who believed them to be a 'buckler of defense', and able 'utterly to depresse malignant and slaunderous tongues'.[6]

How far they were merely following convention in expressing this fear of hostile criticism has already been discussed,

---

[1] STC 11475, sig. B 2ᵛ. Cf. STC 25331, sig. A 2.
[2] STC 6817, sig. A 2.   [3] STC 18665, sig. *3ᵛ.
[4] STC 18136, sig. A 2.   [5] STC 18670, sig. a 3.
[6] STC 21356, sig. A 3.

ROLE OF THE PATRON

and reasons given for thinking the danger less serious than these outbursts would suggest.[1] Authors were quite right, however, in thinking that the name of Lord Burghley or of the Earl of Leicester would serve to assure prospective purchasers that the book was worth buying. Sir Christopher Hatton is told that if he will 'spread the gladsome beames of your favour and well liking cheere' upon *The Philosopher of the Court*, it would 'render to the Reader my author much bettered', and would be more acceptable to the courtiers.[2] Thomas Lodge is also in no doubt about the value of a patron. He tells the Earl of Derby that, 'having resolved with myselfe to publish certaine of my poems, and knowing them subject to much prejudice, except they were graced with some noble and worthie patron, I...with deliberate and advised judgement, wholly devote and offer up my poems to your favour and protection'.[3]

Hence within the stereotype of the convention, we shall find many dedications which emphasize the role to be played by the patron as protector and sponsor. This is perfectly in keeping with the accepted idea of the responsibilities of the upper ranks of society to less-favoured individuals. Rank carried with it the duty of supporting and sustaining learning in all its forms. 'Necessitie maketh men to shroude themselves under the authoritie and countenance of some great personage',[4] writes Thomas Morton, when discussing 'the reasons and respects which usually men follow in dedicating bookes', and it is clear that it was widely held that 'except they were graced with some noble and worthie patron' their books would start at a disadvantage.

Patronage therefore may be viewed, so far as the higher ranks of society are concerned, as a wellnigh inescapable obligation. For the majority it had some attraction, since long-held tradition taught men to believe that they might be eternized by the praise and thanks of writers they had

---

[1] See above, pp. 8–10.   [2] *STC* 19832, sig. A2.
[3] *STC* 16658, *A fig for Momus* (1595), sig. A2.
[4] *STC* 18198, *A treatise of the nature of God* (1599), sig. A3ᵛ.

patronized. 'Neither Princes maye live cleare and knowen to posteritie wythoute the penne and helping hande of learneds Arte: neyther men excelling in learning, woulde be eyther in lyfe reputed or spoken of after death, withoute the countenaunce, defence, and patronage of noble Peeres',[1] declared William Blandie to Leicester. Hence it was that both parties were willing (and often eager) to accept and to perpetuate the tradition.

From this it follows that the more powerful a man was, the more likely he was to attract dedications, and this carried to its logical conclusion meant that the Queen was inevitably the greatest recipient of such attentions. So it was in fact; nearly two hundred books being dedicated to her, while it has been estimated that some two hundred and fifty items would be a nearer figure if both books and works dedicated to the Queen in manuscript were counted. No permission appears to have been necessary, and throughout her reign the Queen found that volumes of the most diverse kinds were dedicated to her, often couched in terms of the grossest flattery.[2]

Great ecclesiastics, great officers of state, and great nobles, all inevitably attracted the attention of writers who hoped for recognition, protection and support. Dr Eleanor Rosenberg has so fully illustrated this in her monograph on *Leicester: Patron of Letters* that it would be superfluous to follow imperfectly in her tracks by making a further detailed examination of the patronage extended by other great notables. Some of them such as Lord Burghley, who was subjected to nearly one hundred dedications, were looked on as patrons of learning in general, and therefore works of all kinds were dedicated to them. To take the years 1582–3 as a random example, we find

[1] *STC* 18886, sig. a3, *The Five Bookes of the Famous, learned, and eloquent man, Hieronimus Osorius, contayninge a discourse of Civill, and Christian Nobilitie* (1576), trans. by W. Blandie.
[2] A chronological list of the books is given in Williams, *Index of Dedications and Commendatory Verses*... pp. 61–2. For the list of books and manuscripts, see E. C. Wilson, *England's Eliza* (Cambridge, Mass., 1939), pp. 413–58.

that of the nine works dedicated to him wholly or in part, three were presented to him and others as members of the Privy Council, and one to him as Chancellor of the University of Cambridge. These were all polemics against the Catholics, as were two others dedicated to him by the Dean of Durham. Of the remainder, three dealt with matters of health and one with problems of surveying. The books dedicated to Leicester in the same years were even more varied in their appeal. As well as four anti-Roman works and two other religious pieces, education was served by a dictionary of Greek, Latin and English, the first part of Mulcaster's *Elementarie*, a treatise on memory and another on law. His interest in current affairs was recognized by a treatise on the troubles in the Low Countries.

An examination of the works dedicated to other political figures, such as Lord Chancellor Bromley or Lord Chancellor Hatton, as well as those accepted by notables such as Lord Hunsdon, the Earl of Oxford, or the Earl of Southampton, confirms the view that patronage was part of the public duty expected from such men. Much was dedicated to them without any reason other than the general belief already touched upon that they provided 'a buckler of defence',[1] or 'a shelter against the stormes and tempests which their malicious enemies raise against the trueth'.[2] Of course, often some reason is given why a particular person is chosen, but the claim is generally a thin one which would apply equally well to others, and this is often tacitly admitted by the practice of dedicating to more than one person. This was not at all uncommon, so that many illustrious persons found themselves yoked with others of similar views as joint dedicatees. Such was the lot of Lucy, wife of the third Earl of Bedford, and also of Burghley on no less than eleven occasions, of Leicester on ten, and of Margaret, wife of the third Earl of Cumberland, on seven. Ecclesiastics were likewise joined with their colleagues on occasion—Grindal (11 times), Parker (9) and Whitgift (10) being notable examples of this. Religious leaders were constantly invited to accept

[1] *STC* 17143, sig. a2.   [2] *STC* 18198, sig. A3.

works whose object was the furtherance of views often passionately held both by patron and author. For instance, Leicester is enjoined to remember that his greatest duty is the protection and advancement of the Church of England, and that

God asketh this at your Honors hands, and this Church of England craves it, that his ministerie may be mainteyned, his trueth may be preserved and continued, the poore people may be taught and enstructed, wicked heretikes may be confuted and abandoned, which (alas) encrease and grow to infinite nombers daily amongst us.[1]

It was in recognition of such a duty that many other supporters of the established Church, or of one of the various anti-Catholic sects, were willing to accept dedications of polemical and devotional works. For example, Henry Hastings, third Earl of Huntingdon, had twenty books dedicated to him, all but one of which were of a religious nature, and much the same will be found to be true if we examine the lists of books dedicated to religious leaders, such as the second and third Earls of Bedford, and their wives, Bridget and Lucy.[2]

As for literature proper, we have only to recall the names of the Sidneys and Herberts to remind ourselves of the importance writers attached to the presence in their midst of rich and influential men with a love of letters. These two families (admittedly outstanding as patrons of literature) received about eighty dedications in some twenty years. The Countess of Pembroke was the patroness of the poets Breton, Daniel and Spenser, as well as of lesser-known writers who were members of her household—Abraham Fraunce, Thomas Howell and

---

[1] These are the words of John Field, a leader of the Puritans, in his dedication of a translation of the work of the Huguenot leader, Philippe de Mornay, entitled *A Treatise of the Church* (1579), and are taken from Rosenberg, *Leicester: Patron of Letters*, p. 248.

[2] To these may be added the names of notables such as Ambrose, Earl of Warwick and his wife, Anne, and ecclesiastics such as Aylmer, Parker and Whitgift.

Thomas Moffett. Tasso's *Amyntas* was dedicated to her, as were Thomas Morley's *Canzonets*.[1] And it was to her that her brother dedicated his *Arcadia* in such moving and humble terms: 'If you keepe it to your selfe, or to such friendes, who will weigh errors in the ballaunce of good will, I hope, for the father's sake, it will be pardoned, perchance made much of, though in it selfe it have deformities. For indeede, for severer eyes it is not, being but a trifle, and that triflinglie handled.'

Sidney's suitors, as might have been expected, were even more numerous. So accomplished a courtier, soldier and man of letters attracted a great variety of writers. 'His prestige was unrivalled', writes Mr John Buxton, 'and besides the poets, there were the nobles and courtiers vying with one another as they strove to emulate the Sidneys as poets or patrons.'[2]

Within the general framework there was still room for the expression of personal and particular reasons for the dedication of a book to one man rather than another. We have already seen how John Bridges hoped to discharge something of his obligations to the Earl of Bedford by dedicating his book to him, and a great many other authors tell us what has influenced them in their choice. Perhaps the most common of the reasons alleged is a desire to put on record the author's sense of obligation for various favours bestowed on him. Men speak of their connexion with the patron's family, as does Thomas Stocker, who records that he was brought up in the house of the Earl of Oxford,[3] while Robert Hill writes to Sir William Fitzwilliam and his lady: 'You have maintained me liberally in your family, and now when I publish this book, I remaine in your family.'[4] Reginald Scot underlines the kind of considerations that

---

[1] In dedicating his *Delia* to her Daniel described her as one 'whome the fortune of our time hath made the happier and judiciall Patronesse of the Muses (a glory hereditary to your house) to preserve them from those hidious Beestes, Oblivioun and Barbarisme'.

[2] J. Buxton, *Sir Philip Sidney and the English Renaissance* (1954), p. 204.

[3] *STC* 4437, J. Calvin, *Divers Sermons... translated by T. Stocker* (1581), sig. *4.

[4] *STC* 13478, R. Hill, *The contents of Scripture* (1596), sig. A 10^v.

animated some writers in the following dedication to his relative Sir Thomas Scot: 'I being of your house, of your name, & of your bloud; my foot being under your table, my hand in your dish, or rather in your pursse, might bee thought to flatter you in that, wherin (I knowe) I should rather offend you than please you.'[1] Some element of flattery there might be, but this does not obscure the fact that by thus dedicating his work Scot hopes to discharge something of his liability to his kinsman.

Some writers go into the matter more thoroughly, and give us details of their obligation. Arthur Hall, later a notorious Member of Parliament, reminds Sir Thomas Cecil that he had been a scholar with him in his father's house, and in recognition of this had long vowed to dedicate a work to him.[2] Others speak of being maintained 'in studie, whereby I have obtained that simple talent, which God hath bestowed on me',[3] or of being kept up at Cambridge as a student,[4] or elsewhere during a period of apprenticeship as a surgeon.[5] John Harmar says he owes to Leicester the 'good procurement of her Majesties gracious favour, whereby I first became a Scholer in Winchester Colledge, afterwards to bee removed to the New Colledge of Oxford, whereof at this present I am a poore member', and therefore he now offers to Leicester his translation from Calvin as something due to one 'unto whom I owe all thankfulnesse and humble dutie'.[6]

Others speak of their indebtedness in adult life to their patrons, and tell of the various ways they have been helped. Some are pensioners, as is John Blagrave, who acknowledges

[1] *STC* 21864, R. Scot, *The discoverie of Witchcraft* (1584), sig. A6.

[2] *STC* 13631, Homer, *Ten books of the Iliades...translated by A. Hall* (1581), sig. A2.

[3] *STC* 4067, H. Bullinger, *A most godly and learned discourse...of the holy Scripture. Translated by J. Tomkys* (1579), sig. A6.

[4] *STC* 17833 F. Meres, *Gods Arithmeticke* (1597), sig. A6.

[5] *STC* 1209, *The composition...of...Oleum Magistrale. Translated by G. Baker* (1574), sig. A2.

[6] *STC* 4453, J. Calvin, *Sermons upon the X Commandmentes*, translated by J. Harmar (1579), sig. *3.

the receipt of a pension or stipend 'most liberally bestowed on me' by Sir Francis Knollys, and who gives a valuable account of a patron's benevolence when he writes:

Your Honour beyond all expectation or cogitation of mine, drawes me forth of the poore countrie Cabin wherein obscurely I lurked, into your more open presence, and there so adorned and beautified me with your Honourable curtesies and favour, so renoumed my name at the Court amongst persons of high regard, and (not content therewith) without any least desart of mine, of purpose, as I take it, to encourage me to proceed: thereby not a litle bewraying your Honours hidden skill and secret good will to the Mathematicke sciences, most liberally bestowed on me a yearley pension or stipend.[1]

Several other writers mention the receipt of a pension or 'a liberall annuitye', or of some form of help, or 'your Lordships liberall hand by which I have so long lived'.[2] George Gifford, in dedicating his Sermon to John Hutton, reminds him that his parents received daily benefits from Hutton, so that 'I think I ought, when I am not able to make any recompence, at least to shew some token of a grateful mind'.[3]

For reasons such as these, we may confidently accept many dedicatory epistles as 'an assured token of dutiful remembrance of many most honourable courtesies, both extended and also daily continued'.[4] 'Courtesies' and 'benefits' are terms continually recurring in these dedications, as when Richard Robinson in dedicating a translation he had made to Sir William Allen, Alderman of London, says that he has received 'manifeste

---

[1] This I take to be essentially true, though subject to the kind of exaggeration to be expected in dedications. Professor E. G. R. Taylor tells us that Blagrave was of 'gentle birth and lived at Southcote Lodge, Swallowfield, Reading'. As a youth he was given access to the mathematical books in the library of Sir Thomas Parry; 'he wrote his *Baculum familliare* (1590) in the summer of 1589 at Grays Court, Oxon, the seat of his patron'. *STC* 3118, sig. A2.

[2] *STC* 649, 7103, 10097, 18889, 21535, 21865, 24631, etc.

[3] *STC* 11863, G. Gifford, *A Sermon upon the parable of the Sower* (1582), sig. A2.

[4] *STC* 2046, T. Beza, *A shorte... Treatize of the Plague* (1580), translated by J. Stockwood, sig. ¶6.

benefites...from time to time these twelve years at your Worshippses bountiful hands', and more specifically, some years later says that in response to the dedication 'my good Master gave mee in money and mony worth xl s.'[1]

Evidence of even greater generosity is occasionally given when the writer speaks of some office or position that he owes to his patron. Thomas Digges, one of the outstanding mathematicians and scientists of his day, dedicated a work on the use of mathematics in making various military calculations to Leicester, to whom he is 'deeply bound, as well for my preferment to her Majesties Service, as for sundrie other favours continuallye powred on me'.[2] As might be expected, the gift of a living was one way in which the great were able to reward their dependants. In dedicating a sermon to Sir Thomas Egerton, John Dove records that the offer of a living came at a time when he 'had set my heart at rest, as one resolved to die within the precincts of the Colledge, like a Monke shut up in his cell...without any hope of ever being called to any Ecclesiastical preferment'.[3] John Downame offers 'the present first fruits of my labours' to his patron, together with his 'obliged duty and humble thankfulness...having had through your honourable bounty...a part of the Lordes vineyard allocated unto mee, his most unworthy workman, by your Honour his most woorthy steward'.[4]

As a further example we may notice the dedicatory letter which John Harmar wrote to the Earl of Leicester in sending him a translation of Beza's *Sermons upon the three first Chapters of the Canticle of Canticles* (1587).

I was requested by manie of my friends, to emploie the time of this last vacation of mine from my publique readinges in the Universitie,

---

[1] *Studies in Philology*, vol. XXI, p. 634. See p. 49n.
[2] About this time, Digges was employed by the Crown in surveying Winchelsea Harbour, and rebuilding the fortifications at Dover. Rosenberg, *Leicester: Patron of Letters*, p. 284.
[3] STC 7087, J. Dove, *A Sermon preached at Paules Crosse* (1597), sig. A 3.
[4] STC 7147, J. Downame, *Spiritual physicke* (1600), sig. A 2.

in the translating of... Sermons... which I had a little before receaved from the Francfurt Mart in French... I did the more willingly emploie both my leasure and my paine, because I would have somewhat to present to your Lordshippe withal for a token and monument of my thankful duety, and dutifull thankfulnesse, upon so manie, so memorable, so utterly undeserved benefits of your Honor, not so much collated, as congested, & heaped from time to time upon me. For extend I the cogitation of my mind to the farthest part of my infancy and childhoode, and drawe it foorth as in a continuall and even threed unto this present time, what part of my age hath not beene honored with the patronage of your Lordships favor and goodwil towardes me? The ground and foundation of my first studies laid in Winchester by your honours onely meanes, in obtaining her highnesse letters for my preferment unto that schoole; the rearing of the farther frame of them in this Colledge, wherein placed by your Lordships favor, I yet continu; my time spent in my great desire & contentment in the parts beyond the Seas by your Honours intercession; my roome and degree I doe nowe enjoie in the Universitie beeing one of her Majesties publique professors, purchased by your Lordships favourable meditation, doe everie of them in particular deserve a volume of acknowledgements in al thankfulnes and humble devotion towards your honour.[1]

The coming in the eighties of the professional man of letters who relied on his pen for his living introduced a more strident note in the dedicatory epistles. Whatever authors had hitherto expected from their patrons, few were optimistic enough to think that they would be rewarded with any large sums or annual pensions. A few pounds, perhaps, were all they hoped for in cash, and in a limited number of cases their patron was able to recommend them to some position in the service of the Crown, or of some influential lord, or perhaps to give them a living or a tutorship.[2]

---

[1] *STC* 2025, sig. ¶ 2.
[2] 'The attempt to live by the pen alone was at the time (*c.* 1589) quite a new thing, indeed I doubt if any had yet succeeded in doing it—unless perhaps Robert Greene for a few hard-worked years.' McKerrow, *Nashe*, vol. v, p. 16. And see E. H. Miller, *The Professional Writer in Elizabethan England* (Cambridge, Mass., 1959), chapter IV.

This was not enough to content the professional writer. Patrons were made aware that something more was expected of them than a benevolent protection, and authors constantly were lamenting the small rewards that they received. Nashe, for example, is never tired of inveighing against the niggardly treatment of authors by their patrons. He invokes the memory of 'gentle Sir Phillip Sidney' who knew what belonged to a scholar, but he adds: 'Thou art dead in thy grave, and hast left too few successors of thy glory, too few to cherish the Sons of the Muses, or water those budding hopes with their plenty, which thy bounty erst planted.' He realizes that

a good Patron will pay for all. I, where is he?...But cap and thankes is all our Courtiers payment: wherefore, I would counsell my frends to be more considerate in their Dedications, and not cast away so many months labour on a clown that knowes not how to use a Scholer: for what reason have I to bestow any of my wit upon him, that wil bestow none of his wealth upon me? Alas, it is easie for a goodlie tall fellow that shineth in his silkes, to come and out face a poore simple Pedant in a thred bare cloake, and tell him his booke is prety, but at this time he is not provided for him: marrie, about twoe or three daies hence if he come that waie, his Page shall say he is not within, or else he is so busie with my L. How-call-ye-him, and my L. What-call-ye-him, that he may not be spoken withall.[1]

He also realizes, however, that the incessant importuning of patrons by so many has spoiled the market, so that nowadays, 'many write bookes to knights and men of great place, and have thankes and promise of further reward for their paines: others come of with a long Epistle to some rufling Courtier, that sweares swoundes and bloud, as soone as ever their backe is turnd"[2]—and that is all!

As a result of all this, these needy professionals were for ever seeking a munificent patron, turning from one man to another in the hope of finding such a person. Robert Greene,

[1] R. B. McKerrow, *The Works of Thomas Nashe* (1904–10), vol. I, p. 241.
[2] *Ibid.* vol. III, p. 341.

for instance, dedicated his seventeen books to sixteen different patrons, while Thomas Lodge changed his patron twelve times between 1584 and 1596. Michael Drayton tried another device when he published *Englands Heroicall Epistles* (1597), for the volume contains no general dedication, but most of the individual epistles are dedicated to one or other of his friends, or else to some person of consequence whose patronage he hoped to win. Another device was to preface the work with a number of dedicatory verses, as Spenser did with *The Faerie Queene*, writing no less than seventeen sonnets to some of the outstanding courtiers of his day. Lesser writers, such as Thomas Churchyard and Richard Robinson, were similarly importunate. Churchyard told Sir Walter Raleigh that although 'I have sixteene severall bookes printed presently[1] to bee bought (albeit they are but trifles) dedicated in sundrie seasons to severall men off good and great credite, but to be plaine not one among them all, from the first day of my labour and studies to this present yeere and hower, hath in anie waye preferred my. sutes, amended my state, or given mee anie countenaunce'.[2] In writing this he seems to have forgotten what he had written eight years earlier in a letter 'To the Friendly Reader' at the beginning of *A light bondell of livly discourses called Churchyardes Charge*, where he lamented how little his efforts had been recognized, but went on to say: 'In one thing I maie rejoice, the honourable persone to whom my *Choice* is dedicated (and others of great callyng) hath bothe been gratefull sondrie waies (in moste bountifull maner) and also hath encoraged me to proceede in the like paines.'[3]

We can come a little closer to what tangible rewards arose from patronship by studying the detailed account left by

[1] Presently, i.e. currently, at the moment.
[2] T. Churchyard, *Sparke of Frendship and Warme Goodwill* (1588). I owe this reference to Professor D. Nichol Smith's chapter on 'Authors and Patrons' in *Shakespeare's England*, vol. II, p. 207.
[3] *STC* 5240, in which he also writes, 'I daily trouble the good Reader with bookes, verses, pamflettes, and many other trifling thinges, as for any matter that I either can gaine glorie by, or deserveth to be embraced'.

Richard Robinson (needy translator and man of letters) of what happened as the result of his various attempts to win the favour of a number of well-to-do patrons of all ranks from the Queen downwards. His own words will best describe his fate when he presented to Elizabeth a copy of his translation of the third part of *The Harmony of King David's Harp*, written by V. Strigelius:

> Dedicated by me unto yow my moste gracyus Soveraigne.... I presented yt unto youre Highnes on all Sainctes day beeyng Saturdsay the first of November Anno 1595 at Richmond youre Majestie then goyng to ye Chappell in ye morning.... It pleased youre moste excellent Majesty to receyve this my pore labor gracyusly. I pore man expected Comfort for the same deservingly. O that yt had pleased youre moste excellent Highnes to have then remembered the Princely Prophet Davids example of gratification in this poynte... So that... I making my humble suite unto youre moste gracyus Highnes for some releef in money, what God mighte move youre gracyus mynde to bestowe upon mee: M. Doctor Caesar then Master of the Requestes returned mee answer, your Majesty thancked me for my good will, youre Highnes was glad yow had a subject coulde do so well, and that I deserved commendacions. But for any gratification for any suche laboures youre Majesty was not in mynde as then to bestow any suche relief uppon mee: for youre Highnes (as hee sayde) had care of the chargeable Voyage to come, of releving youre Needy soldyers and requyting of theyre paynes, fynally youre Highnes sett me not on worck, and therefore yow were not to pay me any wages. Herewith I departed from youre Highnes Court at Richmond, paciently as a pore man before, but now (by this meanes) become a Porer... for I founde now, mo Inconvenyences (by wanting my present releef) then ever I felte before in my lyfe tyme, or at leaste, synce I coulde first handle my penn: For my penury was so greate, that take what paynes I coulde with my pen at home and otherwyse, wryting for my Frendes abroad in the City yea and allso utter as many of these Bookes as I coulde for half a yeare after, trubling my good Benefactors (longer than eyther I thought I shoulde or willingly woulde have done) all was litle ynough and too to litle, to meynteyne mee, my wyfe, and one pore Chylde with meate, drincke, Lynnen, wollen, Rent and necessaries even very meanely.

So as before youre Majestyes Royall Navy went to Cadiz in June followyng 1596, I (still wanting my sayde releef) had solde away certeyne of my howshehould moveables, pawned away dyverse good bookes oute of my Chest, allso my very gowne from my back, yea, and (within two yeares after) was constrayned to sell away the very Leasse of my howse, wherin I then dwelt in Harp Alley in Shoe lane, for the Rent paying due to the Landlord at Michaelmas, 1598....

Onely Gods providence and my owne pore Indeyvour in vertue (for knowledg and releef of my pore estate) helped mee at that instant (so muche as I coulde) by Collecting, wryting oute parfecting and imparting the substance and Circumstance of this happy expedicion... whiche I presenting first unto the Moste Vertuous.... Lord high Admirall of England... liberally gratifying my good will: Dyverse Knightes of ye sayde Cadiz Voyage bestowed upon mee allso bothe they frendly benevolence for the same Copyes, and furthered me in perfecting the Originall for my future benefit amongst others. So as from October 1595, when I presented my Boke unto youre Majesty, untill October 1596, I helped my self with the sale of youre Majestyes booke, and the Copy of this voyage aforesayde: withoute any Consideracion receyved from your Majesty for the dedication therof as aforesayd....

So thoughe youre Majesty at the first, nor second suite of me youre unworthy Supplicant, do not satisfy my present necessity, when possibly some one or other in Auctority aboute your Highnes eyther ys unwilling (or a withholder of your gracyus goodnes graunted or given unto mee), yet I doubte not but (in tyme) God of his greate goodnes & mercy will move youre moste Princely mynde to effect my humble desyer in well deserving.[1]

A similar fate befell him when he approached the Earl of Warwick, 'who receyved (by one Copinger) my Boke at my handes but rendered mee no reward for the same: I was therefore driven to make benefit of one hundred Bookes within two yeares space afterwards to the value of xli. [£10] sterling'.

---

[1] *Studies in Philology*, vol. XXI (1924), G. McG. Vogt, 'Richard Robinson's *Eupolemia* (1603)', pp. 637–41.

On another occasion Sir Thomas Egerton refused to receive the fourth part of *The Harmony of King David's Harp*, presented to him by Robinson

> in the presence of the six clerks in the Chancery: His Lordship grutching to receyve my Booke, or to render mee any rewarde, his eloquent tongue tripped mee in my suite saying 'What have we here? Literae petaces?' I shewing his Lordship yt was a pore mans honest Indeavoure whiche would gladly live in the feare of God and deserve well of all good men what I coulds: He answered me....I shoulde have made him privy to yt before I had dedicated yt unto him. I replyed, both his Honorable Antecessors in office not onely receyved my good will & good workes with lyke good will but also worthely rewarded me for the same....His Booke (or rather my booke) I bestowed upon a vertuous Lady in the City, who gave mee the duble value therof, and I made benefit of 25 Bookes mo, amongst my other good Frendes in the City to some Ls. [50/-]. I will abyde pacyently the redres of my wrong and releef of my necessity untill God the Just Judge of the worlde shall in his grace and mercy move this noble mans mynde to do mee more good by helping mee to some wryting worcke in the Offices of the Chancery which God Graunte. Amen.

He was not always so unfortunate. That 'noble Maecenas', the Earl of Rutland, gave him £3, and Robinson describes him as 'many times before and since, my best Patron', and he was also indebted to another beneficent patron of authors in Sir Christopher Hatton. He names ten others who gave him sums ranging from £2 to ten shillings.

The issue of a new edition sometimes enabled him to dedicate the work anew, and thus to reap a new reward. This was not a substantial source of income, however, as Robinson found when he dedicated the third edition of Leland's *A Record of Ancyent Historyes* to the Bishop of Chichester. Since Robinson had 'perused, corrected and bettered' the original as he claims, the fact that the Bishop gave him a miserable two shillings makes us commiserate with him when he comments that the Bishop was 'not so thankfull as I deserved'.

THE VOGUE OF PATRONAGE

An examination of Robinson's account of what he had received in cash shows that twelve of his books only brought him in about £40—a small sum when spread over some fifteen years. In addition he was given 25 copies of some of his publications, and these he sold at varying prices which perhaps brought him in another £20. No wonder that he had to sell his books and the lease of his house to make ends meet.

Facts such as these were no doubt in Miss Sheavyn's mind when she came to the conclusion that 'only an exceptionally robust literary class could have withstood the withering effects of poverty, official interference, unfair competition, and scorn.... It was the Elizabethan writer's vigorous vitality alone which overcame all obstacles.'[1] But even if this conclusion were true, it deals only with a portion of the output of the age and refers almost entirely to a handful of talented, vociferous men of letters who appeared on the scene in the last two decades of the reign.

If we view the output as a whole, however, it is clear that year in, year out, few books were not being patronized, and I should guess that omitting certain classes of books, only about ten per cent of the remainder appeared without a dedication. So strong was this convention that it expressed itself in a great variety of ways, so that it is impossible to lay down any all-embracing formula to cover its operations. While some dedicated to the Queen or to the great Officers of State, others were content to offer their book to a country neighbour or even to a humble relative. Patronage flourished under many guises and was kept alive for a multitude of reasons which are often explicitly stated. There is little reason to disbelieve what is said of a personal nature in most of these dedicatory epistles, and if men hoped for some material gain by writing them, it is seldom made manifest. Rather they are recognitions of former favours and of former encouragement. 'I have beaten my braines in contriving some device wherein I might yeld you thankes, and after my simple sorte, make you parte of a recom-

[1] *The Literary Profession in the Elizabethan Age*, p. 7.

pence', writes Thomas Twyne, and this idea of the book as a 'recompence' is uppermost in many dedications.[1] So is the notion of the patron as a protector, or as a guarantor of the contents. 'The wel liking of such Noblemen and Magistrates as God hath innobled with the knowledg of his Gospel', Leicester is told, 'is a great furtherance to the good accepting of both of them among the inferior degrees',[2] and this idea was in the minds of many in choosing a patron. Often we are told of how various names were considered before a decision was taken, the choice not being determined by what might be received from the patron, but because he stood out as a supporter of the ideas contained in the book.[3]

A few minor matters call for attention. Very occasionally the patron's name is removed and another substituted. This is generally because of death, and only more rarely because of the downfall of the original dedicatee. Hakluyt's *Voyages*, originally dedicated to Sir Philip Sidney in 1582, on his death were re-dedicated in 1589 to Sir Francis Walsingham, and after his death to the Earl of Nottingham and Lord Burghley jointly. The downfall of the Earl of Norfolk led to the suppression of his name on the second edition of *The vanitie of artes and sciences* by Henry Cornelius Agrippa in 1575, but these are comparatively rare changes and we should not attach too much importance to them.[4]

Nor need we think that authors snatched at the possibility of a second edition as an opportunity for milching a new patron. Needy Richard Robinson did this, as we have seen, but perhaps

---

[1] See, for example, *STC* 2046, T. de Beza, *A shorte... Treatize of the Plague* (1580), sig. ¶6. Cf. *STC* 2962, J. Calvin, *A harmonie upon the three Evangelists* (1584), sig. x2; *STC* 3145, T. Blundeville, *A briefe description of universal Mappes...* (1589), sig. A2, etc.

[2] *STC* 4444, J. Calvin, *Sermons upon Job* (1574), sig. A3ᵛ.

[3] *STC* 4460, J. Calvin, *Two and twentie Sermons...on the 119th psalme* (1580), sig. *2.

[4] See Williams, *Index of Dedications & Commendatory Verses...*, pp. 243–54 for complete list.

the fact that the Bishop of Chichester fobbed him off with a paltry two shillings for a third edition dedication shows that the practice was not a lucrative one. In any case, the number that seem to have done so is very small.

A word should also be said about dedications offered by deputies for the authors. Friends were sometimes asked to do what they thought best, a practice adopted in dedicating Lodge's *Euphues shadow* (1592),[1] or the bookseller was given the task of finding the suitable patron. R. Jones, in his dedicatory letter to Judge David Lewis, writes: 'It may seem a point of great presumption in me to commende to your protection this small booke, being another man's labour', but he does so, as he explains, in 'the absence of the Author, who (not only) delivered the Copye hereof unto mee to be printed, but (also) committed the dedication of it to be disposed (by me) to my best liking'.[2]

It has to be remembered, however, that many were hailed as patrons who knew nothing of the writer or of his intentions until they saw the book in print. The great were particularly subject to this imposition, as a few instances all connected with the Earls of Bedford will illustrate. 'Pardon my boldness herein', writes Thomas Lupton, in dedicating his *A dream of the Devill and Dives* (1584) to Francis, the second Earl of Bedford, since, as he admits, he is 'so simple a person and unknowne of your honour'.[3] Equally so was Thomas Tymme when he dedicated a translation of Guevara's *A looking Glasse for the Court* (1575) to another member of the family, in which he declares that 'it nothing doth dismaye me that I being unknowne to your Honour, have thus far presumed, neyther maye this seeme any rashe attempt for that cause since being warranted under your protection it cannot but carry great

---

[1] *STC* 16656, sig. A3.
[2] *STC* 5615, *The welspring of wittie conceites* (1584), sig. A3.
[3] *STC* 16947, sig. A2. Cf. *STC* 13043, Heliodorus, *An Æthiopian History* (1587). 'It doth nothing dismay me...that I was not knowen to your Lordship' (T. Underdown to the Earl of Oxford).

credit'.[1] This view is set out at greater length in the dedication of *Cooper's Chronicle* (1560) to the second Earl.

> These my labours (ryght honorable), I have bene so bolde to exhibite unto you,... as one whose honour, wysedome, and vertue is suche as can not but favourablie mainteine and further the studious indevours of learned men. For all be it I am a person to your honour so unknowen as ye maie well marvaile at my doynge, and thinke my attempte bothe rashe and impudent; yet the reporte of that gentlenesse and favour, that ye have alway shewed to them that desyre in any wyse to further learnyng, doth throughly perswade me, that you will not onely not mervayle at me, but also take my dooyng in good parte, and gentilly interprete the same. In this perswasion I am muche confyrmed by divers examples of learned men before tyme: whiche have dedicated the fruites of theyr studies to prynces and noble personages, not upon confydence of aqueintance and knowlage, but of persuasion that the state of nobilitee and honour in common weales woulde alwaies be a false protection & defence for knowlage and learnynge. I wyll not therefore in many wordes excuse my boldnesse, lest I shoulde seeme therein to mistrust your honour and gentlenesse.[2]

While a limited number of men were the subject of many dedications, it is not often remarked that there were a considerable number of others who were only thus honoured once or twice in their lives. These single dedications were more frequent than is often realized. A random count made by inspecting about two hundred titles showed that in some twenty per cent of them the dedicatee was only once thus honoured. When we look at such dedications we see that they have been made for reasons such as we should expect. They are not made in the hope of protection or of reward, but as a simple, heart-felt recognition of 'divers benefites', such as the loan of books, or the granting of leisure to read them, or youthful friendship 'that neither length of time, distance of

[1] *STC* 12448, sig. A3. Cf. *STC* 3928, A. Brucioli, *A commentary upon the Canticle of Canticles* (1598), where the translator, T. James, Fellow of New College, writes: 'My selfe being as yet unknown unto your Lordship (Sir T. Egerton) am moved to sue for protection of myself, and defence of mine Author.' [2] *STC* 15218, sig. a3ᵛ.

CONCLUSIONS

place, nor discontents of minde have beene able, I will not say to abolish, but to diminish'.[1] Some dedicate to their friends or relatives, others to their pupils at the University or elsewhere. In short, each of them, as one writer puts it, is dedicated as 'a token of love, or argument of duty, or signe of thankfulnesse'.[2] The study of the mass of evidence afforded by the various types of dedications of which samples have been given above leads to the conclusion that the belief in the efficacy of a dedication, and of a patron to whom it could be offered, still remained strong throughout the period. Men saw in the dedication a means of proclaiming to all their thankfulness for benefits, their affection for their friend or patron and their belief that the fact that they were under the protection of the dedicatee afforded them some protection from the carper and the 'busy reprehenders'.

[1] *STC* 6819, J. Dickenson, *Greene in conceipt* (1598), sig. A2. Cf. *STC* 10499, sig. A2.
[2] *STC* 21672, Saluste du Bartas, *The triumph of faith* (1592), sig. A2. Cf. *STC* 6230, 19148, 21632.

CHAPTER III

THE REGULATION OF THE BOOK TRADE

During the first half of the sixteenth century the Crown had kept a watchful eye on the press, and from time to time issued warnings and had punished printers and booksellers who overstepped the bounds laid down in proclamations and decrees. Matters of religion and politics were especially liable to cause trouble, and 'naughty printed books' were seized by the authorities and their vendors punished. Then on 4 May 1557, Queen Mary, in an attempt to establish a firmer mode of control, promulgated a Charter incorporating the Stationers' Company and giving them authority over nearly all the printers throughout the kingdom. Armed with this power, the Company was able to prohibit printing by any except its own members or those few who had a right given to them by royal warrant. The Company was empowered to seek out unauthorized printers, to seize any printed or bound stock which had been produced 'contrary to the form of any statute, act, or proclamation made or to be made'. The material they seized they could burn, put the printers in prison, and levy a fine of 100s. on each of them. The Charter gave the Company the right to elect its own officers, to enact its own rules for the good conduct of the members and their workmen, to own property, and to sue and be sued as a corporate body.[1]

With this Charter at their backs the Stationers' Company began its new existence by electing a Master, two Wardens and ninety-four freemen as ordinary members. Throughout Elizabeth's reign the Company had complete control of 'the craft

[1] Printed by E. Arber, *A Transcript of the Registers of the Company of Stationers of London*, vol. 1, pp. xxviii–xxxii.

THE INJUNCTIONS OF 1559

and mystery of printing' save that, from time to time, the Queen or one of the great administrative departments, such as the Privy Council, gave the Master and Wardens instructions touching the day-to-day conduct of their trade. By this means the Crown was able to exert pressure as it thought best from time to time, leaving the tiresome and often difficult job of implementing its commands to the officials of the Company.

The first of the royal instructions to the Stationers was given in some *Injunctions* issued in 1559, which read (*inter alia*) as follows:

> Section 51. *Item* because there is a great abuse in the printers of bokes, which for covetousnes cheifly regard not what they print, so thei may have gaine, whereby arriseth great dysorder by publicatyon of unfrutefull, vayne and infamous bokes and papers: The Quenes majestie straytly chargethe and commaundeth, that no manner of person shall print any manner of boke or paper, of what sort, nature, or in what language soever it be, excepte the same be first licenced by her majestie by expresse wordes in writynge, or by .vi. of her privy counsel, or be perused and licensed by the archbysshops of Cantorbury and Yorke, the bishop of London, the chauncelours of both unyversities, the bishop beyng ordinary, and the Archdeacon also of the place where any suche shalbe printed, or by two of them, wherof the ordinary of the place to be alwaies one.[1]

A few years later in 1566 the Court of High Commission (the Star Chamber) put out another set of orders dealing with 'unlawful Books', and laying down fines and punishments for those offending,[2] and this was followed in 1570 by a letter from the Privy Council to the Stationers' Company which did little to alter the general situation.[3] The key document of the latter part of the century was the decree of 1586. Issued in part as a result of a fact-finding commission appointed by the Star Chamber to look into the complaints of a number of aggrieved printers, the decree prohibited the publication of any book

---

[1] *STC* 10095 ff. Printed by Arber, *A Transcript of the Registers of the Company of Stationers of London*, vol. I, pp. xxxviii–xxxix.

[2] Arber, *op. cit.* vol. I, p. 322.   [3] Arber, *op. cit.* vol. v, p. lxxvi.

before it had been perused by the Archbishop of Canterbury or the Bishop of London, and allowed by the Queen's *Injunctions*.[1] This put the responsibility squarely on the shoulders of two men only, but to give practical effect to these instructions it was obvious that the highly placed officials could not possibly read all the books themselves and that they would have to depute the task to members of their entourage. Two years later, therefore, the Archbishop appointed twelve 'preachers and others... to have the perusinge and alowinge of Copies that are to be printed'.[2] For the remainder of the reign this arrangement seems to have been effectively operated.

Two groups of printers remained outside the control of the Company. The two universities were entitled to print by reason of royal licences,[3] while a few individuals held Letters Patent which enabled them to print certain classes of books to the exclusion of others.[4] Although the Company's charter limited its powers to London and the suburbs, since there were no serious provincial printers at the time (other than the two universities) the Company was in virtual control of all the printing done in England, and indeed an authority on the London Guilds has declared that 'no other company... ever attained the same degree of monopoly as that which the State thought it expedient to confer on the Stationers'.[5]

The overall effects of these regulations has been stated by Sir Walter Greg in the following words:

By concentrating the craft of printing books, and to a considerable extent their distribution, in the hands of a single society in London—if we except the authorized printers working for the universities of Oxford and Cambridge—the Government rendered the task of

[1] Arber, *op. cit.* vol. II, pp. 807-12.
[2] W. W. Greg and E. Boswell, *Records of the Court of the Stationers' Company 1576 to 1602—from Register B* (The Bibliographical Society, 1930), p. 28.
[3] The University of Cambridge obtained a licence to print in 1534: Oxford in 1586.
[4] For these Patent holders, see pp. 64 ff.
[5] G. Unwin, *The Gilds and Companies of London* (1908), p. 261.

THE STATIONERS' RECORDS

surveillance and control of the nation's reading comparatively easy. On the other hand, the monopoly it ensured to the members of the Company was valuable and gratifying, and no other interests existed of sufficient weight to form an effective opposition or even raise a vocal protest.[1]

So much for theory: how far and how frequently the injunctions were enforced is another matter, and for information about this we are largely dependent on the records of the Stationers' Company, and since the Company had been charged with the duty of seeing that the royal instructions were observed, and given the power to punish offenders, their records should (in theory) contain a full account of these matters. As soon as they had received their Charter in 1557 the Stationers began to keep a series of books, two of which are our immediate concern—the Wardens' Book, and the Clerk's Book, and in these they entered the names of the apprentices, the freemen, the fines, licences, decrees and ordinances. The Wardens' Book carries us down to 1571 and then there is a gap before the next volume, known as the Clerk's Book, starts in 1576, and gives even more information than does the first volume. All this material was printed by Professor Edward Arber, and the part of the Clerk's Book which he was not at that time allowed to print has since been edited by Sir Walter Greg and Miss Boswell.[2] Most of our knowledge of the day-to-day working of the Company comes from these sources.

The cardinal point of all the royal enactments, it will have been noticed, was the emphasis placed on the necessity that every work should be examined by an authorized agent. This authority varied from time to time, but in all cases the Crown had someone that it could hold responsible if need arose. While in theory it was only some high-ranking officer of State that could authorize publication, it appears that this was not considered necessary in many cases, and for such books the officers of the Company accepted the responsibility of licensing

[1] Greg and Boswell, *Records of the Court of the Stationers' Company*, p. lx.
[2] Greg and Boswell, *op. cit.*

the work. Hence we find entries such as the following: 'Receyvd of Roberte Calye for pryntinge of a boke contrary to our ordenaunces that ys, not havynge lycense frome the master and wardyns for the same the xvii Daye of Decembre [1557] iiiis.'[1] After 1586, however, things were tightened up and most copies were licensed by the bishops or their appointed deputies, although the wardens of the Company still continued to do so, and over half of the copies entered in the Register were licensed by both authorities.[2]

So long as the book was entered, whether or no it mentioned all the conditions that had been fulfilled, the government had something on record. What was much more unsatisfactory from their point of view was the fact that something like a third of the books actually published were never entered at all. The reason for this is hard to understand, since the few pence that were charged for entry cannot have been an obstacle, while on the other hand by doing so a man obtained what we should now call copyright. It must be admitted, however, that according to 'the custom of the trade' copyright was assumed and enjoyed by many who did not trouble to enter their copies, and also that there are very few instances of men being fined for not entering their copies, though there are frequent entries of fines being imposed on them for not getting a licence for the book.

This brings us back to the central point that it was the licence that was all important. Whether or no this fact was recorded (supposing the book to be entered) depended on the degree of care exercised by the clerk of the Company at any given moment. A licence might have been merely endorsed on the manuscript itself, or given in a note or letter, or even by word of mouth without such facts being actually recorded,

[1] Arber, *A Transcript of the Registers of the Company of Stationers of London*, vol. I, p. 70.
[2] Greg, *London Publishing between 1550 and 1650* (Oxford, 1956), p. 49. 'In the sixty-four years from 1576 to 1640 I have counted 9397 new copies entered, of which 1813 bear no indication of licence, 1672 bear only a domestic, 439 only an outside licence, and 5473 have both.

LICENCES TO PRINT

although we have instances which show the Clerk recording just such happenings. For instance, a work might be entered by command of one of the Wardens, given 'in wrytyng under his hand',[1] or by the production of a 'special knowen token sent from master Warden Newbery',[2] or by a note in Master Fenner's hand, 'layd up in the Warden's cupbord',[3] there to be kept as evidence were it so required. For the endorsement on the manuscript it is recorded that Newbery vouched for a ballad 'in his own handwrytinge on the backsyde of the wrytten copie',[4] while Warden Barker did the same on the printed copy of another work.[5] Even the Clerk at times took a risk, as when he accepted the word of R. Waldegrave that the Wardens had licensed *The grounds of Christianity*, and duly entered the work, recording this fact with the words 'as he saieth'.[6]

While the above may be taken as showing the way the entries were generally made, we must not push this too far. A variety of terms, all meaning much the same thing in the minds of the writers, were used. Allowed, granted, assigned, entered, licensed—all occur with nothing to show why one word is used rather than another, and any attempt to read a special significance into this or that form of words is rapidly met by contradictory evidence. All we can assume is that most entries bear their meaning clear on their face, so that 'Licenced to John Charlewood by the Wardens and allowed by the Bishop of London' means that this work has been read by (or probably for) the Bishop of London who allows it to be printed, while the Wardens of the Company license Charlewood to do so, being satisfied that the work belongs to Charlewood and not to some other member of the Company. Similarly hundreds of other entries explain themselves and raise few problems.

---

[1] Arber, *A Transcript of the Registers of the Company of Stationers of London*, vol. II, p. 447.
[2] *Ibid.* vol. II, p. 434.
[3] *Ibid.* vol. II, p. 633.
[4] *Ibid.* vol. II, pp. 440, 448.
[5] *Ibid.* vol. II, p. 443.
[6] *Ibid.* vol. II, pp. 392, 487.

More interesting than the normal entries are those which show the Company's officials taking special care in the way they record an entry which raises some difficulty in their minds. For this reason they enter many works conditionally: the book has not yet got an authorization from a competent person,[1] or it is not yet clear that some other person has not a prior right to the work.[2] Some books are entered conditionally on their being printed by a certain printer,[3] or in impressions not exceeding a certain number, or they are to be printed in French or Italian,[4] and so on.

Translations, particularly those of Spanish works, were hedged about with conditions, as John Charlewood found when he sought to obtain a licence for a translation of *Palmerin of England*. This was granted only upon condition 'that if there be anie thinge founde in the booke when it is extante worthie of Reprehension that then all the Bookes shall be put to waste and Burnte'.[5] Whether Charlewood found these conditions unacceptable is unknown, but no edition by him of the work is known, and it was afterward licensed to Thomas Crede in August 1596, and published by him that year. Another of these Spanish romances, *The second part of the first booke of the Myrrour of Knighthood* was entered, but with the condition that it was to be translated 'and soe to be printed, condiconally notwithstandinge that when the same is translated yt be brought to them [i.e. the Wardens] to be perused, and yf any thinge be amisse therein to be amended'. This was in August 1582,[6] and the book was 'newly printed' in 1585. In his dedicatory letter the printer makes no mention of having found any difficulty in satisfying the Wardens, though he does speak of 'evill luck' which has deferred the preparation of further sections of the

[1] Arber, *A Transcript of the Registers of the Company of Stationers of London*, vol. II, pp. 429, 444, 487.
[2] *Ibid.* vol. II, pp. 336, 405, 435, 439.
[3] *Ibid.* vol. II, pp. 353, 477, 608, 650.
[4] *Ibid.* vol. II, pp. 478, 539, 542, 555, 560.
[5] *Ibid.* vol. II, p. 388.
[6] *Ibid.* vol. II, p. 414.

romance.[1] Again, in 1589 John Wolfe found the officials suspicious when he asked them to enter for his copy Books II–V of *Amadis of Gaul*, yet to be translated. This they did, but added a note stating that 'the lord Bishop of London his hand is to every of the said four French bookes severally for alowance of the printinge therof in English'.[2] Here again no edition by Wolfe appears to exist, although the second book was issued by another publisher in 1595, six years after it was licensed.[3]

To protect themselves should any trouble arise, the officials sometimes added to an entry words such as 'And the said Edward White hath undertaken to beare and discharge all troubles that maie arise from the printinge therof'[4] or they require the printer to agree to the surrender and burning of the whole edition in the Company's Hall if it was thought to be offensive.[5]

While the above may be taken to show the way the entries were usually made, it must be realized that the Registers, extending as they do over the whole reign, reflect the way in which growing experience by the Stationers of their duties, the personal care with which the Clerks made their entries and the varying pressures from time to time of the Crown, all made their mark. The earliest entries generally stated that *A* was given a licence to print *B* and for this he paid so much. Only rarely is anything said concerning any of the people constantly mentioned in the injunctions and decrees—the great lords of the Council, the great ecclesiastics, and the like. For example, in the year July 1559–July 1560 only three books were 'authorized' by such people out of 91 entries in the Register, and in the year 1576–77 out of 103 entries only seven were 'authorized'. It is clear that the officers of the Company were trusted to check the works brought to be entered, and as we see, from time to time they asked for an authorization by a

---

[1] *STC* 18862, sig. A 4.   [2] Arber, *op. cit.* vol. II, p. 607.
[3] *STC* 542.   [4] Arber, *op. cit.* vol. II, pp. 411, 477.
[5] *Ibid.* vol. II, pp. 366, 388.

superior before they would take the responsibility of accepting the work.

After the Star Chamber decree of 1586 had put the responsibility of licensing on to the Archbishop and the Bishop of London, the Clerk was often no longer willing to accept a work 'under the hands of the Wardens', but required the signature of one of the clerics nominated in his order of 1588. From now on well over half the entries were made with both 'outside' and 'domestic' licences (to use Sir Walter Greg's terms), so that the long expressed desire for 'orderly printing' was becoming an actuality.

The control of the Crown on printing was not confined to its licensing regulations, but was also exercised in a more sporadic but discriminating way by means of the privileges which from time to time it conferred on various individuals, giving them the sole right to print a book or books. The author of a legal work, for example, had to get it printed by Richard Tottell; the writer of a dictionary sought out the aid of Henry Bynneman, while the makers of almanacs and prognostications went to Richard Watkins and James Roberts. Various forms of devotional works; a variety of school text-books; books written in Greek, Latin or Hebrew—all had their individual printers, who held grants by Letters Patent valid for a stated number of years, and any infringement of their rights brought down penalties on the head of the offender.

Outstanding in the ranks of the patent holders was the Queen's Printer. When Elizabeth came to the throne this office was held by John Cawood, who had been appointed by Queen Mary on 29 December 1553, who granted 'to the said John Cawood, the office of our printer of all and singular our statute books, acts, proclamations, injunctions, and other volumes, and things, under what name or title soever, either already, or hereafter to be published in the English language'.[1] On Elizabeth's accession, however, a new patent was issued

[1] W. Herbert, *Typographical Antiquities. Begun by Joseph Ames* (1790), vol. II, p. 786 n.

jointly to Cawood and Richard Jugge,[1] and they continued to act as the Queen's Printers until Cawood's death on 1 April 1573, followed by that of Jugge early in 1577. A new patent was issued to Sir Thomas Wilkes, a diplomatist, who sold it to Christopher Barker,[2] and by the terms of the patent Barker was authorized to print the Bible, the Book of Common Prayer, the Statutes and all Proclamations. Then in 1588 Barker appointed George Bishop and Ralph Newbery as his deputies, and on 8 August 1589 his son Robert obtained a patent in reversion, to operate after his father's death, embracing 'all and singular the Statutes, books, pamphlets, acts of Parliament, proclamations, injunctions, as of bibles, New Testaments of all sorts whatsoever translate in the English tongue, imprinted or to be imprinted...also of all books for the service of God'.[3]

This was in theory a most comprehensive patent, but it was not quite so exclusive as it appears to be, since the Queen had already given certain privileges to other printers which infringed upon Barker's patent. For example, Jugge had the right to print the Bible in quarto and the New Testament in decimo sexto,[4] while other Bibles were free to all. As for 'books for the service of God', William Seres had a patent for the printing of primers and the Catechism,[5] while John Day held a similar licence for the Psalms in metre and the little Catechism.[6]

Another most valuable patent was held by Richard Tottell who had the exclusive right to print 'all manner of books of the common law', a concession which gave him complete control over the publication of all legal works save those reserved to the Queen's Printer.[7] As we have seen, the mass and variety of

[1] Jugge printed the proclamation announcing the accession of Elizabeth (*STC* 7886), but in the following February the names of both printers appear on a proclamation (*STC* 7890).
[2] Arber, *A Transcript of the Registers of the Company of Stationers of London*, vol. II, p. 15.
[3] *Ibid.* vol. II, p. 16.
[4] *The Library*, Fifth Series, vol. X (1955), p. 179.
[5] Arber, *op. cit.* vol. II, p. 15. [6] *Ibid.* vols. I, pp. 115–16; II, p. 775.
[7] *Ibid.* vol. II, p. 14.

every kind of law book issued by him is evidence of the extent to which he exploited his privilege. Similarly, the holders of patents for the printing of the more popular school books, or books of psalms, prayers and devotions, chronicles and dictionaries, or the immensely popular almanacs and prognostications, were in possession of a valuable property.[1] 'These monopolies', writes Cyprian Blagden, 'had three important features in common: they covered groups of books, not individual titles; they were therefore capable of expansion: they dealt with books which were cheap and popular; they were therefore vulnerable to piracy: they were enjoyed by printers; they therefore excited opposition both from other printers and from booksellers.'[2]

The Queen also granted patents of a more limited kind. For instance, John Day had the sole right to print Cuningham's *The Cosmological Glass* (1559) for the period of his life, and also for seven years 'all such books and works as he hath imprinted or hereafter shall imprint, being devised, compiled or set out by any learned man at the procurement, costes and charges only of the said John Day'.[3] Christopher Saxton had the sole right for ten years to print the maps he had prepared,[4] and Christopher Ockland's *Anglorum Praelia* (1580), a book in Latin verse, was ordered to be used in all grammar schools and free schools throughout the realm,[5] while Timothy Bright alone could publish not only his book *Characterie* (1588), being the first manual of shorthand in English, but also 'all such other works as he may compile'.[6]

---

[1] Thomas Marshe and Thomas Vautrollier held a patent for these schoolbooks; William Seres for psalms, books of private prayers, etc.: Henry Bynneman for chronicles and dictionaries; Richard Watkins and James Roberts for almanacs and prognostications. For full list, see Arber, *op. cit.* vol. I, p. 111.

[2] C. Blagden, *The Library*, Fifth Series, vol. X (1955), p. 164.

[3] Herbert, *Ames' Typographical Antiquities*, vol. I, p. 631.

[4] *Ibid.* vol. III, p. 1650 n.   [5] *Ibid.* vol. II, p. 910.

[6] Arber, *A Transcript of the Registers of the Company of Stationers of London*, vol. II, p. 16, and see vol. II, p. 746 for patents held by T. Vautrollier.

All these various forms of privilege were not held without challenge from time to time. There were many periods when there was not enough work to keep all the printers busy, and it was only natural that those without work should look askance at their brethren who were prospering by means of the assured trade that came to them by reason of their monopolies. From this it was an easy step for a printer who lacked work to run off for himself an impression of a privileged book, and to hope that he would escape undetected—or more likely that the rightful owner would not think it worth while to challenge the matter.

The patent holders refused to admit that their monopolies were an unmixed blessing. In a report by the Queen's Printer, Christopher Barker, made to Lord Burghley in December 1582, he outlines some of the advantages and the disadvantages that adhered to the holding of one of the patents. For instance, he says that though he has the sole right to print the proclamations, the fact is that the demand for their production often comes without notice, and that they have to be printed in haste, so that he has to take other work off the machines, and as a result he says that 'oftentimes I lose more by one proclamation than I gain by six... and in so many years there happeneth not a proclamation of any benefitt at all'. As for the Bible and the New Testament, the latter has to be sold at so small a price that it scarcely meets the cost of the printing, and at the same time he has had to lay out some £3000 in a year and a half in order to print the Bible, so that he says, 'in which time if I had died, my wife and children had been utterly undone, and many of my friends greatly hindered by disboursing round sums of money for me by suerty-ship and other means... so that now this gap being stopped, I have little or nothing to do, but adventure a needless charge, to keep the journeymen in work, most of them servants of my predecessors'. He goes on to discuss the value of the patents held by other printers, but is nowhere more than lukewarm as to their value. Tottell's patent 'hath been very beneficial.... Nowe it is of much lesse value than before, and is like yet to be rather worse than better.' Bynneman's patent to print chronicles and dictionaries he roundly declares to be 'more dangerous to the Patentee than profitable'.[1]

Many did not believe this, however, and there was much printing of other people's copies, both privileged and unprivileged. The Company tried to check this and the Registers show continuous efforts on the part of the authorities to control their wayward members by fines and sometimes by the confiscation of the printed copies. In many cases the culprit had no answer and could not resist punishment, but there were times when men were in doubt whether or no they could print some item, and the Court from time to time heard claim and counterclaim for the ownership of a book, over thirty such cases being recorded in the Court Book between 1576 and 1602. Sir Walter Greg characterizes these proceedings by observing that 'it may be that as a rule each side had a case of sorts to lay before the Assistants, and no doubt the decisions were given more in accordance with common sense and social diplomacy than with any rigid legal code. It was in fact a Court of conciliation rather than of law. At any rate we are able to observe a marked tendency, while giving an award in favour of one or other claimant, to allow some compensation to the unsuccessful rival, and many of the decisions are in the nature of a compromise.'[2]

The records, therefore, show the work being shared, or one party being given part of the edition at a reduced cost, or being given the right to have a specified number of copies printed for his own use. At times the right to print, but not the right to market the edition was granted, or an unsuccessful claimant was allowed a certain number of copies, and perhaps a cash payment also.

These well-meant attempts to regulate the trade, however, did not mollify a number of members who felt that they were not being given a fair share. As early as January 1578, 'the

[1] Arber, *op. cit.* vol. 1, pp. 115ff. and p. 146.
[2] Greg and Boswell, *Records of the Court of the Stationers' Company*, p. lxxv.

poore men of this Companie' had petitioned the Court for the relief of their sufferings, and their requests were in part granted, more work at adequate rates being promised them.[1] This quietened them down for a while, but did not satisfy the more intransigent rebels. Their leader was John Wolfe, whose outlook can be gauged by the fact that he had declared that 'it was lawfull for all men to print all lawfull bookes, what commandement soever her Majesty gave to the contrary'. A contemporary document states that

> Wolfe being a fishmonger by ye Charter of the Stationers ought not to print at all without her Majesties speciall licence. Wolfe made suite for a priviledge, which being found too large or generall had ye repulse, whereupon he printed what pleased him best of these men's ...priviledges following. Wolfe being friendly perswaded to live in order and not to print men's priviledged copies, for which to their great charge they had provided presses, letters, and other necessaries, answered he was a freeman, and had as great a priviledge as any of them all and that he would print all their bokes, if he lacked work. Wolfe being admonished that he being but one so meane a man should not presume to contrarie her Highnesse gouermente. 'Tush', said he. 'Luther was but one man, and reformed all ye world for religion, and I am that one man, that must and will reforme the government in this trade', meaning printing and bookeselling.

The writer goes on to say that Wolfe's influence on the journeymen and apprentices was very bad, and that he inflamed them to act against their masters.[2]

In an attempt to come to some agreement with Wolfe, Christopher Barker had an interview with him on 14 May 1582, which has often been printed, but is so graphic a picture of the two men and the contemporary position that it must be given again:

> First about Easter last past twelve moneths Barkar wished John Wolfe to live in good order, for ye better increase of his wealth, as

---

[1] *Ibid.* p. 4. In 1584 over eighty titles were surrendered by their owners for the use of the poorer members of the Company. Arber, *A Transcript of the Registers of the Company of Stationers*, vol. II, pp. 786 ff.

[2] Arber, *op. cit.* vol. II, p. 781.

also of his credite, & not to print mens copies priviledged, nor to withstand her majesties gracious favour bestowed upon some of her most dutyfull subjects: Wolfe seeming to take good liking thereof, promised if he might have worke not to print any more any other mens copies. Barkar then perswaded the said Wolfe to translate his freedome from ye Fishmongers to ye Stationers, that ye said Barkar & others might lawfully set him on worke, & then he should be sure to have all ye favour that reasonably he could aske. Wolfe made promise so to doe though he ment nothing lesse appeareth by ye sequele; whereupon Barkar, although he greatly feared and charged him, that he was not able to print anything for him that might stand with his credit, left his owne presses unwrought, & set him on worke, whereby he earned of Barkar to ye value of 80li & more, which work was so untruely & evilly done, that it was not onely to Barkars great hinderance, but an exceeding discredit to all his owne labours. But now Wolfe finding him selfe of more ability then before, printed diverse mens copies without exception & thereupon hath grown much trouble. Notwithstanding all this upon ye 14 day of May last past, Barkar sent for ye said Wolfe, & demanded of him why he printed the Copies belonging to his office: he answered, 'Because I will live': but much more talke having past betwene them, Barkar replyed saying; 'Wolfe, leave your Machevillian devices, & conceit of your forreine wit, which you have gained by gadding from countrey to countrey, & tell me plainely, if you meane to deale like an honest man: what you would have'. Wolfe answered: 'If I should come into your Company I would have allowance of my five Apprentices, I would be provided whereon to live, and I would have the benefite which now I have in mine owne Company'. Barkar answered him: 'Touching your five Apprentices, it is against our order, yet for quitenes sake, I would be a meane as far as I can that you shall injoy them. To provide you a living, that is ye worke of God onely, upon whose providence you must depend, yet I dare promise you after a sort, that being of our Company you shall have good & gainefull copies wheron you may live in measure & yet not print other mens copies. Touching ye lone of 20 li which you have in your Company; we Stationers are very poore & have no land, but the house we sit in, and our whole stock is under 100 li & yet I will do what I may to procure you 20 li therof upon good security.' Wolfe making obscure & doubtfull answeres hereunto, Barkar

BOOK PIRATES

willed him to take adwise and resolve himselfe what he would stand unto. And as for my copies which you have printed, said he you and I will reasonably agree. But even at that tyme, although Wolfe denied to have any more of Barkars Copies in Printing his servants were in work of ye same, as within 4 houres after was manifest. Whereupon Barkar gave him over, as a man unreasonable to deale withall.[1]

After all this it is something of an anti-climax to find as the Committee of the Privy Council puts it 'Wolf hath acknowledged his error and is releved with work'. He was made free of the Company on 1 July 1583, and soon distinguished himself by hunting down his former companions, acting as beadle and in general earning for himself the title of 'Machivill—most tormenting executioner'.

Others were left, however, to carry on the fight, amongst whom Roger Ward was the most conspicuous and intransigent, and a brief account of his career at this time may serve to illustrate the determination of both parties in this struggle. Ward was in trouble as early as February 1582 when an action was brought against him for printing the A.B.C. with the Little Catechism, a work which was part of John Day's patent. In his defence Ward set out the reasons that were activating him and others, and made a frontal attack on the patentees. He declared that

a verye small number in respecte of the reste of the Companye of Stacioners, Prynters havinge gotten all the best bookes and Coppyes to be printed by themselfes by Privyledge wherby they make bookes more dearer than otherwise they wolde be, and havinge lefte verye littell or nothinge at all for the resydue of the Companye of the Prynters to lyve upon, unles they sholde worke under them for suche small wages as they of them selfes please to geve them, whiche is not sufficiente to fynde suche workemen and their famylies to lyve upon, whereby they through their Priviledges inritche themselfes greately and become (some of them) greate purchesers of Landes and owners of large possessyons. And the reste

---

[1] Arber, *op. cit.* vol. II, pp. 780–1. C. B. Judge, *Elizabethan Book-Pirates* (Cambridge, Mass.: Harvard University Press, 1934), pp. 36–7.

of the sayd Prynters beinge manye in number and moste of them howsehoulders so extremely poore, that by reason of pretended Priviledges and restraynte that happenethe therby can scarce earne breade and drinke by their trade towardes their lyuinge, a matter verye grevous and lamentable to the said poore prynters, and suche an enormitye to the Common welthe as if the same were eyther knowne unto this honorable Courte, or unto her Majestie, this Defendante hopeth that the said pretended priviledges wold be eyther restreyned or some suche good order taken as the residue of her Majesties pore Subjectes Printers might by some meanes get their lyvynges in their said trade.[1]

On being closely questioned Ward admitted that he had printed no less than 10,000 copies of the A.B.C. although he knew that the patent was held by Day, but nevertheless he asserted that he did not know that it was illegal to print the book. He also admitted that he had caused Day's name and mark to be printed on the edition, and that he had sold it mainly in London, but that he had sent 1500 copies to Shrewsbury where he also had a shop.

After a term in prison he returned to his illegal activities, for in September 1582 when the Stationers sent a search party to his house 'Warde fainynge himselfe to be absente, hys wyfe and servantes keepeth the dore shut againste them, and said that none should come there to search'. After a number of brushes with the authorities, including a further spell of prison, a search of his premises on Monday 17 October 1586 disclosed that he was printing privileged works which were the property of Flower, Day and Seres, as well as other works the copyright of other members of the Company. The searchers seized much of the printed matter, together with three presses and 'diverse other parcelles of pryntyng stuffe' and brought them to Stationers' Hall, where order was given for the presses and printing stuff to be made unusable, and the type defaced. Three years later a search party found him at work again, his press being hidden in a nearby tailor's house in Hammersmith, and

[1] C. B. Judge, *op. cit.* p. 47.

his type in henhouses near Saint Sepulchre's Church. Destruction again followed, but undeterred Ward set to work again, and erected another press across the Thames on Bankside in a tanner's house from whence the printed sheets, still wet from the press, were hidden near by, and then in due course brought to Ward's own house. Once more, press, printing stuff, type, etc., were destroyed. Lastly in 1596 he was convicted of having set up two presses in 'several obscure places' where he had printed 'contrary to her Majesties priviledge' and as a result the Court ordered 'the said printinge stuff shalbe defaced and made unserviceable for printinge and the stuff therof so defaced to be redelivered to the said Roger'.[1]

Ward was the most determined of the offenders, but the Company had to wage unceasing war against those who refused to recognize the rights of others, were they theirs by Letters Patent, or by the fact that they held the copy by perfectly understood conventions, which in fact gave them what we should now call the copyright. The Company therefore appointed searchers, who were instructed to enter the printers' workshops, and to find out what was being printed, for whom, and in what numbers. On 3 September 1576 twenty-four members of the Company were appointed to go about in pairs, so that every week an inspection could take place and unauthorized printing be detected.[2] Ten years later their number was increased to twenty-seven, and they were ordered to search in parties of threes, and allowed three shillings and fourpence for their dinners. Their doings are recorded from time to time and action is taken against offenders.[3]

---

[1] See Greg and Boswell, *Records of the Court of the Stationers' Company*, passim. For a detailed account of some other important cases in the attempt to put down large-scale piracy, see C. B. Judge, *Elizabethan Book-Pirates*, chapters III, VI.
[2] Arber, *A Transcript of the Registers of the Company of Stationers*, vol. II, p. 41.
[3] *Ibid.* vol. II, p. 42. Bills for meals for various search parties are printed by Arber, *op. cit.* vol. I, pp. 514–15. Greg and Boswell, *Records of the Court of the Stationers' Company*, passim.

'These printers will be the death of me', wrote the Bishop of London late in the reign, and his thought must have been in the minds of many in authority as they tried to control the output of books which for one reason or another fell foul of the authorities. The continual stream of injunctions, edicts and proclamations which were issued from time to time are evidence in themselves that all was not well and that the authorities were trying vainly to stop the output of 'naughty Books' that came on to the market do what they would. Something of their efforts, as we have seen, is reflected in the series of fines, imprisonments, questionings, and destruction of presses and types that are recorded in one place or another, but it must be admitted that control whether by the Crown, or by the City, or by the Company was patchy, uncertain and without any clear direction. The fact that we know that at least one third of the books now extant were never entered in the Register is a tremendous indictment of those entrusted with the task of controlling what was printed, the more so since there were so few printers and their wares were mostly sold in a comparatively small area, so that it should not have been difficult to detect books that had no right to be on the stalls.

Many of these, of course, were innocent enough in so far as they contained nothing that was particularly offensive either to Church or State, their only offence being that they were 'irregularly printed', since they were neither licensed by the Crown authorities, allowed by the Company, nor entered in the Company's Register. While such a state of affairs obtained, no one could feel that the Stationers were masters in their own home. But irregular as this was, it did not offend against the Queen's orders in the same way as did the printing of religious or political matter which set out to controvert or overthrow the *status quo*. What did concern the authorities more seriously was the continual production of books of exactly this nature. We shall see in a later chapter how active the Catholics were in their campaign against the Protestants, and how from their overseas seminaries and centres they never ceased to write and to controvert those put forward by their opponents, so that according to the figures supplied by Allison and Rogers, in their *Catalogue of Catholic Books in English printed abroad or secretly in England*, at least 250 volumes in English, printed at home or abroad, were in circulation between 1558 and 1603.[1]

The production of such a large number of books (and it must be remembered that some of them were very bulky) is a remarkable testimony to the zeal and determination of these authors and those supporting them. The costs of production were always a difficulty, and we find many references to this in the correspondence of the writers and their supporters. A further difficulty arose from the fact that the compositors were setting up manuscript written in a foreign tongue, so that the expense of correction was liable to be heavy, and even so the final result not entirely free from errors. 'Good reader,' says the preface to William Allen's *Defense and declaration of the Catholike Churchies Doctrine, touching purgatory* (1565), 'beare with these small faultes, or other, which in this difficulty of printing where oure tonge is not understanded, must needes be committed';[2] and another publication asks for leniency 'both bicause the printers were unskilfull of oure language, and for that the overseer coulde not be allwaies readie at the presse to make corrections'.[3]

Once printed, the major problem of how to evade the vigilance of the English authorities had still to be overcome. The ports were watched, so that we find the Bishop of Winchester in 1580 advising that 'a diligent watch' be kept at the ports and possible landing places roundabout,[4] while the Privy Council sent orders to the Mayor of Plymouth and others to look out for 'lewde and seditious bookes' coming into that and other western ports.[5] Agents reported the seizing of books on their

[1] *Op. cit.* p. 176.   [2] *STC* 371, sig. A7^v.
[3] *STC* 13250, *The Parliament of Chryste*... (1566), sig. .:.7^v. And see also *STC* 12759, sig. A3, and *STC* 20362, p. 2.
[4] J. Strype, *Annals of the Reformation and Establishment of Religion*, vol. II, p. 635.
[5] A. C. Southern, *Elizabethan Recusant Prose 1559–1582*, p. 36, with many other instances.

being landed, as in a letter to Lord Burghley of 17 February 1598, which tells him that the bearer 'having received order... to take care to such books either bound or unbound as come in this port that they be not such as touch her Majesty or the state, being at the opening of a fall of books, found therein this book I now send you, being a very bad book. I have therefore sent the same sealed up to you by him'.[1] Another agent tells Burghley that South Shields is a favourite landing place for such books, and says that such 'Popish and traitourous books' were sent from Rheims in barrels and fardels, landed at South Shields, and from there sent across the water to Newcastle in baskets covered with fresh fish.[2]

Once the books were smuggled in they still had to be distributed. Our best account of how this was done perhaps is that of an unknown priest writing to Father Agazzari, Rector of the English College at Rome:

So much for the books, which are as difficult and dangerous to publish as to print. The way is, all of them are taken to London before any is published, and then they are distributed by hundreds or fifties to the priests, so that they may be published all together in all parts of the realm. And so the next day, when the pursuivants usually begin to search the Catholics' houses, it is too late; for during the night the young gentlemen have introduced copies into the houses, shops and mansions of the heretics, or even into the court, and the stalls in the streets, so that the Catholics alone cannot be accused of possessing them.[3]

Catholic priests and laymen were constantly moving about distributing these dangerous books, despite the activities of Government agents. Spies and pursuivants were ever on the watch, and constantly pouncing on householders and travellers. There are records of searches in London and elsewhere which provide ample evidence that no one was safe. Stow, the historian, had his study ransacked and a list made of his books,

[1] *Historical MSS Commission. Hatfield MSS*, VIII, p. 53.
[2] *Ibid.* X, p. 203.
[3] R. Simpson, *Edmund Campion* (1896), p. 289.

which included a number of Catholic works.[1] Sudden visits every three or four weeks were advised 'in sundry suspected places', and such visits often produced results. This sort of thing went on up and down the country, and a contemporary Catholic account graphically paints the scene:

> Their serches are very many and severe. The chief times for them are when Catholikes are most busie to serve God, as on Sondaies, holy daies, Easter, Christmasse, Whitsontide and such very great feastes. They come ether in the night or early in the morning, or much about dinner time.... They willingliest come when few are at home to resist them, that they may rifle coffers and do what they list. They locke the servants and mistress of the howse and the whole familie up in to a rowme by them selves while they, like yong princes, goe rifling the howse at their wil.
>
> The maner of searching is to come with a troupe of men to the howse as though they came to fight a field. They beset the howse on every side, and then they rush in and ransacke every corner—even women's beds and bosomes—with such insolent behaviour that their villanies in this kind are half a martyrdome. The men they commaund to stand and to keep their places; and what soever of price cometh in their way, many times they pocket it up, as jewels, plate, monye and such like ware, under pretense of Papistrie.
>
> When they find any bookes, church stuff, chalices or other like things, they take them away.[2]

This vivid (and perhaps heightened) scene of anti-Catholic activities sufficiently illustrates the price that Catholics were willing to pay in order to obtain the books they needed to sustain their faith in these troublous times.

Whatever the dangers and difficulties, the fact that year after year so many books were written and printed abroad and destined for a predominantly English audience, is evidence

---

[1] Arber, *A Transcript of the Registers of the Company of Stationers of London*, vol. 1, p. 393.

[2] Catholic Record Society, vol. 52. *The Letters and Despatches of Richard Verstegan* (c. 1550–1640), ed. by Anthony G. Petti, p. 7. Compare the account given by Rainolds quoted on p. 144.

enough of the demand. We know all too little of the actual numbers in which they were printed, but may reasonably expect that they were editions of 750 to 1000 copies, and much more if the occasion served. At least 5000 copies of the Douay version were printed in the first instance, while some 4000 are said by a contemporary to have been printed of *Newes from Spayne and Holland* by Persons, so that they might be sent to England about Easter 1593.[1] As an example of more normal figures we may note that Thomas Alfield, a priest, confessed to having brought in between 500 and 600 copies of Allen's *True Sincere and Modest Defence* [1584],[2] while 367 copies of *A Briefe Treatise...conteyning sundry worthy Motives...* (1574)[3] by Richard Bristow 'fell into Heretickes handes', among other 'trayterous and popish bookes' in 1574. If these figures may be taken as an indication of what was happening, it is not difficult to understand why the Government took the spread of Catholic books so seriously.

Unfortunately for them, they had also to reckon with the secret presses at home, both Catholic and Protestant, that were disseminating hostile views, for in addition to the books printed abroad, the Catholics also tried to print some works in England. The earliest worker in this cause appears to have been William Carter, who two years after his apprenticeship expired printed *A notable Discourse, plainelye and truely discussing, who are the right Ministers of the Catholike Church: written against Calvine and his Disciples* (1575). This was an anonymous translation of a work by Albin de Valsergues and purported to be printed at 'Duaci. Per Iohannen Bellerum'. This device was employed again and again by Carter, who attempted to throw his enemies off the scent by naming Bruges or Antwerp as the place of publication. At times he gave no indication of place of origin or of the printer's name, and in this way managed to print at least eleven items before he was taken

---

[1] *STC* 22994, *Hatfield MSS*, IV, p. 498.
[2] *STC* 373, Strype, *Annals*, vol. III, p. 310.
[3] *STC* 3799, Strype, *Life of Parker* (1711), p. 477.

by Richard Topcliffe, and imprisoned in the Gatehouse. Bishop Aylmer, writing to Lord Burghley on 30 December, 1579, tells him that

> I have founde out a presse of pryntynge with one Carter, a verye lewed fellowe who hath byne dyvers tymes before in prison for printinge of lewde pampheletes. But nowe in searche of his Howse amongest other nawghtye papystycall Bookes, wee have founde one wrytten in Frenche intytled the inosencey of the Scotyshe Quene, a very dangerous Book.... I can get nothinge of him, for he dyd denye to answere uppon his othe. When your Lordshipp shalbe at any leasure to deale in the matter: I will sende to yow the Wardens [of the Stationers' Company], which will enforme yow further of an other Booke, whych ys abrode wherin her majestie ys towched.[1]

Carter languished in the Gatehouse for eighteen months and was then moved to the Tower. Here he stayed until January 1582 when he was falsely charged with heresy for printing Gregory Martin's book, *The Treatise of Schisme* (1578). For this he was condemned to death and the sentence was carried out the next day.

Little more is known about Carter. Indeed, as recently as 1950, Dr Southern, who has done so much to enlighten us about recusant prose and its printers at this time, wrote: 'Whether Carter printed more than three books I have been unable to discover.'[2] Six years later, however, Messrs Allison and Rogers were able to increase this number to eleven, and a study of their findings shows how carefully Carter covered his traces.[3] All this was in vain, for London was too small a place, and the pursuivants too skilled, so that it was only a matter of time before a change of address was essential if detection was to be avoided. Eventually, however, the constant searches of the Stationers, as well as those of Topcliffe and his assistants, prevailed. The importance to us of such men as Carter is that

---

[1] Quoted from Southern, *Elizabethan Recusant Prose*, p. 351.
[2] Southern, *op. cit.* p. 351.
[3] See their review of Southern in *The Library*, Fifth Series, vol. VI (1951), especially p. 50 and their *Catalogue, passim*.

he kept his press going for several years despite all the difficulties put in his way. 'Underground' printing was possible, given men of determination, furnished with a press, a supply of money and manuscripts to print.

The taking of Carter only preceded by a few months the setting up of another secret press in London. When Campion and Persons arrived in England on their missionary venture in June 1580, one of their projects was to print secretly in England, and on coming to London Persons soon collected both press and printer and established them in a 'large and fair house near a place they call Greenstreet', East Ham. Here, Stephen Brinkley and his assistants printed at least four books before the press had to be moved to the house of Francis Browne where two more works were printed. In March 1581, however, one of the workmen was caught and confessed, whereupon the press was removed to the home of Dame Cecilia Stonor, near Henley. Here a work by Persons and another by Campion were printed, but the latter roused such concern that a strict search was ordered, as a result of which the press was discovered on 8 August, and Brinkley and his four assistants seized and taken to London, where Brinkley was incarcerated in the Tower until June 1583.[1]

Such was the short-lived life of the 'Greenstreet Press'. It only existed as long as it did by operating in three different places in the ten months of its existence; and, as with Carter's press, by the use of false imprints, etc., to disguise the true facts.[2]

The Catholics were not alone in seeing in the printing press a most valuable instrument of propaganda. 'We must root out printing, or printing will root us out' declared Roland Phillips, the Vicar of Croydon, and the fear of subversive literature haunted the authorities. While most of the anti-Establishment

---
[1] See p. 118.
[2] See Allison and Rogers, *Catalogue of Catholic Books in English printed abroad or secretly in England 1558–1640*, nos. 151, 192, 395, 520, 521, 615, 616 and 627; Southern, *Elizabethan Recusant Prose*, pp. 353–8.

MARTIN MARPRELATE

books had a Catholic bias, there were some written by men who felt passionately that reform had not gone far enough in the other direction. Two Puritan clergymen, John Field and Thomas Wilcox, who hoped to see a Presbyterian church government replace that by bishops, had secretly printed at Wandsworth *An Admonition to the Parliament* (1572)[1] setting forth their views and calling on Parliament to act. *A Second Admonition* (by Thomas Cartwright)[2] soon followed, and these outspoken pamphlets caused much excitement, and Parliament did its best to respond. However, the Queen, by using the Lords, beat off the attack and the bill to make the Church more presbyterian was defeated. In the meantime, Field and Wilcox were thrown into prison, and in June 1573 the Queen issued a proclamation ordering the surrender within twenty days of 'the Admonition and all other books made for the defense of it',[3] but when the twenty days had elapsed, the Bishop of London had to admit that not a single copy had been surrendered to him, though, says Strype, 'one need not doubt there were some thousands of them dispersed in the City and other parts of his diocese'.[4]

Some years later, an even more famous attack on the Bishops was staged. Early in October 1588, word got about of a newly printed work that was circulating, in which the bishops were roughly handled by a vigorous, hard-hitting, slangy writer, calling himself Martin Marprelate, Gentleman. Courtiers, members of the universities and of the Inns of Court, as well as the bourgeoisie, were reading copies as fast as they could get hold of them. The stir thus created was rapidly followed by official action, and the pursuivants were eagerly searching for the miscreants who had dared to print and circulate this subversive work. The title-page certainly did not help them, for it

---

[1] *STC* 10847, 10848. Two separate editions, both printed in 1572.
[2] *STC* 4713 [1572], A. F. Scott Pearson, *Thomas Cartwright and Elizabethan Puritanism 1535–1603* (Cambridge, 1925), p. 85, says that the idea that the press was at Wandsworth 'is an assumption'. He also questions Cartwright's authorship of the *Second Admonition*, p. 74.
[3] *STC* 8063.   [4] Strype, *Annals*, vol. II, p. 422.

only bore the mocking ascription 'Printed oversea, in Europe, within two furlongs of a Bounsing Priest, at the cost and charges of M. Marprelate, Gentleman'.[1] We are fortunately not concerned with the identity of Martin, a mystery still not completely resolved. Our concern is to see how it was possible and under what conditions Martin's tracts came to be printed. The story is not unlike that of the Greenstreet press mentioned above—that is, it is the story of a press constantly on the move, constantly but one jump ahead of its pursuers, and finally overtaken. The story begins at Kingston where Robert Waldegrave set up a press sometime in May 1588, having had another press seized and made useless in a raid on his premises in Paul's Churchyard on the night of 16 April.[2] How he came by his new press and some of his types is not clearly understood, but, unperturbed by what had happened in London, he started printing religious pamphlets for two Puritan divines, Udall and Penry, but it soon became clear that agents of the Stationers' Company were hot on the trail, and indeed were at Kingston on 10 June, but had found nothing. However, a move was urgent, and the press found a new home in the house of a sympathizer at East Molesey, a few miles from Kingston. It was here in early October that the first of Martin's pamphlets was printed in a small quarto of 52 pages—a striking contrast to the 1400 page work it set out to contravene, written by Dr John Bridges, Dean of Salisbury.[3] Slight though it was, it was at once evident to the ecclesiastical authorities that it could not be left unanswered and, at a conference at Lambeth Palace, it was decided that Bishop Cooper of Winchester should include an answer to Martin in a book he was writing. This he did, but inevitably it took time, and it was not until the early days of January 1589 that it was on the market.[4]

[1] *STC* 17453, *Oh read over D. John Bridges, for it is a worthy worke* [1588], i.e. 'The Epistle'.
[2] Greg and Boswell, *Records of the Court of the Stationers' Company*, p. 27.
[3] *STC* 3734, *A defence of the government established in the Church of Englande* (1587).
[4] *STC* 5682, *An Admonition to the People of England*.

'SCHISMATICAL AND SEDITIOUS BOOKS'

In the meantime the Queen's authority was invoked, and an injunction was issued which prohibited anyone to possess a copy. 'What then is to become of me?' asked the Earl of Essex, as he drew forth a copy of the book and presented it to the Queen. While all this was going on, the second part of Martin's reply to Dr Bridges was being printed, but not at East Molesey. This was too near London, and a new home for the press was found at Fawsley House, Northamptonshire, the home of Sir Richard Knightley, a sympathizer. Here, early in November, Waldegrave set up and printed the second pamphlet, like its fellow a small quarto of 46 pages.[1] This too was soon in circulation, largely owing to the devoted labours of Humphrey Newman, who personally trudged about the countryside distributing copies to friends and adherents.

Although Bishop Cooper's tract, *An Admonition to the People of England*[2] was on the book-stalls, it could do little to offset the fire and vernacular gusto of its opponent. Richard Bancroft made a vigorous attack on the Puritans and on Martin in a sermon at Paul's Cross on 9 February,[3] and this was followed by a proclamation a few days later against 'certain seditious and ill-disposed persons' who had published 'schismatical and seditious books'.[4] In addition, the pursuivants who were in full cry had tracked the press to East Molesey, and had seized one of the servants of the house, but the press itself still eluded them.

Things were too uncomfortable at Fawsley, however, for Waldegrave and his men to stay after the second pamphlet was printed, and at the end of December 1588 the press was hidden in a farm building in the neighbourhood, and stayed there until a new home was found for it in Coventry. There in late February and March 1589 two more works were printed, one a broadside sheet, the second a small quarto of 58 pages with the punning title *Hay any worke for Cooper* 'wherein worthy

---

[1] *STC* 17454, *Oh read over D. John Bridges for it is a worthy worke* [1588], i.e. 'The Epitome'.
[2] *STC* 5682. Twice reprinted the same year.
[3] *STC* 1346.   [4] *STC* 8182.

Martin quits himselfe like a man, I warrant you, in the modest defence of his selfe and his learned Pistles, and makes the Coopers hoopes to flye off, and the Bishops Tubs to leake out of all crye'.[1] Once this was printed, copies were rapidly stitched, and 900 of them hurried off to London.

By this time the pace was getting too hot for Waldegrave, and he left Martin and his friends to find a new printer. This they did, and John Hodgkins and his two men were brought up from London and found the press in yet another place, for it had moved from Coventry to Wolston Priory, the residence of Roger Wigston. They set to work and by late July had printed two more pamphlets, the *Theses Martinianae*, commonly known as Martin Junior and *The just censure and reproofe*, known as Martin Senior.[2] Probably a thousand copies of each of these were taken off, and a contemporary witness avers that at least 750 of the first were carried off by the indefatigable Newman, while the bulk of the second were made into a bundle and sent by carrier to London via Banbury, as 'a Packe of Leather' and in due course collected by Newman.

No sooner was the last sheet printed than Hodgkins and his men packed up their precious equipment and, despite the pleas of their hostess to stay, set off for Manchester. Misfortune overtook them on the way, for while they were unloading their cart at Warrington, some of the type was spilled, and bystanders who saw it had to be hastily assured that it was shot, and that the carters were 'saltpeter men'. After this misadventure Hodgkins pushed on, hoping for the best, and found a new home just outside Manchester. He started work at once on another pamphlet, but had not even printed the first sheet of *More work for the Cooper* when, on 14 August, he and his men were caught red-handed, and soon were on their way to imprisonment and torture in London.[3]

---

[1] *STC* 17456, sig. A1. [2] *STC* 17457–8.
[3] For the whole of this account of the Marprelate Press I am greatly indebted to the writings of William Pierce: *An Historical Introduction to the Marprelate Tracts* (1908); *The Marprelate Tracts 1588, 1589* (1911); and *John Penry: His Life, Times, and Writings* (1923).

THE MARTINISTS

The widespread effects caused by these pamphlets may be seen in many ways. Martin gives an imaginary picture of the impact that they made on the ecclesiastical authorities—exaggerated no doubt—but in essentials true to life. He pictures the Archbishop as haranguing his pursuivants, scolding them for their lack of success, and instructing them as how they are to hang about Paul's Churchyard so that they might get into conversation with men they saw browsing over the bookstalls, in the hope of learning from them news of the malefactors. They were to attend sermons, listen to talk by members of the Inns of Court, watch at inns when packs were being unloaded, and to open any that seemed to be suspicious. 'Have an eye,' he tells them, 'to all the Puritans' houses in London.... And the preachers' houses.' Others were instructed to go into the country, in particular into those counties where it was believed that the Martinists were strongest, and above all they were enjoined to search diligently for Martin himself. 'I tell you the truth that I do think him and his brood to be worse than Jesuites.' 'These Martinists are all of them traitors and enemies unto Her Majesty; they will overthrow the State.... No warning will serve them; they grow worse and worse', and so on.

Fictitious, of course, but the violent activities of the Archbishop gave Martin every excuse to draw this unflattering picture of his chief opponent. Apart from this, and more to our purpose, we may note how many pens were raised against the pamphlets. Cooper's *Admonition* could do little to counteract the vigour of Martin's attack, and the authorities had to turn to more practised and less scrupulous writers. Lyly, we know, wrote for them, and perhaps Nashe (though to a far lesser extent than has often been asserted), while many pieces were contributed by anonymous writers whose Countercuffs, Pasquils, Whips and the like at least opposed Martin in something of the same slangy, outrageous idiom as he himself employed, and left serious argument to look after itself. One title will be enough to illustrate the spirit in which Martin's opponents set out to demolish him and his arguments. It reads:

A Countercuffe given to Martin Junior: by the venturous, hardie, and renowned Pasquill of England, Cavaliero. Not of olde Martins making, which newlie knighted the Saints in Heaven, with rise up Sir Peter and Sir Paule, But lately dubd for his service at home in the defence of his Country, and for the cleane breaking of his staffe uppon Martins face. Printed betweene the skye and the grounde, Within a myle of an Oake, and not many fieldes off, from the unpriviledged Presse of the Ass-ignes of Martin Junior. Anno. Dom. 1589.[1]

Ballads and plays were also produced, and helped to keep up the excitement, and did all that was possible to deride and vilify Martin and his followers. By September 1589, however, Martin had been silenced, and many of his friends and followers imprisoned or driven into hiding, so that the storm rapidly died down, despite a few late shots by a number of ecclesiastics.

[1] *STC* 19456.

CHAPTER IV

TRANSLATIONS AND TRANSLATORS

In speaking of translations in the first volume of *English Books and Readers*, I noted that in the first half of the century

...every kind of knowledge was laid under contribution and made into books for our early printers, and translations as well as original works were all grist to the mill. 'I se many yonge persones... very studyous of knowlege of thynges, and be vehemently bente to rede newe workes, and in especyall [those] that be translated into the vulgare tonge', writes Robert Whittinton, and it was this desire the printers strove to fulfil. Much of religion, of information and of literary interest was provided by translation. Not only the translation of the Bible itself, but of a host of foreign commentators, both old and new, together with rival bands of eager controversialists kept the printers busy. At the same time, the devout writings of great saints and churchmen, such as Thomas à Kempis or Erasmus, were not likely to be overlooked. Nor were the claims of other moralists, old and new, neglected. All were swept up in the great net of the printers who eagerly competed one with another to meet the market created in part by the vehemence of rival religious opinions, and in part by the traditional belief in the outstanding importance of works of the spirit. These things being so, authors and translators were at one in their desire to see their writings as widely spread as possible, and translations in particular have for their aim the informing of those only able to read the vernacular.[1]

This statement is almost equally true for the second half of the century. Many translators emphasize the fact that their work is for the 'simple', or the 'unlearned and ignorant' who are 'not experte in the tongues', so that the classical and modern languages are beyond them. It is claimed, for instance, that 'Noblemen and Gentlemen, wherof there are no small number,

[1] *Op. cit.* p. 154.

are not well seen in the Castilian tongue', while works in French 'most understand not'. Latin was known to comparatively few, and Greek hardly at all. It was to help such people, especially in making available for their use any religious works, that much translation was undertaken. Some books were translated for the edification of 'all Parents and Children', or to ensure that the works of the great foreign divines, such as Beza, Calvin and others could be readily obtained and studied in English. To this end, for example, the works of Calvin: sermons, catechisms, commentaries and religious treatises were translated and put into circulation. Many of these were of considerable size: *The Sermons on Deuteronomy* ran to 1248 pages in double columns in a small folio, as did those on the *Epistles to S. Timothy and S. Titus*, while many other of his works were formidable in bulk. Writings by Beza, Bullinger, Hemmingsen, Vermigli and Viret may be mentioned among those most frequently appearing on the English bookstalls. The prefaces of printers and of translators help us to understand what was their purpose in publishing many of these books. Beza is published 'as a weapon against the ministers of Satan',[1] or 'to the end that the causes, both of the present dangers of the Church, and also of the troubles of those that are hardlie dealt with els-where, may appear in the English tongue'.[2] Bullinger's *A hundred sermons upon the Apocalips of Christ* (1561), which ran to 759 pages quarto, was recommended as 'a golden spurre' and 'money well spent', while another of his works was 'to no small hartning of the faithfull to continue patiently and steadfastly in their calling, and profession of Christ'.[3] Four Sermons of Calvin are thus advertised by their printer:

There be thre causes specially thar moveth me to printe these sermons of maister Jhon Calvine.... Th'one is the worthines of the matter set furth in these sermons. The other is the plaines and

[1] STC 2013, Beza, *A briefe and pithie summe*... (1589), sig. A2.
[2] STC 2053, Beza, *Propositions and Principles of Divinitie* (1591), sig. A1.
[3] STC 4061, *A hundred sermons upon the Apocalips of Christ* (1561), sig. A4ᵛ.

simplicitie that thys great clarke useth in al his sermons to the people. The third is the reverent handling of the scriptures, without tauntes, skoffes, or jestes, or any trifling tales, wherby our English nacion may se & judge...when it is most naked & bare and void of that painted sheathe that men would put upon it.[1]

We might continue to pile up evidence of the reasons activating the publishers of this kind of work, but it is certain that they were not printing at random, but had a clear idea of the public that they were catering for.

So far as they could, the Catholics retaliated, but as we shall see, they had an uphill task.[2] Nevertheless, they persisted in translating into English works by eminent Jesuit Fathers, such as Loarte and Possevino, or Lives of the Virgin, or of the Saints, or forms of confession, or manuals of prayers. Richard Hopkins makes clear the strategy of these publications in a preface to his translation *Of Prayer and Meditation* (1582), by Luis de Granada. He writes:

It is nowe about foureteene yeares agoe, since the time that Master Doctor Hardinge...perswaded me earnestlie to translate some of those Spanishe Bookes into our Englishe tounge, affirminge that more spirituall profite wolde undoutedlie ensewe thereby to the gayninge of Christian sowles in our countrie from Schisme, and Heresie, and from all sinne, and iniquitie, than by bookes that treate of controversies in Religion: wich (as experience hath nowe plainlie tried) doe nothinge so well dispose the common peoples myndes to the feare, love, and service of almightie God, as bookes treatinge of devotion, and howe to leade a vertuous life doe.[3]

But it was not only religious works that attracted attention. When they turned to the world of antiquity the translators had a wide field to cover. What they thought worthy of giving an English dress has been surveyed in a masterly fashion by Professor H. B. Lathrop.[4] In common with all other investigators, he finds it impossible to explain why this was chosen

---

[1] *STC* 4438 (1561), sig. A 2. [2] See pp. 113 ff. [3] *STC* 16907, sig. a 6.
[4] *Translations from the Classics into English from Caxton to Chapman, 1477–1620* (Madison, 1933), pp. 105–10.

and that neglected, so that the great Greek tragic writers go untranslated while the far inferior Seneca was constantly appearing on the bookstalls. With Professor Lathrop as a guide, however, we may see the range of the translations. This is summed up by Charles Whibley as follows:

The translator's range of discovery was wide. They brought into the ken of Englishmen the vast continent of classical literature. Only a few provinces escaped their search, and, of the few, one was the province which should have had the greatest attraction for them. It is not a little strange that the golden age of our drama should have seen the translation of but one Greek play. Of Aeschylus and Sophocles there is nothing. A free paraphrase of the *Phoenissae*, presented at Gray's Inn under the title of *Jocasta* in 1566 by George Gascoigne and Francis Kinwelmersh, and made not from the Greek but from the Italian of Ludovico Dolce, is the Elizabethan's only and fragile link with Euripides. Plautus fared not much better.... More popular were Seneca and Terence—Seneca, no doubt, for his ingenious maxims, and Terence because he was appointed to be read in schools. Of the historians, both Greek and Latin, there is a long list. An unknown translator, who hides his name under the initials B. R. and who may be Barnabe Rich, published two books of Herodotus in 1584, and Thomas Nicolls... gave to England a complete Thucydides in 1550. Of Livy, we have a fragment by Antony Cope (1544), and a version of all that remains by the incomparable Philemon Holland (1600).... Sallust, as might be expected, was a favourite of Tudor England. His *Catiline* was translated by Thomas Paynell (1541), his *Jugutha* by Alexander Barclay (1557), and both histories by Thomas Heywood, the dramatist (1608). Golding's *Caesar* (1565), Brende's *Quintus Curtius* (1553), and Stocker's *Diodorus Siculus* (1569), by no means complete the tale. What Sir Henry Savile did for the *Histories* and the *Agricola* of Tacitus (1591), Richard Greenwey did for the *Annals* and the *Description of Germany* (1598), and there is no author Englished for us in fuller or worthier shape than the wisest of Roman Historians. Xenophon found other translators besides Holland, and Plutarch's *Lives of the Noble Grecians and Romans* fell happily into the hands of Sir Thomas North, whose skill give them a second and larger immortality.[1]

[1] *Cambridge History of English Literature*, vol. IV, p. 4.

'HOW TO LIVE'

Whibley goes on to point out that 'the philosophers and moralists of the ancient world chimed with the humour of Tudor England', and that the translators understood this in presenting to English readers the riches of Greece and Rome. 'Open this base boxe, and lifte up the lydd of this course casket, wherin so riche and costly a Juell is inclosed; wey it, and weare it, the commoditie issuing from the same is singular, so is the delight redundant and plentifull', says Abraham Fleming to the Courteous Reader, introducing him to *A Registre of Hystories, conteining Martiall exploites of worthy warriours, politique practises of Civil Magistrates, wise Sentences of famous Philosophers* (1576), by Aelianus.[1] Translators sincerely believed that much could be learned from reading the exploits and ideas of great men of the past, and that their experience could serve as a model for the actions of men in Elizabethan England. This is nowhere better expressed than by Thomas Wilson when he writes:

And nowe most gentle Reader thinke that when I was occupied about this worke: to make Athens & the gouverment therof to be knowne to my Countrie men: my meaning was, that every good subject according to the levell of his witte, should compare the time past with the time present, and ever when he heareth Athens, or the Athenians, to remember Englande and Englishmen, and so all other things in like maner incident thereunto, that we maye learne by the doings of our elders howe we may deale in our owne affayres, and so through wisedome by our neyghbours example avoyde all harme that else unwares might happen unto us.[2]

The translators are insistent on the value of these works as providing examples of how men should live and act. The title-page of *Thabridgment of the Histories of Trogus Pompeius* (1564) tells us that it contains 'brieflie great plentie of moste delectable Hystories, and notable examples, worthie not onelie to be read, but also to be enbraced and followed of all men,'[3] just as the

---

[1] *STC* 164, sig. ¶¶3ᵛ.
[2] *STC* 6578, Demosthenes, *Three Orations*...(1570), sig. B1ᵛ.
[3] *STC* 24290, sig. A1.

Institution, schole, and education of Cyrus by Xenophon (1567) has for its 'onlye intent' the exhibition of 'what a noble man by good education may prove unto'.[1]

By the second half of the century, however, it was to foreign literature of a lighter kind that many translators turned their attention. This they found in quantity in the works of Spanish and Italian authors for the main part, and they were careful to give their stories a moral twist if they thought that the contents might otherwise prove a little risky for the puritanical tastes of many of their readers. One of the most successful and most audacious raids made on both ancient and modern literature was that of William Painter who, in 1566 and 1567, published *The Palace of Pleasure*, which he claimed 'will recreate & refresh weried mindes, defatigated either with painefull travaile or with continuall care'. To achieve this end, Painter collected one hundred and one tales, thirty-seven of them from classical authors, the remainder from the great Italian story-tellers—Boccaccio, Bandello, Cinthio, etc. Another similar collection, also published in 1567, was made by Geoffrey Fenton, whose *Certaine Tragicall Discourses written oute of Frenche and Latin, by Geffrey Fenton, no lesse profitable than pleasaunt, and of like necessitye to al degres that take pleasure in antiquityes or foreine reportes* (1567), it has been said, 'loads every rift with rhetorical, proverbial and moral ore' in providing a series of highly exciting stories of passion and violent incident. These books, together with George Pettie's *A petite Pallace of Pettie his pleasure* [1576] were welcomed, as their numerous reprints testify. In addition, there were the translations of the Palmerin series of romances from Spain,[2] so that there was no lack of absorbing and exciting reading material from abroad.

Translations for more practical purposes were very common also. Books on general health, on medicine of all kinds, cures for the eyes, precautions to be taken against the plague, and manuals of surgery (despite the outcries of old-fashioned surgeons) were printed in considerable numbers. Men learnt

[1] *STC* 26067, sig. A3ᵛ.   [2] See p. 253

from foreign writers how to lay out a garden, how to train horses, and how to cure them of various diseases, and so on. Publishers evidently took the view expressed by a contemporary when he wrote:

> I thincke there is no man so bestiall, so rude, or so blunt of wit but that he is (by a certaine instincte of natural inclination) desirous...to understand bokes in his maternall tonge, written first in forein langage, to the ende not to seme altogether ignoraunte in matters both of the liberall sciences, and also of histories, set forth for his rudiment and instruction, as in Cosmographie, in Astronomie, in Philosophie, in Logike, in Rhetoricke and specially in Phisick, wherof we had never so muche neede as in these our daies.[1]

In short, wherever men turned they found available works by ancient and modern writers which could instruct, divert, solace or stimulate them.

From what has been said above, it will be clear that translations formed a large part of the booksellers' stock, and that it was against this that the sons of Zoili fulminated most fiercely. They hated the making common of knowledge, some on narrow professional grounds, as when the secrets of medicine were made available to all,[2] some on the wider ground that certain philosophical or religious matters were not things that the untrained could discuss with any profit.[3] Christian morality, it was thought, might be undermined by making classical stories and the tales of some Italian or French writers easy to come by. These pleas were all answered from time to time by translators who insisted that there was a duty imposed on the learned to help their less-gifted brethren. John Dolman, for example, singles out as deserving help 'a meane sort of men' who are neither the 'raskall multitude', nor the 'learned

---

[1] *STC* 293, Alessio, *The Secretes of Alexis of Piemount*, trans. W. Warde (1558). ✠ iii^v.

[2] See, for examples, pp. 180-1.

[3] *STC* 24290, *Thabridgment of the Histories of Trogus Pompeius* (1564), sig. **3.

sages',[1] while Thomas Hoby asserts that 'the translation of Latin or Greeke authors doeth not onely not hinder learning, but it furthereth it', since it helps men 'to fille their minde with the vertues, and their body with civyll condicions'.[2] Florio carries the war into the enemy's country with the forthright declaration that 'learning cannot be too common, and the commoner the better',[3] and for a final example we may take the indignant reply of Philemon Holland to his critics when he writes:

> Why should any man therefore take offence hereat, and envie this good to his naturall countrey, which was first meant for the whole world? And yet some there be so grosse as to give out, that these and such like books ought not to bee published in the vulgar tongue. It is a shame (quoth one) that *Livie* speaketh English as hee doth: Latinists onely are to bee acquainted with him. As who would say, the souldiour were to have recourse unto the universitie for militarie skill and knowledge; or the scholler to put on arms and pitch a campe. What should *Plinie* (saith another) bee read in English, and the mysteries couched in his books divulged: as if the husbandman, the mason, carpenter, goldsmith, painter, lapidarie, and engraver, with other artificers, were bound to seeke unto great clearks or linguists for instructions in their severall arts. Certes, such *Momi* as these, besides their blind and erroneous opinion, thinke not so honourably of their native countrey and mother tongue as they ought: who if they were so well affected that way as they should be, would wish rather and endeavour by all means to triumph now over the Romans in subduing their literature under the dent of the English pen, in requitall of the conquest sometime over this Island, atchieved by the edge of their sword.[4]

The opponents of translation were on firmer ground when they denied the possibility that the translation could reflect with

---

[1] *STC* 5317, Cicero, *Those fyve Questions which M. T. Cicero disputed...*, (1561), sig. ¶¶4.
[2] *STC* 4778, Castiglione, *The Courtyer* (1561), sig. A4ᵛ.
[3] *STC* 18041, M. de Montaigne, *The Essayes* (1603), sig. A2.
[4] *STC* 20029, Pliny, *The Naturall Historie of C. Plinius Secundus* (1601), (x) 3ᵛ.

accuracy the original. Since they did not often venture into print, we can only guess at their arguments, since they are reported (no doubt with some bias) by their victims, who do not always mince their words, as may be seen in the address to the 'courteous and Christian Reader' by Thomas James, Fellow of New College, Oxford, in introducing his translation of *A Commentary upon the Canticle of Canticles* (1598) by A. Brucioli. He writes:

> But chiefly these spider-catching *Zoilusses* do shoot the venime of their tongues against painfull translators of bookes which seeke other mens profits, & not their owne, reaping not the fruit of that which they have sowne, and like candles spending themselves to give others light. But what saith *M. Momus* with his crue of carping knights, these men mar all with their translations, it was never well with us (that is, that are learned) since so many books were translated into English, their labor were better spared then imployed, they corrupt bookes, misinterpret writers, are enemies unto the common wealth, & enemies to all good learning.... Thus far reacheth their complaint against the abuse of translations, which may in no wise be excused. As for the harme that cometh by making learning too common, men of common judgement may by vulgar examples easily refute them. The sunne & moone, fire and water are profitable, & yet common: the Philosopher saith, *Bonum quò communius, eò melius:* good the commoner it is, the better it is.[1]

Some took the view that translation into English was foolish, since they affected to despise English as an uncouth language. This attitude is strongly combated by George Pettie in his translation of *The civile Conversation of M. Stephen Guazzo* (1586), when he writes:

> There are some others yet who will set light by my labours, because I write in English: and those are some nice Travailours, who retourne home with such queasie stomacks, that nothing will downe with them but French, Italian, or Spanish, and though a worke bee but meanelie written in one of those tongues, and finelie translated

---

[1] *STC* 3928, sig. *7ᵛ. Cf. *STC* 760, sig. A 4; *STC*, 5513, sig. A 2ᵛ, etc.

into our Language, yet they will not sticke farre to preferre the Originall before the Translation: the cause is partlie, for that they cannot so soone espie faultes in a forraine tongue as in their owne, which maketh them thinke that to bee currant, which is but course, and partlie for that straunge thinges doe more delight them, than that which they are dailie used to: but they consider not the profit which commeth by reading things in theyr owne tongue, whereby they shall be able to conceive the matter much sooner, and beare it awaie farre better, than if they reade it in a straunge tongue, whereby also they shall be inabled to speake, to discourse, to write, to indite, properlie, fitlie, finelie, and wiselie, but the woorst is, they thinke that impossible to be done in our own tongue: for they count it barren, they count it barbarous, they count it unworthie to be accounted of; and, which is worse, as I myselfe have heard some of them, they reporte abroad, that our Countrie is barbarous, our manners rude, and our people uncivile: and when I have stood with them in the comparison betweene other countries & ours, & pointed with my finger to many grose abuses, used in the places where we have bene, when by no reason they have bene able to defend them, they have shronke in their necke, and tolde me that it was the fashion of the Countrie: not considering that the manners and fashions of each Countrie, are the onelie things that make it counted barbarous or civile, good or bad. But for our Countrie, I am perswaded that those which know it, and love it, will report it for the civilest Countrie in the world: and if it be thought to be otherwise by strangers, the disorders of those travailers abroad, are the chiefe cause of it.... And for the barbarousnesse of our tongue, I must likewise saie that it is much the worse for them, and such curious fellowes as they are: who if one chance to derive anie word from the Latine, which is insolent to their eares... they forthwith make a jest at it, and tearme it an Inkhorne tearme. And though for my part I use those wordes as little as anie, yet I know no reason why I should not use them... for it is indeed the readie waie to inrich our tongue, and make it copious, and it is the waie which all tongues have taken to inrich themselves.[1]

It will be observed that despite his robust attack, Pettie's use of the English language might well be described as uncouth by his critics, for he is far from able to write

[1] *STC* 12423, sig. A6ᵛ.

THE TRANSLATOR'S APOLOGY

'properlie, fitlie, finelie and wiselie', or to conduct a clear and logical argument, but this does not invalidate his claim that it is good to have works 'finelie translated into our own language'.

The translator of *The Famous Hystory of Herodotus* (1584) in a somewhat literary address to the Gentlemen Readers takes another tack. Even if the English dress is displeasing, he urges that the subject matter is so good that the form in which it is presented may be excused. He writes:

Right Courteous Gentlemen, we have brought out of *Greece* into *England* two of the Muses, *Clio* and *Euterpe*, as desirous to see the lande as to learne the language; whome I trust you wil use well because they be women, and you cannot abuse them because you be Gentlemen. As these speede, so the rest will followe, neyther altogether unwilling to forsake theyr owne Country, nor yet over hasty to arrive into this.... If you lyke them not for the attyre they weare, yet bid them welcome for the newes they bring, which I confesse are in many pointes straunge, but for the most parte true.... Neyther of them are braved out in theyr colours as the use is nowadayes, and yet so seemely, as eyther you will love them because they are modest, or not mislike them because they are not impudent, since in refusing ydle pearles to make them seeme gaudy, they reject not modest apparell to cause them to go comely. The truth is (Gentlemen) in making them new attyre.... I was cutting my cloth by another mans measure, beeyng great difference whether we invent a fashion of our owne, or imitate a paterne set downe by another. Whiche I speake not to this end, for that my selfe coulde have done more eloquently in Englishe than our Authour hath in Greeke, but that the course of his writing beeyng most sweete in Greeke, converted into Englishe looseth a great parte of his grace.[1]

In addition to these reasons, there was the widely held belief, so frequently impressed upon the educated Englishman, 'that we were borne for our selves alone, but that our parents, our friends, or our country have their peculiar and several

---
[1] *STC* 13224, sig. A2. Trans. by B. Rich.

rights and interests in our nativitie and birth, so farre forth as any way we may be able to profit and do them good,'[1] and it was

chiefely and especially for the common utilitie & profyte of my native countrey, the advancement and benefyte where of every man is bound both by nature and conscience to studye for all, by [all] means possible to the uttermost of hys power [2]

that men like Abraham Hartwell set to work to translate a book about the Congo and other far off lands to which the eyes of English Merchants and Adventurers were ever turning, so that he might be 'doing something to help our English Nation that they might know and understand many things which are common in other languages, but utterly concealed from this poore Island'.[3] We must not make too much of this, but undoubtedly religious and nationalistic reasons were often sufficient inducement for men to undertake the exacting and often laborious task of translating. At the same time it would be idle to deny that many translations were put out from a definitely business point of view. Wherever the booksellers saw an opportunity, they quickly made an entry of the work in the *Stationers' Register*, marking the same with the words, 'To be translated',[4] and then proceeded to get the work done, or on reflection abandoned the project. Sometimes we find evidence that the book has been translated on commission for a bookseller, or we are told that the writers were urged by their friends to translate this or that piece of work. Add to this that there was much of ephemeral interest coming in from abroad telling of wars, marvels or adventures and the like, which found a ready sale, and therefore provided some work for the hireling

---

[1] *STC* 6227, L. Daneau, *A fruitfull Commentarie upon the twelve Small Prophets* (1594), sig. ¶ 1. Cf. *STC* 6578, 1178.
[2] *STC* 12191, G. Gratarolus, *The Castel of Memorie* (1562), sig. A 6.
[3] *STC* 16805, sig. ☛ 4ᵛ. Cf. *STC* 5798, Cortes; *STC* 10529, Escalante; *STC* 18005, Monardes; *STC* 647, Peter Martyr.
[4] Arber, *A Transcript of the Registers of the Company of Stationers*, vol. II, pp. 471, 478, 498, 500, 504, etc.

translators, and many of the reasons activating the more commercial side of translations are fairly clear.[1]

For a number of men, no doubt, the term 'the art of translating' had little meaning, but for some it was a serious and challenging matter—'this paynefull and daring enterprise', as one of their number calls it. 'Such a hard thing it is to bring out of one language into another', writes Sir Thomas Wilson, and the difficulty is expressed more fully by John Dolman in the following words:

> It is not possible for any man, to express the writinges of Tullie, in Englishe so eloquently: as he hath uttered the same in Latine. Then, for mine owne translation: forasmuche as it must of necessity be either more simple then, the stile of Tullie, or els more foolishe, and ful of croked termes (for Tullies meane none can attaine) I had rather to be partener of the favour, due to simplicity, and plainenes then, with foolyshe and farre fet wordes, to make my translation seeme more darke to the unlearned, & more foolishe to the wise. By which my playnenes, withoute counterfaite eloquence, if I have gotten no other commoditye: yet, thus muche I am sure of, that I have thereby escaped, the just reproofe, that they deserve, whiche thinke to cloke their ignoraunce, with inkehorne termes.[2]

Most translators, indeed, realized that the way out *via* 'inkehorne termes' was wrong, and the majority go out of their way to emphasize that their skill is so much less than that of their authors that they are content to leave 'the exquisite & curious style to those that have bene brought up in scoles and are seen in oratorie'. Others again prefer to make their writings to be 'as simple and plaine (because of the unlearned) as possibly the matter and phrase of that tongue would suffer', or write in 'plaine and simple rudeness' of manner, rather than trying to be 'untruelye fine'.[3]

In addition to the kind of diction to be employed, the translators had also to decide how closely they would endeavour to

[1] See pp. 220 ff.
[2] *STC* 5317, Cicero, *Those fyve Questions, which Marke Tullye Cicero, disputed in his Manor of Tusculanum* (1561), sig. ¶ 4. Cf. *STC* 15488, sig. A 2.
[3] *STC* 11725, *The Lawes and Statutes of Geneva* (1562), sig. *5.

follow their original. Two widely contrasted examples may serve to illustrate how differently authors viewed this question. Thomas Drant thus describes the way in which he translated two of the Satires of Horace:

> I have done as the people of god wer commanded to do with their captive women that were hansome and beautifull: I have shaved of his heare, & pared of his nayles (that is) I have wyped awaye all his vanitie and superfluitie of matter. Further, I have for the moste parte drawen his private carpyng of this or that man to a general moral. I have englished thinges not accordyng to the vain of the Latin proprietie, but of our own vulgar tongue. I have interfarced (to remove his obscuritie and sometymes to better his matter) much of myne owne devysinge. I have peeced his reason, eekede, and mended his similitudes, mollyfied his hardnes, prolonged his cortall kynd of speeche, changed, & much altered his wordes, but not his sentence: or at leaste (I dare say) not his purpose. For shorte if thou canste credit me: do so.[1]

Drant asks too much of us, and we turn with relief to read what Philemon Holland tells us of his notion of what is the true duty of a translator:

> I proposed to myselfe in making [Livy] English... to come as neere as possibly I could, to the true meaning of the Author: making this account, that if I could approve my diligence that way to men of reason and understanding, all my other wants and defects might sooner be passed by and pardoned. A desire I had to performe in some sort, that which is profitable to the most, namely, an English Historie of that Common Wealth which of all others... affordeth most plenteous examples of devout zeale in their kind, of wisedome, pollicie, justice, valour, and all vertues whatsoever. According to this purpose & intent of mine I framed my pen, not to any affected phrase, but to a meane and popular stile. Wherein, if I have called againe into use some old words, let it be attributed to the love of my countrey language: if the sentence be not so concise, couched and knit togither, as the originall, loth I was to be obscure and darke: have I not Englished everie word aptly? ech Nation hath severall

[1] STC 13805, *A Medicinable Morall, that is, the two Bookes of Horace his Satyres* (1566), sig. A3ᵛ.

THE TRANSLATOR'S DUTY

maners yea and tearmes appropriate, by themselves: have I varied in some places from the French and Italian? censured I looke to be, and haply reprooved: but like as *Alcibiades* said to one...even so say I...Find fault and spare not; but withal, read the original better before ye give sentence.[1]

The whole matter was well summed up in 1603 by Francis Marbury who put the translator's position and responsibility in the following words:

Comparatively the author is the light, and the translator is, as it were, another candlesticke to translate the light into, and that for those which through ignorance of the tongue could not attaine to the light when it shone out of the authors owne lampe. Now although there seeme no great gifts to be required in a translator, yet the truth is that if he be not of good discretion to choose the fittest wordes, of good speech to expresse the authors sentence with fittest wordes...his defectiveness will bring him in danger of showing what gifts are required in a translator, for a good translator is neither a paraphrast nor a periphrast, which is committed to needles chaunging or adding wordes. He so behaveth himselfe that the comparing of the originall will command his fidelity, and that they which know of no originall would take the translator for the authour himselfe. He must naturalise his translation for the reader without injuring the gift of the author in the native worke.[2]

'He must naturalise his translation'; it was the great merit of the best of the Elizabethan translators that they did this with such skill that Charles Whibley could write of them: 'They have turned their authors of Greece and Rome not merely into a new language, but into the feelings of another age and clime. In other words, their books carry with them the lively air of originality.'

Not much can be said by way of generalization about the translators themselves, since they come from too wide a range

---

[1] *STC* 16613, T. Livy, *The Romane Historie* (1600), sig. A 4ᵛ.
[2] *STC* 21286, R. Rollock, *A Treatise of Gods Effectual Calling* (1603), sig. *3.

of callings to be easily classified. Obviously there were many well-educated men amongst them, both the universities and the Inns of Court providing many recruits. Men going into the Church, in particular, were able to find time from their parochial duties to translate works which they felt would be of value to their fellow Christians. John Field, for example, a well-known Puritan, translated seven works by Beza, Calvin, L'Espine, De Mornay and Olevian dealing with a variety of religious topics. Many other examples of translations made by incumbents might be quoted, even if few were so diligent as Field. Other active workers came from the ranks of the schoolmasters, who somehow found time for such work, though as Thomas Stockwood, schoolmaster of Tonbridge School, says, this was not done 'without great painstaking, as wel in rising up early, sitting long at it, and going late to bed'.[1] As for the Inns of Court, which Professor Conley thinks contributed so many translators, we may readily agree that many who were enrolled in the various Inns found time enough to interest themselves in the absorbing art of translation, especially when we remember that quite a number of them had no serious intention to make themselves expert in the law.[2]

But much translation was done, especially from modern languages, by men whose linguistic abilities had probably been acquired by the 'direct method', and had never reached a high standard. Their attainments, however, were sufficient to enable them to translate a news letter from France or the Low Countries, or to give a version of the latest pamphlet telling of some wonder or unusual event reported from abroad. Not much more was required here than a racy version of the original, and publishers of such wares, especially John Wolfe, had a number of hack translators, including Edward Aggas, Anthony Munday, Anthony Chute and others who rapidly adapted the copy given to them into an English form in which the interest and excite-

[1] *STC* 6227, L. Daneau, *A fruitfull Commentarie upon the twelve Small Prophets* (1594), sig. 5ᵛ.
[2] Conley, *The First English Translators of the Classics, passim.*

CONCLUSIONS

ment of the narrative meant more to the reader than any niceties of translation.[1] To move from these to the achievements of Florio, North or Holland is to appreciate something of the range of Elizabethan translations, and the difficulty of characterizing them in any meaningful way.

Nevertheless, a few general points emerge. First, neither translators nor readers seem to have been much concerned whether or no the work was made from the original or from a translation. 'I have my wares at second hand, as by Fraunce out of Greeke, because I am not able to travaile so far for them', writes Arthur Hall, concerning his translation of Homer, and indeed perhaps the most famous of all these translations was North's *Plutarch*, which was translated from the French of Jacques Amiot. Nor was he alone in this practice, for other notable Greek works which came to us from a French intermediary were histories by Diodorus Siculus, and Thucydides, natural history from Pliny, politics from Aristotle, orations by Isocrates and pastorals by Moschus and Longus. Works by lesser Greek authors were generally translated from the Latin.

As to Latin authors, they were in constant demand, and many notable translations were forthcoming. The prose works of Cicero, Livy and Tacitus: the poetry of Horace, Ovid, Terence and Vergil, as well as the drama of Seneca were all given an English dress, and we shall not be overstating the case if we take it that about fifty Greek and one hundred Latin translations were made. Add to this the fact that a number of them were reprinted (some of them more than once) and it appears that the total number of such publications cannot have fallen below two hundred items. If we assume that an average edition consisted of not less than 750 copies at this time, this implies that there were some 150,000 copies of classical works alone printed in England to be disposed of by the booksellers during this period.

Secondly, it is clear that the level of competence in translation was much more various than is often supposed. A few

[1] See p. 234.

hours' reading of translations selected more or less at random will show that much of such work reached a mediocre level at best, and much fell even below that. The literary critics have naturally concentrated on the most gifted versions, such as those of Florio, North or Holland, and the same may be said of the works gathered together to form the two great series of *The Tudor Translations*.[1] This, however, is not our main concern: it is the quantity not the quality of the translations that is our chief interest. A careful (but probably far from complete) search shows that over one thousand items were translated in Elizabeth's reign, while in addition some of them were reprinted several times, so that they represented at least a fifth of the printers' total output. The importance of this to the economy of the trade needs no emphasizing.

It is not within the purpose of this book to consider the stylistic achievements of the translators, and therefore no extended examination of the works of the outstanding practitioners is necessary.[2] It is worth while, however, to note that the practice of translating was widespread, so that we have the names of many hundreds of translators, although most of them are credited with one or two works only. Either they found the task too laborious, or their work did not win approval enough to encourage them to persevere, or else their professional life became too exacting. There were, however, a limited number who were constantly at work, so that at least a dozen can be named who were responsible for ten or more translations. We must not attach too much importance, however, to these figures, since many of the pieces they translated were but slim pamphlets. E. Aggas, for example, translated some thirty works but most of them were little pieces of twenty-four to thirty

[1] *The Tudor Translations*, first series, ed. W. E. Henley (1892–1909); second series, ed. C. Whibley (1924–27).
[2] For information about the stylistic merits of the Elizabethan translations, see the chapter by Charles Whibley in the *Cambridge History of English Literature*, vol IV (1909), pp. 1–19; C. H. Conley, *The First English Translators of the Classics*; F. O. Matthiessen, *Translation: An Elizabethan Art* (Cambridge, Mass., 1931).

pages only, while the works of some of his contemporaries ran to many hundreds of pages, and at times to over a thousand.

Among the most prolific of translators was Arthur Golding, who was notable, not only for the high quality of his work, but also for its volume. He was responsible for at least thirty translations, many of which were very large, the greatest of them—Calvin's *Sermons on Deuteronomy*—running to 1248 pages in double columns. An examination of his output is revealing, for it gives us valuable information concerning the way in which he managed to produce such a large body of work.[1]

Golding was the son of one of the Auditors of the Exchequer. His place of education is unknown, but in the sixties he was receiver for the youthful Earl of Oxford, a ward of Sir William Cecil, and it was to Cecil that Golding dedicated his early work, a translation of Leonardo Bruni's *The Historie of Leonard Aretine, concerning the warres betwene the Imperialles and the Gothes* (1563). The book was dedicated to Sir William 'under whose roofe it hath bene harboruged & fostered from the infancie untyll suche time as it came to his full growth'. The dedication was 'finished at y^r house in the Strond the second of April, 1563', and Golding says that if Sir William will accept the work it will encourage him to make further efforts. It was an ambitious undertaking for a beginner, since it ran to 360 pages of text, which the title-page declared to be 'pleasant and profitable'.[2]

The next year (1564) another publisher printed a translation by Golding made from the Latin entitled *Thabridgment of the Histories of Trogus Pompeius*. Golding had long vowed to dedicate this to the late Earl, but that no longer being possible, he offers it to the young Earl, whose love of history he records, and whom he encourages to learn herein from the example of great men of the past. He has written it, he says, to eschew the

---

[1] Much of value concerning Golding's life and work will be found in L. T. Golding's *An Elizabethan Puritan: Arthur Golding* (New York, 1937), to which I am indebted.

[2] *STC* 3933, sig. a3.

vice of idleness and for love of his country. Again it made a sizeable volume of 380 pages quarto.[1]

In 1565 Golding returned to his first patron, and dedicated to him his translation of Caesar's account of his exploits in Gaul. He says that his earlier work had been well received by Sir William, and that he had at some time handed to him a translation by John Brende of the first four books of the Caesar made before his death. After having 'deeplye weyed' the reasons for setting aside Brende's version, Golding did so and made a new translation of the whole work, fortified by the knowledge that he had sufficient leisure for the task, and had 'also overcome a pece of no lesse difficultye alreadye'. He added: 'How my doings may be liked of others I know not.'[2] He need not have feared, for the work was reprinted in 1590.

The same year saw the appearance of part of his masterpiece, the first four books of Ovid's *Metamorphoses*, which he dedicated to Robert Dudley, Earl of Leicester. It was reasonable for Golding to turn to the Earl, who was well known as a friend to translators and one whose religious views were similar to Golding's own. The work was offered as a sample, 'the wiche if it please you to take in good part, I accompt my poore travaill herein sufficiently recompensed, and think myselfe greatly inforced to persever in the full accomplishment of the whole worke'.[3] The Earl was evidently satisfied, and in 1567 Golding published *The XV Bookes of P. Ovidius Naso, entytuled Metamorphosis*, with Leicester's device on the title-page and a long dedication in verse to him, setting out the contents of the book, and begging for his further support, since he was well known as a protector of translators. The work was popular, being reprinted four times by 1603, and came under the eye of Shakespeare.

[1] *STC* 24290, *3ᵛ. This was reprinted in 1570 and 1578 by the same printer, Thomas Marsh.
[2] *STC* 4335, *The eyght bookes of Caius Julius Caesar conteyning his martiall exploytes in Gallia*, sig. *2, 3. It contained 568 pp. octavo.
[3] *STC* 18955, *The Fyrst Fower Bookes of P. Ovidius Nasos worke, intitled Metamorphosis* (1565).

This marks the culmination of Golding's classical translations. Henceforth, his main preoccupation was with religious treatises, and in the same year as the Ovid was printed, a very different work, *A little booke concernynge offences*, translated from Calvin, made its appearance. This was dedicated to Francis, second Earl of Bedford, then Governor of Berwick, and it is from there that Golding dates his dedication on the first of October 1566. In this he says that 'the matter defendeth rather than craveth defence',[1] and it marks the fourth publication by William Seres of Golding's works.

His reputation as a translator was evidently growing, for in 1569 he was approached by two booksellers

> Lucas Harrison and George Bishop Stationers, men well minded towardes godlinesse and true Religion, taking uppon them too Imprint this woorke at their proper charges, requested mee too put the same intoo English, I willingly agreed too their godly desire.[2]

The work was by the Danish theologian, Nicholas Hemmingsen, entitled *A Postill, or Exposition of the Gospels that are usually red in the churches of God, upon the Sundayes and Feast dayes of Saincts*, and in dedicating the work to Sir Walter Mildmay, sometime Chancellor of the Exchequer, and founder of Emmanuel College, Cambridge, Golding says that he has made the translation not only as a thanksgiving tribute to Mildmay for his 'great Goodnesse', but also to be 'a furtherance and helpe to the simple and unlearned sorte of our ministers in England'. When one recalls that Mildmay was later to found his College with the primary purpose of training men for the Ministry, one can see why Golding's book made a special appeal to him.

The booksellers were taking a considerable risk in this venture, for the translation runs to close on seven hundred large quarto pages, but they were evidently satisfied with their bargain, for the next year they asked Golding to complete his work by translating *A postil, or orderly disposing of certeine*

---

[1] *STC* 4434, sig. *4ᵛ.   [2] *STC* 13061, sig. *3.

epistles by David Chytraeus. This he did, again dedicating the work to Mildmay. Many, he tells him, have read the earlier work with 'great willingnesse and diligence', and the new work of some five hundred quarto pages he hopes will 'come into the handes of all men, as well of the rudest, unskilfullest and unlearnedest sort...as to the hands of the skilful and learned sort'.[1] Whether this wish was granted we have no means of telling, but a second edition was called for only seven years later.

In 1571, although he complains that 'my continuall troubles and sutes in the Lawe (as yet unended after more than three years travel) have bereft mee of the greatest part of my time, so I could not dispatch things with such expedition as otherwise I might have done',[2] he nevertheless somehow found time to translate another large work *The Psalmes of David and others. With John Calvins commentaries.* This he dedicated to his old patron, the Earl of Oxford, and in so doing makes some interesting remarks on the art of translation. In commending the work to the Earl he writes:

Onely this muche I may safely say of it, that in all pointes (to the uttermoste of my power, and according to the abilitie which God hath given me to edifie withal) I have sincerely performed the dutie of a faithful Interpreter, rather indevouring too lay foorth things plainlie (yea and sometimes also homely and grossely) too the understanding of many, than too indyte things curyously too the pleasing of a fewe. For in this and suche other workes, the rude and ignorant have more interest than the learned and skilful.[3]

This was the third work published by Harrison and Bishop, and again it was of considerable size, running to nearly five hundred and fifty pages quarto; but clearly by now they knew what they were doing, and were satisfied that there was a market for works of this description made by a tried translator.

About the same time he was also at work on a version of Beza's *Booke of Christian Questions and Answers. Wherein are*

[1] *STC* 5263, sig. Hhh6ᵛ. [2] *STC* 2389, sig. *2.
[3] *STC* 2389, sig. *5.

Set foorth the chefe pointces of the Christian Religion (1572). The title-page states it to be 'a worke right necessarie and profitable for all such as shall have to deale with the captious quarellings of the wrangling adversaries of Gods trueth'. In the form of question and answer, it gave information on a number of points much in dispute at the time, and evidently filled a need, for it was reprinted five times by 1586.[1]

'Presuming upon the apparent signes of your Lordships former favour and great good will towardes me', writes Golding to Leicester, he ventures to dedicate to him Bullinger's *Confutation of the Popes Bull which was published more than two yeres agoe against Elizabeth*.[2] It was hoped by this translation to make Bullinger's views 'more largely and plenteously available' to English readers, for whom the work was mainly intended. It was a quasi-official publication and, with Government support and Leicester's backing, Golding had every reason to make this comparatively small translation.

Golding's labours on behalf of religion were intensified over these years, and in 1574 three more volumes, sponsored by the same two booksellers, Harrison and Bishop, appeared. Two of these were by Calvin and one by Marlorat. Calvin's *Sermons upon the Booke of Job* made a large folio of 752 pages in double columns and was again dedicated to Leicester. In so doing Golding says that it is a work of 'greater substance, importance and travell than Diverse works of mine' formerly accepted by the Earl. He is anxious about it, for it is 'the first of any great weight that ever I translated out of the French tongue to be published', so that he asks that 'as a special favour to myselfe... that where any faultes shal be found I may be made privie to them'.[3]

The second volume of Calvin's Sermons to appear this year dealt with the epistle to the Galatians, and made a volume of

---

[1] *STC* 2037–43.
[2] *STC* 4044 (1572). The Latin version was printed by J. Day in 1571.
[3] *STC* 4444, *Sermons upon the Booke of Job*, sig. a3ᵛ. Despite its size it was four times reprinted by 1584.

660 pages quarto. In his dedication to his old patron Sir William Cecil, he thanks him for help in a protracted lawsuit, which now being put aside has enabled him to return to his 'accustomed exercise of translating'.[1] His letter from Cripplegate is dated 14 November 1574, but before this, the third volume sponsored by the two booksellers had been issued. This was Augustine Marlorat's *Catholike Exposition upon the Revelation of Sainct John*. Again he asks Mildmay 'of your accustomed goodnesse towardes mee, or rather of your love of the setting forth of Gods glorie...to accept this travell of mine'.[2]

After a number of smaller books in the intervening years Golding put out another large volume in 1577 consisting of Calvin's *Sermons upon the Epistle too the Ephesians*. It was dedicated to the Archbishop of Canterbury, Edmund Grindal, and Golding declares that: 'Forasmuch as it is the dewtie of all them that publishe things too the world, whether as first authors, or as translators, too deale in such sort as most folke may reape profite and commoditie by their dooyings, specially in matters of religion.'[3]

Six years later he concluded his work on the writings of Calvin by the production of a version of the sermons upon Deuteronomy. This required no less than 1247 folio pages in double columns and was dedicated to Sir Thomas Bromley, the Master of the Rolls on the last day of December 1582.[4] Once again the work was printed for the bookseller George Bishop.

This detailed survey of many of Golding's translations brings to light a number of facts which illustrate the business side of the translator's trade. In the first place, successful though he was, Golding was careful to obtain the backing of men who were eminent in Church or State, and generally well known as leaders in religious matters. Sir William Cecil, Leicester, Mildmay, Grindal—to mention only the chief of them—formed

---

[1] STC 4449, *Sermons...upon the Epistle of Saincte Paule to the Galathians* (1574), sig. ¶2ᵛ.
[2] STC 17408. [3] STC 4448, sig. *2.
[4] STC 4442, *The Sermons of M. John Calvin upon Deuteronomie* (1583).

a body of supporters on whom a writer could safely rely, and this must have helped Golding to work away at the gigantic tasks that he essayed. It has been estimated that there were one and a half million words in his translation of Job, while that of Deuteronomy was considerably larger.[1]

Furthermore, for much of his work he had the backing of influential members of the book trade. John Day, whose strong religious views were well known, printed four of Golding's works, while Harrison and Bishop were responsible for no less than eight large volumes. Without the financial backing of these men Golding could never have made the name for himself that he did, since it is unlikely that he would have persevered with his heroic tasks without a publisher at his back.

Translators, as we know, had many enemies, and the story of Golding is clear evidence that both patron and publisher were immensely important, if not essential, to the writer who hoped to do more than make the kind of hack translations required by printers such as J. Wolfe. The patron implicitly vouched for the soundness of the matter: the publisher or printer assured the author of an audience, especially for these 'works not broached in the seller of myne owne brayne, but drawne out of the most pure and clear fountains' of other and greater men.

[1] The extent of Golding's labours on the text of Calvin alone may be estimated from the following figures. In folio form: Deuteronomy, 1248 pp. d.c.; Job, 752 pp. d.c. In quarto: Ephesians, 694 pp.; Psalms, 546 pp. In octavo: Galatians, 640 pp.

CHAPTER V

THE VARIETY OF BOOKS

The above chapters have given some account of the conditions and circumstances prevailing in the second half of the sixteenth century. It now remains to examine the variety of literary wares that were laid before the public.

1. *Religion*

In the first half of the sixteenth century in England, the book trade depended to a great extent on the sale of religious works of various kinds for its prosperity. Something like half the printer's output was of a religious nature: liturgical books necessary for the conduct of the various services of the Church, works for the instruction of the clergy, helps for priests in their parochial duties, books of moral instruction for the young, lives of saints, sermons, devotional treatises for the ordinary Christian man and woman—these and many others were to be found on the stalls of the booksellers and gave help and instruction to those in need.

During the reign of Elizabeth the demand for books of a religious nature still remained great and it was only as the reign wore on that the claims of other kinds of literature equalled those of religion. While the demand remained, however, the nature of the output changed fundamentally. The split between England and Rome meant that the bookstalls no longer carried editions of breviaries, missals, books of hours and all the rest of the Catholic service books, but in their place they displayed the Book of Common Prayer, the Psalms in prose and verse, and in ever-growing numbers the Bible in English. Gone were the Lives of the Saints, the treatises of the Four Last Things, or the helps to those devoted to the cloistered

CONTROVERSIAL RELIGIOUS WORKS

life of monk or nun, and in their place were the 'home helps' to godly living, the various Catechisms, the manuals of devotion, the commentaries and the books of exegesis. And as the controversy between England and Rome grew sharper, both sides eagerly availed themselves of the services of the printing presses to put forward their own views and to controvert those of their opponents. Controversy was in the air, for naturally many did not surrender the religion in which they had been nurtured without a struggle, and despite every attempt to stamp out the Catholic religion and all its practices, this did not prove to be an easy task, and the control of Catholic writings was particularly difficult. Since this was so, there was nothing for it but to see that Catholic propaganda was answered, and hence a continuous flow of books and pamphlets from both sides resulted.

Controversial religious writings

Quite early in Elizabeth's reign many Catholics went into exile, and Louvain soon became their headquarters. Here exiles, especially from Oxford and Cambridge, congregated, and from here they published many of their counter-blasts to the Protestant opinions. By 1568 William Allen had set up a college at Douay, which was to become a great training school in dogmatic theology and for missionary activities. These crusaders for the Catholic faith infiltrated into England, teaching, encouraging the faithful, celebrating the sacraments and helping to disseminate the controversial works of their colleagues secretly imported into England from Douay and Louvain.[1]

Almost before the earliest of the exiles had left, however, the first salvoes of the engagement which was long to occupy both sides (and the presses) had been fired by John Jewel, Bishop of Salisbury, in what came to be known as the 'Challenge Sermon'

---

[1] A. C. Southern, *Elizabethan Recusant Prose*, pp. 25 ff. Throughout this chapter I am greatly indebted to Dr Southern, whose work is a model of accuracy and completeness.

preached at Paul's Cross on 26 November 1559.[1] After setting out twenty-seven articles of the Roman faith the Bishop concluded:

If any man alive were hable to prove any of these articles, by ani one clear, or playne clause, or sentence, eyther of the scriptures, or of the olde doctours, or of ani olde generall Counsell, or by any example of the primitive church: I promised then that I would geve over and subscribe unto hym.[2]

In his book on *Elizabethan Recusant Prose, 1559–1582*, Dr A. C. Southern has shown that this challenge led to the publication during the next ten years of some fifty items for and against the Bishop's views. Jewel published his sermon in the autumn of 1560, together with his correspondence with Dr Henry Cole, a learned Catholic theologian. Nothing more appeared in print until 1562, although Jewel's opponents were busy circulating replies to various parts of his case. Jewel returned to the attack in 1562 by publishing his *Apologia Ecclesiae Anglicanae*,[3] while a translation under the direction of Archbishop Parker made by Anne, Lady Bacon, was printed the same year by the printer of the Latin version.[4] By 1564 the Catholics were ready with their replies, and Thomas Harding in *An Answere to Maister Juelles Chalenge*[5] traversed all the twenty-seven points of Jewel's challenge. Three more Catholic replies to Jewel were printed in the same year, while in 1565 almost each month saw one book more added to the list, sixteen in all being issued, only two of them by Catholics. There was a slight falling off the next year when two Protestant and eight Catholic pieces were printed, while in 1567 the score was two and seven respectively, including Jewel's *Defence of the Apologie*.[6] After one more shot on each side the next year the matter was nearly at an end, a second and enlarged edition of Jewel's *Defence*[7] closing this extraordinary series of exchanges, made

---

[1] It was repeated at Court on the following 18 March 1560, and at Paul's Cross on 31 March.
[2] *STC* 14612, sig. F5ᵛ.   [3] *STC* 14581.   [4] *STC* 14590.
[5] *STC* 12758.   [6] *STC* 14600.   [7] *STC* 14602 (1571).

the more extraordinary since the Catholic books were written and printed overseas and smuggled into England and circulated with much difficulty.

Not only the number of books but the extent of some of them was equally remarkable. To take the two chief opponents, Jewel and Harding, only. Harding's *Answere to Maister Juelles Chalenge* occupies 386 pages quarto, or 472 pages in the octavo reprint, and his reply to Jewel's *Apologia* is even longer, taking up 752 pages quarto. In the next year his *Rejoindre to M. Jewels Replie* was nearly as lengthy, running to 635 pages quarto although it deals only with the first of Jewel's twenty-seven articles. Three further works the next year took up 524 pages quarto, and in his final effort in 1568, *A Detection of sundrie foule errours*, he apologizes for the brevity of his reply which occupies some 900 pages quarto![1]

Another example of the way in which the rival religious parties kept the presses busy may be seen if we look at what was happening some ten years later. About June 1580 the two Jesuits, Campion and Persons (or Parsons), had arrived in England on their proselytizing mission, and as part of their activities Persons wrote *A Brief Discours contayning certayne reasons why Catholiques refuse to goe to Church*, 'in which booke he showed by divers reasons, that conscience and not obstinacy or other evill meaning was the true cause of Catholikes refusing to goe to Protestant Churches'.[2] This work was surreptitiously printed at Greenstreet House, East Ham, and gave nine reasons against churchgoing. It was introduced by an address to the reader by W. Howlet, professing loyalty and

---

[1] *STC* 12763, sig. *4ᵛ. 'The booke of the *Defence* being alreadie so great as it is, by the time a just answer should be added unto it, every man that hath any judgement in these thinges maie soone conceive of what an huge quantitie my new Printed Volume would be. In deed, were every idle point answered and treated of at ful, it would seeme to match yea farre to outmatche Foxes Huge Booke of his false Martyrs.'

[2] Southern, *Elizabethan Recusant Prose*, p. 461, quoting Persons's memoirs. The *Discours* (*STC* 19394) was published in 1580, with the false imprint 'Imprinted at Doway by John Lyon, 1580'.

accusing their opponents of falsely misrepresenting the Catholic position. In the course of the next year there were three answers printed, which vied one with the other in abuse and derision of Persons and Howlet, calling them 'that darke broode and uncleane cage of papists', jeering at the 'untimely flights and scriching in the cleare day light of the Gospell', and calling on people to bear in mind 'the Papists traiterous and treacherous doctrine and demeanour towardes our Soveraigne and the State'. In the meantime Campion had also fallen foul of various Protestants, for soon after their arrival, both he and Persons were advised by their friends to make declarations of their beliefs, so that something should be on record should they be imprisoned and their views silenced or misrepresented. This they did, Campion's taking the form of 'a Letter to the Council', one copy of which he gave into the safe keeping of a fellow Catholic, Thomas Pounde. 'But my said friend', wrote Campion, 'kept it not close long, but divulged it and it was read greedily: whereat the adversaries were mad.' By December 1580 William Charke, a rabid Puritan, had written a reply to 'Campions Challenge', as it came to be called, under the title of *An answere to a seditious pamphlet lately cast abroade by a Jesuite, with a discoverie of that blasphemous sect,*[1] while a month later Meredith Hanmer, 'Master of Art, and Student in Divinitie', published his attack, entitled *The great bragge and challenge of M. Champion...contayninge nyne articles here severallye laide downe, directed by him to the Lordes of the Counsail, confuted and aunswered.*[2] In this, as the title suggests, Hanmer follows the familiar device of the time by printing the words of his opponent in extenso, and then controverting them passage by passage, thus giving the appearance at least of treating an opponent fairly. As far as the Catholics were concerned, this gave a wider circulation to their books than they could have achieved by their own means, since they could do nothing openly to print or circulate their views.

At this point Persons took up the cudgels in defence of

[1] *STC* 5005 (Dec. 1580). [2] *STC* 12745 (1581).

Campion, and to the surprise of the authorities had a book written and 'imprinted at Doway', and a copy left on the doorstep of William Fleetwood, Recorder of London (an active enemy of the Catholics) only ten days after Hanmer's book had been entered.[1] Despite the imprint of 'Doway', the book was actually printed at the Greenstreet House Press (now lodged with Francis Browne), but even with this aid it was a notable achievement, and a sign of the vigour and determination with which the Jesuits were conducting their campaign. They were almost forced to do so, since their opponents were unsparing in their attacks. Persons thus characterizes the treatment of Campion by Charke:

Whatever he says or does you will have it taken in evil part: if he speak humbly, he dissembleth: if he yield commendation, he flattereth: if he show confidence in his cause, he vaunteth: if he offer trial, he meaneth not perfomance: if he protest his meaning, he must not be credited: if he desire audience, he must not be admitted: whatever he urges for himself or his cause must avail nothing. William Charke will have him condemned for unlearned, proud, wicked, and traiterous to the state.

Needless to say, neither Charke nor Hanmer was willing to let Persons have the last word, and a little later in the year each came back with replies. Both of these were entered in August 1581, so that Persons must have been well abreast of what was going on before leaving England that summer. The Catholic press was seized on 8 August at its new hiding place in Oxfordshire when Persons had written only part of his reply, as he states in a moving epistle to Charke, printed in his *Defence of the Censure, gyven uppon two bookes of William Charke and Meredith Hanmer*, printed in Rouen in 1582. He writes:

In generall, every one can imagine by hym selfe, how difficult a thing yt is in England at this daye, for a Catholique man to write any book: where nether libertie, nor rest, nor librarie, nor conference, nor beinge is permitted hym. And in particular, this muche I must adde,

---

[1] *STC* 19393 (1581), *A Brief Censure uppon two bookes written in answere to M. Edmonde Campions offer of disputation.*

whiche you alredie in part doe knowe: that soone after the publishinge of your reply to the Censure, the Author therof addressed hym selfe to a defence, and had in greate part dispatched the same, redie for the printe, in suche sort as the rigorous tyme of your persecution permitted hym. But God sufferinge at that verie instant, that the sayd print so long sought, and muche feared by you, should be taken: there was taken, lost, and dispersed ther-withall, not onelie all furniture there redy for this booke, but also for sundry other thinges, partlie printed, and partlie in printing, concerning our defence of trueth and equitie, against your falsehood and violent oppressions.[1]

In the meantime, Campion distressed by the charge of insolence which had been made against him for his letter to the Council in which he offered to sustain the Catholic position against all comers, wrote a work entitled *Rationes Decem*: 'Ten reasons for the confidence with which Edmund Campion offered his adversaries to dispute on behalf of the Faith, set before the famous men of our Universities.'[2] The work was secretly printed at Stonor Park, Oxfordshire, whither the Greenstreet Press had been forced to move, and on 27 June 1581, those attending the Commencement ceremonies in St Mary's, Oxford, found copies of the work lying on the benches. This was too grave a matter to be ignored, and the authorities through Aylmer, Bishop of London, instructed the two Regius Professors at Oxford and Cambridge to answer Campion. Whitaker of Cambridge did so later in the year:[3] Humphrey of Oxford took longer, and it was not until March 1582 that the first part of his reply was published,[4] followed by a second part in the summer of 1584.[5] By this time, however, his more energetic colleague was once more in the field, for John Drury,

---

[1] *STC* 19401, sig. A2.
[2] Not in *STC*, but four copies have now been located. See A. F. Allison and D. M. Rogers, *A Catalogue of Catholic Books in English*, no. 192. This is a work of first-class importance and has been of the greatest help in compiling this chapter.
[3] *STC* 25358 and 25359 both published in 1581.
[4] *STC* 13961, *Jesuitismi pars prima: sive de praxi Romanae Curiae*.
[5] *STC* 13962, *Jesuitismi pars secunda*.

a Jesuit, had already attacked his reply to Campion in a work printed in Paris in 1582, and this provoked an answer of 887 pages quarto from Whitaker!

Persons also found time in the summer of 1581 to deal with the impudent attacks on the Faith by the turncoat John Nichols. After some disagreement with his ecclesiastical superiors, Nichols had made his way to Rome, and after further difficulty because of his slender qualifications, was admitted into the English College at Rome in 1577. In good time 'the Colledge began to be werie of him' and he left for Rheims, but seems to have changed his mind *en route* and arrived back in England about 1580. Only eight days after landing he was clapped into the Tower, and rapidly found himself wishing to be a member of the Church of England once again. As we have already seen, while there and under threats from his captors, he wrote *A declaration of the recantation of John Nichols...*,[1] and this he followed a few months later by *The Oration and Sermon made at Rome by commaundement of the fowre Cardinalles...upon paine of death...Now by him brought into the English tongue, for the great comfort and comoditie of all faithfull Christians. Herein also is aunswered an infamous Libell, maliciouslie written and cast abroad, against the saide John Nichols, with a sufficient discharge of himselfe from all the Papists lying reports, and his owne life, both largelie and amplie discovered.*[2]

Both these works were a tissue of lies, or at best half-true statements, designed to show the Catholic religion and its practitioners in the worst light, and Persons thought it was necessary to answer them, which he did later that same year in a pamphlet printed at the Greenstreet House Press in Oxfordshire. The reply to Nichols 'contayned a ful answere to his recantation, with a confutation of his slaunders, and proofe of the contraries, in the Pope, Cardinals, Clergie, Studentes, and private men of Rome'.[3] In the course of the work Persons

---

[1] *STC* 18533 (1581).   [2] *STC* 18535 [1581].
[3] *STC* 19402, *A Discoverie of I. Nicols minister, misreported a Jesuite* [1582?], sig. A 1.

takes occasion to attack Thomas Lupton, who had recently published a book entitled *A Persuasion from Papistrie, wrytten chiefely to the obstinate, determined and dysobedient English Papists.*[1] As might have been expected, Persons's reply in its turn only provoked another book by Lupton, who denounced Persons and his like as men who 'call themselves Jesuites, but they rather deserve to be called Judaites, for they follow Judas in betraying, not Jesus in saving'. Lupton characterizes the work of Persons as 'a pernicious book in praise of the Pope and Papisterie in reproache of M. Nicols, lately converted from Papisterie to the Gospel....' Furthermore', he adds: 'He doth also detract a booke by mee pende and published called *A Perswasion from papistrie*...without disproving or confuting any one part therof, whose namelesse worke in such pointes as I know to be false I have not only taken upon me to reprove, but also to defend myselfe and my saide bookes by him therin depraved and slandered.'[2]

Persons's attack on Nichols also brought forth another defence early in the spring of 1583, in which Dudley Fenner wisely leaves the matter of Nichols as soon as is decent, and gives the larger part of his 80,000 word treatise to a defence of the Protestant cause in general.[3]

I have taken these two groups of conflict—admittedly two important groups—in which the clash between the rival parties is clearly and quickly reflected in the book market, but many more centres of controversy could be instanced. It is even more significant to watch the number of works published over a series of years, since it is only by so doing that their ubiquity and their importance to the booksellers can be fully realized. An examination of a period that we have not hitherto drawn on to any considerable extent, namely the years from 1570 onwards, is revealing. During 1570 there appeared on the bookstalls a little work of some eighty pages entitled *The*

[1] *STC* 16950 (1581).
[2] *STC* 16946, *The Christian against the Jesuite* (1582), sig. ¶ 2.
[3] *STC* 10764, *An answere unto the Confutation of J. Nichols, his Recantation.*

Hatefull Hypocrisie and rebellion of the Romishe prelacie by Lewys Evans. Evans was an apostate, whose writings while still a Catholic vie with those written after his conversion in their unbridled use of invective, bitterness and general abuse. The book now offered for sale was just the thing for the most rabid Protestant partisans in which the hypocrisy of the Roman prelates, together with their ignorance, iniquity and blasphemy, get a rough handling.[1] A more general attack on the Romanist position was printed the same year, having been translated from the Latin of Thomas Kirchmeyer. Barnaby Googe, the translator, tells us that this seemed to read 'so eloquentlye in Latin... and so plainley and truely hath described the fayned sanctitie of the Romishe religion' that he thought it worthy of an English dress in the hope that it would be 'for the benefite of the common, and simpler sorte'.[2] Its nature may be judged from the following passage describing the elaborate ceremonial of the Catholics, so hated by many of the opposing party:

> But who is able then to shew the gesture straunge, and grace,
> And shuffling up and downe of Clarkes, herein from place to place?
> With what a great solempnitie, he liftes his looke on hie,
> His Myter now he putteth of, and on immediatly,
> And at his hande there standeth one with still attentive eyes,
> To put it on and of againe, according to the guise.
> Sometime he standes, sometime he sittes, and sweetely oft doth kisse,
> His Altar, Chalice, Booke, and Glasse, enclosed here for this.
> Some whiles....[3]

So it runs along for over a hundred pages, and it was evidently popular, for another edition was called for in 1577.

In the same year another versified attack on the Catholics was put out by John Phillips which he called *A frendly larun or faythfull warnynge to the true-harted Subjectes of England. Discovering the Actes and malicious myndes of those obstinate and*

---
[1] *STC* 10591.
[2] *STC* 15011, *The popish kingdome, or reigne of Antichrist* (1570), sig. A 1ᵛ, E 2ᵛ.
[3] *STC* 15011, sig. E 2ᵛ.

rebellious Papists that hope (as they terme it) to have theyr Golden day. Phillips warns his readers that 'If thou looke for any Eloquence or fine Phrases of Rhetoricke, thou art deceaved', and perhaps his opening lines are sufficient to convince us of the truth of his statement:

What meanes the ragynge mindes of cruell carelesse sorte?
To range with rage whose choller hot, thet deame a sweete disporte?
Or why do Papistes mutter so, in every corner nowe?[1]

Less easily come by in the same year were two Catholic pieces, the first of which by Thomas Butler was entitled *A Treatise of the Holy Sacrifice of the Altar, called the Masse*.[2] This was a translation of an Italian work and is described by Dr Southern as 'a straightforward exposition of doctrine without controversial bias'. The other was printed by Laurence Tomson in his *Answere to certein Assertions of M. Fecknam, somtime Abbot of Westminster, which he made of late against a godly Sermon of M. John Goughes, preached in the Tower the xv. of Januarie, 1570.* The circumstances of its production are of interest. Feckenham, who had been a prisoner since 1563, having refused to take the Oath of Supremacy, was forced to attend Gough's sermon, and as he came from the church he was asked by the Lieutenant of the Tower and other notables for his opinion of it.

I answered: that I was very lothe to finde any faulte with the sayings or doings of any man, being already in trouble as you knowe. You replied and sayd: that I was not able to finde fault, where no fault was. I had then no leisure to make any further answer, you departing homewardes, and I to my prison. But now considering... uppon your lycence graunted and obteyned,[3]

Feckenham set out his objection to the sermon, and this, under its four heads, is printed by Tomson before he turns to answer

[1] *STC* 19870 (1570), sig. A6.
[2] Not in *STC*. No. 659 in A. F. Allison and D. M. Rogers, *A Catalogue of Catholic Books in English*.
[3] *STC* 24113, sig. A2.

Feckenham. He finds Feckenham to be ignorant of the scriptures and lacking in logic, but nevertheless takes 160 pages octavo for his reply. For good measure, Gough also issued a reply, but contented himself with a third of the space.[1]

The next year (1571) saw a book by that hardened controversialist, William Fulke, entitled *A confutation of a Popishe and sclaunderous libelle, in forme of an apologie: geven out into the courte, and spread abrode in diverse other places of the Realme.* He was induced to write, he tells us, since

> there was found in the court, either cast of purpose, or lost of negligence, a certain small pamphlette conteinynge an Apollogie, or aunswere of a Papist to some frends of his that persuaded him to conforme hymself to the Religion now received in the realme by publike authoritie, which when it came to my handes, supposing it might do some hurte emonge those that are ignoraunte, I thought good briefly to confute it.[2]

Fulke first prints the Apology which was written by Feckenham setting out his reasons for refusing to attend church services as laid down by the new Book of Common Prayer. This takes up about twenty pages and is refuted by Fulke in the remaining ninety-six pages of the book. He goes out of his way to try to be fair to his opponent by stating that

> because the copie whiche was founde was unskilfully written, I had some difficultie to reade it in certaine places, and sometimes I mighte plainely perceive that the authours meanyng was chaunged by untrue writynge, so that the authour and his frendes maie have some occasion to cavill at my publishing of the copie whiche was so muche corrupted. In consideration wherof, I would have been verie glad to have had the principall copie of the authours owne hande if I could have knowen how to come by it. But seyng I was out of hope of that, I perused, and restored the copie that I had, as faithfully as I could, desiryng the aucthour, or his frendes that have

---

[1] *STC* 12131, *The aunswer of John Gough to maister Fecknams objections against his sermon lately preached in the Tower* (1570).

[2] *STC* 11426, sig. A1.

the originall, if I have erred in any woorde of any momente to lette me have knowledge therof, and I will thereby reforme the apologie and alter myne answere therto accordingly.[1]

A less controversial note is struck by Richard Cavendish in his book, *The image of nature and grace, conteyning the whole course and condition of mans estate*, written 'to all that throughe simplicitie of conscience and lack of true knowledge embrace the doctrine of the Papistes'. In his attempt to persuade, he writes that 'I have therin offered no doctrine unto you but that which is witnessed by the lawe, and the Prophetes, 'namely the Scriptures'.[2] Another controversial but temperately written book appeared this year, written by Christopher Carlile, in which he attempts to show that St Peter was never at Rome, and that neither St Peter nor the Pope can rightfully be called the Head of the Church. For some reason this sober work is preceded by verses of a highly offensive nature, lampooning the Pope in words such as 'His nose doth snuff forth hellish fumes | His tungue is stinge of death'.[3]

Ignoring the books that appeared the next year, 1574 saw the arrival in England of a book printed in Antwerp, but not readily available in England, partly we are told 'because there were but few printed and partly because some of them fell into heretickes handes'. This was a work written by Richard Bristow, sometime Fellow of Exeter College, Oxford, and now one of the most energetic and learned of Allen's associates at Douay. *A Briefe Treatise of diverse plaine and sure wayes to finde out the truthe in this doubtful and dangerous time of Heresie*..[4] was in fact an enlargement of the Articles of the Christian Faith which had been written by William Allen some years earlier and had circulated in manuscript. These Articles had become known to the English authorities, who considered them dangerous and tried to suppress them. Knowing this, and knowing how few of the original edition of his work had escaped the

---

[1] *STC* 11426, sig. A2.   [2] *STC* 4879 [1571], sig. A2.
[3] *STC* 4655, sig. A3.   [4] *STC* 3799.

enemy,[1] Bristow reissued his book in an enlarged form in 1576 with a new title which read: *Demaundes to be proponed of Catholiques to the Heretikes*.[2] Bristow, commenting on its comparatively small size, says that to some it may 'for the quantitie seme but a trifle, yet whosoever will voutsafe to peruse it, shal finde it (I trust) full of most just & weightie considerations to beleeve the Catholikes, of this time also, & not the Heretickes'. Needless to say this did not go unanswered, and Fulke published in 1577 *Two Treatises written against the Papistes*...,[3] the first of which purported to be an answer to Bristow, but the latter denied this, saying that 'in trueth it toucheth me not at all'.[4]

Although Bristow's version of the Articles of William Allen was first printed in 1574, the next year also saw another version of them put out as the second part of a work secretly printed in England. Their author was Edward Rishton, who entitled his work: *An offer made by a Catholike to a learned Protestant, wherin shall appere the difference betwixte the open knowen Church of the Catholikes, from the hid and unknowen Congregation of the Protestantes*.[5]

Since it was printed in England it may be that this edition had a much wider circulation than was the lot of Bristow's first venture, and kept things going until the revised *Demaundes* were issued in 1576. No reply seems to have been made to the *Offer* until 1588, when Robert Crowley wrote *A Deliberat answere made to a rash offer, which a popish Antichristian Catholique made to a learned Protestant (as he saieth), and caused to be publyshed in printe: Anno D. 1575*. Crowley tells us that he got a copy of the *Offer* in 1586, and that 'in May 1587 having more spare time than in long time before', he took the book in

[1] From Arber, *A Transcript of the Registers of the Company of Stationers*, vol. I, p. 492, we learn that actually 367 copies of the edition were seized.
[2] Not in *STC*. No. 148 in A. F. Allison and D. M. Rogers, *Catalogue*. The quotation I owe to Southern, *Elizabethan Recusant Prose*, p. 392.
[3] *STC* 11458.
[4] *STC* 3802, *A reply to Fulke* (1580), sig. A2.
[5] *STC* 274; part 2. The imprint 'Douai' is false. The work was printed on W. Carter's secret press in London. See pp. 78–80.

hand, and having read it now answers the 'Offers' there made, and dedicates the book 'To all and singular popish Recusants'.[1]

Hard hitting as are many of the works mentioned, they were in the main serious attempts to state a case, and to appeal to reason. The same cannot be said for a work obviously intended to inflame opinion against the Catholics published in 1574. Written in Latin some twenty years earlier, it was a characteristic specimen of the work of that violent anti-Catholic, Bishop John Bale. 'Now Englished with sundrye additioons by John Studley', it was published with the title *The Pageant of Popes...shewing many straunge, notorious, outragious and tragicall partes played by them, the like whereof hath not els bin hearde.* It is hard, however, to believe that 'straunge, notorious, outragious' as may have been the behaviour of the Pontiffs, it could have possibly exceeded that of Bale, whose outlook may be judged from a sentence of his preface: 'If an hundred of the rankest hellhounds that ever raigned on the earth might be mustered out of hell, foure score and nineteen of them should be Popes.'[2]

Perhaps enough has been quoted from these few years to show the steady warfare that went on and the vigour with which each side conducted its campaign. The severe handicaps under which the Catholics laboured were often overcome by their persistence and their courage.[3] When they could not print openly or secretly in England they fell back on their presses across the Channel and endeavoured to smuggle their wares into England and circulate them as best they could. In this they were obviously successful to a considerable extent as is obvious from the above account of how seriously and continuously their opponents felt it necessary to answer them. Sometimes as we have seen the replies were written at the instructions of someone in authority, but more generally they

[1] *STC* 6084, sig. A2.   [2] *STC* 1304, sig. b4ᵛ.
[3] The Catholic output was naturally much smaller than that of their opponents, but it was by no means insignificant. I estimate that over 250 editions of controversial works in English, printed abroad or secretly at home, were published between 1558 and 1603. See pp. 74 ff.

seem to come from the sincere convictions of their authors, whose strenuous and at times acrimonious wrestlings with the arguments of their opponents are the best evidence of their belief that these heretical views must be met openly and in full detail.

All this it must be confessed often makes dusty enough reading for us nowadays. There is a great deal of logic chopping, straining for dialectical victory, trivial scoring off an opponent and so on. To the devoted Protestant or Catholic, however, it was another matter, and men were prepared to buy and to read through these considerable tomes, each side believing that what was done was all *ad majorem gloriam Dei.*

As a horrible commentary on the passions that were aroused in many by the more extreme anti-Catholics we have to remember that from time to time the bookstalls displayed broadsides or little pamphlets which related to what frightful ends these religious controversies could lead. For example, in the early summer of 1570, there appeared a little piece entitled *The Several Confessions of Thomas Norton and Christopher Norton, two of the Northern Rebels who suffred at Tyburn, and were hanged, drawen, and quartered for Treason,*[1] while later in that same year the end of another religious victim was chronicled by John Partridge. In his account of the proceedings Partridge outlines *The end and Confession of John Felton, the rank Traytour, that set up the Traiterous Bull on the Bysshop of London his gate,* and says that in spite of all argument, Felton insisted that 'he believed the ancient and catholic faith which the holy father, the Pope hath long defended, and said that whosoever believed any other faith or held any other opinion it was most wicked and erroneous'. Partridge goes on to describe the scene at the gallows in the following graphic words:

Then he came down the stair, having on a satin doublet and a gown of gograin. Then being come to the place of execution he was loosed off the hurdle by two sergeants and then stripped by the

[1] *STC* 18683.

hangman of his gograin gown and satin doublet. Then he, standing up and shaking for fear said: 'Ah, ah, Lord, have mercy upon me'... and then he said 'O Lord, into thy hands I commend my spirit' in English, and as he was saying it in Latin he was turned off the ladder, and hanging there six turns, he was cut down, and carried to the block, and there his head was smitten off and held up so that the people might see it, whereupon the people gave a shout, wishing that all Traytors were so served. Then was he quartered and carried to Newgate to be parboiled and so set up as the other rebels were. God save the Queen.[1]

While battle was thus joined on the main front, these were not the only controversial works to be issued. Within the Protestant party things were far from easy, since some wanted to follow moderate lines, but many, and those the most active, were eager for reform and a dismissal of everything that savoured of Rome. Hence we have the manifestos of the extreme sects, such as the Brownists, or the Family of Love, or the advocates of a Presbyterian form of Church government, or those who wished to abolish all forms of State control and allow the utmost freedom of conscience. Opinions ran high, and plea and counter plea were published, often supported by the views of eminent foreign divines whose opinions carried great weight. But for the main part it was the voices of Englishmen at home that were heard discussing the propriety of the wearing of vestments,[2] the marriage of the clergy,[3] the power to remit sins,[4] the doctrine of predestination,[5] and many

[1] *STC* 19421. The next year saw the publication of two tracts concerning the execution of Dr Story: *STC* 23297, *A declaration of the lyfe and death of John Story, Late a Romish Canonicall Doctor, by professyon*; *STC* 23296, *A copie of a letter lately sent by a gentleman, student in the lawes of the realme to a frende of his concernyng D. Story.*

[2] *STC* 6079, 10387–91, all in 1566.

[3] *STC* 20176 (1549), 20175 (1555), 24687 [1562?], 17519 [1567?] all in favour, and *STC* 17517 (1554) against.

[4] *STC* 372 (1567), by William Allen, answered by W. Fulke in 1586 (*STC* 5009).

[5] *STC* 11885 [1575?], 24680 [1561], *A fruteful treatise of predestination... against the swynyshe gruntings of the Epicures & Atheistes of oure time.*

other religious matters, great and small. The general climate of opinion in which all these works were liable to find themselves was well expressed by James Bell in 1581:

> Experience hath taught me (gentle Reader) that it is very daungerous in this troublesome age to committ any thyng to printe for thy behoofe. So farre forth hath that frettyng canker of carping curiosity prevailed: so busily pryeth in every Printers shoppe that wayward churle Zoilus: so divers and variable are the wittes and dispositions of our age, readyer to breake downe open roades through other mens hedges than to stoppe never so little a gappe with any frythe of their owne. To such be it aunswered, that the greatest barkers be not commonly the best byters: and it falleth out for the more parte, that such bytesheepe curres smell of the cudgell, when the gentle houndes feede of the croomes. And so I leave them to them selves, whose sinister judgement as I litle regarde, so I groape not after their prayse. Onely my purpose is to profitt the unlettered English men: emongest whom the gentle natured will interprete the best, and findyng ought amisse, will with courtesie rather correct (I trust) than with carpyng condemne the course of my labours, for whose onely behoofe and benefit I adventured upon this translation, and published the same in Printe. Some bytternesse of speache will now and then occurre, which at the first blushe may happely breede some offence.... This offence will be lesse offensive in respect of the oppressed adversary, whose mouth ruffleth and runneth over every where, with more then ruffianlike and rascallike tearmes agaynst our most dread Sovereigne... which no true harted Englishman can endure to read without greevous anguishe of mynde. This licentious lavishenesse of rayling toungue sithence outraged so monstruously, was convenient to be mette withall with some libertie of free speache.[1]

Devotional literature

These fierce contentions must not blind us to the fact that simultaneously with all this, there was the ordinary devout man and woman to whom their religion was all important, since as time went on and the new generation grew up in the Protestant

---

[1] *STC* 12594, W. Haddon and J. Foxe, *Against Jerome Osorius Byshopp of Silvane in Portingall and against his slaunderous Invectives* (1581), sig. 2. Translated by James Bell.

faith, they wanted nothing better than to live and die according to its tenets. So there was a real demand for works of devotion among other kinds of literature, and every year saw many books issued from the press designed to help the ordinary devout laymen in all sorts of ways. Some writers definitely catered for the more unlearned of readers, and couched their instruction in the simplest possible terms:

> I have set down the principall pointes of Christian Religion in as plaine sorte as I coulde possible, for their sakes especially, whose capacities are small and memories unable to containe much.... If this come to the handes of such as are already past such A. B. Cees, let it not offend them that children are ledde, though they being men can goe alone.[1]

Another ingenious author, Edmund Bunny, advertises his book on its title-page in these words:

> *The whole summe of Christian Religion, given forth by two severall Methodes or Formes: the one higher, for the better learned, the other applyed to the capacitie of the common multitude, and meeter for all: yet both of them such, as in some respect do knit themselves together in one.*[2]

With an eye to the humble reader, some authors, such as Edward Vaughan, deliberately kept their books 'so short & of so small price... that the poorest should have the profit of my paines',[3] while others were written particularly for the young, as was Thomas Pritchard's *The schoole of honest and vertuous lyfe*, which he says is 'profitable and necessary for all estates and degrees... but cheefely for the pettie Schollers, the yonger sorte of both kindes, bee they men or women'.[4]

Clearly this was a highly important market for the book trade, and, as we see, they tried to meet it by publishing works

---

[1] *STC* 11832, J. Gibson, *An easie entrance into the principall points of Christian religion* (1579), sig. A2.
[2] *STC* 4096 (1576), sig. *1.
[3] *STC* 24598, *Nine observations howe to reade the Bible* (1591), sig. *7ᵛ.
[4] *STC* 20397 [1579], sig. Ai.

HOMILETIC WORKS

designed to attract all kinds of readers. In addition to the cheap, comparatively short pieces mentioned above, there were also to be seen on the stalls large folios, such as the works of Thomas Becon, which were published in three volumes between 1560 and 1563. Each of these contained over one thousand pages, collecting the large number of homiletic and devotional works that their author had put out from time to time under such titles as *The Castle of Comfort*, or *The Pommander of Prayer*, or *The sycke mans salve*, and so on,[1] the last named being so popular that it was printed eleven times between 1561 and 1603.[2]

The main purpose of these productions was to set out and to explain the tenets of the Protestant faith and to give advice as to how the Christian could best observe them. Sometimes this took the form of question and answer, or a dialogue between two or more speakers,[3] or concerned itself with the explanation of some doctrine, such as the Mystery of the Eucharist;[4] or, descending to a lower and more practical level, discussed how men 'ought to lead their lyves in that vocation which is fruitfull and necessary, as well for the masters as also for the servantes, agreeable to the holy scriptures'.[5] A more compendious work by Abraham Fleming called *The Diamond of Devotion. Cut and squared into sixe severall points* offered the reader brief instruction in a number of treatises fancifully named *The Footpath to Felicitie*, *A Guide to Godliness*, etc. Each book contains a number of aphorisms, set out in an orderly fashion so that they could easily be memorized.[6]

Other helps to a Christian way of life were plentiful. Manuals on how to live and die well; on the reading of the

[1] *STC* 1710, *The worckes of T. Becon, whiche he hath hytherto made and published*.
[2] *STC* 1757–67.
[3] *STC* 6130, C. A. Curio, *Pasquine in a Traunce: a Christian and learned Dialogue* [1566?].
[4] *STC* 10593, L. Evans, *A short treatyse of the mysterie of the Euchariste* (1569).
[5] *STC* 10929 (1577), sig. A1.   [6] *STC* 11044 (1602), sig. A1.

Bible; on meditation; on marriage; on the active and the contemplative life were published from time to time, all helping to enforce the lessons and teaching which preachers were giving from their pulpits. These things being written down and given a more permanent form in these books were an invaluable help to the earnest Christian.

Since it would be impossible to treat all these many types of spiritual help separately, it must suffice here to look at a few of the works of one group—the aids to meditation and prayer. Their *raison d'être* is clearly set forth in the words of Thomas Rogers in a preface to his translations (or rather versions) of S. Augustine's prayers. There he writes:

I do cal this booke, as also the author doth, a Manuel, because my wish is that Christians would use it and have it in their hands, not onlie when they are at home in their chambers and studies privatelie but also when they are abroad in the fields, gardens, and elsewhere idlelie: and that not to dandle and to handle onlie, but diligentlie and zealouslie, as the part of Christians is, to reade the same for their spiritual exercise.[1]

This and other works attributed to S. Augustine were translated by Rogers, who took care to render them inoffensive to Protestant minds ('purged from divers supertitious points') in a fashion similar to that in which he had dealt with the most important of all works of this nature—*The Imitation of Christ*, which he said he had translated by 'leaving out the corruption of it, and taking onlie that which was sound'.[2]

As an example of the kind of meditation that was so popular at this time we may take the writings of John Bradford, 'the constant martyr of God', who was burnt on 3 July 1555, and whose writings were afterwards published in various collections, and were on the bookstalls as late as 1633. A list of some of the contents of a volume with the title *Godly meditations upon the ten Commaundements, the Articles of Faith, and Lord's Prayer* will show what it was that attracted the pious reader, and made

[1] *STC* 950 (1581), sig. A 2ᵛ. [2] *STC* 23973 (1580), sig. A 2.

books of this kind so much sought after. Bradford first gives some instructions concerning prayer, and then begins his meditation on the Lord's Prayer, which he discourses upon clause by clause. Next he deals with the Apostle's Creed in the same way, and follows this by an explication of the Ten Commandments. He follows all this with a series of meditations upon such things as the pleasures of life; of 'death and the commodities it bringeth forth'; of the passion of Christ and so on; concluding with a treatise on election and free will. The title-page of this volume did not exaggerate therefore when it declared that within men might find 'Certayne godly exercises, meditations and prayers, very profytable for all persons and for all times, set forth by certayne learned men to be used dayly'.[1] A letter to the reader by Thomas Lever indicates the ways in which it was hoped that such a book might be used:

And for that everie man can not have all scriptures, and no man ought to be without the ten commaundementes, the articles of the beliefe, and the Lordes prayer, to meditate in hys minde: therfore the meditation of them shoulde be in such sorte, as we might best finde and feele the sicknes and daunger of our sinne by the commaundementes: then see the remedie and salve for sinne, which is the goodnes of God confessed in the articles of the beliefe: and so, as followeth in the Lords prayer, use the maner and forme of desiring and joyning the medicine and salve of Gods mercifull goodnes, unto the sicknes and sores of mans sinful wretchednes.[2]

The Catholics did not let this kind of religious activity go unchallenged. Whether they were printed in England on a secret press or smuggled into the country, they put into circulation a number of books written from their own point of view 'that would afford the confused and perhaps wavering Christians the information they needed'. In 1576 there appeared with a false imprint a book with the title *Certayne devout Meditations. Very necessary for Christian men devoutly to*

[1] *STC* 3485 (1567), sig. A1.
[2] Quoted from H. C. White, *The Tudor Books of Private Devotion* (Madison, 1951), p. 180.

meditate vpon Morninge and Eveninge, every day in the weeke; Concerning Christ his lyfe and Passion and the frutes therof.[1] The book is simply written without any great attempt to impress by rhetoric or imagery, and was admirably suited to meet the needs of the ordinary reader. More impressive books were translated from the writings of eminent Catholic divines and quietly put into circulation here. Two outstanding names may be mentioned—those of the Spanish Jesuit, Gaspare Loarte, and of the Spanish Dominican, Luis de Granada. Three works by Loarte were secretly printed in London by William Carter; the first about 1576 under the title of *The godlie garden of Gethsemani, furnished with holsome fruites of meditation & prayer upon the blessed passion of Christ our Redemer*, while about 1579 there followed *The Exercise of a Christian Life*, and about the same time *Instructions and Advertisements, how to meditate the Misteries of the Rosarie*. These titles, perhaps, sufficiently indicate the nature of their contents, while a brief quotation from *The Exercise* will demonstrate the practical nature of these works and explain in part their popularity, and why they were reprinted from time to time.

The residue of time from supper til thou goe to bed, thou maiest bestowe in some honest talke, or other good exercise and recreation, taking heede yet of occupying thy selfe in any suche thing as may hinder and disturbe the quietnes of thy minde. Afterwardes having made some smal pause and resting awhile, see thou prepare thy selfe to bedward, considering that a good Christian ought to dispose him selfe in such wise therto, as if he were that night to depart this life.[2]

More important still for English readers were the translations from the works of Luis de Granada. In 1582 there appeared a translation, printed in Paris, and made by Richard Hopkins, of the *Libro de la Oracion y Meditacion* with the title

---

[1] *STC* 17775, *Duaci, apud Iohannem Bojardi*, i.e. London, W. Carter.
[2] Not in *STC*. No. 462 in Allison and Rogers, *Catalogue*. My quotation is taken from Southern, *Elizabethan Recusant Prose*, p. 194.

Of Prayer and Meditation. Wherein are conteined fowertien devoute Meditations for the seven daies of the weeke, bothe for the Morninges and Eveninges.[1] This was followed by another translation by Hopkins in 1586, *A Memoriall of a Christian life*,[2] and finally in 1599 a translation by Richard Gibbons, of Granada's *A spirituall doctrine, conteining a rule to live wel, with divers praiers and meditations*.[3] Several of these volumes were of considerable size, *Of Prayer and Meditation*, for example, making a book of about 650 pages. Nevertheless, they were sufficiently esteemed to attract the notice of Protestants, and a number of adaptations of some of them began to appear, in which Catholic doctrine was quietly eliminated and the works given a Protestant outlook. Two well-known writers, Francis Meres,[4] and Thomas Lodge,[5] both lent themselves to this kind of dubious 'borrowing', but here, as in a number of other instances, the means evidently were thought to justify the end.

The *locus classicus* of this kind of action is to be seen in the history of *The First Booke of the Christian Exercise, appertayning to resolution*, written by Robert Persons and published in 1582, having been printed in Rouen.[6] The work was well received, and soon out of print, and Persons put out a revised edition in 1585.[7] Before he could do this, however, two versions of his work had appeared:

I was enformed of two other editions come forth of my foresaid booke without my knowledge, the one by a Catholique (as it seemeth) who perceving al copies of the former print to be spent, for satisfying of them that desired the booke, procured the same to be set forth againe, albeit somewhat incorrected, and very disorderly, not having the consent or advise of such, as therein should have given him the best direction. The second was published by

---

[1] *STC* 16907.   [2] *STC* 16903.   [3] *STC* 16922.
[4] *STC* 16902, *Granados devotion* (1598); *STC* 16918, *The sinners guyde* (1598); *STC* 16920, *Granadas Spirituall and heavenlie exercises* (1598).
[5] *STC* 16901, *The flowers of Lodowicke of Granado* (1601).
[6] *STC* 19353.
[7] *STC* 19362, *A Christian directorie guiding men to their salvation* (Rouen, 1585).

one Edmund Buny minister at Bolton Percy (as he writeth) in the liberties of Yorke; who with publicke licence under my Lord Archbishop of Yorke his protection, set forth the same to the benefite of his brethren; but yet so punished and plumed (which he termeth purged;) as I could hardly by the face discerne it for mine when it came unto my handes, and I tooke no smale compassion to see how pitifully the poore thing had bene handled.[1]

The first of these two need not bother us: it was a more or less straight reprint, and although the title-page said that it had been corrected, this was only a salesman's point, and as Persons himself said, in fact it was 'somewhat incorrected and very disorderly'. The work of Bunny was quite another matter, for the original had been very seriously tampered with (or purged), and Persons had every reason to be concerned with the result. Bunny had the effrontery to reproduce much of the title-page of Persons's original edition of 1582, adding the words; '*by R. P. Perused, and accompanied now with a Treatise tending to Pacification: by Edm. Bunny*'. What Bunny meant by perused is made clear in his preface:

I perceived that the booke issuing was willingly read by divers for the persuasion that it hath to godlines of life, which notwithstanding in manie pointes it was corruptly set downe, I thought good in the end to get the same published againe in some better manner than now it is come forth among them, that so the good that the reading thereof might otherwise do, might carrie no hurte or danger withal, so far as by me might be prevented. For this cause I have taken pains, both to purge it of certain points that carried either some manifest error, or else other inconvenience with them, and to join another short treatise withal, to exhort those who are not yet persuaded to join with us likewise in the truth of Religion.[2]

Despite Persons's natural protests against this high-handed treatment of his book, Bunny refused to make any apology, speaking of 'those idle and frivolous quarrels of R.P. against the late edition of the *Resolution*', which he characterized as 'much a doe about nothing'.

[1] *STC* 19362, sig. A 4.   [2] *STC* 19355 (1584), sig. +2.

This has taken us a long way from the books of meditation from which we started, and from the work of Loarte which was the starting-point of Persons when he first contemplated writing what in effect turned out to be *The First Booke of the Christian Exercise*, but it is an instructive example of the interplay of Protestant and Catholic, didactic and homiletic, that filled so much of the religious life of this period, and is from time to time reflected in its literature.

Side by side with books of meditation went the books of prayer—indeed, the two were often to be found printed together. The prayer book had become of great importance: 'This type of book', writes Professor Helen White:

> was of peculiar interest and value to the reformers, both Catholic and Protestant. To the former, it offered a fresh way of carrying out an old evangelical purpose. And it afforded a way of satisfying those middle class interests and ambitions to which the 'English books' had been appealing with such disturbing success. But the type was of even greater importance to the Protestant reformers. The middle classes were a field of great promise for their propaganda of criticism of the established order and their suggestions of new points of view. This was true in every field of religious activity, but it was perhaps more urgent in the field of private devotion than any other. For the Protestant reformers had expressly repudiated the monastic way of life, and the premises on which it had been erected. They, therefore, faced with peculiar urgency the problem of organizing the life of prayer within the framework of ordinary domestic life lived in the contemporary world.[1]

Conditions such as these gave a clear lead to writers and the book trade, and this was readily followed, on religious as well as on financial grounds. The old Roman Catholic primers were out of place and dangerous as they stood, and it was highly important to put into the hands of faithful Protestants books which they could use with confidence. This was done in a variety of ways, each of them varied to meet the needs of some particular public. The task was not entirely a new one, for in

[1] White, *The Tudor Books of Private Devotion*, pp. 149–50.

the reigns of Henry VIII and Edward VI a number of books of prayer had been forthcoming—outstanding, perhaps, being those of Katherine Parr, the first commonly known as 'the Queen's Prayers', first published in 1544,[1] and the second *Prayers or medytacions*, 1545.[2] These had been very popular before Mary came to the throne, and as soon as Elizabeth succeeded her they were reissued.

Shortly after this came a work by the energetic and voluminous writer, Thomas Becon, who returned from exile when Elizabeth came to the throne. In 1558 he had given to John Day, the printer, a book of prayers 'as are most meet for in this our age to be used of all degrees and states', to which he gave the fanciful title *The Pomander of Prayer*.[3] From time to time, Becon altered and enlarged its contents so that the book could be turned to on a great number of occasions by those in need of a helpful prayer.

The success of this work seems to have encouraged others, and in 1568 Henry Bull published his *Christian Prayers and Holy Meditations*,[4] a much more extensive work than any preceding it. This, Bull had put together from a variety of sources, foreign and English, so that it included 'traditional material, almost contemporary Catholic material as passed through translation, like Bradford's version of the prayers of Vives, and of course, contemporary materials from some of the Protestant reformers'.[5] The result was a comprehensive work which found much favour and ran to at least five editions between 1568 and 1596.

While all these authors drew some of their material from the old prayer books, it was left for John Day to put out a series of prayer books which in format and general appearance resembled the older primers. The pages were decorated with borders which showed scenes from the Old and New Testament, a

---

[1] *STC* 3002, *Psalmes or prayers taken out of holye scripture* (1544).
[2] *STC* 4819, *Prayers or medytacions, wherin the mynd is stirred, paciently to suffre all afflictions here* (1545).
[3] *STC* 1744. [4] *STC* 4028.
[5] White, *The Tudor Books of Private Devotion*, p. 185.

BOOKS OF PRIVATE DEVOTIONS

series depicting the Dance of Death, and other allegorical and decorative devices. The title-page had an elaborate design of the tree of Jesse and, all in all, the book bore a remarkable physical resemblance to the Primers of the Old Religion. Day's first volume, entitled *Christian Prayers and Meditations in English, French, Italian, Spanish, Greeke, and Latin*,[1] was published in 1569, but after the first edition he dropped all the prayers in foreign tongues, and put out the work again in 1578 with a new title: *A booke of Christian Prayers, collected out of the aunciert writers, and best learned in our tyme, worthy to be read with an earnest mynde of all Christians, in these daungerous and troublesome dayes*.[2]

One other collection that gained some favour was printed by Middleton in 1574, having for its title *A godly Garden out of the which most comfortable herbs may be gathered for the health of the wounded conscience of all penitent sinners*.[3] This was a small book, about four inches by three in size, so that it could easily be slipped into a pocket, and again contained prayers appropriate for various times of the day, for the several days of the week, and for many important occasions throughout the year. Professor Helen White draws attention to the 'traditional' nature of its contents, and thinks that for some people this harking back to some of the older prayers said in their youth was a proof of 'that tenderness for tradition and antiquity that has often manifested itself in the aesthetic and religious life of the English'.[4]

In addition to these works, there were a number of volumes of prayers written and published to attract suitable audiences. Thomas Tymme prepared one such book for the simple reader which he called *The Poore Mans Pater noster, with a preparative to prayer*,[5] while Edward Dering's *Godly private*

---

[1] *STC* 6428.
[2] *STC* 6429. This book was popularly known as 'Queen Elizabeth's Prayer Book,' since the verso of the title-page showed the Queen at prayer in her apartment.
[3] *STC* 11555.   [4] White, *op. cit.* p. 187.
[5] *STC* 24419 (1598); 'newly imprinted the second time', it was entered 5 July 1591.

praiers for householders to meditate upon, and to say in their families (1576) was also a popular little book which was four times reprinted within the next fourteen years.[1] One more popular work must be mentioned, which was written by John Norden and published in 1584. Its title well suggests its contents: *A Pensive Mans Practise. Very profitable for all personnes; wherin are conteyned very devout and necessary prayers for sundry godlie purposes, with requisite perswasions before every Prayer.* First published in 1584, it had run to above forty editions by 1627, and there were at least two further editions before 1640.[2] Norden's work with its eminently straightforward and practical approach evidently provided just what many people wanted.

In one way or another then, Protestant families were well provided with books of prayer for their everyday needs in the home. At the same time, their needs whenever they attended public service were met by the revised *Boke of common praier, and administration of the Sacramentes, and other rites and Ceremonies in the Churche of Englande.*[3] It was published in 1559, and was in fact the Prayer Book of 1553 with a few alterations; and, unsatisfactory as it was to both Papists and Puritans, it remained unchanged throughout Elizabeth's reign, and at least forty editions of it had been printed by the time of her death.

The Bible

When all these kinds of religious literature have been surveyed, however, we have still to recall the two most significant contributions to be seen on the stalls, namely the Bible and its auxiliaries in the shape of commentaries, concordances and the like, and also the sermons. As is well known, these aids to religion were fundamental to the Protestant cause, and

---
[1] *STC* 6685.
[2] *STC* 18616–26a. The above title is taken from the edition of 1627 'newly corrected and amended by the Author after above forty Impressions'.
[3] *STC* 16291.

as soon as Elizabeth came to the throne the booksellers began to cater for the needs of an eager body of devout readers who were anxious to imbibe the word of God from the Bible, and the teaching of the Church from the ministers, especially as it was set out in their sermons. 'To be ignorant of the Gospels is to be ignorant of Christ', the Lollards had proclaimed and, although their words fell upon stony ground at the time, nearly two centuries later their view was to prevail.[1]

First, then, the Bible and all the accompaniments that it was realized were necessary if the ordinary layman was to make use of the scriptures in an intelligent and fruitful way. The more that men began to rely upon themselves to read and interpret the scriptures, the more their leaders saw that it was incumbent upon them to provide guides and aids in the way of commentaries, works of exegesis, concordances and the like. This they did, partly by the written word, and partly by sermons, which it was soon realized were so vital to the ordinary Christian that it was not sufficient for him to hear them, but he must also be able to read them and ponder over what they had to teach. In consequence of these conditions, the output of religious works springing from the Bible and the pulpit grew tremendously, and kept the presses in constant employment.

During the reign of Mary the printing of the Bible came almost to a standstill. The only known issue is a translation of the New Testament by William Whittingham, one of the many exiles at this time, whose work was printed in Geneva by Conrad Badius in 1557.[2] This was in startling contrast to the output in the previous brief reign of Edward VI, when nearly forty editions of the Bible or the New Testament had appeared. With the accession of Elizabeth things took a turn, and slowly

---

[1] The most helpful general account of the history of the Bible will be found in A. W. Pollard, *Records of the English Bible* (1911). A great deal of bibliographical and historical information is given by T. H. Darlow and H. F. Moule in their *Historical Catalogue of the printed editions of the Holy Scripture* (1903–11), to which I am indebted.

[2] *STC* 2871, *The Newe Testament of our Lord Jesus Christ, Conferred diligently with the Greke and best approved translations*.

the printing presses began to issue the Scriptures once again. The first new edition to appear was one of great importance, for it had been prepared in Geneva by a number of exiles, including Whittingham, and was destined to play an outstanding part in the Englishman's knowledge of the Bible throughout the reign. The 'Genevan Bible', as it was called:

> showed a distinct advance on its predecessors, and appearing as it did in compact form, with roman type and verse divisions, obtained speedy and permanent popularity. Its arguments and explanatory notes (often distinctly Calvinistic in tone), which amount to a running commentary, endeared it especially to the Puritans, and for three generations it maintained its supremacy as the Bible of the people.[1]

In addition to the text there were twenty-six engravings, five maps and a plan of the Garden of Eden, together with aids to the understanding of the subject-matter, such as a description of the Holy Land and of other countries and places.

The church authorities could hardly allow this to go unchallenged, and a committee of revisers under the leadership of Archbishop Parker got to work on the existing 'Great Bible', which had appeared in 1539 and had gone through a number of editions without very much change. Now in 1568 was first published the results of the labours of the Archbishop and his colleagues in a large folio which has been described as 'perhaps the most sumptuous in the long series of folio English Bibles',[2] both for its typography and illustrations. Commonly known as the 'Bishops' Bible', in April 1571, the Convocation of Canterbury ordered that copies of this edition should be placed in every cathedral and as far as possible, in every church.

These two versions of the Bible were reprinted again and again throughout the reign with comparatively little revision. The New Testament was often printed as a separate volume, while both Bible and Testament were printed in various sizes

[1] *STC* 2093 (1560). The quotation is from Darlow and Moule, *Historical Catalogue*, vol. I, p. 61.
[2] *Ibid.* vol. I, p. 69.

THE BIBLE

to meet differing demands. Even so, the Bishops were not altogether satisfied with the demand for their edition, for in 1587 we find Archbishop Whitgift writing to Bishop Wickham of Lincoln as follows:

Whereas I am credibly informed that divers, as well parish Churches as Chapels of Ease, are not sufficiently furnished with Bibles, but some have either none at all, or such as be torn and defaced, and yet not of the translation authorised by the Synods of Bishops: These are therefore to require you strictly in your visitations, or otherwise, to see that all and every the said Churches and Chapels in your diocese be provided of one Bible or more, at your discretion, of the translation allowed as aforesaid, and one book of Common prayer, as by the laws of this realm is appointed. And for the performance thereof, I have caused her Highness's Printer to imprint two volumes of the said translation of the Bible aforesaid, a bigger and a less: the largest for such Parishes as are of ability, and the lesser for Chapels and very small parishes, both which are now extant and ready...[1]

However disappointed the Archbishop may have been, the fact remains that at least one hundred editions of the Bible and thirty of the New Testament were published during Elizabeth's reign, so that there was scarcely a year that did not see at least one new edition of the scriptures on the bookstalls.

Against this tremendous output of the Protestant Bible, the Catholics could make but little headway. In 1582, however, they did produce and print at Rheims the *editio princeps* of the Catholic version of the New Testament

with Arguments of bookes and chapters, Annotations, and other necessarie helpes, for the better understanding of the text, and specially for the discoverie of the Corruptions of divers late translations, and for cleering Controversies in religion, of these daies.[2]

---

[1] Darlow and Moule, *op. cit.* vol. I, p. 99, quoting Cardwell, *Documentary Annals*, vol. II, pp. 31–2.
[2] STC 2884, *The New Testament of Jesus Christ, translated faithfully into English*, sig. a1. This was popularly known as the Douay Version.

The translation was the work of Gregory Martin, moved by compassion to see our beloved countriemen, with extreme danger of their soules, to use onely such prophane translations, and erroneous mens mere phantasies, for the pure and blessed word of truth, much also mooved thereunto by the desires of many devout persons: have set forth, for you (benigne readers) the new Testament to begin withal, trusting that it may give occasion to you, after diligent perusing therof, to lay away at lest such their impure versions as hitherto you have ben forced to occupie.[1]

It is said that five thousand copies of this edition were printed (an unusually large number), but to get them into the hands of 'our beloved countrymen' was another matter, as William Rainolds declared in 1583, saying that

every corner of the realme was searched for those bookes... the portes were layed for them, Paules crosse is witnes of burning many of them, the Princes proclamation was procured against them, in the Universities by soueraigne authoritie, Colleges, chambers, studies, closets, coffers, and deskes, were ransackt for them... aunciente men and students of Divinite were imprisoned for having of them.[2]

Even when we have made some allowance for rhetorical exaggeration it is clear that the Catholics had a hard task in disseminating copies of the work, and what copies did get abroad were challenged by a Protestant fusillade from John Rainolds, Whitaker, Fulke, Bilson, Bulkeley, Wither and Cartwright. Immensely important and valuable as this translation is in the history of the English Bible, there can be no doubt that for the majority of Englishmen of this period, when they spoke of the Bible they were referring to the Genevan or the Bishops' versions.

Since the Bible meant so much to so many people, it was natural for them to welcome any aids to its understanding.

[1] *Ibid.* sig. b2.
[2] Southern, *Elizabethan Recusant Prose*, p. 235, quoting from *STC* 20632, W. Rainolds, *A Refutation of sundry reprehensions, cavils, and false sleights, by which M. Whitaker laboureth to deface the late English translation and Catholike annotations of the new Testament (1583)*, sig. F6ᵛ.

THE SCRIPTURES EXPOUNDED

These they got in some measure from the pulpit, where the Christian message was interpreted by the preacher, who often took a book, or a chapter, or even a few verses from one book of the Bible as the subject of his sermon.

Some sixty to seventy volumes at least of sermons expounding the scriptures in detail were published between 1558 and 1603, and while some of these were of a modest dimension, many of them were really remarkable for their size. Calvin's works afford the most notable example of the avidity of the devout Protestants for works of this kind. He preached no less than 200 sermons on the book of Deuteronomy which required 1248 pages printed in double columns to contain them;[1] his 157 sermons on the Book of Job occupied 752 pages of print, also in double columns and, despite its size, it was four times reprinted in ten years.[2] The sermons on Timothy and Titus ran to 1248 pages, also in double columns,[3] and a number of other collections of his made very large volumes. Another Genevan preacher, Michel Cope, wrote *A godly and learned exposition uppon the Proverbes of Solomon*, occupying 1278 pages of print.[4] Naturally there were not many volumes that reached such proportions, but there were a great many large enough to provide the reader with materials for many hours of reading and study.

As well as these books formed out of sermon material, there were a good many writers who felt that what they had to say did not readily lend itself to the spoken word, but required close reading. To this end they devoted their talents, carefully and fully annotating parts of the Bible, or to use a contemporary phrase, they 'truly opened and explained by paraphrase according to the right sense of every Psalme'.[5] Their purpose was to reveal the Scriptures 'teaching every man how to order his life,

[1] *STC* 4442 (1583). Tr. A. Golding.
[2] *STC* 4444–7 (1574–84). Tr. A. Golding.
[3] *STC* 4441 (1579). Tr. L. Tomson.
[4] *STC* 5723 (1580). Tr. M. Outred.
[5] *STC* 2033, T. de Beza, *The Psalmes of David*...(1580). Tr. A. Gilbie.

so that they may come to true and ever lasting happiness',[1] or 'opening by time and place such things as are both necessary and profitable for the time present'.[2] Some books were written with an eye on a definite public, such as one 'for the better help and instruction of the unlearned', while others had a specific aim, such as to explain in simple terms these 'Chapters of the olde testament as usually are redde in the Churche as common praier on the Sundayes'.[3] Here again, as with the printed sermons, many of these works were translations from the writings of such great divines as Beza, Calvin and others, whose works were frequently to be found on the book stalls with titles explaining their purpose, such as *The Comentaries of M. John Calvin upon the first Epistle of Sainct Jhon, and upon the Epistle of Jude: wherin according to the truthe of the wordes of the holie Ghost, he most excellently openeth & cleareth the poinct of our justification with God, and sanctification by the Spirit of Christ, by the effects that he bringeth forthe in the regeneration.*[4]

As a result of the publication of books such as these it was possible at the end of the century for a man to write:

Thou hast...[in] the holie Bible, the most necessary, the most profitable booke, even the Booke of Life, and that dispersed in infinit numbers, easie to be gotten. Thow hast also even in thy mother tongue, Expositions, Readings, Comments, Sermons, Catechismes innumerable, which all tend to the opening of that booke, and to make the understanding therof easie unto thee.[5]

Catechisms

From readings and comments we must turn to say something about catechisms and sermons. Few things were of more importance to the devout man and woman and to the clergy than the upbringing of the young in virtuous ways and godly

---

[1] *STC* 2764, T. de Beza, *Ecclesiastes, or the Preacher* [1593?].
[2] *STC* 3810, J. Brocard, *The revelation of S. Jhon reveled* (1582). Tr J. Sanford.
[3] *STC* 5684, T. Cooper, *A briefe exposition of such Chapters of the olde testament...* (1573).   [4] *STC* 4404 [c. 1580]. Tr. W. H.
[5] *STC* 17843, P. Merlin, *A most Plaine and profitable Exposition of the Booke of Ester* (1599), sig. A2.

learning. To this end, divines and other zealous teachers sent to the printers books and pamphlets in which parents and householders were instructed what they should teach those in their care, and how they should examine by means of question and answer the knowledge of the Christian faith that their children and servants had acquired.

The most famous of the catechisms were those compiled by Alexander Nowell, Dean of St Pauls, but other 'Catechismes innumerable' appeared on the stalls. Indeed, Andrew Maunsell, the bookseller, listed in 1595 between eighty and ninety such works written in the time of Elizabeth, so that we may confidently say that at least one hundred catechisms, great and small, appeared in half a century. Nowell's own work took a number of forms of varying length, written in English, Latin, or at times in editions in which both Latin and English appeared *en face*. Very early in Elizabeth's reign the Church authorities had felt the need for a catechism which would set out the official doctrines which the faithful should hold, and in 1562 Convocation had advised that 'there should be authorised one perfect Catechism for the bringing up of the youth in godliness, in the schools of the whole realm'. It was in response to this that Nowell drew up his catechisms, and laid them before the Archbishops and others. Not until 1570, however, was official sanction forthcoming, but in that year both the Latin and the English versions appeared, and henceforth the works were in constant circulation.

The many other catechisms that appeared were addressed to a variety of readers. Edward Dering compiled one 'verye needfull to be knowen of all Housholders, whereby they maye the better teach and instruct their families in such pointes of Christian Religion as is most meete';[1] R. Bird's was 'to be learned of the ignorant folk',[2] while S.S. called his 'a briefe instruction for all families'.[3] Of course, the accent in most was on youth, so that we have 'a briefe instruction for the exercise

[1] *STC* 4794 (1575), sig. A1. [2] Not in *STC*. Maunsell, *op. cit.*
[3] *STC* 21518 (1583).

of youth',[1] or 'short questions betweene the father and the sonne',[2] or Calvin's 'manner to teache children the Christian Religion',[3] or the Roman Catholic 'Catechisme, or a Christian doctrine, necessarie for Chyldren and ignorant people'.[4] In *A Rule how to bring up Children*, John Lyster sets out 'a treatise wherein is declared how the Father opposeth his Sonne in the holy Scripture, whereby parentes may be taught how to bring up their children',[5] while another work by Josias Nichols was designed to help householders in their attempts to explain the Bible to their families and apprentices.[6]

Sermons

As early as 1561, Goddred Gylby, in an address to the Reader, which he wrote as a preface to his translation of an epistle of Cicero, gave it as his opinion that:

Men are now a days here in England glutted as it wer with gods worde, & therfore almost ready to vomit up again yt which thei have receyved, lothing ye sermons & despising the preachers, some turning to curious arts...som Atheistes, & few or none do stand forth as fathers to us yonglings to byd us folow their fotesteppes in vertues and godlines.[7]

Could he but have looked forward to the end of the century, he would have found an even more 'glutted' scene, since it has been estimated that over one thousand sermons in more than five hundred separate publications were on the market during the reign of Elizabeth, and that this figure does not include sermons preached in Latin, even though these were later translated into English. Nor does it include the large number of translations of the sermons of the great foreign preachers, such as Beza, Bullinger, Calvin or Hemmingsen, to name but

[1] *STC* 5455, T. Cobhead (1579).   [2] *STC* 5829, W. Cotes (1585).
[3] *STC* 4380. First translated and published in England in 1556, this work was constantly reprinted until 1628.
[4] *STC* 4801, L. Vaux [1568].   [5] *STC* 17122 (1588).
[6] *STC* 18540, *An order of household instruction* (1596).
[7] *STC* 5306, Cicero, *An Epistle or letter of exhortation* (1561). Tr. G. Gylby, sig. A2.

SERMONS

a few of these.[1] To omit such preachers from any survey of what was made available by the booksellers is to give a very incomplete picture, since their writings were widely in evidence and in considerable demand. It would therefore be possible, I believe, to double the figure of one thousand, and still be on the safe side in an estimate of the number of sermons from all sources printed in English in England during Elizabeth's reign.

The reasons for this state of affairs are many, and are often stated by the printers themselves. Undoubtedly there were many rich and influential men who desired to see what they thought to be the truth given the widest publicity. To this end they patronized the sermons of writers whose views chimed with their own, and who had shown an ability to hold their audiences when they were preaching, for preaching was fundamental to both Protestant and Puritan. It is related of Laurence Chaderton, the first Master of Emmanuel College, Cambridge, that 'having preached for two hours, he said that he had tired his hearers' patience and would leave off; upon which the whole congregation cried out: "For God's sake, sir, go on, we beg you, go on". He accordingly continued the thread of his discourse for another hour, to the great pleasure and delight of his hearers.'[2]

The delight in the spoken word inevitably created a desire in some hearers to have the sermon available for private reading and meditation, and it is common to find that the preacher was at times 'earnestly urged and entreated both by word and letters of good bretheren to commit to writing and so to print' what he had preached.[3] At times this kind of statement may be no more than a polite convention, and not much reliance therefore should be placed on prefaces which go no further than to say that the sermons are printed at the request of 'many and sundry friends',[4] or 'divers well affected in-

[1] A. F. Herr, *The Elizabethan Sermon: a survey and a bibliography* (Philadelphia, 1940), p. 117.
[2] *Life of L. Chaderton* by W. Dillingham, trans. E. S. Shuckburgh (1884), p. 13.
[3] *STC* 23023 (1594), sig. A2.   [4] *STC* 23284 [1578], sig. A2.

habitants of the place' Cirencester, where the sermon had been preached.[1] We are on safer ground when the applicants are said to have been 'the Mayor of London and others the Aldermen his brethren',[2] or such persons as 'that noble and wise Councillor, Ambrose, Earl of Warwick',[3] or the Earl of Derby who personally sent a sermon which had been preached before him to London to be printed.[4]

It would be unfair, therefore, to regard the output of sermons as mainly a reflection of the vanity of their authors. While this may have been true of many, it is clear that it was not only nor mainly the preachers who pressed for publication. Indeed, for many of them the labour involved in having their sermons printed was simply not worth their while. This may seem to be a surprising statement at first sight (once the demand for the sermon is admitted), but it has to be remembered that it was not the normal custom to preach from a carefully prepared manuscript, but more often from notes and schemes, or even *extempore*. Some preachers went so far as to declare that they would rather preach ten sermons than write one.[5] To write out a sermon meant not only the labour of composition and transcription, but it involved first of all the recalling and ordering of what had already been said. This would have been a difficult matter enough even from notes, but when the preacher had little but his memory to guide him, he was faced with a formidable task. John Foxe frankly acknowledged this difficulty when he wrote:

Although I have not, nor could not fully folow in speach and forme every thing so precisely as was spoken: yet so far as remembrance

---

[1] *STC* 14728 (1588), sig. 4. Other preachers mention that the sermons were 'earnestlie desired in print'; were asked for by 'divers well affected and godly persons', or were 'earnestly intreated by nobles to be put in writing'. 'A daily request for the printed copie' is reported, while 'many Christians by word and letter', or 'those who were present', or 'divers who heard it', are said to be the occasion of others, as was 'the request, persuasion and counsel of a friend', or the advice of 'a learned Father', etc., etc.
[2] *STC* 13465 (1595), sig. A2.   [3] *STC* 19731 (1604), sig. A2v.
[4] *STC* 4367 (1577), sig. A2v.
[5] *STC* 11422 (1574), sig. A2v. Cf. *STC* 23027 (1594), sig. A2.

could serve me, I have not much digressed from the sentence, order, and principall points in the said Sermon contained: adding withall some things more which I thought before to have spoken, and either for plentie of matter, or lacke of memorie were forgotten.[1]

'So far as remembraunce could serve me' is an important reservation, and a reminder that at best the preacher's version of this type of sermon depended entirely on his memory. Some were scrupulous in their efforts to keep to the exact wording of what they thought they had said. For example, Robert Crowley tells us that: 'I caused my Memorie to searche out all her corners, and to bring forth that which she found, and so I have penned (as my Memorie telleth me) almost the same words that I then spake, and in the same order.'[2]

This was only possible if the preacher had a good memory and got to work soon after the delivery of the sermon. A man well trained in this kind of exercise might well produce a close copy of what he had said, but these conditions did not always obtain, and sometimes there was considerable delay, as is admitted by John Bradford in an epistle prefixed to a sermon on repentance, preached probably in 1552. He writes:

Last summer as I was abroad preaching in the Countrey, my chaunce was to make a Sermon of Repentence, the which was earnestlie of dyvers desired of mee, that I should give it to them written, or else put it forth in print. The which thing to graunt, as I could not (for I had not written it) as I tolde them that had so earnestlie desired it.

But when no nay would serve, but I must promise them to write it as I could, I consented to their request they should have it at my leysure. This leysure I prolonged so long that as (I weene) I offended them, so did I please myselfe, as one more glad to reade other mennes wrytinges than in such sort to publish mine owne, for other men to reade.[3]

[1] *STC* 11245 (1585), sig. A4ᵛ. Cf. *STC* 568 (1576), sig. A2ᵛ.
[2] *STC* 6092 (1575), sig. A3. Cf. *STC* 11450 (1571), sig. A2ᵛ, where Fulke emphasizes the fact that he has observed 'as neare as I could, not onely the substance of the matter, but the phrase of words which I then used'.
[3] *STC* 3501 (1581), sig. B2.

Bradford, like others, was clearly an unwilling author, who only under pressure, and then at his own time, would go to the labour of putting on to paper what he could recollect of last summer's sermon. His unwillingness (and unworldliness) are the more remarkable when we see that the sermon was reprinted no less than eight times before men lost interest in it.

Even if the preacher had retained his notes they may well have been 'short and imperfect', as Laurence Humphrey confessed his to have been when he began to recreate the seven sermons that he had preached in various parts of Hampshire and at Paul's Cross.[1] Others were not even fortunate enough to have anything to refer to, and had to write from memory, and to admit that what ensued was 'not word for word, what I preached, but materially the same'.[2]

Sometimes, however, the preachers were not forced to rely on memory or notes since their discourse may well have been taken down by one or more listeners. Men were good listeners in those days, since many were trained from youth to follow a discourse, and to memorize the main points of an argument, and sometimes to get phrases by heart. Add to this that they were adroit, experienced note takers, and could set down on their 'tables', or 'tablets', which they carried for the purpose, enough to enable them to work up at leisure the tenor of their discourse, and we can understand how some sermons came to the printer. Not all, of course, were so experienced; it was the 'special appeal of some poor Christians, afflicted in conscience, which came to me since the sermon was preached with their imperfect notes of their own gathering', which persuaded William Burton to write out his sermons.[3] Printers, naturally, were not so scrupulous as the preachers themselves, so that even if the copy was 'not altogether in such sorte as it was by the reverend Father preached, yet as nigh thereunto as could be remembered', this seemed sufficient for the printer to go ahead, while if he were lucky he might have 'not only received

---

[1] *STC* 13966 (1588), sig. xx.   [2] *STC* 3064 (1599), sig. A 2.
[3] *STC* 4171 (1596), sig. A 4.

notes, but almost the whole discourse... from those who could pleasure him in this behalf'.[1]

A more accurate text was forthcoming when the work was the result of one 'being somewhat of a readie hande who hath taken from the mouth of the Preacher, certaine of the Sermons which he hath preached', which were 'againe over seene and corrected', probably by the preacher himself.[2] Certainly that is what happened on another occasion when eight sermons on Ecclesiastes were printed, for George Gifford says in a dedicatory letter to Anne, Countess of Warwick, that after his Sermons had been 'noted by one that did write', he was requested 'to peruse and perfect them in some better sort for the Printer, which as leisure served he performed'.[3]

The facilities for obtaining an accurate text were carried further in the 1580's when at least one early system of shorthand came into use, and was put on the market by Timothy Bright, its inventor, in 1588. This he called *Characterie: an arte of shorte, swifte and secret writing by character*. The possibilities of this system appear to have been limited, according to modern investigators, but there can be no doubt that it was used by some who attended the sermons and reproduced a text from what they had taken down. If this was worked over by the preacher as is suggested by the title-page of Henry Smith's *The examination of Usurie, in two Sermons. Taken by Characterie, and after examined*,[4] then something approaching the actual words of the sermon resulted. This was undoubtedly the case when a sermon by A. Tyrell came to be printed, which was 'taken by Characterye', says the title-page, while the preacher elaborates on this in his dedicatory letter to the Archbishop of Canterbury when he writes:

At the time I made my exhortation publicklie in Christ his Church in London, my wordes were no sooner out of my mouth but a yong youth had penned my Sermon *verbatim* by Characterie, an arte newly invented. It was at this youthes pleasure, for the manifesting

[1] *STC* 6137 (1579), sig. A2. [2] *STC* 11858 (1582), sig. 2ᵛ.
[3] *STC* 11853 (1589), sig. A3ᵛ. [4] *STC* 22661 (1591), sig. H3.

of his skill in that swift kind of writing, to publish my Sermon in print, yet honestlie he came unto me to enforme me first of the matter. Hee was to me a meere straunger, of whom, after I had understood his intent and purpose, I craved respite to pause of the matter before I would give my consent.

Evidently Tyrell was convinced of the accuracy of what had been taken down, for he says later in his preface 'He that penned my Sermon as I uttered it in pulpit, did it most exactly, writing it word for word'.[1]

Smith, the most popular preacher of his day, must have welcomed the aid that 'characterie' gave him. Even if imperfect, it was more accurate than the mangled versions of his sermons which were printed without any authorization. He speaks of his *Sermon on the Benefit of Contentation* as being 'miserably abused in printing, as it were with the whole limmes cut off at once, and cleane left out';[2] while of *The Wedding Garment* he says that in order

to controll these false coppies of this Sermon whiche were printed without my knowledge (patched as it seemeth out of some borrowed notes), and to stoppe the printing of it again without my corrections, as it was intended, because they had got it licensed before, although utterly unwilling for some respects to have it published, which made mee withstand their inportunity for so long, yet seeing more inconvenience than I thought of, I suffered that which I could not hinder.[3]

Such was the demand for his works that edition after edition was printed from unauthorized texts, so that in time later editions had to be put on the market bearing the words 'published by a more perfect copy than heretofore',[4] or 'examined by the best copies and corrected'.[5]

A number of preachers frankly abandoned the attempt to recreate what they had said, as closely as possible, and seized

---

[1] *STC* 24474 [1589], sig. A6ᵛ.
[2] *STC* 22720, *The Sermons of Maister Henrie Smith* (1594), p. 107. The first edition is dated 1592.
[3] *STC* 22713 (1590), sig. A2.   [4] *STC* 22749 (1602), sig. A1.
[5] *STC* 22688 (1591), sig. A1.

the opportunity to enlarge their discourse and print it 'not now altered but augmented',[1] as reads the title-page of a sermon by Tobias Bland, or as is said more explicitly by Richard Bancroft, who declares his sermon to contain 'some things which were omitted, either through want of time, or default of memorie'.[2]

Sometimes the reason for this enlargement is given, as may be seen from the title-page of a sermon made by Thomas Rogers *to the Confutation of so much of another Sermon* [*by T. Cartwright*] *entituled A frutful Sermon... as concerneth both the deprivation of our present government, and the perpetual and uniforme regiment of our Church.* In the printed version, he elaborates his original argument, so that now it is

more fully penned than could by mouth be expressed, the tyme being limitted to the speaker being verie short.[3]

But once we enter the realm of controversy (and many Elizabethan sermons were deliberately controversial), the necessity for an exact version of the preacher's words becomes most important. Preachers found that false or misleading accounts of what they had said were in circulation, so that they were forced to put their sermon into print to vindicate themselves, or 'in order that this Sermon may be the more advisedly considered by Readers, which was not well taken in part by some of the hearers when it was spoken'.[4] Obviously, when publication was undertaken for reasons such as this it was essential that the printed copy should faithfully reproduce what the preacher had said, even if it went on to enlarge the original utterance. This was expressly the purpose of William Burton in printing a sermon which he had preached in Norwich Cathedral on 21 December 1589, and now 'published for the satisfying of some who took offence when they first heard it'. The author assures his readers that 'as for the sermon itself, it is

[1] *STC* 3127 (1589), sig. A 1.
[2] *STC* 1346 (1588), sig. A 3. Cf. other title-pages of Smith's sermons which read 'printed from the true corrected copy sent by the author to a Lady', or 'Sickness allowed him to correct false copies', etc.
[3] *STC* 21240 (1590), sig. A 1. [4] *STC* 22239 [1575], sig. A 1.

faithfully translated from the pulpit to the pen, save that at some points he hath now much enlarged than he could have then for lack of time, but for these things whereof he was accused, and which were taken so grievously, they be set downe even as they were uttered, as nigh as he could, word for word, without adding or detracting'.[1]

Similarly, William Kethe prints the sermon which he delivered at Blandford in 1571, because some:

so much misliked my sayd sermon, that they thought I spake somwhat more then became me, [and] by their sinistrall reportes of my Sermon, would very faine cause others who heard me not, to be of their owne corrupt and perverse judgementes. I have therefore thought it expedient... to call to my remembraunce my sayd Sermon, and to commit the same to writing (and to the judgementes of the godly) wherein I have used such diligence, if I be not deceaved, that such as heard it shal finde not very many things added, but yet lesse left out or omitted, certainly to my knowledge not one sentence.[2]

Long as it is, this account only outlines some of the main topics that filled the minds of many Englishmen. Religion was all important to them: to know and to expound the truth as they saw it was vital. They naturally turned to the printers as one of the main ways in which to attain their ends. As the above shows, the printers and their associates did not fail them. Some members of the trade were devout men and gladly put their resources at the service of their religion, but devout or otherwise, the printing trade was an essential agent in the production and dissemination of religious ideas.

2. *Law*

When the practising lawyer looked about his chambers, there, ranged in order, he would see the tools of his trade—his books. Pride of place went to his copy of the *Statutes at Large*, in one or two folio volumes, a work published several times during Elizabeth's reign. Side by side with them stood the slim

[1] *STC* 4178 [1591?], sig. A3ᵛ.
[2] *STC* 14943 [1572], sig. A2ᵛ. Cf. *STC* 7083 (1601) and *STC* 11839 (1584).

LEGAL TEXT BOOKS

volumes containing the statutes promulgated year by year since the last collected edition was published. Near them also there would probably be one or more of the various abridgements or abstracts of the statutes which made reference to them a great deal easier. Equally valuable were the series of Year Books, since these were an essential authority for the medieval common law, and these too were accompanied by volumes of abridgements.

Next to these primary sources of the law, there would stand a number of well known text-books, such as Littleton's *Tenures*, together with collections of writs of various kinds, books of formulas, precedents, terms of the law, etc. These were well-nigh indispensable to the active lawyer, and thus a most valuable property to those printers who issued them. In Elizabeth's reign, however, these were few, since here, as elsewhere, printing monopolies had been established, and the right to print had been strictly reserved by royal mandate to one particular person or persons. Books on the law had long before this been made a matter of privilege, and Richard Tottell had held such a privilege so far as the printing of law books was concerned from the time of Edward VI, who had authorized him to print for the space of seven years 'all manner of books of the temporal law... so as the copies be allowed, and adjudged mete to be printed, by one of the Justices of the law, or two serjeants, or three apprentices of the law; whereof the one to be a reader in court. And that none shall imprint any book which the said Richard Totell shall first take and imprint, during the said term, upon pain of forfeiture of all such books.'[1] Elizabeth increased his privilege by giving him a monopoly 'to imprint all manner of books concerning the common laws of this realm' for his life.[2] As a result, Tottell was able to enter in the *Stationers' Register* of 1583 the titles of twenty-five law books which no one but himself could print. Since this figure excludes the Year Books, of which he printed at least 175 between

---

[1] Herbert, *Ames' Typographical Antiquities*, vol. II, p. 806.
[2] Arber, *Transcript*, vol. II, p. 15.

1558 and 1593 (when he ceased to print), the total value of his monopoly is apparent.

Tottell was aware, however, that privilege also implied responsibility, and that the keeping of a series of legal texts available meant a good deal more than putting out a series of straight reprints. In fact, law books were constantly being revised, as better or more perfect exemplars of the original text became known, or as new cases or new judicial decisions clarified or extended the law. So important was this that many books bore on their title-page some such words as 'lately perused over', or 'newly corrected with divers additions', or with 'divers new and later statutes, most convenient to be had perfect and ready'. Something of what this might mean can be seen from a preface written by Tottell to his edition of *Magna charta cum statutis quae Antiqua vocantur*, first published in 1556, and afterwards put out several times in the next forty years. He writes:

To stuffe a preface with praise of this boke, or with exhorting you to reading of it, were in a manner not doubtfull to take fond peine not nedefull.... Onely touching myselfe, and my labours in this and other, I praye ye suffer that I maye somewhat use your pacience, as ye shall alway use my diligence.... How unperfit the bokes of the lawes of England were before, what price the scarcenes had raysed, the most part mervelously mangled, and no smale part no wher to be gotten, ther be enow, though I rehearse it not, that do freshlye remember, & can truely witnes. Likewise how, sithens I toke in hand to serve your uses, the imperfections have been supplied, the price so eased as the scarcenes no more hindreth but that ye have them as chepe (notwithstandinge the common dearth of these times) as when thei were most plentiful, the print much pleasanter to the eye in the bokes of yeres than any that ye have ben yet served with, paper & margine as good & as faire as the best, but much better & fairer then the most, no smal nomber by me set forth newly in print that before were scant to be found in writing, I nede not myself to report it.... But now to say also somewhat of this present work, albiet it might seme superfluous and nedelesse to have emprinted it againe so sodeinly, being lately done in so faire paper &

letter by another [Thomas Marshe]: yet when ye shal wey how in sundry places much here is added out of bokes of good credit, as examined by the roules of parliament; how echwhere the truth even of the best printes is overmatched by theire faultes not fewe not a litle reformed, the light of pointing adjoined, the chapiters of statutes truly devided, & noted with their due nombers, the alphabeticall table justly ordred & quoted, the leaves not one falsly marked, with mani other helps to correct it & further you, when (I say) ye shal have weyed both al these by me performed, and the want of these in al other heretofore, I hope your wisedoms wil sone espie that nether I have newe printed it for you causelesse, nor ye shal bye it of me frutelesse. This thought I fit in min own behalf first to have sayd unto you: and so now I cesse further to trouble you from your more earnest studies.[1]

It is well to know that Tottell took his responsibilities seriously, since his monopoly was so nearly complete. He published very little else but law books throughout his career, and a review of his publications is very nearly a review of the legal publications of his day. One great exception must be made however, since the *Statutes of the Realm* did not fall within his privilege, but were printed by the Queen's Printer of the day. The *Statutes* were an important part of any lawyer's equipment, and had been so from the earliest times. Chaucer's Man of Law, it will be remembered, knew all the statutes word for word, even at a period when they were only available in manuscript: the printed volumes had made matters easier for his successors who could turn to compilations such as *The whole volume of statutes at large...since Magna Charta, until the xxix yeere of...Elizabeth...with marginal notes,*[2] published by Christopher Barker in 1587. These two massive folio volumes were the ultimate authority, and lawyers were taught to consult them in any matter of importance, and not to rely on the lesser authority of text books or abridgements.

The abridgements, however, were of the greatest help, since they presented much that the lawyer wanted to know in a

[1] *STC* 9278, sig. † i[v].   [2] *STC* 9316.

convenient form. Such works had been much in demand since the first days of printing, and just before the accession of Elizabeth, William Rastell, son of old William Rastell, the printer, published in 1557 his *Collection of all the Statutes from the beginning of Magna Carta unto...1557*.[1] This work gave almost uncut, and in the original language, the text of the enacting parts of the statutes; but, as Rastell explained, omitted the preambles, together with the private and obsolete acts. For quick reference he arranged the statutes under alphabetical headings, with marginal notes as to their contents. Although Rastell did all he could to keep his volume within bounds, nevertheless it ran to over one thousand quarto pages of text in double columns. Despite this, it was very popular, and after eight reprints it was printed entirely in English for the first time, together

with two verie necessarie Tables. The one declaringe by order of Alphabet, all the severall Titles, with the speciall and most necessarie matters contayned therin. Whereby Justices of peace, Coroners, Eschetors, Mayors, Sheriffs, Bayliffes, Constables, &c. and all other her Hyghnes Subjectes shall (under their apt Titles in the same Table) finde what, and wherwyth they are charged by any manner of Statute. In the other Table, being at thend of the Booke are set downe the severall times of the Parliaments, wyth the Titles at large of every one of the Statutes made therein, whereby the Reader may easilie finde what Statute it shall please him to seeke for...[2]

Next to the Statutes in importance came the Year Books, 'absolutely necessary to all students of law' as Sir William Holdsworth says, and 'by far the most important source of, and authority for, the mediaeval common law'.[3] Some 260 volumes of these Year Books had been published by 1560, and they formed one of the most valuable of all Tottell's legal properties. His presses were constantly at work producing Year Books of different years from the time of Edward III to that of 27 Henry VIII, and in all he printed some 225 editions

[1] *STC* 9306.   [2] *STC* 9314 (1579), sig. ¶ 2.
[3] Holdsworth, *A History of English Law* (1923 ed.), vol. II, p. 525.

and issues of these books. Many of them were so much in demand that they were reprinted several times, and furthermore Tottell issued some volumes which collected together the reports of a number of years, as in 1562, when he reprinted in this fashion all the reports for the 14 years' reign of Henry IV.[1]

In addition, the lawyer found his path smoothed by a series of abridgements of the Year Books. The most important of these had originally been compiled by Anthony Fitzherbert, and was published in 1516. When Tottell first issued it in 1565 it consisted of two large folio volumes, containing 1428 pages of print, which, we are told, had been 'dernierment Conferre avesque la Copy Escript, et par ceo Correcte'. Aided by a very full table of contents (which ran to 132 pages in the 1577 edition), lawyers could find what the Year Books could tell them about many hundreds of matters from *Abbe* to *Withernam* with ease.[2] Further help came in 1573/4, when Sir Robert Brook published his edition of Fitzherbert, which divided the table of contents more thoroughly, and also referred to works other than the Year Books.[3] Despite its size (two volumes of some 1400 folio pages in Norman French) it was reprinted in 1576 and 1586, while in 1578 Richard Bellewe had extracted some of the cases dealing with matters arising since the time of Henry VIII, and set them down chronologically.[4] Lastly, we may note a work by William Fleetwood, Recorder of London, to which he gave the title *Annalium Edwardi Quinti...Henrici Octavi elenchus*,[5] which also gave assistance to those using the Year Books, which it has been said, 'must have seemed an uncharted waste to the student of the sixteenth and seventeenth centuries'.

In addition to all these books, which were so useful to those practising in the superior courts, there were a number of others

[1] *STC* 9608. Tottell had originally published this collection in 1553. For other collections of the Year Books, see *STC* 9565–7, Edw. III, 22–8; *STC* 9582–5, Edw. III, 40–50, etc.
[2] *STC* 10956–7.   [3] *STC* 3827.
[4] *STC* 3821. And in 1585, 1587 and 1597.
[5] *STC* 11034 (1579). And in 1597.

which were much in demand. Among these we may notice *Les plees del Coron diuisees en plusiours titles*, compiled by Sir William Stanford, and first printed by Tottell in 1557 and again on four subsequent occasions.[1] Another useful book, entitled *A colleccion of entrees, of declaracions, barres, replicacions,...and divers other matters* (1566) was a book of precedents in pleading which, despite its size, also called for two reprints by 1596.[2] Then in 1579, Simon Theloall of the Inner Temple edited *Le Digest des Briefes Originals*,[3] which 'contains all the Year Book learning on the writs therein contained', and is 'the most orderly treatise on procedure, founded on the Year Books, that had yet appeared'.[4]

Other sides of the lawyer's work were assisted by manuals, such as Littleton's *Tenures*, originally compiled about 1480. This treatise had been continually reprinted and revised since then, and also had been translated into English. It has been described by Sir Edward Coke as 'the most perfect and absolute work that was ever written in any humane science', and Sir William Holdsworth adds: 'It summed up and passed on to future generations the land law as developed by the common lawyers of the Middle Ages,'[5] which probably accounts for its continuous popularity from the first editions and throughout the sixteenth century. Both versions were printed by Tottell, and by 1591 he had reprinted the French version at least thirteen times, while the English version had also run to nine editions since 1556. Another popular work, which had long been in circulation, was originally entitled in about 1543 *A newe boke of Presidentes...in manner of a Register: wherin is comprehended the very trade of makynge all maner of evidences etc.* Thomas Phaer, in a foreword to this, claimed that

> every person that can wryte and reade and entendeth to have any thynge to do amonge the common weale must of verye neede, for

---

[1] *STC* 23219–23 in which various kinds of offences, indictments, methods of trial, sentences, etc., are treated.
[2] *STC* 20730–2.   [3] *STC* 23934.
[4] Holdsworth, *History of English Law*, vol. V, p. 381.
[5] *Op. cit.* vol. II, p. 574.

COLLECTIONS OF PLEADINGS

his owne advantage, applie his mind somewhat unto this kynde of learning...It shewith the makyng of those thynges, whereupon dependeth the welth and lyvynge of men, wythout which thinges there can no tytle lawfullye be claymed, no landes nor houses purchased, no right recovered....Finally no man can be sure of his owne livelod without help of evidence which, as a trusty anker, holdeth the right of evry man's posessions safely and surely agaynst al troubles and straunge tempestes of injuries not of men only, but of time also, the consumer of al.[1]

Other useful and practical collections of pleadings commonly in demand were the volumes known as the *Natura Brevium*, the *Nova Narrationes*, the *Articuli ad Novas Narrationes*, the *Diversite des Courtes*,[2] etc., which were all found to be 'commodyous and profitable unto gentil men studentes of the lawe', who for further help could consult *The Exposicions of the Termes of the Lawes...with diuers rules...*[3] printed in French and English by Tottell in 1567 and constantly reprinted during the next fifteen years, when it passed to his successors and was still widely used in the first few decades of the seventeenth century.

A much longer and more ambitious work was compiled by William West under the title of *Symbolaeographia. Which may be termed the Art, Description, or Image of Instrumentes, Covenants, Contracts, or the Notarie or Scriuener...in fower severall bookes* (1590).[4]

Help for those engaged in the administration of the law up and down the land was forthcoming in various ways, the most important being perhaps a manual for the use of the Justices of the Peace. This was available in two forms. An anonymous author as far back as about 1506 had compiled *The Boke of Justices of Peas*, and this was continuously reprinted until 1580.[5] Then in 1538, Robert Redman printed *The newe Boke of Justices of the peas*, written by Sir Anthony Fitzherbert. This is

---

[1] *STC* 3333, sig. A2ᵛ.   [2] See p. 157.
[3] *STC* 20704 (1567). Tottell's edition of 1567 appears to be the first with the text both in French and in English.
[4] *STC* 25267. Later editions were published in parts: 'Newly corrected', or 'Lately amended', etc.   [5] *STC* 14862–87.

shorter and simpler to follow than its predecessor, and was also very popular, so that at least 47 editions or issues of the two works were published in the sixteenth century. By the time of Elizabeth, however, the earlier treatise was being published as part of an omnibus volume, as appears from the title-page of Tottell's edition of 1559, which reads:

The Contentes of this Boke. Fyrst the booke for a Justice of peace. The boke that teacheth to kepe a Courte Baron, or a lete. The boke teachinge to kepe a courte hundred. The boke called returna Brevium. The boke called Carta feodi, conteynynge the forme of dedes, releases, Indentures, obligations, acquitances, letters of attorney...testamentes and other thynges. And the boke of the ordinaunce to be observed by the offycers of the Kynges Escheker for fees takynge.[1]

Fitzherbert's work was only printed twice in Elizabeth's reign, and then was replaced by an enlargement by Richard Crompton in 1583, *Loffice et aucthoritie de Justices de peace...enlarge per R. Crompton.*[2] This 'never had a wide circulation, certainly not among practising justices, and in spite of its mass of information was speedily neglected because of its chaotic arrangement and impossible language'.[3] The earlier treatises were in fact replaced by a work by William Lambard, historian, lawyer and antiquary, entitled: *Eirenarcha: or of the Office of the Justices of peace, in two bookes: Gathered in 1579, and now revised, and firste published, in the 24. yeare of the peacable reigne of our gratious Queene Elizabeth: by William Lambard of Lincolnes Inne Gent...*[4] 'It met', writes Professor Putnam, 'the needs of the country gentleman on the commission', and together with the complementary volume, also by Lambard, *The duties of Constables, Borsholders, Tithing-men, and such other lowe Ministers of the Peace...*,[5] 'exactly supplied a want

---

[1] STC 14882.   [2] STC 10978.
[3] B. H. Putnam, *Treatise on...Justices of the Peace* (Oxford, 1924), p. 215.
[4] STC 15163 (1581).
[5] STC 15145 (1583). Eight editions had been published by 1599.

which had long been felt by that numerous and important class who were called on either to act as justices of the peace, or to advise them as to their powers and duties.'[1]

Apart from matters concerning the Queen's peace and causes which could be tried in the superior courts only, landholders were still holding their own courts to deal with the administration of their estates. The conditions under which their tenants held their various parcels of land, and the intricate communal customs which governed their cultivation called for constant supervision and for the holding of courts to regularize and to control their use. Littleton's *Tenures* had for long been the main guide available, but valuable as this work had been, it was at least one hundred years old by 1580, and the publication in 1580 of John Kitchen's book, *Le Court Leete et Court Baron... et les cases et matters necessaires pur Seneschals de ceux Courts a scier, et pur les students...* at once was seen to be a worthy replacement of the older work, and it was reprinted five times by 1598.[2] In his preface, dedicated to the students of the Inns of Court, Kitchen says that his book was designed in the first place to instruct those who hold such courts, and in the second place to encourage lords of manors to appoint properly qualified stewards and officers to hold such courts so as to ensure that the law was not in the hands of serving men, whose object was not to administer the law, but merely to administer it in such a way as they thought would most please their masters.

Of a more limited appeal, but sufficiently popular to call for three editions between 1562 and 1573, was *The offices of Sheriffes, Bayliffes of liberties, Escheatours, Constables and Coroners, and sheweth what everyone of them may doo by vertue of their offices....*[3] These officials still played their part in the government of the country, and this manual, attributed to Sir A. Fitzherbert, sets out their duties for them.

[1] Holdsworth, *History of English Law*, vol. IV, p. 118.
[2] *STC* 15017–22.
[3] This is the title of *STC* 10993 (1573). It was first published in [1535?]. The edition of 1573 is the eleventh recorded in *STC*.

In addition to works such as these, the more advanced and erudite students of the law could turn to a number of other treatises. The great lawyers of the Middle Ages were represented by editions of Bracton (1569); Britton (1540); Fortescue (1537, in Latin; 1567 with R. Mulcaster's English version); and Glanvill (1554). More modern writers, such as Sir Thomas Smith in his *De Republica Anglorum* (1583), with three reprints within ten years, discoursed on 'the form and manner of the government of Englande and the policie thereof',[1] while special aspects of the law were the concern of writers such as William Clerke, *The triall of Bastardie* (1594),[2] or John Manwood, *A Brefe Collection of the Lawes of the Forest* (1592),[3] or *A briefe treatise of testaments and last willes* (1590),[4] by Henry Swinburne.

This summary account must suffice to indicate the busy traffic in law books that went on in this period. Although before Elizabeth came to the throne legal printing was becoming more and more the preserve of a few, it was only after the turn of the century that the Queen's Printer and Tottell obtained such a monopoly. As a result, Tottell used over 90 per cent of his printing capacity in the production of legal works, and he has with justice been called '*the* publisher of Year Books'. He used his privilege with a proper sense of his responsibilities. His long explanation of the care he took in preparing a new edition of the statutes has already been quoted, while many of his books tell his prospective readers that they have been 'conferred with divers true written copies and purged of sundry cases, having in some places more than ye authour wrote, and lesse in some other'. Both he and the Queen's Printer of the day may be said to have well discharged their duty to see that both the original documents and the many treatises dealing with the law were reasonably available. The Elizabethan lawyer, in short, had reason to bless the printers of his day.

[1] *STC* 22857–60. [2] *STC* 5411.
[3] *STC* 17290. [4] *STC* 23547.

3. *Education*

During the reign of Elizabeth schools increased in number, and more and more people learned to read. Instruction was commonly provided in the first stages by the Petty Schools (as they were called)—which taught reading, writing and sometimes arithmetic as well. Reading matter was obviously required, and began with the horn-book. This was generally a single leaf of print, containing the alphabet, the vowels, some simple combinations of letters, such as ab, ba, etc., and the Lord's Prayer. This leaf was pasted on to a board and covered with a thin sheet of horn. From this the beginner passed to the 'Absey book'—that is *The ABC with the Catechism*, which contained the alphabet, the catechism with other religious teaching and a few prayers. This in its turn led to the *Primer and Catechism*, which was 'set forth by the Queenes majesty to be taught to children'.

Clearly here was a good market for the book trade, but here again, as with the law, the field was a closed one, since the Crown had given a monopoly in these books to the printer John Day. Renewing a previous patent by Edward VI, the Queen gave to Day on 28 October 1559 the sole rights for seven years to print the ABC and the Catechism, and this was extended on 6 May 1567, for a further ten years to cover 'the Psalmes of David in Englishe Meter with notes, the A.B.C. with the little Catechism, appointed also by our Injunctions for the instruction of Chyldren'.[1] Then on 26 August 1577 there was a new privilege which gave to Day and his son Richard a sole right to print

the psalmes of David in English meeter with notes to singe them, the A.B.C. with the little cathechisme...the Cathechisme in englishe and lattyn compiled by...Alexander Nowell...with all other books in englishe or lattyn which the said Alexander Nowell hath made or hereafter shall make write or translate.[2]

[1] Arber, *Transcript*, vol. I, p. 111.
[2] Arber, *op. cit.* vol. I, pp. 115–16; vol. II, p. 775.

These books covered the early stages of learning, and beyond this the majority of children never ventured. For those who did, their future lay in the Grammar Schools, where an ability to read and write was regarded as a *sine qua non*. By grammar, of course, was meant Latin, and the Master had the duty of ensuring that everything was done to see that his pupils acquired a competent use of this language. This they learnt with the help of 'Lily's Latin Grammar', a time-honoured work, known in Elizabethan times as *A Shorte introduction of grammar, generally to be used; compiled and set forth for the bringing up of all those who intend to attain the knowledge of the Latin tongue* (1549).[1] No other book could be lawfully used; all Grammar School masters were required to teach from it, and Bishops at their visitations were accustomed to ask whether this work and no other was used in the schools. After about a year on the first part (*A Short Introduction*), the pupil tackled the second part of the volume (*Brevissima institutio*), or the grammar proper in Latin.

This book again was the monopoly of one man—at this time Reyner Wolfe—and a most valuable monopoly it was, for many thousands of this and of the other school texts, such as the *ABC with the Catechism*, were printed every year. Since the rewards were considerable, piracy was inevitable. For example, in 1582, John Day went to the Star Chamber saying that his patent had been infringed and that ten thousand copies of the *ABC with the Catechism* had been printed by Roger Ward, who admitted the offence. Again in 1585, Richard Day alleged that 'great numbers of the *ABC with the Little Catechism* had been printed and put on sale to the number of fifteen thousand of the saide book by three men, while two others had printed ten thousand ABCs in the space of eight months'. Furthermore, it was claimed that two men had sold four thousand copies of the Psalms in metre, while eleven others had put out for sale two thousand Psalm books and ten

[1] *STC* 15611–24.

thousand ABCs.[1] These figures are sufficient evidence of the large numbers of books of this kind that were printed, and are a striking confirmation of the fact that the commoner the book, the more likely it is that it will disappear, as seems to have happened to these pirated works. Thus it is that a recent investigator can write:

Of the many thousands of copies of the little manual *The ABC with the Catechism*, printed in the reign of Queen Elizabeth and handled by wellnigh every school-child of that period, only four imperfect leaves, now in the library of Worcester College, Oxford, have come down to us, and they only survived because they were made to serve as binding material for an obscure Latin volume...printed in Cologne, 1582.[2]

So far as books printed in England are concerned, the further progress of the Grammar School boy is not of such importance, since the books he studied were classical texts, or works based upon them which were printed abroad. But some crumbs fell to the English book-trade, since once the preliminary foundation was laid, further reading matter was required so that the rules of construction could be studied and practised. Among these, works by Cato and Aesop were favourites.

In his translation of the *Mimi* of Cato, Taverner had explained to the 'tender youth of Englande' that

The cause, gentle Chyldren, that hathe impelled me to take these paynes in thys booke, is youre weale and commoditie. I perceyved, that thys boke...as it is in dede very apte and accommodate for youre education in vertue and learnynge: so it is also verye muche frequented and borne in youre handes. But agayne I perceyved, that of the most part it is rather borne in the handes, then imprynted and fixed in the memorie. The cause hereof, I coulde conjecture to be nothynge els, but that the moste parte of thys boke is composed not in solute oration, but in metre, which to ye rude chyld must nedes be obscure and full of dificultie, and consequentlye unpleasaunt

---

[1] H. Anders, 'The Elizabethan ABC with the Catechism', *The Library*, Fourth Series, vol. XVI (1935), pp. 36–7.
[2] H. Anders, *op. cit.* p. 32.

and unsaverye. For the redresse therefore of thys inconvenience, I beynge moved, good chyldren, with the love that I beare unto you, have not disdayned to playe as it were the chylde agayne, attempering my selfe to youre tender wyttes and capacities. I have not translated the boke worde for worde, for then I shuld have taken awaye the office of your schole maister, and also occasion you to be [the] more negligent and slacke in your studie upon truste of the translation therof. But I have with brief scholies onely illustrated and opened the sense of the verses.... Nowe it shalbe your partes (swete children) so to embrace thys booke, and to beare it hence forth, not onely in hande, but also in mynde, as I maye thyncke my laboure well imployed uppon you.[1]

Half a century later the Cato was still in use, and the bookseller Maunsell tried to attract a public by putting out an edition with the title:

Cato construed, Or A familiar and easie interpretation upon Catos morall Verses. First doen [sic] in Laten and Frenche by Maturinus Corderius, and now newly englished, to the comforte of all young Schollers.[2]

As for Aesop, Brinsley in his *Ludus Literarius* (1612) concurred with the opinion and practice of the previous century that Aesop was the next book to be used after Cato. Not only was it useful grammatically, but the fables served as valuable material for moral instruction. The booksellers, however, do not seem to have grasped their opportunity here, for the texts were imported for the main part, and were plentifully produced for a large market. Professor Baldwin has noted no less than twenty editions by one editor by 1573, and gives good reasons for believing that it was this compilation that was used by Shakespeare.[3]

---

[1] Quoted by T. W. Baldwin, *William Shakspere's Small Latine and Lesse Greeke* (Urbana, 1944), vol. I, p. 597, from the edition of 1553, *STC* 4844.
[2] *STC* 4858 (1584), sig. A 1.
[3] Baldwin, *op. cit.* vol. I, p. 615, and pp. 616 ff. For contemporary foreign editions see, for example, the lists in the B.M. Catalogue. For English editions, see *STC* 171 a (1591) and *STC* 172 (1596).

LATIN TEXTBOOKS

Translations and construes were certainly available, but here we can speak with little precision, since many versions appear to have been lost. For example, Simon Sturtevant, in *The Etymologist of Aesops Fables* (1602), speaks of the 'many editions' of the books of 'maister Haines', the schoolmaster, yet no single edition of them is recorded in *STC*, save a translation of Cicero in 1611.[1]

As greater efficiency was required, other textbooks were called for. Terence was adapted by Nicholas Udall in his *Floures for Latine spekynge* (1533),[2] which was much used as a phrase book, and thrice reprinted in the latter half of the century, while more advanced students used texts of the comedies in the original.

More to the taste of struggling schoolboys were the books designed to make their lot an easier one; sometimes by giving them a direct translation, and sometimes by a detailed explanation of how to parse or construe the passage. In his *Terence in English: fabulae Anglicae factae opera R. Bernard* the translator entices his readers as follows:

I offer you here, that which *Fortune* hath vouchsafed to favour me withall, a Latin authour taught to speake English; a comicall Poet, pithie, pleasant, and very profitable: as merry as Eutrapeles. as grave as *Cato*, as ethicall as *Plato*. He can play craftily the cousener, and cunningly the clowne: he will tell you of the nature of the fraudulent flatterer, the grimme and greedie old Sire, the roysting ruffian, the minsing mynion, the beastly baud; that in telling the truth by these figments, men might become wise to avoid such vices, and learne to practice vertue: which was *Terence* purpose in setting of these comedies forth in latin; mine in translating them into english; & this end I desire you to propound to yourselves in reading them, so shall you use them, & not as most doe such authors, abuse them.[3]

[1] *STC* 5304, *Certaine Epistles of Tully Verbally Translated.*
[2] *STC* 23899, reprinted in 1538, 1560, 1575 and 1581. For texts in the original, printed in England, see *STC* 23886, *Comoediae sex* (1583); *STC* 23887, *P. Terenti Afri Comoediae sex* (1589), and again in 1597.
[3] *STC* 23890 (1598), quoted from H. B. Lathrop, *Translations from the Classics into English from Caxton to Chapman, 1477–1620.* University of Wisconsin Studies in Language and Literature, no. 35 (Madison, 1933), pp. 291-2.

Further help for the schoolboy was provided by books instructing him how to write the Latin tongue, of which two were widely used and were printed in England. First, there was the work of Baptista Mantuanus, 'a Poet both for style and matter, very familiar and grateful to children', whose *Adolescentia seu Bucolica* was introduced fairly early in the curriculum. First printed by Wynkyn de Worde, it acquired a new popularity in Elizabeth's time, and called for five editions between 1569 and 1590,[1] while as additional evidence of its popularity we may note that a translation by George Turberville was printed in 1567 and 1572.[2] The other author who was almost compulsory reading at the same stage was Marcellus Palingenius, whose *Zodiacus vitae* (1572), 'that is, concerning the life of man, study and the inculcating morals the best way' as the title-page has it, was printed six times between 1572 and 1602.[3]

From this point on, the Grammar School boy was fairly launched, and his further studies in Logic and Rhetoric introduced him to the great classical masters of these arts. For the non-specialist, however, there was a good deal done to make these works available in translation. Professor Lathrop has treated this side of the matter very fully and only brief reference is required here, save to emphasize that the output of translations from the classics was considerable. Professor Lathrop lists some 116 such works between 1558 and 1603, and this does not include about fifty reprints. He summarizes what the translators accomplished as follows:

It was of course to Latin authors that the translators turned, and first of all to the poet-narrators consecrated by long tradition—to Vergil and Ovid, the beloved story-tellers of the schools, and to Seneca, whose name had been consecrated during the Middle Ages like the names of Vergil and Statius by his supposed contact with Christianity. From Ovid to the late Greek writers of amatory romances was a natural step; the French had set the example of taking it, and had given translations which the English writers could

[1] *STC* 22980–4.   [2] *STC* 22990–1.   [3] *STC* 19139–44.

LOGIC AND RHETORIC

exploit. And finally there were versions of epigrams from the Anthology, from Martial, and from Ausonius, and of a few pastorals, also under the leading of the French.[1]

As for the intensive study of logic and rhetoric in the Grammar Schools, this is reflected in the output of works in English dealing with these matters. Before 1558 there had been works by Leonard Cox, Sir Thomas Wilson, and Richard Sherry.[2] Then in 1563 Richard Rainolde published his treatise, *A booke called the foundacion of Rhetorike, because all other partes of Rhetorike are grounded thereupon...verie profitable to bee knowen and redde*,[3] which was followed in 1577 by Henry Peacham's *The Garden of Eloquence, conteyning the Figures of Grammer and Rhetorick from whence maye bee gathered all maner of Flowers, Coulors...*, compiled 'to profyte this my country and especially the studious youth of this Realme, and such as have not the understanding of the Latyne tongue, sure I am, it may profyte many, and I dare be bold to say, it can hurte none'.[4] Another work meant for a more sophisticated audience was compiled by Abraham Fraunce, entitled *The Arcadian Rhetorike*. This, writes Miss Ethel Seaton, combined 'the virtues of a useful textbook and an elegant anthology'.[5]

Not only sophisticated audiences, however, were envisaged: Anthony Munday, in his translation of *The Orator* by Alexander van den Busche, tells the reader that the book contains a collection of

certaine Rhethoricall Declamations, the use whereof in every member in our Commonweale, is as necessary, as the abuse of wilfull ignorance is odious. In these thou maiest learne Rhethoricke to inforce a

---

[1] Lathrop, *op. cit.* p. 106.
[2] *STC* 5946, L. Cox, *The arte or crafte of Rhethoryke* [1524]; *STC* 25799, Sir T. Wilson, *The Arte of Rhetorique* (1553), and *STC* 25809 *The Rule of Reason*(1551); *STC* 22428, Richard Sherry, *A Treatise of Schemes & Tropes* [1550], and *STC* 22429, *A treatise of the Figures of Grammer and Rhetorike* (1555).
[3] *STC* 20604.   [4] *STC* 19497, sig. A 3.
[5] *STC* 11338 (1588). Reprinted by the Luttrell Society, ed. E. Seaton (1950), p. li.

good cause, and art to impugne an ill. In these thou maiest behold the fruits and flowers of Eloquence, which as *Tully* saith in his Orator, *Bene constitutae civitatis est quasi alumna*: use them to thy profit good Reader, and accept them with as good a mind as I present them with a vertuous intent. If thou studie law, they may helpe thy pleadings, or if divinitie (the reformer of law) they may perfect thy persuasions. In reasoning of private debates, here mayest thou find apt metaphors, in incouraging thy souldiours fit motives. Fathers here have good arguments to move affections in their children, and children vertuous reconcilements to satisfie their displeased fathers: briefly every private man may in this be partaker of a generall profit, and the grossest understanding find occasion of reformation.[1]

With this wholesale puff for the general usefulness of a knowledge of rhetoric we may turn to the books on logic. Here the situation was enlivened by the fight between the traditionalists, who adhered to the logic of Aristotle, and the newer school who swore by the system of Ramus. For the Aristotelians, Ralph Lever published in 1573 *The Arte of Reason, rightly termed Witcraft, teaching a perfect way to argue and dispute*, in which for the most part he follows Aristotle whom, he says, in his judgement, 'far surpasses all prophane writers'.[2]

The other outstanding work on the same side was by Thomas Blundeville, whose *Art of Logike. Plainely taught in the English tongue* (1599), he tells the reader, is 'a very necessary boke for all young students in any profession to find out thereby the truth in any doubtfull speech, but especially for such zealous Ministers as have not beene brought up in any University and yet are desirous to know how to defend by sound argumentes the true Christian doctrine...and how to confute false Silogismes & captious argumentes'.[3]

The logic of Ramus was printed in England in translation in 1574, and this was followed two years later by the text in its

---

[1] *STC* 4182 (1596), quoted from Baldwin, *William Shakspere's Small Latine and Lesse Greeke*, vol. II, p. 45.
[2] *STC* 15541.   [3] *STC* 3142, sig. A 1.

original form.[1] This in turn led to the composition by Dudley Fenner of *The Artes of Logike and Rhethorike, plainelie set foorth in the Englishe tongue, easie to be learned and practised, together with examples for the practise of the same* (1584).[2] Then in 1588 Abraham Fraunce published his work, entitled *The Lawiers Logike, exemplifying the precepts of Logike by the practise of the common Lawe*. He began the work, he says in a letter to the Earl of Pembroke, some seven years ago 'with a generall discourse concerning the right use of Logike, and a contracted comparison betweene this of Ramus and that of Aristotle. These small and trifling beginnings drewe both him to a greater liking of, and my selfe to a further travayling in, the easie explication of Ramus his Logike.'[3]

The attraction of the new logic is explained by Fraunce to lie in the fact that 'logike is nowe six leaves longe & eyght daie laboure, which before was seven yeres studye, and fylled the world with volumes almost infynite: herby it comes to passe that every cobler can cogge a syllogisme, everye carter cracke of propositions'.[4]

In addition to these various books on logic and rhetoric, there was still room for an English version of one of the many works such as the *De Ratione Conscribendi Epistolas* of Erasmus to help struggling letter writers. For such people William Fulwood, 'Merchant', published in 1568 his book, *The Enimie of Idlenesse: Teaching the maner and stile how to endite, compose, and write all sorts of Epistles and Letters: as well by answer, as otherwise.*[5] This was followed in 1576 by *A Panoplie of Epistles, Or, a looking Glasse for the unlearned, Conteining a perfecte plattforme of inditing leters of all sorts, to persons of all estates and degrees...* written by Abraham

---

[1] *STC* 15242, *Dialecticae libri duo*. And again in 1584 and 1588. For the English version, see *STC* 15246, *The logike of P. Ramus, translated per M. R. Makylmenaeum Scotum* (1574). And again in 1581.
[2] *STC* 10766. And again in 1588.
[3] *STC* 11343, quoted from Baldwin, *William Shakspere's Small Latine and Lesse Greeke*, vol. II, p. 57.
[4] *Op cit.* vol. II, p. 58.   [5] *STC* 11476, sig. A1.

Fleming.[1] 'He is thus similar in purpose to Fulwood, but the latter had much less of the flower and more of the business and practical thorn idea' in its composition.[2] By far the most important of works of this kind, however, was Angel Day's *The English Secretorie* (1586). His letters are classified according to types, and are planned he says 'for the unlearned... to whom the want therof breedeth so divers imperfections', and who know 'how greevous it is to participate their moste secreat causes to an others credite'.[3] From manuals such as these, as Fleming writes, 'whatsoever thou art disposed to do by letter, eyther to thy friend or to thine enemie, thou hast this Panoplie to guide thy head in devising, and thy penne in disposing. To the unlearned I likewise offer it as sufficient furniture to arme and enable them against ignorance.'[4]

In addition to the books mainly designed to meet the use of students, there were others written to help those who wished to acquire a knowledge of one of the modern languages, especially French. Miss Lambley has shown how teachers of French were in demand, and that French had become a part of the education of the nobility and gentry.[5] Others, however, were finding the knowledge of one of the European tongues useful for business purposes, and a number of books were written to meet this demand. Perhaps the most important writer of such books was the Huguenot refugee, Claude Desainliens, or as he anglicized it, Holyband. Soon after settling in England he wrote *The French Schoolemaister, wherin is most planlie shewed*

---

[1] *STC* 11049. 'Not broched in the cellar of myne owne brayne, but drawne out of the most pure and cleare fountaines of the finest and eloquentest rhetoricians' (sig. ¶5). The list of contents gives the names of 57 such rhetoricians.

[2] Baldwin, *William Shakspere's Small Latine and Lesse Greeke*, vol. II, p. 51.

[3] *STC* 6401, sig. A2. Also in 1592, 1595 and 1599.

[4] *STC* 11049, sig. ¶5. For a full treatment of this subject, see 'The Complete Letter Writer in English 1568–1800', by Katherine G. Hornbeak, *Smith College Studies in Modern Languages*, vol. XV (Northampton, Mass., 1934).

[5] K. Lambley, *The Teaching and Cultivation of the French Language in England during Tudor and Stuart Times* (Manchester, 1920), p. 65; a most valuable work.

the true and most perfect way of pronouncinge of the Frenche Tongue.[1] This work appeared most probably, Miss Lambley thinks, in 1565, although no edition exists before 1573. The work was immensely popular, as was the succeeding one, entitled *The Frenche Littelton; a most easie, perfect and absolute way to learne the frenche tongue*,[2] which appeared in 1576. Both works were reprinted again and again well on into the next century. Holyband adopted the dialogue form, a familiar device, which enabled him to interest his students by the lively conversations which he invented, and which made the learning of French as painless and as free of tiresome grammatical hurdles as was possible.

Another Huguenot who settled in London was Jacques Bellot, who published *The French Grammar, or An Introduction orderly and Methodically by ready rules, playne preceptes and evident examples, touchinge the French Tongue* (1578). This was a more exclusively grammatical work than those of Holyband, but which the author claimed was 'not so leane and voide of fruite, but there is in it some taste. The bee gathereth honey from the smallest flowers, and so may the wise man from this small work'.[3] Bellot published other little books in French as helps to students, but none of them had the popularity of those by Holyband, whose only rival was G. De la Mothe, another refugee, who published about 1592 *The French Alphabet, teaching in a very short tyme by a most easie way, to pronounce French naturally, to reade it perfectly, to write it truely, and to speake it accordingly, Together with the Treasure of the French tung.*[4] The volume was evidently found to be useful, since it was reprinted several times in the next fifty years.

Other languages attracted less attention from the book trade. Italian and Spanish works were frequently translated, but little appeared in print to help those wanting to learn these languages. In 1550 William Thomas had published his *Princi-*

---
[1] *STC* 6748. [2] *STC* 6738.
[3] *STC* 1852, quoted from Lambley, *op. cit.* p. 158.
[4] The first extant edition is that of 1595, *STC* 6546.

pal Rules of the Italian Grammer, with a Dictionarie.[1] This was a well-written and well-arranged work, and was reprinted in 1562 and 1567. Holyband also concerned himself with Italian, and attempted to provide an elementary reader by printing the Italian and English texts *en face*, but he asks the reader first 'for the better understanding of the Italian phrase, to note certaine profitable rules touching the pronunciation of the same tongue, and after let him take a little paine in the Dialogues and familiar speeches, there following. Then let him repaire to ye History of Arnalt and Lucenda, in the reading wherof using a good discretion, he may attaine great profite.'[2] About the same time was published *An Italian Grammar written in Latin by Scipio Lentulo, and translated into English by H. Grantham* (1574). 'Such as it is, rudely attired with this Englishe habit', nevertheless the translator calls it 'a very necessary booke for all suche as are studious of the Italian tongue',[3] and his view seems to have been that of students, for it was reprinted in 1575 and again in 1587.

The first book printed in Spanish in England appears to have been that of Antonio de Corro, entitled *Reglas Gramaticales para aprender la lengua Española y Francesa*, printed at Oxford by J. Barnes in 1586, although some copies bear the imprint 'Paris'.[4] This was translated by his pupil John Thorius in 1590 under the title of *The Spanish Grammer, With Certeine Rules teaching both the Spanish and French tongues... With a Dictionarie adjoyned....*[5] It was probably this work that was referred to the next year by W. Stepney who commends the publication of a grammar and dictionary, and publishes himself *The Spanish Schoolemaster, Containing Seven Dialogues, according to every day in the weeke, and what is necessarie*

---

[1] *STC* 24020–2.
[2] *STC* 6758, *The Pretie and wittie Historie of Arnalt & Lucenda with certen rules and dialogues for the learner of the Italian tong* (1575). Reissued in 1597 as *The Italian Schoolmaister*, and again in 1608, 'revised and corrected by F.P. an Italian professor and teacher of the Italian tongue', from which my quotation is taken.
[3] *STC* 15468, sig. A2.   [4] *STC* 5789 and 5789a.   [5] *STC* 5790.

SPANISH TEXT BOOKS

everie day to be done.[1] Stepney believed that there was a great future for a knowledge of Spanish by Englishmen, and his book was twice reprinted. The same year saw the publication of *Bibliotheca Hispanica: Containing a Grammar, with a Dictionarie in Spanish, English, and Latine, gathered out of divers good Authours: very profitable for the studious of the Spanish toong*, compiled by Richard Percyvall,[2] who tells us that his work incorporates that of the physician Dr Thomas D'Oylie, and that he had the assistance of two Spanish gentlemen who had been taken as prisoners-of-war at the time of the Armada. This work was sufficiently popular to attract the attention of John Minsheu, a professional teacher of languages, who reissued it in 1599, 'now enlarged and amplified'. Another work by Percyvall appeared in the same year entitled *A Spanish Grammar, first collected and published by Richard Percivale Gent. Now augmented...by J. Minsheu*. This little book of 84 folio pages was dedicated to 'the Gentlemen Students of Grayes Inne'. It also contained *Pleasant and delightfull Dialogues in Spanish and English, profitable to the learner, and not unpleasant to any other Reader*.[3]

Little need be said about the polyglot phrase-books which circulated in England but were printed abroad. They seem to come from an Antwerp schoolmaster, Noel de Barlement, who wrote early in the sixteenth century, and whose work was enlarged from time to time by the addition of another language. In 1557 Edward Sutton entered a volume 'intituled Italian, Frynsche, Englesshe and Laten', and other editions of this book were entered in 1568 and 1578, but whether they were ever printed is not known, since they do not appear to be extant today.

4. Medicine

The production of medical and allied books was much greater after 1558 than in the previous half century. This increase is the more notable since it was effected in the teeth of a good deal of

[1] *STC* 23256. [2] *STC* 19619. [3] *STC* 19622.

opposition, which took two main forms. In the first place there were those who felt that the mysteries of the medical art were mysteries and should remain so. 'What a great detriment is this to the noble scyence of phisicke, that ignoraunte persons wyll enterpryse to medle wyth the ministracion of phisicke',[1] writes Andrew Borde; and many were of his view, or believed that the 'Secretes of phisicke ought not to be participated unto the common sorte, but onely knowne of such as be professors of the arte', as Leonard Mascall puts it.[2] For those who ignored views such as these trouble ensued, as we are told by the well-known surgeon, Thomas Gale, when he writes:

Since the first time that I beganne to sette out anie parte of this arte in English tongue, I have both susteined great displeasure, and also lost manie profites, of those which were in times past my speciall friendes, and the greatest matter that they have to saie against mee, is onelie that I goe about to make everiebodie cunning in the arte of medicine, with setting foorth of these my workes in the English tongue.[3]

It can be well understood, therefore, that the usual practice of the time, whereby writers put themselves under the 'protection' of a patron, certainly had some reason behind it so far as medical writers were concerned. In dedicating Gesner's *The newe Jewell of Health* to the Countess of Oxford, George Baker, its translator, and himself another outstanding surgeon, claimed that in so doing, 'it maye more easily bee defended against Sycophants and fault finders, because your wit, learning, and authoritee hath great force and strength in repressing the curious crakes of the envious and bleating Babes of Momus'.[4]

In mentioning the offence he was alleged to have committed in 'setting forth my workes in the English tongue', Thomas Gale touched on the other main obstacle that the old brigade sought to put in the way of those anxious to make medical works

---

[1] *STC* 3375, *The Breviary of Healthe* (1557), sig. A2ᵛ.
[2] *STC* 17977, *Prepositas his Practise* (1588), sig. A2.
[3] *STC* 11531, *Certaine Workes of Galens...Translated by T. Gale* (1586), sig. A2ᵛ.
[4] *STC* 11798 (1576), sig. *2ᵛ.

of repute more easily available. There had long been opposition to the writing of such things in the vernacular, but the case against this view had been vigorously stated by William Turner in 1551 when he declared that to translate into English the works of foreign writers could do no harm for, as he said, to their original readers they had been in the vernacular, and

if they gave no occasyon unto every olde wyfe to practyse Physike, then gyve I none. If they gave no occasyon of murther, then gyve I none. If they were no hynderers from the study of lyberall sciences, then am I no hynderer, wrytyng unto the English my countremen, an Englysh herball.[1]

Some opposition, however, continued, and writers were conscious of the suspicion that fell on them if they did not keep to the traditional Latin for their writings. The Latinists fought a losing battle, however, and although as late as 1588 John Read could indignantly ask: 'Why grutch they Chirurgerie should come foorth in English?'[2] the fight was really over, and as a result, almost as many works by foreign as by English authors were to be seen on the stalls, and the position held by these translations is indicated by the number of times that they were reprinted, so that foreign reprints actually exceeded the reprints of English writers. Among foreign authors whose writings were translated may be noted the following names: Alexis (Alessio of Piedmont), Franciscus Arcaeus, Bertholdus, Fioravanti, Gaebelkhover, Galen, Gesner, Goeurot, Guido de Chauliac, Guillemeau, Hermanni, John XXI, Lemnius, Pythagorus, Roesslin, Vasseus, J. de Vigo and others.

Reprints, indeed, are perhaps the most remarkable feature of the medical book trade at this time, and I estimate that many books, first published before 1558, were constantly in demand after that date, and indeed made up about one-third of the total output of medical works. The Elizabethans, in short, were

---

[1] *STC* 24365, *A new Herball*, sig. A3ᵛ.
[2] *STC* 723, F. Arcaeus, *A most excellent...method of curing woundes...* (1588), trans. by J. Read, sig. A2ᵛ.

living on their past, and this is particularly well illustrated by the fact that a number of old-established works still remained in demand well into the second part of the century. For example, Elyot's *Castel of Helth*, first published in 1539, called for six editions before 1558, and then ran to seven more by 1595. Roesslin's *Byrth of Mankynde* (1540) is even more remarkable: its three editions of the earlier period were surpassed by a demand for six more later. Goeurot's *Regiment of life* (1544) ran to five editions in each period, and other striking examples could be given. None of these works was less than sixteen years old when it was reprinted, and there was a demand for years for works such as *The Treasure of Pore men*, which had first been printed about 1526.[1]

It might well be thought (and indeed the title-pages of many of these books would give support to such a view), that these ancient editions had been revised from time to time before they were reissued. The 1571 edition of Elyot's *Castel of Helth* says that it is 'corrected and in some places augmented'— a statement which might encourage a prospective buyer to think he was obtaining a recently revised work, if he were unaware that these words had first appeared to assist the sale of the work some twenty years before. Goeurot's *Regiment of life*, reprinted in 1560, claims to be 'newly corrected and enlarged'—but the edition of 1544 (the earliest recorded) says just the same. The *Schola Salernitana* of 1575 claims to be 'Ammended, augmented and diligently imprinted', which is exactly what the title-page of the 1541 edition had also claimed. Clearly these books had survived, not because of amendment or the like, but because their pages gave help and comfort to the ordinary person on matters of health or hygiene such as he could understand.

It is against this background that we have to view the output as a whole. It was considerable, both in size and in variety.[2]

---

[1] *STC* 24199–24207.
[2] Much information relative to this section will be found in W. S. C. Copeman, *Doctors and Disease in Tudor Times* (1960), to which I am indebted.

An average of three to four books a year was maintained, and I suspect that it was greater than this, since the number of editions of some of these comparatively small works that have not survived must be very considerable. Not all were small, however: *The Secretes of Alexis* ran to nearly nine hundred quarto pages, and this was exceeded by *The whole worke of J. Vigo* (1586). On the other hand, *This Lytell Practyce* of the same writer only ran to thirty-two octavo pages in the 1564 edition, while Elyot's *Castel of Helth* was equally small and easily carried in the pocket. Occasionally the stalls saw finely produced folios, principally intended for the use of professionals which, furnished with plates and erudite information, were a far cry from the little manuals intended to attract the ordinary public.

Here, as we have seen before, the book-trade cast its net widely in its search for custom. A great many books, such as a small thirty-two page octavo by Nostradamus, dealt briefly with pestilence, fevers, catarrh, and other common ills, and most of them contained recipes for their treatment. These and similar works appealed to the ordinary man and woman as useful first-aid manuals, so much so that the more scrupulous of authors were concerned to think that their works might be used in place of a doctor's advice, and said that this should only be done 'in tyme of necessity when no learned Phisicion is at hande, or els conferryng wyth some learned man, and usynge hys councel, mynister the thinges herin conteyned'.[1] An even clearer declaration of the audience the writer hoped to reach is made by Andrew Borde, whose *Breviary of Healthe* (1552) was four times reprinted in Elizabeth's reign, and who writes: 'I do not wryte these bokes for learned men, but for simple and unlerned men that they may the better have some knowledge to ease themselves in theyr diseases and infirmities.'[2]

[1] *STC* 14652a, John XXI, *Treasury of healthe* [1550], translated by Humphrey Lloyd, sig. A3.
[2] *STC* 3375 (1557), sig. R1ᵛ.

Experience had shown the book-trade that there was a steady demand for simple books setting out the basic rules of hygiene and dietary, or making 'observacions and preceptes very necessary and profitable to the prolonging of life', and also that there was a continuous sale for the works of the best sellers of the first half of the century, as the works of Elyot, Goeurot and Borde could bear witness. To meet the demand for new books of this type the presses turned out a series of books by William Bullein: *Bulleins Bulwarke of defence againste all Sicknes, Sornes, and woundes* (1562),[1] or another dealing with the *Governement of Healthe...Reduced into the forme of a Dialogue for the better understanding of thunlearned* (1558).[2] These and works such as those on *The Haven of Health* (1584),[3] by Thomas Cogan, and *An Hospitall for the diseased*, by T. C.,[4] did much to give the public what they wanted—that was books of a reasonable size which they could understand and which they could turn to in times of trouble. The booksellers were better judges than some authors, such as Bullein, who feared that his work might be judged by many to be 'pouring water in the sea, where aye plentie is'.[5]

Other works assured of a popular sale were books of recipes such as the *Secrets* of Alexis, or books on distilling of 'Water, Oyles, Balmes, Quintessences', or first-aid manuals such as *A Rich Store-house or Treasury for the Diseased. Now set foorth for the great benefit and comfort of the poorer sort of people that are not of abilitie to go to the Physitions*.[6] Less generally in demand were the treatises which dealt with specific complaints, such as pleurisy, fistula, syphilis. These and a number of others are witness to the book-trade's endeavours to give the public what they wanted.

More technical manuals were also available, and were far more common than they had been in the earlier part of the century. To help those anxious to become really proficient as

[1] *STC* 4033 (1562).
[2] *STC* 4039 [1558].
[3] *STC* 5478 (1584).
[4] *STC* 4304 (1579).
[5] *STC* 4039 [1558], sig. A2.
[6] *STC* 23606 (1596).

SURGICAL MANUALS

surgeons a number of books were written, either in English or translated into English, since the 'unlatined Surgeon', or the 'Young Student' was constantly in the minds of writers, and a really remarkable supply of surgical manuals in particular was forthcoming. Not all of them were by contemporary authors, since even in the middle of the century medieval texts were in demand. Galen's *Methodus Medendi* was a set book for candidates taking the examination of the newly founded United Company of Barber Surgeons (1540). Part of this had been translated by Dr Caius, although it does not seem to have been printed, so that the way was open for the translation of Thomas Gale which he published in 1586.[1] Another well-known work, this time by a famous medieval surgeon, Guido de Chauliac, was also prescribed, and was translated in 1542 under the title of *The questyonary of cyrurygens*, and was reissued as *Guydos Questions newly corrected* in 1579.[2] Then there was *The most excellent workes of Chirurgerye*,[3] by Joannes de Vigo, recommended by Dr Robert Record as 'most surest for you to follow in the arte of surgery'—also a set book—first translated by Bartholomew Traheron in 1543, and reprinted three times in the next forty years. Candidates in the latter part of the century were examined on the writings of great contemporary surgeons, such as John Banister's *A needefull, new, and necessarie treatise of Chyrurgerie* (1575).[4] They also studied his book entitled *The Historie of Man, sucked from the sappe of the most approved Anathomistes...compiled in most compendious forme...for the utilitie of all godly Chirurgions* (1578),[5] which has been called 'the textbook of surgery until the modern period'. His colleague, William Clowes, besides publishing *A prooved practise for all young chirurgians* (1588),[6] was also the author of a number of other successful surgical works. Most

[1] *STC* 11531, *Certaine Workes of Galens called Methodus Medendi* (1586).
[2] *STC* 12468–9. Edited by G. Baker.
[3] *STC* 24720–3 and *STC* 24724–6 for *Vigo's Lytell Practyce*, published in 1535?, 1550? and 1564.
[4] *STC* 1360. [5] *STC* 1359.
[6] *STC* 5444. For other works by Clowes, see *STC* 5442–8.

important of all perhaps was Thomas Gale's *Certaine workes of Chirurgerie* (1563),[1] in three parts; the first in dialogue form dealt with the Institution of a Surgeon; the second was a manual of surgery, while the third dealt with the treatment of gunshot wounds. With works such as these to study, the apprentices of the Barber-Surgeons Company of London had much to be grateful for.

One of the most remarkable features about the surgical literature of this period was the number of works by foreign writers which appeared on the stalls. Men could buy translations of Lanfranc (1565), Guido de Chauliac (1579), J. de Vigo (1571), J. Guillemeau (1597), L. Fioravanti (1580), C. Galen (1586), and C. Schilander (1596), all of whom had written manuals of surgery. At the same time there were translations of works which dealt with specific complaints, such as F. Arcaeus on the cure of wounds (1588), Vesalius on anatomy (1559), and E. Roesslin on midwifery (1540).

By the end of the century therefore the booksellers had done much to put medicine on a better footing than it was in 1565 when John Halle had asserted that

where as there is one Chirurgien, that was apprentice to his arte, or one phisicien, that hath travayled in the true studie, and exercise of phisique: there are tenne, that are presumptious smearers, smaterers, or abusers of the same: yea, Smythes, Cutlers, Carters, Coblars, Copers, Coriars of lether, Carpenters, and a great rable of women: which (as the moste excellent Galen feared to happen) forsake their handicraftes, and for filthy lucre abuse phisick and chirurgerie.[2]

Connected to some extent with the books setting forth rules of health and giving recipes and directions as to diet were the herbals.[3] At first these were comparatively small books without

[1] *STC* 11529. Reprinted in 1586, and issued in the same year as part of J. de Vigo's *Whole Works*.
[2] *STC* 15192, Lanfrancus, *A most excellent and learned woorke of Chirurgerie* (1565), sig. *3.
[3] See, for example, *STC* 18060, P. Moore, *The hope of health, wherein is conteined a goodlie regiment of life: as medicine, good diet, and the goodly vertues of sondrie herbes, doen by P.M.* (1565).

illustrations, of which the one generally known as 'Banke's herbal' in its various forms was the best known, and had run to some fifteen editions before it came to an end in 1561. A much more ambitious work which first appeared in 1526 was a translation from the French, a folio volume of 372 pages entitled *The grete herball*. This had many illustrations in its first two editions, and was published again in 1539 and 1561 without them. The only other work in circulation early in the reign of Elizabeth was *The Booke of Secretes of Albertus Magnus, of the vertues of herbes*. This little book was continually reprinted from 1549 onwards, but its value can be guessed from the frank statement in the 1595 edition, which reads: 'Use this booke for thy recreation (as thou art wont to use the book of Fortune), for assuredly there is nothing herein promised but to further thy delight.'[1]

Up to about 1550 most herbals were of little consequence, since they were a survival to some extent from medieval times, and the earliest herbals were printed with little additional matter straight from manuscripts which contained information going back through the centuries. The first work published in England which really broke new ground was the work of William Turner, *A new Herball*, of which two parts were published in 1551 and 1562, while the third part was not forthcoming until 1568. Turner's contempt for earlier herbals was considerable: they were, he said, 'full of unlearned cacographies and falselye naminge of herbes'. His work really put the study of plants on a new footing, for by his personal observation, his accurate descriptions and his systematic survey, he raised the English herbal to a hitherto unknown level.[2]

The herbalists of the second half of the century had a high standard to keep, and the day of the cheap, ill-informed little

[1] *STC* 263, sig. A1.
[2] For an account of William Turner's scientific achievements, see C. E. Raven, *English Naturalists from Neckam to Ray* (Cambridge, 1947), pp. 48–137, and for the early herbals in general, see my *English Books and Readers, 1475 to 1557* (Cambridge, 1952), pp. 98 ff.

book was over. The few herbals that were printed were for the most part large and well-illustrated volumes, and also for the most part translations. First came the work of the well-known Flemish herbalist, Matthew de l'Obel (from whom the lobelia takes its name). This was printed by Thomas Purfoot, but being in Latin had only a limited audience.[1] Greater success came to Henry Lyte, who translated the herbal of another Flemish herbalist, Rembert Dodoens, which by reason of its arrangement, and its descriptions of the various species, their habitats, and their medicinal virtues, as well as by the increase in the number of plants described was a great advance on the work of Turner, and after its first publication in 1578 was again reprinted in 1586, 1595 and in 1619.[2]

The popular herbal of the period, however, was that of John Gerard, well known for twenty years as superintendent of the gardens of Lord Burleigh, both in London and in Hertfordshire, and also for his own garden in Holborn. His folio volume, *The Herball or Generall Historie of Plantes* (1597), ran to 1464 pages and included no less than 1800 woodcuts of the various plants he described.[3] 'Some have solicited me,' he writes, 'first by my pen, and after by the Presse to make my labors common', and he does so, for he believes that it will be 'a ready Introduction to that excellent art of Simpling, which is neither so base and comtemptible as perhaps the English name may seem to insinuate.' His friends warmly commended the work in the fashion of the day, both in verse and prose, George Baker claiming that 'to this day never any in what language soever did the like, first for correcting those faults in so many hundreds places being falsely named, mistaken the one for the other, and then the pictures of a great number of plants now newly cut'. Not only this: 'Manifold will be the use both to the Phisitian and others.... This booke above many others will suite with the moste, because it both plentifully administrateth knowledge...and doth it also with a familiar and

---

[1] *STC* 19595, *Stirpium Adversaria Nova*...(1570-1).
[2] *STC* 6984-7.   [3] *STC* 11750.

pleasing taste to every capacitie', writes Dr Stephen Bredwell to the Reader.[1] The Reader concurred, and the book was a success. In the meanwhile, Gerard was aware that he was taking credit undeserved, since in fact much of the work was not original, but a translation of the *Pemptades*[2] (1583) of Rembert Dodoens, which had been translated before his death by a Dr Priest. However, this was not known at the time, and those interested were glad to get hold of so useful a volume, which held the field until the appearance of Parkinson's *Paradisi in sole* in 1629.[3] Even so, the publisher thought it worth while to commission a new and enlarged edition of Gerard, which was made and published in 1636. In this the Editor, Thomas Johnson, revealed the true facts concerning Gerard's work, and pleaded on his behalf that 'his chief commendation was that out of a prepense good will to the public advancement of this knowledge, he endeavoured to perform therein more than he could well accomplish, which was partly through want of sufficient learning'.[4]

5. *Information*

The growth of literacy in this period is again shown in the increased demand for works of information. It was clearly in the interests of the book-trade to do what it could to meet such a demand, and accordingly we find works of all sizes, destined for very different audiences, on the stalls. And once again, as was seen in the provision of books on the law or on medicine, men were still living on the past. Works of information, such as Fitzherbert's treatises on *Husbandry* and *Surveying*, were reprinted to the end of the century without much alteration, although they were both first printed about 1523.

This reliance on the past is strikingly illustrated by the re-issuing in 1582 of the only encyclopaedia in English available

---

[1] *STC* 11752 (1636), sig. ¶7ᵛ.
[2] R. Dodoens, *Stirpium historiae pemptades sex, sive libri xxx*. Antwerp (1583).
[3] *STC* 19300.   [4] 11752, sig. ¶¶¶i.

to the Elizabethans. This was the *De proprietatibus rerum* of Bartholomew Anglicus, translated into English late in the fourteenth century by John Trevisa, and printed by Wynkyn de Worde in 1495, and in an improved form by Thomas Berthelet in 1535. In 1582 Thomas East put out a folio edition of 854 pages in double columns, entitled *Batman Uppon Bartholome... newly corrected, enlarged and amended: with such Additions as are requisite, unto every severall Booke.*[1] The editor was Stephen Batman, 'Professor in Divinity and chaplain to the Bishop of London', who in his address to the reader says he has taken account of the writings of fairly recent authors, but as a matter of fact the additions are a very small part of the whole, and the work remains a vast repository of medieval lore covering subjects as diverse as the nature of the angels, the properties of air or of water, of beasts and their qualities, or of the conditions of a good servant.

Large volumes such as this are not characteristic of the books produced to inform or instruct, which were generally octavos or smaller sizes, seldom running to more than 150–200 pages. Books on farming and agriculture may serve as an example. As already mentioned, two works by John Fitzherbert were popular enough to call for several reprints in Elizabeth's reign: *Husbandry*, seven times printed before 1560, called for four more editions by 1598, while its companion volume *Surveying*, also eight times printed by about 1555, was reprinted in 1567 and 1587(?). The treatise on husbandry is admirably practical, and to this, no doubt, it owed its long life, for men found Fitzherbert's advice (say) on how 'to carry out donge or mucke and to sprede it', with its knowledge of special practices 'used in the farther syde of Darbyshyre, called Scaresdale, Halomshyre, and so northwarde towarde Yorke and Ryppon', just as valuable at the end of the century as it had been at the beginning. It was not merely an author's vanity that caused Fitzherbert to write towards the end of his treatise of it as 'a shorte information for a yonge gentyl-man,

[1] *STC* 1538.

that intendeth to thryve. I avyse hym to gette a copy of this presente boke, and to rede it frome the begynnynge to the endynge...and by reason of ofte readyng, he maye waxe perfyte what shulde doone at all seasons'.[1] A man who took Fitzherbert's advice had an invaluable handbook in *Husbandry*.

As for *Surveying*, it had a more limited interest, but a very practical one: 'to thentent that the lordes, the freeholders nor theyr heires shulde not be disherited, nor have their landes loste, nor imbeseld, nor encroched by one from another'. It sets out methodically how a manor should be 'surveyed and viewed, butted and bounded on every parte, that it may be knowen for ever whose every parcel thereof was, at the makyng of this boke'. It contained useful models for the preparation of documents, and much historical information and advice on procedure in manorial courts. It will thus be seen that it was of great value to all landowners of any size, and lost little of its value by the passage of time.[2]

The Elizabethans can take credit for producing one outstanding work on husbandry—*A hundreth good pointes of husbandrie* (1557),[3] written by Thomas Tusser and twice reprinted before it was enlarged to *Five hundreth points of good husbandry united to as many of good huswiferie*... (1573), and reprinted no less than eleven times before the end of the century.[4] The secret of its success lay in its gossipy, commonsense, practical appeal to men and women all over the country. It is mostly in four-lined stanzas, taking the reader month by month through the farmer's year, digressing at times to discuss varieties of soil and what they will grow best, children's education or the menu for feast days. Edition after edition changed as Tusser's experience grew, but Southey's description of him as a 'good, honest, homely, useful old rhymer', sums up the man and the reason for his continued appeal to his age.

[1] *STC* 10994–11004.
[2] *STC* 11005–15.
[3] *STC* 24372.
[4] *STC* 24375–86.

For those requiring something more scholarly, Barnaby Googe translated the work of Conrad Heresbach of Cleves: *Foure Bookes of Husbandry...Conteyning the whole arte and trade of Husbandry, Gardening, Graffing and planting* (1577).[1] Googe expressly says that he has no intent to deface or darken the enterprise of Fitzherbert or Tusser, and the work with its constant reference to the ancients such as Pliny, Varro, Palladius and others lives in a world far removed from that of Tusser. It was popular, however, and was reprinted four times by 1600, and twice later before 1640.

Dr Louis B. Wright has suggested that 'one can be reasonably sure' that the popularity of the works mentioned above, and of others discussed later in this chapter, was connected with the fact 'that many a London merchant, having made his money in trade and invested in a country place, was buying the books which described methods of leading successfully a rural life'.[2]

There was certainly a considerable market for such books, among the most popular being the works of Thomas Hill 'Londoner', who was a great provider of handbooks on a number of topics. The most sought after of these were two works on gardening, and the title-page of one of these will explain the nature of these books: *The proffitable Arte of Gardening, now the third time set fourth: to which is added much necessarie matter, and a number of secretes* [recipes] *with the Physick helpes belonging to eche herbe... To this annexed two Treatises, the one entituled The marveilous Government, propertye & benefit of the Bees, with the rare secretes of the honny & the waxe. And the other, the yerely conjectures, meete for husbandmen to knowe* (1568).[3] Hill completed this work by adding in 1574 'a treatise of the Arte of graffing and planting of trees'. Hill, like Heresbach, made much use of earlier authors, and gives a

[1] *STC* 13196.
[2] L. B. Wright, *Middle-Class Culture in Elizabethan England* (Chapel Hill, N.C., 1935), p. 565 n. 29.
[3] *STC* 13491. The first recorded edition is *STC* 13490 (March 1563). Hill's other work on gardening was *The gardeners labyrinth, STC* 13485 (1577).

formidable list of them (perhaps as guarantees of his trustworthiness) at the beginning of his books. Not that he felt himself to be nothing but a purveyor of other men's wares, for he claims that 'I have performed in such sorte, as the like hitherto hath not been published in the English tung'.[1]

The grafting and planting of trees was obviously a matter of interest to many, and besides Heresbach's and Hill's treatises already mentioned, Leonard Mascall translated in 1572 *A Boke of the Arte and maner, howe to plante and graffe all sortes of trees....*[2] This was a practical handbook of some 124 quarto pages, well organized, with a 'table to find out quickly all general parties afore mentioned', and called for five reprints by 1596.

Two works of a more general agricultural nature came from the pen of Leonard Mascall. The title of the first sufficiently displays its contents. It reads: *The first Booke of Cattell; Wherein is shewed the government of Oxen, Kine Calves, and how to use Bulles, and other cattell to the yoke, and sell; with remedies. The seconde booke intreating of the government of horses, gathered by L.M. The third booke intreateth of the ordering of sheepe and goats, hogs and dogs; with such remidies to help most diseases, as may chaunce unto them.*[3] This work was popular and there were at least eight reprints by 1630. Mascall also put together another work entitled *The Husbandlye ordring and Governmente of Poultrie* (1581). Mainly a translation from the French, Mascall says that 'poulterie and other foule is a good thing for the common wealthe, and specially to them that are housekeepers, as well for the Gentlemen as the husbandemen, and to further the mayntainaunce of the same I have taken some paynes therein... for such government thereof as hath not here before bene written or revealed in our English tongue'.[4]

---

[1] *STC* 13497 (1608), sig. A 4. Hill also claims that his *Pleasaunt instruction of the parfit Ordering of Bees* is 'a thing very rare, and seldome seene in the Englishe tongue', *STC* 13491 (1568), Part 2, sig. A 3ᵛ. There was at least one other treatise on bees (1593), by E. Southerne, *STC* 22942.
[2] *STC* 17574.
[3] *STC* 17580 (1587). The title-page is quoted from the third edition of 1596.
[4] *STC* 17589, sig. A 3.

Although the books already mentioned say something about animal husbandry as well as about agriculture in general, it was not until about 1560 that a substantial book on horses appeared. In *The Arte of Ryding and Breaking Greate Horses*, Thomas Blundeville tells us how after attempting a straight translation from the Italian of Grisone, he decided to adapt the work freely as seemed best to him. There was need for such a work he felt, since good horsemen and good horses were most necessary if the realm was to be properly protected by efficient troops.[1] Blundeville's book was well received ('it pleased not onlie you [Lord Dudley] but also the most part of the Gentlemen of the Realme'), and this encouraged him to embark on a larger work entitled *The fower chiefyst offices belongyng to Horsemanshippe* (1565-6) in which he incorporated his first book with three others which set out to instruct the breeder, the horse-keeper and the farrier in their avocations 'as are of capacitie to conceive reason, and not to the ignorant sort, who have neither letters, judgment nor good understanding'. He confesses to a further aim, and tells his patron, Lord Dudley: 'Truely my chiefe intent is to instruct the Gentleman so that he may be able to judge both of the keeper and of the Ferrar, and to teach them their office (if need be) rather than be taught of them.'[2]

The markedly practical nature of Blundeville's writings may be gauged from some remarks in his *The order of curing horses disease* (1566) where he writes that the farrier's art

is so playnely taught, as every playne smith if he wil applie his minde therunto, may soone learne the same to his owne prayse and the great benefite of you Jentilmen that delighte to keepe good Horses, and to have them well shodde, and the rather through your good

---

[1] *STC* 3158. 'Very necessary for all Gentlemen, Souldyours, Servingmen and for any man that delighteth in a horse.' Blundeville returns to the necessity of keeping up the training of horses and horsemen for military purposes in the preface to his second work, *The fower chiefyst offices belongyng to Horsemanshippe*.

[2] *STC* 3152. My quotation comes from the edition of 1593, sig. P5^v.

instructions after that you have once red and well considered this booke, for I am sure that fewe or none of the countrey smithes can reade.[1]

He concludes his preliminary remarks with the words: 'I trust that thys my travell will cause such Ferrers as can reade and have some understanding already, to be more diligente in seeking after knowledge than they have bene heretofore.'[2]

No book seems to have rivalled that of Blundeville until 1593 when Gervase Markham published his *Discource of Horsmanshippe*, in which the breeding and riding of horses is 'more methodically sette downe than hath been heretofore', while Markham also included sections on cures for the diseases of horses, and how to choose, train and diet them.[3] If we add to these two outstanding writers two works mainly concerned with the art of riding, one from the Italian of Claudio Corte, *The Art of Riding* (1584), and another by Christopher Clifford, *The Schoole of Horsmanship* (1585), we shall have well-nigh completed the supply of books on this subject available to the Elizabethans.

Outdoor sports, which had been sadly neglected earlier (save for *The Book of Saint Albans*, *Toxophilus* and one or two minor works), received much better treatment in the second half of the century. Fishing, hunting, falconry and archery all were written about. Fishing, it is true, came off rather badly, for Leonard Mascall's *Booke of Fishing with Hooke & Line*[4] (1590) is little more than a rehash of a 'treatise of fyshynge with an angle' of 1496, but both hunting and hawking were handsomely treated by George Turberville in *The Noble Arte of Venerie or Hunting*[5] and also in his work *The Booke of Faulconrie or Hawking*. Turberville admits that the latter book is only a 'collection out of sundry Authors as well Italians, as

---

[1] *STC* 3159, sig. A2ᵛ.   [2] *Ibid*. sig. C1.
[3] *STC* 17346. There was evidently room for both Blundeville's and Markham's works, for Blundeville was reprinted five times by 1609, and Markham four times by 1606. The others were never reprinted.
[4] *STC* 17572.   [5] *STC* 24328 [1575].

French, from whome I have gathered some chiefe points of Falconerie to pleasure my Country men withall'.[1] It is a handbook for falconers and gives a very full description of the various kinds of hawks, their training, diet, etc. The work on hunting is again mainly a translation from the French authorities, adorned with many woodcuts 'wherein is handled and set out the Vertues, Natures, and Properties of fourteene sundrie Chases, together with the order and maner of how to Hunte and kill every one of them'. Both books were 'translated and collected for the pleasure of all Noblemen and Gentlemen'.

There were few books obtainable concerning other outdoor sports. Ascham's book on archery, first printed in 1545, was 'newlye perused' in 1571 and appeared again in 1589, and remained unchallenged as a practical guide on the subject.[2] Firearms, however, were becoming more and more the standard weapon, and the relative merits of the two arms in warfare were discussed and formed the subject of a number of books.[3] Pastimes such as bear-baiting, cock-fighting, swimming and fencing, all provoked the attention of a few writers, but it was not until the seventeenth century that any considerable number of books on sports and pastimes appeared.[4]

6. *Arithmetic, astronomy and popular science*

We have already seen the successful efforts that were made to write books in the vernacular so that they could reach a public ignorant of Latin or of the various European languages. A

[1] *STC* 24324 (1575), sig. A2ᵛ.
[2] *STC* 837–9. See also *STC* 21512, *A briefe treatise of the use of archerie* (1596).
[3] See, for example, *STC* 1542, H. Barwick, *A Breefe Discourse concerning the force of all manuall weapons* [1594?]; *STC* 22883, Sir J. Smythe, *Certain Discourses concerning...divers sorts of weapons* (1590).
[4] Bear-baiting was described in R. Laneham, *STC* 15191, *A letter...* [1575]; cock-fighting in *STC* 25768, G. Wilson, *The Commendation of Cockes and Cockfighting* (1607); swimming in *STC* 6839, E. Digby, *De Arte Natandi* (1587), trans. in 1595, and fencing in *STC* 12190, G. di Grassi, *True arte of defence* (1594); *STC* 21788, V. Saviolo, *His practise* (1595) and *STC* 22554, G. Silver, *Paradoxes of Defence* (1599).

similar effort may be observed in the fields of mathematics, astronomy and popular science. By a stroke of fortune, England possessed a popularizer of genius in Robert Record—a man of first-class mathematical ability with an equal skill as a teacher. In a series of works on arithmetic, geometry and astronomy, he set a standard no one else could quite rival, for in addition to his scientific knowledge and pedagogical skill he wrote in so clear an English, and used the method of question and answer so skilfully, that his books and influence were a dominating factor in mathematical thought and teaching for well over a generation.

In 1542 he had published his work *The Grounde of Artes; teachyng the Worke and Practise of Arithmetike, bothe in whole numbers and Fractions, after a more easier and exacter sorte than any like hath hitherto bin set foorth*,[1] and this work intended for 'the simple and ignorant' remained the most popular book of its kind for the next century, being reprinted again and again. It was followed by *The Whetstone of Witte, whiche is the seconde parte of Arithmetike*... (1557),[2] and by *The Pathway to Knowledg, containing the first principles of Geometrie, as they may moste aptly be applied unto Practise, bothe for Instrumentes Geometricall, and Astronomicall*... (1551).[3] The two latter works were not nearly so popular as *The Grounde of Artes* which held the field throughout the century, although in 1568 *The Well-spryng of Sciences, whiche teacheth the perfecte woorthe and practise of Arithmeticke*, written by Humphrey Baker, a noted teacher of arithmetic, was published. This work, according to the author, was 'beautified with moste necessarie rules and questions, not only profitable for Marchauntes, but also for all Artificers'. Baker had written an earlier arithmetic, he tells us, but has yielded to the importunities of his friends

to adde sum thinge more ther unto, and to amplifie the same. Which ernest and freindlye sute of theirs for extreame just causes seeming nedefull unto me, suerly I could in no wise deny. For when

[1] *STC* 20798. It was reprinted thirteen times by 1640.
[2] *STC* 20820.   [3] *STC* 20812. Twice reprinted by 1602.

I perceaved the inportunitye of certayne straungers...that they advanced and extolled themselves in open talk and writinges, that they had attained such knowledge and perfection in Arithmeticke, as no English man the like, truly me thought that the same report not only tended to the dispraise of our Countrymen in generall, but touched especially some others & me that had trauailed & written publiquely in the same facultye. For unto this same effecte they have of late painted the corners and postes in every place within this Citie with their peevishe billes, makinge promise and bearinge men in hande that they coulde teache the summe of that Science, in briefe Methode and compendious Rules, suche as before their arrivall have not bene taughte within this Realme.[1]

The book was a great success, and survived with little change until the end of the next century.

Apart from two works invoking the use of verse as an aid to students,[2] the only serious competitor came late in the century in the person of Thomas Masterson, who in 1592 published *Thomas Masterson his first booke of Arithmeticke. Shewing the ingenious inventions, and figurative operations, by which to calculate the true solution or answeres of arithmeticall questions...verie necessarie for all men.* Masterson says that his book is designed to help traders and merchants, and for this reason he writes, 'I have placed needefull questions, applied to paying, receiving, buying, selling, bartering...'.[3] Notwithstanding his care in this respect, and his claim that 'the Art of numbers is so common and necessarie in all actions of this life, that it is almost impossible to find any part of them which can be exercised without the use thereof',[4] his work was not successful and only three of a projected six volumes of his arithmetic were ever published.

These comparatively simple works paved the way for others in which the mysteries of the spheres and the astrolabe, the use of the compass and the theory of magnetism, the art and craft

---

[1] *STC* 1210a, sig. A6 (1574).
[2] *STC* 12201, D. Gray, *The store-house of Breuite in woorkes of Arithmetike* (1577) and *STC* 13480, T. Hill, *The Arte of vulgar arithmeticke* (1600).
[3] *STC* 17648, Book II, sig. E2.   [4] *Ibid.* Book I, sig. A3.

of mensuration and of surveying, and the steadily advancing ideas in astronomical thought were all expressed in English, and indeed in many cases by men lacking in any advanced form of education, but who had been able to benefit from the writings of men such as John Dee and Leonard Digges, so that in time they could make their own contributions to works on navigation and magnetism. They were greatly helped by the determination of some of the leading scientists to explain their ideas in English. Digges announced in 1591 that his future work, 'if I publish the same at all, I doe constantly resolve to doe it onely in my Native Tongue', and, as we have seen, all Record's works were in English, as indeed were most of those of Digges. Their students and followers had no doubts about the help given to them by works in the vernacular. Robert Norman writes:

For albeit they have not the use of the Greeke and Latine tongues, to searche the varietie of Aucthours in these artes, yet have they in English for Geometrie Euclides Elements, with absolute demonstrations: and for Arithmeticke *Record's* workes, both his first and second part: and diverse others, both in English & in other vulgar languages, that have written of them, which bookes are sufficient to ye industrious Mechanician to make him perfect and ready in those sciences.[1]

These writers in their turn wrote for men of limited book learning who were glad to get advice and instruction concerning the tools of their trade. Hence it is that William Borough dedicates his *Discours of the Variation of the Cumpas* (1581), 'to the Trauelers, Seamen and Mariners of Englande',[2] while Robert Norman and William Bourne have similar readers in mind.[3]

The practical effects of the teaching of the professionals may be illustrated in many ways, of which we may deal briefly with

[1] *STC* 18647, R. Norman, *The new attractive* (1581), sig. B1ᵛ.
[2] *STC* 3389.
[3] *STC* 18647 and *STC* 3422, W. Bourne, *A Regiment for the Sea* [1574]; ed. by E. G. R. Taylor.

one topic as an example. The study of mensuration and of the art of surveying was set out by Leonard Digges in *A Geometrical Practise, named Pantometria* (1571), which may be described as a 'full introduction to surveying, range-finding and other uses of mathematical instruments',[1] and in an earlier work *A boke named Tectonicon briefely shewynge the exacte measurynge all maner lande* (1562), which Digges calls 'a treasure unto the Masons, Carpenters, Landmeaters, correcting their old errours wrongfully reckened of them as infallible grounds, teaching faithfully, sufficiently, and very briefly, the true mensuration of all maner land, timber, stone, bord, glass...'.[2]

The exact measurement of distances also concerned military men, who turned to the mathematicians for help. The most important book on military mathematics was written by Thomas Digges, mustermaster general of the English forces in the Low Countries. In his dedication to the Earl of Leicester, Digges says that he has long been engaged in making mathematics available in a practical form, and mentions works on navigation, naval construction, dialling, fortification and ballistics either begun or ready for the press 'had not the Infernall Furies, envying such his Felicitie and happie Societie with his Mathematicall Muses, for many yeares so tormented him with Lawe Brables that he hath bene enforced to discontinue these his delectable studies'.[3] In this work, after setting out such arithmetical knowledge as was 'requisite for the profession of a Soldiour', Digges turns to the application of mathematical methods to problems of fortifications and ballistics, etc. The other outstanding work of this nature was a translation of *Three Bookes of Colloquies concerning the Arte of Shooting in great and small pieces of Artillerie* (1588), written by Niccolò Tartaglia, with an appendix in which the translator

[1] STC 6858. The quotation is from Taylor, *Mathematical Practitioners of Tudor and Stuart England*, p. 320.
[2] STC 6864, *A Prognostication*...(1576), sig. [χ2ᵛ].
[3] STC 6848, *An Arithmeticall Militare Treatise, named Stratioticos* (1579), sig. A2. The work was commenced by his father, L.D.

Cyprian Lucar has added much additional material gathered from many authors, enriched with many plates and tables.[1]

'Astrology is the foolish daughter of a wise mother, Astronomy', wrote Kepler, and the foolish daughter found many friends among the Elizabethans. Judicial astrology, as it was called, that is the foretelling of human affairs by the study of celestial bodies, was widely practised: eminent scientists, among them John Dee, professed astrology, and their advice was much sought after by those rich enough to pay for it.[2] At the same time a minority were sceptical: 'As for your Astrology, it is thought of many better unknown than known.'[3]

All this is reflected in books which appeared from time to time often as the result of some *cause célèbre* or public disturbance. In 1561, for example, the practices of Francis Coxe led to his arrest 'being accused of certayne sinistral & Divelish Artes', for which 'with vii mor', he was condemned to stand in the Pillory in Cheapside there to declare his recantation of what he had professed, and a few days later this was published by John Awdeley. At the end of his recantation he declared that

As a true declaracion of my unfayned repentaunce in these Divelish practices, I have caused this my Retractacion to be put in print, to have it openly published to all sorts of People. Purposing (by Gods helpe) within these fewe dayes to set forth a small peice of woorke to the utter defasing of those divelish sciences, with the declaration of the horrible practises and deathes of such as have used those Diabolical Artes, which (as I trust) shall fear all other to practise the lyke.[4]

---

[1] *STC* 23689. In the previous year there appeared *STC* 3420, W. Bourne, *The Arte of shooting in great Ordnaunce*.

[2] See C. Camden, 'Astrology in Shakespeare's Day', *Isis*, vol. XIX (1932), pp. 50ff.

[3] *STC* 6275, C. Dariot, *A breefe Introduction to the Astrologicall Judgement of the Starres* [1583?], sig. A2ᵛ.

[4] *STC* 5951, F. Coxe, *The unfained retractation of F. Coxe* (1561), quoted from Herbert, *Ames' Typographical Antiquities*, vol. II, 885.

He was as good as his word, and later that year published *A short treatise declaringe the detestable wickednesse of magicall sciences, as Necromancie, Conjurations of spirites, Curiouse Astrologie and suche lyke*. This was probably produced under duress, and is characterized by the *Dictionary of National Biography* as being 'a grovelling and panic-stricken pamphlet'.

A really serious attack on judicial astrology had already been made by William Fulke, who published a Latin tract entitled *Antiprognosticon contra inutiles astrologorum Predictiones* (1560), which four months later was also put out in an English translation, 'whereunto is added a short treatise in English, as well for the better subversion of that faigned arte, as also for the better understanding of the common people'.[1] This was the most serious attack on judicial astrology in Elizabethan times, and the publication of Calvin's *Admonicion against astrology iudiciall and other curiosities, that raigne now in the world* [1561][2] was perhaps scarcely necessary.

Not that anything writers such as Fulke or Calvin could say seems to have had much influence, as a work translated from the French during the next year showed. *Arcandam*, as it was called, purported 'to fynd the fatal desteny, constellation, complexion and naturall inclination of every man and childe by his byrth; with an addition of Phisiognomie very delectable to reade'.[3] Twenty years later Claude Dariot was asserting that 'Judicial astrology was most necessary and most avaylable: expressing very certenly and perticularly the complexion of the body, & the nature of the infirmity, & consequently the causes of the same'.[4]

At the same time there was another crop of books for or against astrology, occasioned by the predicted conjunction of Saturn and Jupiter which was thought to presage great danger. Richard Harvey, brother of Gabriel, led off with

---

[1] *STC* 11420, sig. A 1.   [2] *STC* 4372.
[3] *STC* 724 [1562], sig. A 1.
[4] *STC* 6275, *A breefe Introduction to the Astrologicall Judgement of the Starres* [1583]. Part II, sig. A 2.

ASTROLOGY

An Astrological Discourse vpon the great and notable Coniunction of the two superiour Planets, Saturne & Iupiter, which shall happen the 28 day of April, 1583.[1] This was written and published Harvey tells us, 'partely to supplie that is wanting in common Prognostications: and partely by prædiction of mischiefes ensuing, either to breed some endevour of prevention by foresight, so farre as lyeth in us: or at leastwise, to arme vs with pacience beforehande'. This discourse, Dr McKerrow says, 'seems to have awakened immense interest, and, among the vulgar at least, a great deal of perturbation', and it is of some interest to note that when a second edition was called for later in the same year the passages in Latin were all translated into English.[2]

Harvey was answered by Thomas Heth in *A manifest and apparent confutation of an astrological discourse lately published to the discomfort of the weake and simple sort* [1583].[3] Heth did not differ greatly from Harvey as to the date of the conjunction, but thought that the result would not be the catastrophe that Harvey feared. He was supported by Henry Howard, Earl of Northampton, in *A defensative against the poyson of supposed Prophesies: not hitherto confuted by the penne of any man...very needefull to be published at this time, considering the late offence which grew by most palpable and grosse errours in Astrology* (1583).[4]

Harvey returned again to the fray in 1588 when he attempted to answer 'the horrible threatenings and menaces peremptorilly denounced against the kingdoms and states of the world, this present famous yeare, 1588, supposed the Great, Woonderfull and Fatall yeare of our Age'. He laments

how notoriously and perilously the world hath continually from time to time beene abused, and in sort cosened with supposed prophesies, and counterfet soothsayings, devised either for unknowen, or for ungracious, and lewed causes: intending at least

---

[1] *STC* 12910.
[2] R. B. McKerrow, *The Works of Thomas Nashe* (1910), vol. v, p. 167.
[3] *STC* 13255. [4] *STC* 13858.

Comicall sturs [i.e. comets] but commonly fostering tragicall commotions, not onely forraine histories, both old and new, in all languages...but also our owne British and English Chronicles.... beside a number of other famous books, and many old smokie paperbookes, are very copious and over plentiful in affoording examples of this covenous and imposturall kinde. Amongst which notwithstanding, no examples ever were, or are more dangerous, and jeoperdous, than those which daily experience both in England, and in every other state or Commonwealth of the world, eftsoones suggesteth; upon every new occasion, strange accident, perilous exigence, or whatsoever other notable occurrence, againe and againe revived, by way of fresh, and currant matter to serve present turnes, and to feede the working humour of busie and tumultuous heads, continually affecting some innovation, or other. But of all the residue, what comparable to the terrible pretended prophesie, even now notoriously in *Esse*, concerning the imagined, mightie and wonderfull casualties and hurliburlies of the present yeere 1588. In which respect of so universall fame, I was earnestly mooved, and importuned...to undertake some little travell in examining the naturall causes, and artificiall reasons of the said supposed prophesie.[1]

The 'many old smokie paperbookes' which Harvey mentions are unknown to us now, for they seem not to have survived. Probably they were small pamphlets of an ephemeral nature, which spread alarm and encouraged the belief in the powerful influence of the stars, for it was common belief, as Leonard Digges puts it, that 'Cometes signifie corruption of the ayre. They ar signes of earthquakes, of warres, chaunging of kingdomes, great dearth of corne, yea a common death of man and beast.'[2]

Lastly, something must be said about the 'poor man's practical Astronomy', as the almanacs and prognostications have been called. *The Short-Title Catalogue* gives the names of some 140 authors and compilers of these works, while Mr Bosanquet has calculated that there were at least 600 books of this nature published by 1600, and this is certainly an underestimate. By the time of Elizabeth the almanac, calendar and

---

[1] *STC* 12908, *A Discoursive Probleme concerning Prophesies*, sig. A 4.
[2] *STC* 6860, *A Prognostication of right good effect* (1555), p. 5.

prognostication were issued in one pamphlet, to be used for a time and then thrown away. Such as have survived have often done so in a torn and fragmentary form—their soiled and battered pages testifying to their sometime popularity.

In time a rather more substantial booklet was evolved which acted as a perpetual prognostication. Erra Pater, Leonard Digges and Richard Grafton may be mentioned as the outstanding providers of this sort of book, and their productions in various forms were printed and reprinted throughout the reign. To take one example: Richard Grafton in 1571 published *A litle treatise conteyning many proper Tables and rules: very necessary for the use of al men.* It contained first of all the Calendar with the Saints' Days, 'not because all are Saints', but because it is customary and useful in dating deeds and in finding the dates of fairs and markets, etc. There followed the Almanac, Tables of Leap Years; Phases of the Moon; the dates of Easter and other movable feasts; the names of the Colleges and Halls of the Universities; and at what time to purge and to let blood.[1]

The usefulness of these Elizabethan 'Whitakers' is obvious, and it is no wonder that in their various forms they were so popular, or that many booksellers published their own version 'referred to the meridian of Chester', or useful 'generally for all England, but especially for the meridian of this honourable citie of London'.[2]

7. *Geography*

The first half of the sixteenth century saw few books in English dealing with geographical matters, either in the form of works designed for seamen, such as Pierre Garcie's *The rutter of the sea*, translated by Robert Copland [1555?], or in accounts

[1] *STC* 12153, sig. A2.
[2] For a detailed survey of these books, see E. F. Bosanquet, *English Printed Almanacks and Prognostications: A Bibliographical History to the year 1600* (1917), and also for supplementary information, *The Library*, Fourth Series, vol. VIII (1928), pp. 456–77. See also Carroll Camden, 'Elizabethan Almanacs and Prognostications', *The Library*, Fourth Series, vol. XII (1932), pp. 83–108, 194–207.

of recent discoveries and voyages to Africa or the New World. The second half of the century, however, saw a great change, for the exploits of the Elizabethan seamen all over the world, the growing knowledge of geography and navigation, the pleasure men took in learning of the manners and customs of distant lands, all helped to stimulate the book-trade and to call for a constant flow of works bearing on these subjects.

Pride of place must be given to the exploits of the Elizabethan seamen, although these have frequently been surveyed and eulogized,[1] and also the narratives of some of those who took part in these voyages and discoveries have been printed. At the same time, however, any survey such as this cannot overlook the part played by Richard Hakluyt ('a man that laboureth greatly to advance our English Name and Nation') in making much of this material available in print. He tells us how

> I do remember that being a youth, and one of her Majesties scholars at Westminster that fruitfull nurserie, it was my happe to visit the chamber of M. *Richard Hakluyt* my cosin, a Gentleman of the Middle Temple, well knowen unto you [Sir Francis Walsingham], at a time when I found lying open upon his boord certeine bookes of Cosmographie, with an Universall Mappe: he seeing me somewhat curious in the view therof, began to instruct my ignorance, by shewing me the division of the earth into three parts after the olde account, and then according to the latter, & better distribution, into more: he pointed with his wand to all the knowen Seas, Gulfs, Bayes, Straights, Capes...of ech part, with declaration also of their speciall commodities, & particular wants, which by the benefit of traffike, & entercourse of merchants, are plentifully supplied.[2]

'In Oxford', he continues,

> my exercises of duety first performed, I fell to my intended course, and by degrees read over whatsoever printed or written discoveries or voyages I found extant either in the Greeke, Latine, Italian, Spanish,

---

[1] See Sir Walter Raleigh, *The English Voyages of the Sixteenth Century* (Glasgow, 1906).

[2] *STC* 12625, *The principall Navigations, Voiages and Discoveries of the English nation, made by sea or over Land, to the most remote and farthest distant Quarters of the earth*...(1589), sig. *2.

Portugall, French, or English languages, and in my publike lectures was the first that produced and shewed both the olde imperfectly composed, and the new lately reformed Mappes, Globes, Spheares, and other instruments of this Art for demonstration in the common schooles, to the singular pleasure, and generall contentment of my auditory. In continuance of time... I grew familiarly acquainted with the chiefest Captaines at sea, the greatest Merchants, and the best Mariners of our nation.[1]

For years after this, he continued to collect information concerning maritime discoveries and enterprises, putting some of this into books. First came the *Divers voyages, touching the discoverie of America*...(1582), which served as a prelude to the folio *Principall Navigations* (1589), this in its turn giving place to the three noble folios of 1598–1600, which enshrined not only printed matter but much manuscript material. He writes movingly of his labours in producing

into this homely and rough-hewen shape, which here thou seest, what restlesse nights, what painefull dayes, what heat, what cold I have indured; how many long & chargeable journeys I have traveiled; how many famous libraries I have searched into; what varietie of ancient and moderne writers I have perused; what a number of old records, patents, privileges, letters etc., I have redeemed from obscuritie and perishing; into how manifold acquaintance I have entred; what expenses I have not spared; and yet what faire opportunities of private gaine, preferment and ease, I have neglected; albeit thyselfe canst hardly imagine, yet I by daily experience do finde & feele, and some of my entier friends can sufficiently testifie.[2]

Hakluyt was sustained in all these labours by his desire to inform his readers of what had been done, and to make them proud of their countrymen and worthy of them. In an exalted passage he recounts their exploits:

For, which of the kings of this land before her Majesty, had theyr banners ever seene in the Caspian sea? Which of them hath ever dealt with the Emperor of Persia, as her Majesty hath done, and

[1] *STC* 12625, sig. *2.   [2] *STC* 12626, sig. *4.

obteined for her merchants large & loving privileges? Who ever saw before this regiment, and English Ligier in the stately porch of the Grand Signor at Constantinople? Who ever found English Consuls & Agents at Tripolis in Syria, at Aleppo, at Babylon, at Balsara, and which is more, who ever heard of Englishmen at Goa before now? What English shippes did heeretofore ever anker in the mighty river of Plate? passe and repasse the unpassable (in former opinion) straight of Magellan, range along the coast of Chili, Peru and all the backside of Nova Hispania, further then any Christian ever passed, travers the mighty bredth of the South sea, land upon the Luzones in despight of the enemy, enter into alliance, amity, and traffike with the princes of the Moluccaes, & the Isle of Java, double the famous Cape of Bona Speranza, arrive at the Isle of Santa Helena, & last of al returne home most richly laden with the commodities of China, as the subjects of this now florishing monarchy have done?[1]

But Hakluyt's collections come at the end of the century, and form the grand finale of a steadily increasing interest in geographical works of all kinds, especially those that told

> Of moving accidents by flood and field;
> Of hairbreadth scapes i' th'iminent deadly breach;
> Of being taken by the insolent foe
> And sold to slavery; of my redemption thence.
> And portance in my travel's history;
> Wherein of antres vast and deserts idle,
> Rough quarries, rocks, and hills whose heads touch heaven,
> It was my hint to speak—such was the process;
> And of the Cannibals that each other eat,
> The Anthropophagi, and men whose heads
> Do grow beneath their shoulders.

This is Othello speaking; but his speech is the poetical paraphrase of many a title-page, such as that of

The Rare Travailes of Job Hortop, an Englishman, who was not heard of in three and twentie yeeres space. Wherein is declared the dangers he escaped in his Voyage to Gynnie, where, after hee was set

---
[1] *STC* 12625, sig. *2ᵛ.

on shoare in a wildernes nere to Panico, hee endured much slaverie and bondage in the Spanish Galley. Wherein also he discouereth many strange and wonderfull things seene in the time of his travaile, as well...of sundrie monstrous beasts, fishes, and foules, and also Trees of wonderfull forme and qualitie.[1]

But while works with such an alluring title-page were appealing to some book buyers, more serious authors lamented the sensationalism 'whereby, by sundrie mens fantasies, sundrie untruths are spread abroad' and 'trifling Pamphlets have bin secretly thrust out, not only without the consent of the captaynes and executioners of the same, but also rather to the greate disgrace of the worthy voyage than otherwise'.[2] Attempts were made to get authentic accounts from actual partakers of what they recorded, so that *A true report of the third and last voyage into 'Meta Incognita,' atchieved by the worthie Captaine M. Martin Frobisher Esq, 1578* was 'written by T.E., Sailer and one of the company' in the belief that his 'countrymen will be no lesse earnest and desirous to learne & enquire, than attentive to knowe and heare as well of our travelles, troubles, toyles, and daungers, as of our late adventures, happes and good successes'.[3]

This puts one side of the case for the publication of books such as these clearly enough, but we may also add that they were often of importance to those venturing and those financing the great series of voyages and expeditions of that time. There were adventures in all directions—to the Near and to the Far East; to the Americas from the far north to the south, and beyond into the Pacific, and so on. There was no limit to the schemes that were afoot, and any book, however brief and vague, was of interest and perhaps of importance. And it

[1] *STC* 13828 (1591), sig. A1.
[2] *STC* 1972, G. Best, *A True Discourse of the late voyages*...(1578), sig. V3.
[3] *STC* 7607, sig. A1. Cf. *Voyages to the East Indies*... 'from the mouth of Edmund Barker', or *STC* 12925, *Strange and wonderfull things Happened to Richard Hasleton. Penned as he delivered it from his owne mouth* (1595).

was not only English sources that were drawn on, but many translations from French and Spanish sources appeared, as for example, Jean Ribaut's *The whole and true discoverye of Terra Florida* (1563), which gave an account of the voyage which had ended in 1562, and was 'now newly set forthe in Englishe',[1] or the Spanish account of *The Pleasant Historie of the Conquest of the Weast India... Atchieved by Prince Hernando Cortes... and most delectable to Reade* (1578), made by his secretary Lopez de Gomara, who gives a first-hand account of the conquest of Mexico.[2] Another Spanish work had a more peaceful note, and gave *Joyfull Newes out of the newe founde worlde, wherein is declared the rare and singuler vertues of diverse and sundrie Hearbes, Trees, Oyles, Plantes, and Stones, with their applications, as well for Phisicke as Chirurgerie*. This was one of the earliest books to tell of tobacco, and for long remained a valued source of information about the medicinal plants of America.[3]

Nor was travel to the East neglected. There was, for example, *A discourse of the navigation which the Portugales doe make to the Realmes and Provinces of the East partes of the worlde* (1579), whose practical importance is urged by the translator, John Frampton, who says he was asked to translate it 'by diverse moste excellent pilotes, maisters and towardly young mariners, muche exceeding in knowledge and godly life many of that profession that have been heretofore',[4] while three years later another work on 'the East Indies, enterprised by the Portingales in their daungerous Navigations' was said on its title page to be 'very profitable for all Navigators, and not unpleasaunt to the Readers',[5]—the printer obviously hoping to attract a double audience. A more specific reference to a hoped-for audience is to be found in *The Historie of the great and mightie kingdome of China* (1588), which Robert Parke, the translator,

---

[1] *STC* 20970. [2] *STC* 16807.
[3] *STC* 18005a (1577). [4] *STC* 10529, sig. A 2ᵛ.
[5] *STC* 16806, Lopes de Castanheda, F., *The first Booke of the Historie of the Discoverie... of the E. Indias* (1582), sig. A 1.

says is 'for the illuminating the minds of those that are to take the voyage next at hand to Japan, China and the Phillipines'.[1]

So much for this aspect of the geographical literature of the age. We must also, however, notice a number of books of a more general nature, such as the translation published in 1575 of *The Traveiler of Jerome Turler*... *A Woorke very pleasaunt for all persons to reade; and right profitable and necessarie unto all such as are minded to Traveyll*. It was written 'in the behalf of such as are desirous to traveill, and to see forreine Cuntries, & specially of students'. It contains not only directions concerning travel but also a great many incidental pieces of information such as 'The Arte of Printing is as much frequented in England as in Germanie, and Fraunce: in Ireland it is nothing so'.[2] Another similar work, *The post for diuers partes of the world*, was translated by Richard Rowlands in 1576. Originally composed 'in the high *Almaine* tongue, and the like also to be seene in the *French*, and *Italian*', it was a road book 'very necessary & profitable for Gentlemen, Merchants, Factors, or any other person disposed to travaile. The like not heretofore in England.'[3]

A more comprehensive work, giving an account of some eighty countries and provinces, was made by Robert Johnson from Giovanni Botero's *The Travellers Breviat, Or an historicall description of the most famous kingdomes in the World: Relating their situations, manners, customes, civill government and other memorable matters* (1601). In justification of his translation the author says that 'there is no book extant touching the same argument which can aequalize it',[4] so that it was evidently meant to supplement Archbishop George Abbot's smaller work, *A Briefe Description Of The whole worlde* (1599). Both works had their own public: Dr Wright says that Abbot's

[1] This work was translated at the suggestion of Hakluyt, while the organization of direct trade with the East began in October 1589.

[2] *STC* 24336, p. 25.

[3] *STC* 21360, sig. A 1, 2. Cf. *STC* 12425, A de Guevara, *A Booke of the Invention of the Art of Navigation* (1578), giving advice to those that travel in galleys. [4] *STC* 3398, sig. A 2ᵛ.

summary was used apparently as a textbook, and both remained in circulation until the 1630's, being constantly reprinted.[1]

Geography had in fact arrived, and had claimed and obtained a place for itself, thanks in part to the enterprise of the booktrade, and in part to the pressure of the times. In 1577 Richard Willes had felt able to declare that

> Geography laye hydden many hundred yeeres in darkenesse and oblivion, without regarde and price: of late who taketh not uppon him to discourse of the whole worlde, and eche province thereof particulerly, even by hearesay, although in the first principles of that arte, he bee altogeather ignorant and unskylfull. This tyme is now.[2]

Although Willes laments that men wrote of geography, despite being 'altogether ignorant and unskylfull', the study of geography on a scientific basis was being actively pursued. In 1559 William Cuningham had published *The Cosmographical Glasse, conteinyng the pleasant Principles of Cosmographie, Geographie, Hydrographie, or Navigation*. 'I am the firste that ever in our tongue have written of this argument' he declared, but his work, despite its tables, charts and pictures, was too academic to be popular, and was never reprinted. Perhaps Cuningham betrayed his theoretical attitude to his subject by his naïve declaration:

> I had almoste forgotten to resight the benefits we receive of Cosmographie: in that she delivereth us from greate and continuall travailes. For in a pleasaunte house, or warme study, she sheweth us the hole face of all th' Earthe, withal the corners of the same. And from this peregrination, thy wife with sheadinge salte teares, thy children with lamentations, nor thy frendes with wordes shal dehort & perswade the. In travailing, thou shalt not be molested with the inclemencye of the aere, boysterous windes, stormy shoures, haile, Ise, & snow. Comming to thy lodginge, thou shalt not have a churlish & unknowne hoste, which shall mynister meate twise sodden, stinking fish, or watered wine. Going to rest, thou shalt not feare lowsy beddes, or filthy sheates.[3]

---

[1] Wright, *op. cit.* p. 535.
[2] *STC* 649, sig. (.) 2ᵛ.
[3] *STC* 6119, sig. A6.

AIDS TO NAVIGATION

There followed in 1561 *The Arte of Navigation, Conteyning a compendious description of the Sphere, with the makyng of certen Intrumentes and Rules for Navigation*, translated at the expense of the Muscovy Company by Richard Eden.[1] This gave much practical and theoretical help to navigators and was frequently reprinted, despite the production of later rivals, such as *A Regiment for the Sea, conteyning most profitable Rules, Mathematical experiences, and perfect knowledge of Navigation for all Coastes and Countreys* (1574). William Bourne, its author, says it is 'a necessarie booke for the simplest sort of Seafaring men... with the names of diverse things meete for Navigation, together with their uses, which the moste part of seamen do mistake or missecall'.[2] In another work the same author declares himself to be only 'a poore Gunner' whose only reason for writing books is 'to instruct and teach them that are simple and unlearned'. Then there were also books of charts and maps such as *The Safegard of Sailers, or the great Rutter* (1584),[3] a useful work for those sailing around the coast of England and in Northern waters, or a collection of 'divers exact sea charts' entitled *The Mariners Mirrour* (1588) made by Lucas Jansen Wagenaer 'and now fitted with necessarie additions for the use of Englishmen by Anthony Ashley'.[4]

While all this attention was being given to countries and to continents far away, there were also books being published which gave information about the geography of nearer countries such as France, Holland, Germany, Portugal, and others, although it must be admitted that they were few in number and did not attract very much attention. Of England itself little had been written: we have *The laboryouse*

---

[1] *STC* 5798. Reprinted seven times by 1615.

[2] *STC* 3422, sig. A3ᵛ. The sixth edition of 1596 also contained *The Mariners guide... wherin the use of the plaine Sea card is brieflie and plainlie delivered to the commoditie of all such as have delight in Navigation*. A full account of Bourne's life and works will be found in *A Regiment for the Sea*, ed. by E. G. R. Taylor, Hakluyt Society, Second Series, no. CXXI (1963).

[3] *STC* 21545 and frequently reprinted.

[4] *STC* 24931, sig. A1.

journey & serche of J. Leylande (1549)[1], but little else before Humphrey Llwyd's *The Breuiary of Britayne* (1573), written he says, 'for the English Reader's sake whiche understandeth not the Latine tongue. To whome I thought it was much appertaining to know the state and description of his owne country as to the learned'.[2] Then in 1576 came the first county history, *A Perambulation of Kent*, by William Lambard,[3] and in 1586 William Camden's *Britannia, sive...chorographica descriptio*,[4] both works being a combination of history and geography. A more purely geographical work was produced by Christopher Saxton in the form of a series of thirty-five coloured maps of England and Wales,[5] and in 1593 John Norden began to publish another series of county maps entitled *Speculum Britanniae*, the first part being a description of Middlesex (1593), which was followed by a description of Hertfordshire in 1598.[6]

8. History

On 5 April 1559 William Seres displayed for sale on his stall at the sign of the Hedgehogge, a new book printed for him by Thomas Marshe, entitled *An Epitome of Cronicles. Comprising the whole discourse of histories as well of this realme of England as al other countreys, with the succession of their kinges, the time of their reigne, and what notable actes they did: much profitable to be redde, namelye of Magistrates, and such as have auctoritie in common weales, gathered out of most probable auctours*.[7] This title-page is revealing of the reasons encouraging men to read history at this time. Such a study, it was thought, was profitable 'to such as have authoritie in common weales', since it taught by example how men should live and govern, and it set out the main events that had occurred here and in other countries 'in such forme and order that a diligent reader may as

---

[1] *STC* 15445. [2] *STC* 16636, sig. A 7.
[3] *STC* 15175.
[4] *STC* 4503. The Latin original was first published in English in 1610.
[5] Herbert, *Ames' Typographical Antiquities*, vol. III, pp. 1651–2.
[6] *STC* 18635, 18637. [7] *STC* 15221.

in a mirrour behold the state and condicion of all realmes at all tymes'.[1] Furthermore, as Stow wrote:

Amongst other Bookes which are in this our learned age published in great numbers, there are few eyther for the honestie of the matter, or commoditie which they bring to the common wealth, or for the pleasantnesse of the studie and reading, to be preferred before the Chronicles and Hystories. What examples of men deserving immortalitie, of exploites worthy of great renowne... is not plentifully in them to be found.[2]

History was, in fact, sufficiently popular for the bookseller to put out a work such as the above, even though it ran to some 750 quarto pages, and even though it was not a new work, but one based on an earlier work of Lanquet and Cooper which had been published in 1549 and was presumably hard to come by some ten years later. Not unreasonably, however, Thomas Cooper, who was still very much alive, objected to this unauthorized use being made of his material by the new editor, Richard Crowley, especially as he found 'almost five hundred fautes and errours eyther of the prynter, or els of hym that undertooke the correction; yea, and many of them in those thynges that are in this worke chiefly to be regarded. I cannot therefore doe otherwyse but greatly blame their unhonest dealynge, and openly protest that the Edicion of this Chronicle set forth by Marshe and Seres... is none of myne, but the attempte of certayne persons utterly unlearned.'[3] To put matters right Cooper published a new edition of his book, *Coopers Chronicle... unto the late death of Queene Marie*. This was popular enough to call for two further editions in 1565, and carried the story forward as far as October 1564.[4]

All this is worth rehearsing at length, since it is indicative of the interest that there was at this time in history. No other decade of the reign showed so many historical productions as came from the presses between 1560 and 1570. It is true that

---

[1] *STC* 15217, sig. A3ᵛ.   [2] *STC* 23333, sig. ¶4.   [3] *STC* 15218, sig. a1ᵛ.
[4] *STC* 15218–20. For a good modern account of this quarrel, see Rosenberg, *Leicester: Patron of Letters*, pp. 66ff.

for the main part this was the outcome of a rivalry between the two men which became more and more embittered as the years passed. Richard Grafton, in addition to his work as a publisher, had also helped to write *Halles Chronicle* (1548 and after), and in 1562 put together a work of his own, which Richard Tottell published under the title of *An Abridgement of the Chronicles of England*. This was a comparatively small book, aimed at a comparatively uneducated public, which was easy to read and inexpensive. It won some success for it was reprinted again in 1563, and in 1564, while a revised and expanded version appeared in 1570 and 1572.[1]

Grafton's work, however, did not satisfy some readers, and an approach was made to the well-known antiquary, John Stow, who tells us that 'many sitizens and others, knowynge that I had bene a searchar of Antiquities...moved me to travaille in setting forth some other abrydgment or summarye'. As a result, Stow compiled *A Summarie of Englyshe Chronicles* (1565), which because of its brevity and its novelty in places he hoped would be 'not altogether unwelcome. For though it be written homily, yet it is not (as I trust) written untruly.'[2] Stow's book was obviously a challenge to that of Grafton who quickly responded with 'a brefe colation' of history, which he called *A Manuell of the Chronicles of Englande. From the creacion of the worlde, to this yere, 1565*. This was a smaller and cheaper book than his former work, and was designed to ensure that the public 'which covets such little collections...may not be abused as heretofore they have been'.[3]

Stow's reply to this challenge was to compile an abridgement of his own *Summarie* 'digested into a new forme such as may both ease the purse and the caryage, and yet nothing omitted convenient to be knowen'.[4] Finding his attempt to corner the

[1] *STC* 12148–52.   [2] *STC* 23319, sig. a 2.
[3] *STC* 12167, sig. A 2ᵛ. It comprised a little over 200 pages and was only four inches by three inches in size.
[4] *STC* 23321, sig. a 1. The *STC* does not distinguish between these two works. The one Stow called *A Summarie*... and the other *The Summarie* (the abridgement), both of them about four inches by three.

small book market a failure, Grafton put all his energies into a long work in narrative form, running to over 800 pages in two folio volumes. This he called *A Chronicle at large and meere History of the affayres of Englande...unto the first yere of the reigne of Queene Elizabeth* (1569).[1] This work won but little favour, and has been characterized by a modern historian as 'a monstrous compilation', and of no value. Stow was more fortunate, for his writings were well received, and both his *Summarie* and the abridgement were revised and reprinted many times until the end of the century and later. In addition, he was working at a large-scale work which he finally published in 1580 under the title *The chronicles of England, from Brute unto this present yeare of Christ, 1580*.[2] At the request of the publisher he put aside a larger work on English history that he was writing in order to revise the *Chronicles* which were then put out under the title of *The Annales of England from the first inhabitation untill 1592*.[3] The way was now clear for his last great publication, *A Survay of London*, first published in 1598, embodying a lifetime of loving observation and research in his native City, or as he puts it himself—'a dutie that I willingly owe to my native mother and Countrey'.[4]

Stow was obviously a most important figure in the story of Elizabethan historical publishing, and the continued reprints of his works reflect this. The only other historian to be mentioned alongside him is Raphael Holinshed whose *Chronicles* have preserved much that otherwise might have been lost. Their great historical importance is not our primary concern. What is to our purpose is to note, as Holinshed tells us, that the original idea was not his, but only part of a grandiose scheme that Reyner Wolfe, the printer, had conceived and worked at for 25 years, in an endeavour to compile a universal cosmography, for which he had enlisted the help of Holinshed to put

---

[1] *STC* 12147. He had published a shorter version the previous year.
[2] *STC* 23333. This was a large quarto of 1223 pages, and was not reprinted.
[3] *STC* 23334. And many times again. See *STC* 23335–40.
[4] *STC* 23341. Also in 1599 and 1603. 'Continued and enlarged', 1618, etc.

together the historical material. On the death of Wolfe, Holinshed was asked to carry on the whole enterprise, but the volume grew so great that those who were to defray the charges for the impression were not willing to go through with the whole, and resolved to publish the histories of England, Scotland and Ireland, together with a topographical description of Britain. This was done in 1577 in a large folio, and after the death of Holinshed the work was reissued in a greatly increased form which required three folio volumes and ran to some 1800 pages of print in double columns.[1]

Nor was the history of other countries neglected. Ancient history bulked large, since the Elizabethans looked with interest on the history of the past, for as a contemporary wrote: 'In them men may see the groundes and beginnynges of commen wealthes, the causes of their encrease, of their prosperous mayntenaunce, and good preservation: and againe by what meanes they decreased, decayed and came to ruyne.'[2] Not only was this general consideration urged, but men were encouraged to read for particular reasons, as when the history of Appian is recommended, since it shows 'how God plagueth them that conspire againste theyr Prince...the which this Author hathe pleasure to declare, bycause he would affray all men from disloyaltie toward their Soueraigne'.[3] The Æthiopian History of Heliodorus is published as an antidote to the many 'wanton allurements to leudnesse' that were commonly to be found on the stalls, since

while *Mort Darthure, Arthur of little Britaine*, yea, and *Amadis of Gaule* etc., accompt violente murder...for no cause, manhoode, and fornication and all other unlawfull luste, friendely love. This booke punisheth the faultes of evill doers, and rewardeth the well livers. What a king is Hidaspes! What a pattern of a good prince! What happy successe had he! Contrariewise, what a leawde woman was Arsace! What a paterne of evil behaviour! What an evill end had shee....[4]

[1] STC 13568 (1577); 13569 (1587). See also p. 273.
[2] STC 6142, *The historie of Quintus Curcius* (1553), sig. A 2.
[3] STC 713, *An auncient historie...of the Romanes warres* (1578), sig. A 2.
[4] STC 13043, ed. by C. Whibley in *Tudor Translations* (1895), p. 4.

The works of Aelianus, Appian, Herodotus, Polybius, Quintus Curtius and others were also printed with a similar purpose.

As for more modern history, here again the presses were active. The religious wars in France and the Low Countries encouraged the translation of works such as that of Jean de Serres, which set out *The Commentaries of the Civill Warres in Fraunce and the low Countrie of Flanders* (1573–6),[1] as well as the many ephemeral pamphlets which gave the most recent accounts of civil and military happenings in these countries.[2] The past and present histories of various countries also interested the Elizabethans sufficiently for a good number of volumes to be published such as *The Historie of Philip de Commines* (1596),[3] a work which had long been in circulation in manuscript form, and cried out for publication by reason of the vigour and liveliness of the narrative of the author who had been an eyewitness of much that he recounted. Other works such as *The State of Spaine* (1594), *The historie of Italie* (1549), *The Mahumatane or Turkish historie* (1600), *The History of the Jewes* (1558); or *A notable Historie of the Saracens...as also of the Turkes* (1575) may serve as examples of the interest there was in the history of countries other than England; an interest, be it noted, sufficient to persuade the book-trade to go to the trouble of getting translations made of all these works named above, as well as others, believing that many felt as did 'certaine gentlemen to whose hands the booke happened to come', who 'tooke so great pleasure and delight therein, that they determined to put it to the presse, supposing it a great dishonor to our nation, that so woorthy an historie being extant in all languages almost in Christendome, should be suppressed in ours'.[4]

---

[1] *STC* 22241–3. Cf. *STC* 5590, A. Colynet, *The true History of the Civill Warres of France...from 1585 untill October 1591* (1591).

[2] See pp. 234–9.

[3] *STC* 5602. Trans. T. Danett.

[4] *STC* 5602, sig. A 2. Cf. *STC* 5642 (Venice); *STC* 17943 (Turks and Persians), etc.

In addition, it should be noticed that the lives and deeds of various historical personages were thought to merit attention. George Whetstone writes: 'English historiographers are bound to eternise the memories of the good Magistrates disseased who were the instruments of our blessings, that the dead may have their right, and the living incouragement to virtue.'[1] To some such end were published *Aelianus on the Martial exploits of worthy warriors & others* (1576); Henri Estienne on the *Lyfe, deedes, and behaviours of Katherine de Medicis* (1575); writings by Daniel, Lodge and Hayward on various historical worthies, and works by a number of others.[2] Furthermore, some authors gathered together collections of the lives of the great, such as that of the Spaniard Pedro Mexia, whose book was translated in 1571 under the title *The Foreste; or Collection of Histories, no lesse profitable than pleasant and necessarie*,[3] or that of Antonio de Guevara, *A Chronicle, conteyning the liues of tenne Emperours of Rome...worthie to be read, marked and remembered* (1577).[4] The most famous of all these compilations needs little more than a brief reference. The incomparable portraits of noble Grecians and Romans painted in 'North's Plutarch' exhibit, as Thomas Norton said of another chronicle of ancient history, 'glasses of experience, scholehouses of wisedome...terrible threateners and warners to flee vice and follie'.[5]

9. *News*

In dedicating his *Second Frutes* (1591) to Master Nicholas Saunders of Ewell, Giovanni Florio writes: 'Everie man is busilie woorking to feede his owne fancie: some by delivering to the presse the occurrences & accidents of the world,

---

[1] *STC* 25345, sig. A2.
[2] See, for example, *STC* 12997a, J. Hayward, *Henri the IIII* (1599). 'By setting before us the actes and lives of excellent men, it is the readiest way to fashion our qualities according to the same' (sig. A3ᵛ).
[3] *STC* 17849, translated by T. Fortescue.
[4] *STC* 12426.
[5] *STC* 785, *Orations, of Arsanes agaynst Philip* [1560?], sig. A1.

newes from the marte, or from the mint, and newes are the credite of a travailer, and first question of an Englishman.'[1] So it had been throughout the century, for news was always in demand, whether it came from the traveller fresh from the Spanish Main, or from the battlefields of Europe. Rumour with her many tongues was ever active in producing news of sorts, whether gleaned from a chance conversation overheard in the ordinary or at the tavern, or from a letter coming from a country friend, or from an eyewitness, eager to tell his story to all who would listen. Obviously all these ways of learning what was going on were unsatisfactory. Yet there was little else that could be done to dispel the fog of ignorance that clung about most affairs. Since there were no newspapers at this time, the printers and booksellers had an open field, and were doubly lucky, since many of them had stalls in Paul's churchyard, and Paul's was the recognized centre for the exchange of news and gossip. So without taking more active steps than to let it be known that they were interested in the publication of news of this sort, they would naturally attract those who had a tale to tell, or who had received information of interest from some source or other. A man such as John Wolfe, for example, had by the late eighties come to be known as a ready receiver of items of news which he was prepared to print for himself, or for sale by others. In 1588 he printed at least ten pamphlets or broadsides giving news, and the next year he raised the number to some fifteen, not including those which he entered in the *Stationers' Register* but which he apparently never printed. In 1590 the number was even greater, and while no one else was so active in this field as Wolfe, yet when we add together the output of all the presses it certainly makes a respectable figure.

But while news and rumour circulated freely, it was not very easy for the printer to know what credence to attach to it. Many printers, no doubt, did not bother much about this. If the report was interesting and told of exciting national events, that

[1] *STC* 11097, sig. A2.

was good enough. Correction, if necessary, could come later. In the meantime, speed was of importance, and the energies of the printer were directed to getting the news into print at the earliest moment. Whether this was an easy task or not depended on the nature of the copy. The garbled story of an illiterate narrator had to be put into a readable form, while accounts of battles and the like were often little more than lists of those killed and the barest outlines of the course of events, since the narrator could justly plead that he was a soldier and not an author. Some accounts reached the printer just as they were received from a correspondent writing to a friend or acquaintance, having been penned with no thought of publication. Others again had a more literary flavour, and had been carefully prepared by a writer of some skill. Much of the news came from abroad and had to be translated, often from a printed copy, although manuscript copy was not unknown. All these various ways in which material came to the printing house presented problems: how long would it take to get a piece translated and cut down or augmented to fill a given number of pages? How much rewriting would be required to turn an illiterate recital into a reasonable narrative? What likelihood was there of some other printer getting in first? These and other considerations made the publication of this kind of literature something out of the ordinary, and it is not surprising that only a comparatively small number of men ventured into this field, and that what seems to us to have a lively market was not more thoroughly exploited.

In dealing with the output of news, however, we have always to remember that, even more than with other classes of literature, we have only a part of what was available to the Elizabethans—how large a part it is impossible to tell. Our best measure of control is the *Stationers' Register* in which there should have been entered all the titles of all writings intended for publication. The briefest glance, however, shows that many works were published which were never entered—a number estimated by Sir Walter Greg to be 'something like a third of the copies actually printed'.[1] On the other hand, many titles were registered of which there is now no trace. Either they have perished or they were never printed at all. It is true that the majority of the pieces were printed on broadsheets, and were peculiarly liable to be quickly destroyed, as to a lesser extent were many of the little pamphlets of relatively few pages in which news of various sorts was usually published. Consequently we are operating in an imperfectly charted area.

With these considerations in mind we may turn to survey the variety of news that was available throughout the reign. Some news could be gained from time to time by reading the royal proclamations which were publicly displayed. Most of these, it is true, were concerned with matters in which there was little that could be called news, dealing as they did with the prices of victuals, or of wines, or setting out the sumptuary regulations concerning the wearing of excessive apparel. A few, however, were more informative, such as those which gave the government's reasons for sending an army into Scotland, or declared how the realm was troubled by certain priests and Jesuits. This last was a four-page proclamation headed:

A declaration of the great troubles pretended against the Realme by a number of Seminarie Priests and Jesuits, sent and secretly dispersed in the same, to worke great Treasons under a false pretence of Religion, with a provision very necessary for the remedy thereof.

The declaration 'recites the malice of the King of Spain for thirty years. He is now stirring up war against France. He has procured a Milanese [a vassal of his] for Pope Gregory XIV, has made war in Italy, has encouraged rebels in England. These, though using spiritual threats and inducements, have been tried for treason, and not for saying they will take part with any army sent by the Pope against us. There are many Roman Catholics in England who are not tried. The Jesuits have lately promised the King of Spain that many thousands will aid him if he invades this year. Certain

---

[1] W. W. Greg, *Some Aspects and Problems of London Publishing between 1550 and 1650* (Oxford, 1956), p. 68.

scrolls have been shown to the King by Parsons, and to the Pope by Allen (who has been made a Cardinal) containing the names of those likely to join in revolt, which have been drawn up by the Seminary Priests and Jesuits on their visit this last year. The King has promised to invade England next year. Precautions are to be taken etc.[1]

The formal legal phraseology of the Proclamations was often felt to be too limited a way of informing the public of the state of national affairs, and of the methods the government proposed to adopt to deal with them. This is explained very clearly in the preamble of a Declaration by the Queen concerning her intention to send troops to the support of the Protestant forces in the Low Countries in 1585. The Declaration states that:

Although kinges and princes soveraignes, owing their homage and service onely unto the Almightie God the king of al kings, are in that respect not bounde to yeeld account or render the reasons of their actions to any others but to God their only soveraigne lord...yet we are notwithstanding this our prerogative at this time specially mooved, for divers reasons hereafter briefly remembred, to publish not onely to our owne naturall loving subjectes, but also to all others our neighbours, specially to such princes and states as are our confederates...what our intention is at this time, and upon what just and reasonable grounds we are mooved to give aid to our next neighbours the naturall people of the Lowe Countreis.[2]

Another little 24-paged octavo pamphlet set out the reasons that had led to the seizure of some ships at Lisbon laden with 'Corne and other provisions of warre, bound for the said citie, prepared for the service of the King of Spaine'.[3] This was printed in English and in Latin, a not uncommon practice, while on some occasions, as with the declaration given above, as many as four or five languages might be used, so that the

---

[1] For a full account of the history of these documents and a most valuable list of them see R. Steele, *A Bibliography of Royal Proclamations of the Tudor and Stuart Sovereigns*, 2 vols. (1910). The abstract quoted above is by Mr Steele. [2] *STC* 9188. [3] *STC* 9196 (1589).

widest publicity possible might be obtained.[1] A further indication of the importance attached by the government as a means of disseminating information can be seen in the 'Stop press' matter at the end of the above Declaration concerning the Low Countries. This reads as follows:

After we had finished our declaration, there came to our hands a Pamphlet written in *Italian*, published in *Milan*...conteyning a report of the expugnation of *Anwerpe* by the Prince of *Parma*: by the which we found ourself most maliciously charged with two notable crimes.... The one, with ingratitude towards the King of Spaine...the other, that there were some persons procured to be corrupted with great promises, and that with our intelligence...the life of the Prince of *Parma* should be taken away.... Now, knowing how men are maliciously bent in this declining age of the world... we found it very expedient, not to suffer two such horrible imputations to passe under silence, least for lacke of answere, it might argue a kind of guiltines, and did therfore thinke, that what might be alledged by us for our justification in that behalfe, might most aptly be joyned unto this former declaration now to be published, to lay open before the world the maner and ground of our proceeding in the cause of the Lowe Countries.[2]

In addition to such pamphlets, vouched for by authority, the government found it useful from time to time to put out information which they wished to be as widely distributed as possible, without attaching to it the name of any particular officer of state. Throughout the reign anonymous pamphlets were published, justifying government action in this or that matter. The most well known of these, perhaps, were first, *The Execution of Justice in England for maintenaunce of publique and Christian peace, against certeine stirrers of sedition* (*STC* 4902 (1583)), and secondly, *A Declaration of the favourable dealing of her Majesties Commissioners appointed for the examination of certaine Traitours, and of Tortures unjustly reported to be done upon them for Matters of Religion* (*STC* 4901 (1583)). The latter is said to be the work of a 'verrie honest gentleman',

[1] See *STC* 9190–3.   [2] *STC* 9188, sig. D1.

known to 'have good and sufficient meanes to delyver the truth against such forgers of lies and shameless slanders in that behalfe, which he and other that know and have affirmed the same will be at all times justifie'. It is now generally agreed that both pieces were written by Lord Burghley.

Other works of this kind are said to be 'a true and perfect account', or 'Verie true by such as have cause to knowe them' and contain information which could only have come from well-informed persons, either official or semi-official. Such, for example, is *A true and summarie reporte of the declaration of some part of the Earle of Northumberlands treasons, delivered publikelie in the court at the Starre-chamber by the Lord Chancellour and others...together with the examinations and depositions of sundrie persons* [1585]. The writer of this pamphlet says that 'for the help of my memorie, comming then to the star chamber...I tooke note of the severall matters declared by the Lord Chancellor', and follows this up by a circumstantial account of the proceedings, together with the statements of witnesses, and copies of official documents. Since the work was published by the Queen's Printer there can be little doubt that it set out for the public exactly what the authorities wished to be known about the Earl's death.[1]

The hand of authority is even more clearly to be seen in the many accounts of trials for treason which were published from time to time. No doubt there was a public ready for these pamphlets which spared no item of the gory proceedings which culminated with the horrid barbarities at the gallows. Take, for example, *A discoverie of the treasons practised and attempted by Francis Throckmorton* (1584). It is printed, we are told, because

the case of Throckmorton at this time hath been subject to... sinister constructions, and considering that lies and false bruites cast abroad are most commonlie beleeved until they be controlled by the trueth, it hath been thought expedient in this short discourse

---

[1] *STC* 19617.

to deliver unto your view and consideration a true and perfect declaration of the treasons practised and attempted by the said Throckmorton...by him confessed.

There follows a detailed account of the interrogations, the trial itself and letters to the Queen.[1] The tract finishes with the words: 'Now judge all yee, that be not perversely affected, whether Throckemorton be justly condemned.' Although this is said to be a letter by 'a gentleman of Lions Inne' which hath been 'sent into the Countrie', giving 'more particular knowledge' which had come to hand 'by the meanes of a secret friend', there seems little reason to doubt the opinion of the *DNB* that it was written to order.[2]

Another good example may be seen in the officially inspired pamphlet entitled: *A true report of the Araignement and execution of the late Popishe Traitour, Everard Haunce* (1581). The preface reads as follows:

It is not well that men of more neediness than discretion or understanding, being not instructed in the truth of matters, do take uppon them, for a smal rewarde at a Printers Hande, to sette downe matters of fact in writing, and the Printers like wise for gaine do publish the same being not true: whereby bothe the state is in many things offended, religion and the procedings thereof laid open to some infamie among its affected persons, and the orders of her Majesties Injunctions and commandements broken.... Of this sort of untrue reportes is a pamphlet lately published, as gathered by M.S. and printed by Charlewood and White, touching the arraignment and execution of a wilful and obstinate traitor, named Everard Ducket alias Haunce. Bycause the moste of the same booke is untrue, and manye partes thereof do lay open the honor of our justice to slaunder, and the cause of religion to some disadvantage of cavailous speeches, it hath bin thought good that the trueth bee more certainly delivered by some yᵗ have better meane to knowe it and better cause to be creditted, and the Readers required to impute

---

[1] See also the trials of Essex (*STC* 1133); Lopez (*STC* 7603); Squire (*STC* 10017); Norfolk (*STC* 11504); Parry (*STC* 19341); Story (*STC* 23296–8).

[2] *STC* 24050, sigs. A 1 and C 4.

the errours of the former booke to the audacitie of some one greedy man, and not to any publique defacement of authoritie. Thus it is. There was one Everard Haunce, a Papist....[1]

There follows a clear, factual straightforward narrative of the trial, the more impressive by the seeming impartiality of the writer, as when he notes early in the trial that, being ordered to hold up his hand, Haunce held up his left hand, which at once caused the prosecutor to suspect some subterfuge on Haunce's part, but which in fact he did (as the narrator explains) 'in truth...because his right hand was occupied in holding his shackles to ease his legges'. It may well be as the preface suggests that this is an account which had some official sanction.

Although not officially inspired, the abject confession of Henry Arthington is not free from suspicion of being so. Arthington had been implicated with William Hacket in a conspiracy to murder the Queen. Hacket was hanged in July 1591, but for some reason in February 1592 it was thought necessary to publish Arthington's account of the affair. In a foreword to the Christian Reader written 'from my poor chamber in the Counter prison' he says:

I am to give thee to understand, that the Epistle before, and the booke following, were both perused and allowed by authoritie: and after sent mee agayne to examine, that I might see and testifie what upright dealing I founde therin. In verie trueth, I finde nothing in substance added to the originall, but certaine wordes and sentences chaunged for the better. The rest (I protest) is mine owne doinges, as I was directed by the spirite of God.[2]

This may be true, but it is impossible to tell how much he was writing under duress, especially in the light of the following. In 1581 was published by the Queen's Printer a work by the turncoat John Nichols, entitled *A declaration of the recantation of John Nichols...which desireth to be reconciled and received*

---
[1] *STC* 12934, sig. A 2.
[2] *STC* 799, *The seduction of Arthington by Hacket* [1592], sig. A 3.

as a member into the true Church of Christ in England.[1] This he dedicated to Sir Owen Hopton, lieutenant of the Tower, and speaks of his repentance and desire to be received into the true Church. Two years later, however, he found himself in prison in Rouen, and there he repudiated his *Declaration*, which he said was not his own, but was inspired by others.

He explained what had happened as follows:

Sir Owen Hopton the Lieutenant of the Tower commaunded me with threates, to write mine examination according to his will & pleasure, and willed me (when I published the names of Papists, many of whose names I never heard of before) not to be afraid to affirme them to be the fautors of the Pope, or of the Queene of Scots, to be mortal ennimies to the Queenes Majestie, to her Counsellors, & to al those which were defendors of the religion which is now publickly taught in England...

If thou wilt do this (quoth he) the Queene will promote thee, and thou shalt find me most ready to helpe thee.... If thou wilt not do this, thou shalt be tormented. [Nichols went on to say that] M. Stubs gave me the matter of my booke in the Tower...M. Wilkinson did write in the margent the notes: and also added to that which I wrote, and corrected the faults by me escaped.... I answered truly, if I had been permitted by M. Lieutenant so to do. For when I said so, *I told M. Kirkby that I wrote these bookes for ambition*, say not so (quoth M. Lieutenant) write (quoth he to his Secretary) after this manner: *That he was sorie that he wrot his bookes so rudely as he did.*[2]

Nichols, of course, is a most untrustworthy witness, and it may well be that he was willing to write whatever suited his case at the moment, but that some pressure was placed on him seems clear, and instances such as this suggest that the Queen's agents were not overscrupulous as to what they caused to be printed.

Even when we come to the many pamphlets not directly inspired by the government, it remains true that they must

---

[1] *STC* 18533.
[2] *STC* 18537, *A true report of the late apprehension of J. Nicols minister, at Roan* (Rhemes, 1583), sig. C3.

have been written with the knowledge that nothing that was seditious or offensive to the Queen had any chance of being given permission to print. If it was published without permission, all involved in its production and circulation were liable to be prosecuted. On the other hand, the authorities welcomed any printed matter that put before the public narratives of events of public importance, or which gave explanations of public policy, or drove home with suitable moralizings the fate of traitors or other disaffected persons. This can be seen very clearly at times of crisis, such as the Rebellion of the North of 1569–70. Without going into the details of the rising, it is enough to say that it was fairly quickly subdued, and the leaders and many of their followers drastically dealt with. For us the interest of the Rebellion is that it illustrates the usefulness to the authorities of the Press, and the readiness with which they met the popular demand for news. There were ballads for the simple, and for the more serious reader pamphlets which set out the case against the rebels with much righteous outcry against the horrid sin of disloyalty to the Crown. The actual news that is given in ballad or tract was pretty limited: the writers were seldom in a position to retail much more than was common gossip unless they were favoured by being given some piece of information, or a copy of a document or two that those in authority thought safe to release. But whether there was much reliable material available or not, the booksellers saw in the Rebellion their opportunity, and over thirty pamphlets and ballads were issued in a little over twelve months. The most important of these was a pamphlet of 56 quarto pages, written by Thomas Norton, best known to fame as part-author of *Gorboduc* (1561). In this work, entitled *To the Quenes Majesties poore deceived Subjectes of the North Countrey, drawn into rebellion by the Earles of Northumberland and Westmerland*, Norton denounced the rebellion and the rebels, and stated the case for the Crown so convincingly that not only was his work reprinted three times in 1569 but it formed a source book from which others could draw ideas and argument.[1] Both during the Rebellion and after it had been put down, the ballad writers were hard at work, reproving the rebels, or rejoicing in their overthrow, and missing no opportunity to preach the doctrine of lawful obedience. It was poor stuff, but suited to its public of simple folk, starved of news and easily swayed by the catch-penny verses of the balladists. Finally, the end of the Rebellion was greeted by works such as the ballad headed: *The Severall Confessions of Thomas Norton and Christopher Norton: two of the Northern Rebels who suffred at Tiburne, and were drawen, hanged and quartered for Treason May xxvii, 1570.*[2]

Other great national events, such as the long-drawn-out struggle against Mary Queen of Scots, or the threatened attack and defeat of the Armada, were splendid opportunities for the booksellers, and the ballad writers. Their wares were eagerly bought, but being only single sheets for the most part, and dealing with matters of strictly temporary interest, they were frequently thrown away, or used as wrapping material, so that in many instances they have disappeared entirely, and are only known to us by an entry in the *Stationers' Register*, or by a chance reference in a contemporary writing. Thus it is that the memorable summer of 1588, when England awaited the coming of the Armada, produced a shower of ballads and short poems describing such scenes as the Queen's coming to inspect the 'Martiall Shewes of Horsemen and Footmen before hir Majestie at St James', or later in the year we have an account of the 'Riall Entertainment of Quene Elizabeth at the City of London the 24th day of November, 1588, and of the

---

[1] *STC* 18680–2.

[2] *STC* 18683. Cf. verses on the same topic by Sampson Davie (*STC* 6325) and by William Gibson (*STC* 11843). By far the most complete list of ballads is to be found in the work of Hyder E. Rollins, 'An Analytical Index to the Ballad-Entries in the Registers of the Company of Stationers of London', *Studies in Philology*, vol. XXI (1924), pp. 1–324. Reference to the 'Index of Names and Subjects', pp. 279–324, will enable the reader to see what ballads are noted there which deal with traitors, murderers, etc., as these topics are discussed in this chapter.

Solemnity used by her Majestie to the glory of God, for the wonderful overthrow of the Spanyards'. So ephemeral, however, were such publications, that although we know the titles of at least twenty-six of them, only four appear to have survived in print to this day. Even when we recall the imperfect nature of the *Stationers' Register*, and make allowances for this, the loss is considerable and reminds us that we are dealing with only part of the material put out to meet such a popular demand.

Popular demand was also responsible for the outpouring of ballad and pamphlet that set forth the details of the trial and execution of traitors and murderers. The ballads were pretty skimble skamble stuff, but headed by a grisly woodcut and then followed by a series of easily understood verses, often marked to be sung to some popular tune, such as 'Fortune my foe', or 'Weston's verse', they were very much in demand. A few facts, the criminal's last words and repentant advice to others not to follow in his footsteps, and a verse or two of moralizing—these were the ingredients which were the staples of dozens of ballads which found a ready sale on the booksellers' stalls, or from the pack of the itinerant pedlar as he trudged from fair to fair, and market to market.

The pamphlets were of a slightly superior nature, though often written hurriedly to catch the market and over-full of the horrifying scenes at the gallows. This is, of course, exactly where the Elizabethans would have wished the emphasis to be. One such pamphleteer ends in dialogue form with the words: 'My eies saw their traiterous harts burned, and bodilesse heads advanced to the view and comforte of manye thousands of people', to which his friend replied: 'You sawe a happie sight.' The writer agreed, and added: 'The whole multitude, without any signe of lamentation greedylye behelde the spectacle from the first to the last.'[1] An even more dramatic scene was reported which marked the end of William Hacket, a religious maniac, whom we have already mentioned. After an account of the frenzied scenes that marked his progress to the gallows, the

[1] *STC* 25334, sig. A3.

narrator describes how that Hacket on his arrival there, after 'rayling and cursing of the Queenes Majestie most villainouslie' and using the 'most execrable blasphemie against the divine Majestie of God', then turned to the hangman and said to him:

'Ah thou bastards childe, wilt thou hange *William Hacket* thy king?' The *Magistrates* and people detesting this subtill, seditious, and blasphemous humour, commanded and cried to the Officers to dispatch with him, or to have his mouth stopped from blaspheming: but they had much adoe to get him up the ladder: And when he was up, he struggled with his head to and fro (as wel as he could) that he might not have the fatal noose put over his head. Then he asked them (very fearefully) *O what do you, what doe you?* but seeing by the circumstance, what they intended, he beganne to rave againe, and saide, 'Have I for this my kingdome bestowed upon thee? I come to revenge thee, and plague thee', and so was turned off. But the people unwilling that so traitorous and blasphemous a wretch should have any the least favour: cryed out mightily to have him cut downe presently [i.e. instantly], to be quartered, and seemed very angrie with the Officers, that made no more haste therein: but as soone almost as he was cut downe, (even with a trice) his heart was taken foorth, and shewed out openly to the people, for a most detestable, blasphemous traytors heart.[1]

As for murders, the catch-penny titles of many of these pamphlets indicated to the prospective purchasers what to expect. They could read of *The trueth of the most wicked and secret murthering of John Brewen, Goldsmith of London, committed by his owne wife, through the provocation of one John Parker whom she loved: for which she was burned, and he hanged in Smithfield.*[2] Another pamphlet told of: *Two notorious Murders. One committed by a Tanner on his wives sonne, nere Hornechurch in Essex. The other on a Grasier nere Ailsburie in Buckinghamshire. With these is intermixt another murdrous intending fellonie at Rislip in Middlesex. All done this last month.*[3] The accounts of these are gruesome enough, but for good measure the booksellers got from abroad such pieces as *A Strange Report of Sixe*

---

[1] *STC* 5823 (1592), sig. L3.   [2] *STC* 15095 (1592).   [3] *STC* 18289 (1595).

most notorious witches, who by their divilish practises murdered above the number of foure hundred small children.[1] The details of the punishment and execution of these women reaches a degree of savagery reminiscent of the treatment of the Jews, Poles and Russians by the Third Reich.

Naturally the Elizabethans were not content with home news only, especially if it told of what was happening in the countries nearest to England, so that the affairs of France and of the Low Countries were continually in the public eye. The success of the Protestant cause was of special interest through much of the reign, and there was a continuing demand for news, not only of battles and persons but also of policies and diplomatic affairs. It is indeed surprising to note the number of items which the English booksellers displayed on their stalls which are nothing more than royal proclamations concerning the internal affairs of France, as for example the various declarations of Henry III, 'consernyng the new troubles in his realmes', or 'concerning the observation of his edicts'. Many other items could be cited which would seem to be of limited interest to an English reader, such as the 'Ordinances set foorth by the King (Henry IV) for the rule and government of his Majesties men of warre', or 'The Kings Declaration, imposing a Revocation of all such letters for ennoblishment, as have not been verified in the Chamber of accounts of Normandy'. The fact that the booksellers found it worth their while to print works such as these, either in the original, or in translation, and sometimes in both, reflects the public interest in affairs abroad.

The news value of such items as these may well be thought to be small, and we are on firmer ground when we turn to survey the many ballads, tracts and pamphlets that recorded such matters as the religious wars in France and the Low Countries. It has been said that the booksellers did not concern themselves much with the defeats sustained by the Protestant cause, and there is some truth in this and much good business

[1] *STC* 20890 (1601).

sense on their part. What they wanted for their customers was good rousing stuff telling of the superior virtues as fighting men of the Protestant forces. And if there were any Englishmen engaged, it was a pleasure, if not a duty, to report as does an eyewitness in *Newes from Brest* (1594) how well the English fought, and how poorly the French. The accounts of eyewitnesses, especially if larded with phrases such as 'the thundering shot of the canon calleth me to my place, and therefore I am constrained to cut short my narrative',[1] encouraged readers to take what they read as true. So did statements such as 'a week since came from Diepe a certaine Bark the which reporteth...'.[2] Many of these reports were hastily put together and published without anyone bothering much about their accuracy, a condition glanced at in the epilogue of an account of the Victory of the King of Navarre over the Duke of Maine in August 1591, which reads:

> The former discourse is not forged or feigned as some perhaps for malice will peevishly report: neither is it fetched from flying or fabulous letters, ordinarie reports on the Exchange, and published uppon rash warrant as some, I knowe, will not stick to utter: but the same is set forth for such credit as cannot be disproved, being agreeable to intelligence sent from His Majestie into England to the Ambassador for Fraunce. And although the same bee not put with such eloquent phrases as some newes which hath lately been published, yet will I assure you... that this is of more trueth, and without error, notwithstanding that much trueth was promised and little found but untrueth.[3]

These reports of battles and campaigns fascinated the Elizabethans who were always eager to hear of how their religious compatriots were faring. One or two extracts from the title-pages of the pamphlets will best indicate the kind of interest they attempted to satisfy. The massacre of St Bartholomew's Day is recounted in full in a work entitled: *A true and plaine report of the Furious outrages of Fraunce, & the horrible*

---

[1] *STC* 18654, sig. B2. [2] *STC* 11265, sig. A2.
[3] *STC* 13142·1, sig. B3ᵛ.

and shameful slaughter of Chastillion the Admirall, and divers other Noble and excellent men, and of the wicked and straunge murder of godlie persons, committed in many Cities of Fraunce, without any respect of sorte, kinde, age, or degree.[1] The battle of Ivry was made known to Englishmen in a number of pamphlets, one of which has as its title: *The true discourse of the wonderfull victorie, obteined by Henrie the fourth, the French King, and King of Navarre, in a battell against those of the League, neere the towne of Yurie, on the Plaine of Saint Andrew, the foureteenth day of March (according to the French account) in the yeare 1590.*[2]

Confining ourselves to France for the moment, it is instructive to look at the news the booksellers provided during the year 1590. Within a week of the battle of Ivry a ballad was entered and was presumably soon printed for sale, while during the next month no fewer than four separate accounts were prepared for the English market from French originals. A few weeks later there appeared a couple of ballads on the siege of Paris by Henry of Navarre, and of the conditions within the City itself. The sending of an English force to aid the Protestants was celebrated in a ballad in May, while in June a little eight-page pamphlet gave an account of the most recent news of the fighting. During the next three months four more pieces kept Englishmen up to date with the progress of events, and four more carried on the story until the end of November. Finally, early the next year another pamphlet carried matters as far as mid-January. The year 1590 was not perhaps a normal one, but it shows what could be done by the booksellers if they thought it worth while.

For more serious moments there were the books and pamphlets which supported or attacked the causes of various participants in the affairs of France and the Low Countries. A good example may be seen in a work by Innocent Gentillet entitled *An apology or defence for the Christians of Fraunce which are of the Evangelicall or reformed Religion, for the satisfying of*

[1] *STC* 13847 (1573).   [2] *STC* 13145.

such as wil not live in peace and concord with them (1579),[1] while an anonymous Italian translator wrote *A Politike Discourse most excellent for this time present; composed by a French Gentleman against those of the League, which went about to perswade the King to breake the Allyance with England, and to confirme it with Spaine* (1589). This latter work was so liked, we are told, that although a new translation was prepared the same year, 'the former copies were for the most part alreadie distracted'.[2] While works such as these were not strictly news, they contained much in their pages that was illuminating to the English reader, and at the same time tried to influence him in favour of a particular cause.

Similarly the sieges and battles in the Low Countries were recounted, sometimes in detail, sometimes in little more than bare lists of names and places, and only occasionally were they written with a graphic pen such as that of the experienced writer, George Gascoigne, who compiled *The Spoyle of Antwerpe. Faithfully reported by a true Englishman, who was present at the same* [1577?] immediately on his return from the city. A brief quotation will show the justice of Professor C. T. Prouty's verdict that 'reporting of this description has no parallel in Elizabethan days'.[3] After his account of the attack and taking of the city by the Spaniards, Gascoigne goes on to describe the scenes that followed as the Spaniards had their will.

I forbeare also to recount the huge numbers, drowned in ye new Toune: where a man might behold as many shapes and formes of mans motion at time of death: as ever *Mighel Angelo* dyd portray in his tables of Doomes day. I list not to recken the infinite nombers of poore Almains, who lay burned in their armour: some thentrailes skorched out, & all the rest of the body free, some their head and shoulders burnt of: so that you might looke down into the bulk & brest and there take an Anatomy of the secrets of nature. Some standing uppon their waste, being burnte of by the thighes: and

---

[1] *STC* 11742.   [2] *STC* 13101, sig. A 4.
[3] C. T. Prouty, *George Gascoigne, Elizabethan Courtier, Soldier, and Poet* (New York, 1942), p. 238, from which the passage quoted is also taken.

some no more but the very toppe of the brain taken of with fyre, whiles the rest of the body dyd abide unspeakable tormentes. I set not downe the ougly & filthy polluting of every streete with the gore and carcases of men and horses: neither doo I complaine, that the one lacked buryall, and the other fleing, untyl the ayre (corrupted with theyr caryon) enfected all that yet remained alyve in the Towne.... But I may not passe over with sylence, the wylfull burning and destroying of the stately Townehouse, & all the monuments and records of the Citie.[1]

Among other countries, as might have been expected, it was Spain that attracted the attention of the printers the most, whether to supply such a masterpiece of reporting as Sir Walter Raleigh's account of the last fight of the *Revenge*, 'truly set down and published without parcialitie or false imagination' (1591),[2] or to give up-to-date information about the Spanish Armada, together with a detailed account of its encounters with the English fleet, as related by a Spanish officer.[3] Ballads for the man in the street told of the 'straunge whippes which the Spanyards had prepared to whippe English men',[4] or of 'the happie obtaining of the great Galleazzo'.[5] Those requiring more factual information found it in works such as *A true discourse of the Armie which the King of Spaine caused to be assembled in the Haven of Lisbon against England*,[6] or in *Certaine advertisements out of Ireland concerning the losses and distresses happened to the Spanish navie*,[7] or in the *Orders set downe by the Duke of Medina to be observed in the voyage toward England*.[8] Nor was it only in 1588 that Spain was in the news: throughout the reign of Elizabeth men were constantly finding on the bookstalls ballads and pamphlets telling of encounters on land or sea with the Spaniards, or terrifying stories of men escaped from the Inquisition and the dungeons of Spain. As

---

[1] *STC* 11644. Ed. by J. W. Cunliffe, *George Gascoigne* (Cambridge, 1910), vol. II, pp. 596–7.
[2] *STC* 20651.
[3] *STC* 19935 (1588).
[4] *STC* 6558 (1588).
[5] *STC* 6557 (1588).
[6] *STC* 22999 (1588).
[7] *STC* 14257 (1588).
[8] *STC* 19625 (1588).

mentioned above, there was no lack of news of the struggles between the Spaniards and the men of the Low Countries, whether recounted by the gifted pen of a Gascoigne, or by some less skilled writer. Nor were the internal affairs of Spain entirely without interest to Englishmen, for we find publications which discuss the present state of Spain in 1594 (*STC* 22996), or print an edict of 1597, setting out the conditions governing the exchange of money,[1] or a relation of the King's reception in Valliodolid (*sic*), and at the English College there, in 1592.[2]

Most other countries, however, do not seem to have attracted much attention. We have a few accounts of coronations, or of royal baptisms, but other than sensational news (which will be treated later) only fights against the Turks and scraps of news from Rome, or Vienna, or Switzerland apparently provided worthwhile news.

Not only the events themselves, but anything that concerned those who took part in them interested the Elizabethans who were eager readers of little pamphlets which told of the tragic death of the Admiral Châtillon, or of William of Nassau, or most celebrated of all, of course, that of Sir Philip Sidney. This latter event called forth at least a dozen pieces extolling his noble life and valiant death. For lighter moments there were works such as a 32-page quarto, telling of the reception of the Earl of Leicester by the Landgrave of Hesse to whom he had been sent in 1596 by the Queen. This work, the preface tells us, may be read as 'matter of pleasure, fit for a spare houer in an afternoon', since it gives an eyewitness's account of the Earl's journey to Hessen to take part in the christening of the Landgrave's daughter.[3]

We still have to consider the kind of news that circulated freely, generally in ballad or broadsheet form, and catered to the tastes of a comparatively uneducated public. Such news was mainly concerned with wonders and portents, with mon-

---

[1] *STC* 19833. [2] *STC* 19836a.
[3] *STC* 18013. E. Monings, *The Landgrave of Hessen his princelie receiving of her Majesties Embassador* (1596), sig. A 2.

sters, with witches and other manifestations of the unusual. Writers of such pieces told of *Wonderfull straunge sightes seene in the element, over the citie of London*,[1] or of comets and blazing stars. From Suffolk and Essex in 1583 there came a report of the sky raining wheat for six or seven miles,[2] while other accounts told of earthquakes at home or abroad or of 'tempestuous and outrageous floods' in 1570,[3] or of tempests such as that at Bungay in August 1577, when there was a violent rain, with lightning and thunder 'the like whereof hath been seldome seene. With the appearance of a horrible shaped thing, sensibly perceived of the people then and there assembled', which instantly killed a number of people.[4] All these things were signs of God's displeasure it was said, so that after feeding the credulity of people to the full, the writers generally went on to emphasize the need for repentance and reform. Thus the scene at Bungay was said to be 'a spectacle no doubt of God's judgement, which as the fire of our iniquites hath kindled, so by none other meanes then by the teares of repentance it may be quenched'.[5]

Then again, at Beccles in Suffolk, in 1586, the great wind on St Andrew's Eve was followed by a fire which was said to have done twenty thousand pounds worth of damage, and to have destroyed some eighty houses. Nicholas Colman of Norwich, not otherwise known to have been a bookseller, had two accounts of this fire printed for him by Robert Robinson of London[6]—an interesting example of local enterprise.

Another group of writings dealing with unusual events told of happenings such as *A notable and prodigious Historie of a Mayden, who for sundry yeeres neither eateth, drinketh, nor sleepeth, and yet liveth* (1589), a story imported from Germany, but vouched for by the Commissioners of the County Palatine of the Rhine, we are told.[7] Another tells of the 'striking

---

[1] *STC* 6433 [1583].
[2] *STC* 982.1.
[3] *STC* 15032.
[4] *STC* 11050, sig. A1.
[5] Sig. A2.
[6] *STC* 6564 and 23259.
[7] *STC* 5678.

dumme of two of the cheefe of the Holyhouse, as they were pronouncing sentence of death against two English Mariners, unto whom they had offered great promotions to have them serve against the King of France, and their own Countrie'.[1] Perhaps the most remarkable of these stories concerns a young child who was heard to cry in its mother's womb, eight days before it was born on New Year's Eve 1599, and on the following 14 January 'it fell sick, and casting up its eyes to Heaven cried out "O my God" three times. This is vouched for by a Seemster and another woman who were present. At two o'clock in the morning other words were spoken, among which there seemed to be these: "Aye me" repeated, and then the child died.'[2] Like so many other pieces of this nature, this story has its moral: 'By this may be seene, that the little babes also have the Holy Ghost, although some (and especially the Anabaptists) say no. Which now appears to the contrary.'

Another unfailing source of popular news was provided by accounts of the birth of human monsters of various sorts. Broadsheets told of Siamese twins, or of 'a monstrous deformed infant...a notable and most terrible example against Incest and Whoredom', in which it was begotten.[3] Another told of an infant born out of wedlock 'living and like to live', but lacking legs and arms, for 'Nature cropped his limbs to wreak her spite on the parent's sin',[4] while a child born at Maidstone in 1568 is described as having 'first a mouth fitted on the right side, like a libardes (leopards) mouth, terrible to behold'. Occurrences such as these the moralists used as examples and warnings to the age. 'If we will not be warned neither by His word, nor yet by His wonderful workes, then let us be assured that the strange monstrous sights do demonstrate unto us that His heavy indignation wyl shortly come upon us for our monstrous living.' With this for an excuse, the booksellers poured forth ballads and broadsheets, telling of children with ruffs, or of a 'woman (now to be seene in London)...in the

[1] *STC* 15704 (1591).   [2] *STC* 20511.
[3] *STC* 20575 (1600).   [4] *STC* 12207.

midst of whose forehead there groweth out a crooked horne of foure inches long', and other sights, some of which were said to be on view at various places in London.

Animals with anatomical peculiarities were described, such as a pig with a dolphin's head, born at Charing Cross, or a 'Herring, having on the one side the picture of two armed men fighting, and on the other most strange Characters, as in the Picture here expressed'. Pictures, indeed, were an important part of these productions, since their boldly drawn woodcuts made an immediate appeal to the illiterate, and whetted the appetite for the detailed account which accompanied them. But even these pictures (vivid as many of them were), the reader is assured, are but a poor indication of the full horror of the actual specimen itself, since as one writer put it:

> No Carver can, nor Paynter maye,
> The sam so ougly make,
> As doth itself shewe at this daye
> A sight to make thee quake
>
> But here thou hast by Printer's arte
> A signe thereof to se,
> Let eche man saye within his harte
> It preacheth now to me.[1]

Among the many kinds of popular news in circulation, none perhaps was more popular than that which told of witches and of witchcraft. Up and down the country wretched men, but mostly women, were brought before the Assize Courts where they were charged and generally convicted of the most outrageous doings. Some sort of transcript of these proceedings, often accompanied with an alleged confession by the accused, made exciting reading, and fed the fears and prejudices of the credulous reader, for as a writer of 1574 puts it: 'This Realme is known by common experience to be troubled with Witches, Sorcerers, and other such wise men and women.'[2] One such

[1] STC 6177. J. D., *A description of a monstrous Chylde born at Chichester* (1562).   [2] STC 3738, sig. A 2.

WITCHCRAFT

woman was 'Margaret Hacket, a notorious witch, who consumed a young man to death rotted his bowels and back-bone asunder, and was executed at Tyburne 19 February 1585', while another account tells of one Peter Stubbe, 'a most wicked Sorcerer, who in the likeness of a woolfe, committed many murders, continuing this divilish practise twenty-five yeeres'.[1] Other accounts tell of the sufferings of the victim of the agents of the Devil, such as Alexander Nyndge, at Herringswell in Suffolk in 1573. An evil spirit entered into him, and for three days tried to carry him away, so that six men could scarcely hold him down. To the truth of this the names of many witnesses are appended.[2] Only the reading of the scriptures finally exorcized this devil, who flew out of the window crying 'Bawe, wawe, bawe, wawe'. In 1584 there was reported the case of Margaret Cooper, 'a woman possessed with the Devill, who in the likenesse of a headlesse beare fetched her out of her bedd, and in the presence of seven persons, most straungely roulled her thorow three Chambers, and doune a high paire of staiers'.[3] The number of printed pieces extant is quite considerable, but a survey of the *Stationers' Register* reminds us of how many of these slender pieces we have lost which were evidently often read till they fell to pieces.[4]

Although they do not concern us here as news, the publication of a number of works (some of them of considerable size) which dealt with the whole subject of witchcraft should be remembered. These books set out the case for and against the belief in witchcraft, and in the course of doing so, give many

---

[1] *STC* 23375.   [2] *STC* 18752.   [3] *STC* 5681.

[4] The following are some of the items printed during the reign of Elizabeth concerning witches and witchcraft: *STC* 19845 (1566) at Chelmsford; *STC* 24099 (1566), J. Walsh at Exeter; *STC* 3738 (1574), R. Pinder and A. Brigges at London; *STC* 18752 (1578), A. Nyndge, Suffolk; *STC* 23267 (1579), E. Stile and three others at Windsor and Abington; *STC* 5681 (1584), at Ditchet; *STC* 10841 (1591), Dr Fian; *STC* 25019 (1593), three witches at Warboys; *STC* 6281 (1598), W. Sommers; *STC* 6282 (1599), J. Darrell; *STC* 18070 (1600), seven persons in Lancs.

243   16-2

examples of alleged possession and of the practices of witches.[1]

Some indication of the interest shown by the public in the provision of news can be gained from the speed with which copies were entered in the *Stationers' Register*. For example, the traitor, Everard Haunce, was condemned to be executed on 31 July 1581. Within five days, one pamphlet had been published telling of his end, while another had been entered, which complained that most of the matter of the first pamphlet was untrue.[2] Only two days after Edmund Campion was lodged in the Tower, a ballad and a pamphlet were entered describing his capture in the summer of 1581, while only one day elapsed between his execution and an account of it being lodged at Stationers' Hall. Christopher Barker, the Queen's Printer, took time by the forelock when he entered *A true and plaine declaration of the horrible Treasons, practised by William Parry, The manner of his arraignment, Conviction and Execution* on 27 February 1585, three days before the actual execution.[3] In a number of cases of trials for treason or murder the matter was scarcely concluded before the stationers were at Stationers' Hall making their entries. Thus, when Arnold Cosby was condemned to be executed on 27 January 1591, Edward White two days before entered a work entitled *The Araignment, Examination, Confession and Judgement of A. Cosbye: who wilfully murdered the Lord Burke...and was executed the 27 of [January] 1591*.[4] This he followed by another pamphlet entitled *The manner of the death and execution of Arnold Cosbie...at Wandsworth townes end on the 27 of Januarie 1591* (1591).[5] White was only one jump ahead of another of his rivals. Robert Robinson, who also entered an account of the affair, to which the Wardens gave

---

[1] Outstanding amongst these are the works of R. Scot, *The discoverie of Witchcraft* (1584); James I, *Daemonologie* (1597), and S. Harsnet, *A Discoverie of the fraudulent practises of John Darrel* (1599). John Darrel, the celebrated exorcist, put out a series of books between 1598 and 1602, defending his belief in witches (*STC* 6281–8).

[2] *STC* 12934, sig. A2.   [3] *STC* 19342.
[4] *STC* 5813.   [5] *STC* 5814.

a provisional licence, 'Provyded alwayes that yf it be hurtfull or prejudiciall to the copie entred the last day for Edward White touchinge Cosbyes Condemnacon and arraygnement... this entrance to be voyd as though it had never ben entred.'[1]

To turn to other types of news. The burning of the steeple of St Paul's by lightning on 4 June 1561 was recorded in a work entered by William Seres entitled *The true report of the burnyng of the steple and churche of Paules* only seven days later,[2] while the great earthquake of 6 April 1580 led to two books and three ballads being entered, one the next day and four more two days after the event, and before the end of June ten others had followed. The need for speed in reporting sensational news was evidently clearly appreciated by the book-trade.

As we have seen, there was news from overseas constantly arriving in England by one means or another; and in particular that dealing with the Protestant fortunes against the Catholics in the Low Countries and France was always sure of a welcome and quickly put on to the market. We have but little evidence of what steps were taken to get hold of these accounts of foreign affairs, but we can tell something of the speed with which they were given an English dress and put into print. Indeed, it is at first startling to read that *The true coppie of a letter written from the leager by Arnheim the 27 day of July 1591* was entered on the 20th of the same month until we recall that England still adhered to the old calendar, while many continental countries had adopted the Gregorian or New Style calendar, and were therefore ten days in advance of the English dating. Nevertheless, this meant that the entry was made only three days after the letter was written.[3] An even more complete record is to be seen on the title-page of a little pamphlet in the Folger Library which reads: *A true rehersall of the Honorable and Triumphant Victory which the defenders of the Trueth have had against the tyrannical and blood-thirsty heape of ye Albanists. Which came*

---

[1] Arber, *Transcript*, vol. II, p. 574.
[2] *STC* 19930. Written by James Pilkington, Bishop of Durham.
[3] *STC* 781.

to passe withouten the worthye Cyttie of Harlem in Holland, the xxv. daye of Marche. 1573. Translated out of Dutch into English the thirde day of Apryll: the which copy in Dutch was Printed in Delft, the xxvii. day of March laste paste. Since the title-page of the English version is dated 6 April, the whole transaction took a bare three weeks.[1] Later in the same year, a letter from the Low Countries, which was not written before 13 August, was in the hands of an English publisher by the 24th, that is allowing for the ten days difference between the Old Style and the New, only three weeks later.[2]

A great deal of similar evidence might be quoted from the rapidity with which French news was published in England, and once again we may take the year 1590. As might have been expected, the Battle of Ivry, fought on 4 March (O.S.), gave the book-trade an opportunity that was greedily taken. On 10 March an 'excellent ditty' was entered by William Wright,[3] while on 6 April there was entered for Richard Oliffe an account of the battle, dated from Dieppe, 20 March.[4] Four days later another account, which carried on the narrative of events up to 14 March, was set down at Stationers' Hall, so that there again little time was lost.[5]

Later events in the same year were also quickly recorded. St Dennis surrendered to Henry of Navarre on 19 June (O.S.) and this was known in England by 10 July when an entry concerning it was made.[6] At the end of the next month on 30 July, Henry made a declaration before the city of Paris in which he roundly asserted that 'Neyther this crowne, nor the Empire of all the whole earth were able to make me chaunge the Religion wherein I have been brought uppe and instructed from my mothers pappes, and the which I uphold to be true', and this was entered on 24 August.[7] A few years later Henry found that 'Paris is worth a Mass', and on 23 April 1594, John Windet entered for his copy a translation of the French account

---

[1] *STC* 13578.   [2] *STC* 18438.   [3] *STC* 13135.
[4] *STC* 13131.   [5] *STC* 13145.   [6] *STC* 13128.
[7] *STC* 13114.

of *The Order of Ceremonies observed in the anointing and Coronation of...Henry IIII* which had taken place at Chartres on 17 February.

Even news from farther afield was given an English dress with remarkable quickness. An eight-page pamphlet, telling of the fights against the Turks in Malta and elsewhere up to 27 June 1565, was translated into English and printed in Ghent by 27 August.[1] Further news of the defeat of the Turks in Hungary on 5 August 1566 was translated into German and printed in Augsburg, and afterwards translated into English and entered by John Awdeley on 21 September.[2]

So the list might be continued, but enough perhaps has been said to show how comparatively quickly the English book market snapped up whatever it thought might interest its readers. While it is not possible in most cases to tell the exact day that the work was on sale on the bookstalls, the delay after the entry in the *Stationers' Register* could only have been a matter of a few days, since most of these news items are a few pages only, and everything encouraged the trade to get them on sale as quickly as possible.

10. Literature

To turn to the literature of the Elizabethan age is to confront an age responsible for much of the greatest of our verse and prose. Any critical assessment of this is not the concern of this study which is mainly interested to note the volume and variety of the output in an endeavour to form some estimate of the various kinds of readers that the book-trade had to cater for.

First as to volume. If we take the decennial figures given by Miss Edith Klotz under the heading 'literature' in her 'Subject analysis of English Imprints for every tenth year from 1480 to 1640',[3] we find that whereas before 1560 only 13 per cent of all publications fell into this class, from then till the end of the century the number rose to 25 per cent. To put it another way,

---

[1] *STC* 17214·1.   [2] *STC* 24716.
[3] *Huntington Library Quarterly*, vol. 1 (1937–8), p. 417.

the decennial figures for 1480–1550 total 89 volumes, while those for 1560–1600 amount to 266 volumes, the output for 1550 being 21 and that for 1600 being 84. This sharp rise is confirmed by a detailed analysis of 'prose fiction' made by Mr Sterg O'Dell, from which it can be calculated that the production of such writings from 1588 to 1603 was three times that of the period 1475 to 1558.[1]

At the time of the incorporation of the Stationers' Company in 1557 its members could feel assured that a considerable and eager reading public was awaiting its activities, and there is every reason to believe that this public increased during the next half century. Writing in the 1580's, William Harrison declared that 'there are great number of Grammer Schooles through out the realme, and those verie liberallie indued, for the better reliefe of poore scholers, so that there are not manie corporat townes now under the Queenes dominion, that hain not one Grammar schoole at the least'.[2] The fact that there were these grammar schools postulates the existence of inferior schools where reading and writing were the staple subjects of instruction, although many of their pupils never went farther than learning to read and to write.[3] They knew enough, however, to make them a valuable element in the booksellers' clientele, and widened the range of prospective customers. The increase in the number of books published noted above indicates this, but fails to reflect the degree to which all classes of the public were being catered for, or that for one work such as the *Arcadia* there were a dozen ballads, or news pamphlets available for those whose ability to read and to reach any serious intellectual level was limited.

It was in response to this demand for an ever-widening range of publications that the booksellers increased their activities,

[1] *A Chronological List of Prose Fiction in English...1475–1640*. (Cambridge, Massachusetts Institute of Technology, 1954). Mr O'Dell defines 'prose fiction' as 'imaginative narrative not in verse'.

[2] *STC* 13569, 'The Description of England', prefixed to 'Holinshed's Chronicle' (1587), p. 151, col. 2.

[3] See pp. 167–8.

and nowhere was this more noticeable, to take one example, than in their provision of reading matter of a literary interest for the bourgeoisie. Dr Louis B. Wright has shown how this interest was catered for in such detail that it would be superfluous to retail it all over again, but a few lines from his conclusions may be usefully quoted:

The Elizabethan middle class had an eager craving for stories, a craving which was satisfied by a voluminous literature of fiction that ranged from chivalric romance to realistic tales of London life.... Entertaining stories, then as now, were abundant, and those which received the greatest acclaim were filled with a multitude of incidents, for the Elizabethan relished action. One quality more obvious in Elizabethan fiction than in modern novels and short stories was the didactic element which occupied such a conspicuous place in the literature appealing to the bourgeoisie intent upon improvement. Some of the most popular fiction professed to improve the mind, help the purse, and save the soul.... Surely even the grimmest Puritan could laugh in defense of his health. Given proper justification for the reading of stories, the Elizabethan middle-class reader consumed fiction as voraciously and as uncritically as his modern descendant.[1]

In the same way, other sections of the reading public had their own special interests: the sonnet sequences, the poetical anthologies, the books of Lyly and his followers making an appeal to one set of readers, while another group eagerly fed upon exciting, event-packed, frightening short tales, ballads and news pamphlets. It would be impossible here to survey in any detail all these various groups of writings, and a few general points, and a few special groups of writings, must serve as examples of the services rendered by the book-trade to their readers in the provision of literature.

First it should be noted that this increased demand was selective, for some forms of writing that had hitherto been popular were going out of favour. For instance, the day of the

---

[1] Wright, *Middle-Class Culture in Elizabethan England*, chapter XI. The quotation will be found on p. 417.

medieval romance was coming to an end. It is true that a few still survived,[1] but most of these only appeared once during the whole of the period, a striking contrast from the earlier part of the century, by when at least fifty editions of various romances had been published since Caxton's time. An even more remarkable indication that medieval literature was no longer in favour is to be seen in the failure of Chaucer and his contemporaries to attract. Langland, Gower, Hoccleve all go unpublished: Lydgate, outstandingly popular in the first half of the century, survives only in a reprint of one poem, *The Churl and the Bird* (1561), and Malory only appears in the edition of 1585. Even Chaucer himself was no longer popular enough to warrant a separate edition either of *The Canterbury Tales* or of *Troilus and Creseyde*, so that readers wanting a copy of these were forced to buy the folio of his 'Works' published in 1561, and again in 1598 (revised 1602). These volumes, it is true, contained many 'Chaucerian' pieces, so that they served as anthologies of medieval verse rather than editions of Chaucer only.[2]

This is perhaps the more surprising, since it cannot be said that the writings of the past, *tout court*, were rejected by the Elizabethans. On the contrary, among serious writings none were so popular as the works of the great classical authors. While some of these had appeared by 1557, the remainder of the century saw the booksellers busily exhibiting the works of many famous Greek and Latin writers. It may be that they shared the view of John Dolman, who believed that 'besydes the raskall multitude, and the learned sages, there is a meane sort of men: which although they be not learned, yet, by the quicknes of their wits, can conceive al such points of arte, as nature could give. To those, I saye, there is nothing in this book to darke.'[3]

[1] For example, *Bevis of Hampton, Blanchardine, Guy of Warwick, Huon of Bordeaux*, and *Octavian*. See for full treatment, R. S. Crane, *The Vogue of Medieval Chivalric Romance during the English Renaissance* (Menasha, Wis., 1919).

[2] See also pp. 277–8.

[3] *STC* 5317, Cicero, *Those fyve Questions, which M. T. Cicero, disputed in his Manor of Tusculanum*, translated J. Dolman (1561), sig. ¶ 4.

CLASSICAL TRANSLATIONS

Professor Lathrop, in his admirable study of the translations from the Classics from Caxton to Chapman, writes that at this period

the literature of delight takes precedence over the literature of instruction; and the center of interest turns from didactic essays on conduct to imaginative works dealing with adventurous or amatory subjects, whether in prose or verse.... This change in interest involves not merely the selection of new authors and books for translation, but expresses a different view about the classics from that held by the graver humanists of the earlier era. It turns to the classics for variety and excitement, for color, for the enrichment of life, and not for its guidance and restraint. The better translators wrote in that flush of joy at the revelation of the world of poetic delight which a long succession of youths, acolytes of verse, have felt first of all when Vergil's magic revealed it to their newly enlightened eyes.... The new translators were not in general men of affairs.... They were students, young professional men, enthusiastic for letters, or elder pedants, with the dry and warped interest in crochets which marks the tribe.[1]

A glance at the list of translations given by Lathrop will be indication enough of the continuous output of classical works, both in prose and verse. By the end of the century some of the best of ancient literature was available to those who had no Greek or Latin at their command. But we must not forget that this output was very patchy and unpredictable. How, for example, are we to explain the comparative neglect of the classical drama? That of England was in its heyday, towards the end of the sixteenth century, so that we might confidently have expected to find that the plays of Greece and Rome had all been made available to those who could not read them in the original. Not a bit of it. Neither the works of Aeschylus, nor of Sophocles, nor of Euripides were translated until the seventeenth century; and similarly the comic writers such as Aristophanes were neglected. Nor were things much better where the Roman authors were concerned. 'In spite of the

---

[1] H. B. Lathrop, *Translation from the Classics into English*, pp. 105-6.

Plautine influence on English comedy, but one drama of Plautus was translated. Terence is a school-book, and but one play of his was translated before the end of Elizabeth's reign.'[1] It was the second-rate Seneca that attracted attention, so that by 1581 Thomas Marshe was able to bring together in one volume all the ten tragedies, and thus established in the minds of readers and playwrights an idea of tragedy that certainly had a great effect on the plays produced over the next few decades. But no other Roman dramatist had anything like the same effect on the English writer or reader, and here again it was left to later centuries to make their works available in the vernacular. If we turn to lyric or narrative poetry the picture is much the same. The *Iliad* was badly translated in 1581, and had to wait until 1611 for Chapman's version of all twenty-four books, while it was not until five years later that all the *Odyssey* appeared in English. The *Aeneid* of Virgil fared better, so that the whole work was translated by 1584. So we might go on, putting together piece by piece the classical writings made available to the English reader.[2]

Not only were classical authors rifled to instruct and amuse the Elizabethans, but booksellers and writers searched eagerly among the works of French, Spanish, Portuguese and Italian authors for materials that they thought would attract an English audience. Some of these they found, for example, in the immensely long romantic tales which replaced the old romances. One or two examples will suffice perhaps to illustrate this. In 1578 Margaret Tyler translated *The First Part of The Mirrour of Princely deedes and Knighthood*, by Ortuñez de Calahorra, and for the next twenty-three years the story of the adventures of various peers of chivalry and their ladies entranced a public that followed the extraordinary exploits and unending adventures which befell them. They have a specific intention, so their translator tells us, namely to show 'the just reward of mallice & cowardise, with the good speede of honestie and courage',

[1] Lathrop, *op. cit.* p. 309.
[2] For earlier discussion of translations from the Classics, see pp. 90 ff.

but also she has to admit that the stories 'have bene rather devised to beguile time, then to breede matter of sad learning'.[1]

Another group of stories was translated by Anthony Munday—the Palmerin series. These works kept his readers entertained over some two decades while he recounted the story of Palmerin D'Oliva and his offspring, and their amazing adventures. Munday, as was his custom, is deliberately exploiting a market, and he frankly admits this when he writes at the beginning of the *First Part of Palmerin d'Oliva* explaining that

a Booke growing too bigge in quantitie, is Profitable neither to the minde nor the purse: for that men are now so wise and the world so hard, as they love not to buy pleasure at unreasonable price. And yet the first Part will entice them to have the second, when (it may be alledged) the cost is as great [as] though it had come altogether: yet I am of the minde, that a man grutched not so much at a little money, payd at severall times, as hee doth at once, for this advantage he hath, in the meane time he may imploy halfe his money on more needfull occasions, and raise some benefit toward buying the second part.[2]

This is a give-away indeed, so Munday rapidly moves to safer ground in declaring that these stories 'hath so highly pleased the Emperours, Kings, and mighty Potentates, if then the Inferiour sort mislike, it is because they are not capable of so especiall deservings'. The 'Inferiour sort' did like them, no doubt not influenced very much by the feelings of Emperors and potentates, but for the reason given above by Margaret Tyler.

The mention of the great by Munday reminds us that, while literature no longer remained the preserve of the aristocracy and the wealthy, there was still a large enough market among them to encourage the publication of anthologies, or books of

---

[1] *STC* 18860, sig. A 4. The first part of this series was printed in 1578, the ninth and last in 1601.

[2] *STC* 19160. The passage is quoted from Wright, *Middle-Class Culture in Elizabethan England*, p. 380.

verse, or writings such as those of John Lyly. Lyly's euphuistic works, with their 'unnatural natural history', their word play and their characteristic sentence structure were clearly for a sophisticated audience. They set the fashion for a period, so that to speak and write 'pure Euphues' was very much *à la mode*, and while edition after edition of Lyly's works came from the press, imitators, such as Munday, tried their hands with works of a similar nature.[1]

For even more refined tastes there was Sidney's *Arcadia*. It was written in the first instance ('onlie for you, onely to you') and then sent to his sister. As for the manner of its composition, Sidney writes to her: 'Your deare selfe can best witnes the maner, being done in loose sheetes, of paper, most of it in your presence, the rest, by sheetes, sent unto you, as fast as they were done.' It was first published in 1590, 'augmented and ended' in 1593, and issued 'with sundry new additions' in 1598. Despite its aristocratic origins, R. Waldegrave thought it of general enough interest to warrant a cheaply produced edition which he also published in 1599. Further editions of the book were called for, so that the edition of 1638 carries on its title-page the words: 'Now the ninth time published.'[2]

To go to the other end of the scale we have the ballads, published for the most part on single sheets, sometimes with a crude woodcut at their head, and sometimes mentioning the popular tune of the day to which they could be sung. They celebrated a wide variety of events, generally sensational, often reported for their crude, emotional interest, or as 'hot news' items. They told of 'moving accidents', of murders, robberies,

---

[1] See, for example, *STC* 18283, A. Munday, *Zelauto, the fountain of Fame* (1580); *STC* 6817, J. Dickenson, *Arisbas, Euphues amidst his slumbers* (1594); *STC* 12269, R. Greene, *Mamillia; a looking glass for the ladies of England* (1580).

[2] See the edition by A. Feuillerat of *The Prose Works of Sir Philip Sidney* (Cambridge, 1912, reprinted 1962), vol. I, pp. 522–3. For some 'Arcadian imitations' by R. Greene, see *STC* 12217, *Arbasto, the anatomie of fortune* (1584); *STC* 12224, *Ciceronis amor, Tullies loue* (1589); *STC* 12285, *Pandosto. The triumph of Time* (1588).

THE PUBLICATION OF PLAYS

battles, etc. As was inevitable, hundreds of them have perished. Read and re-read, passed from hand to hand, and rapidly decreasing in interest as the event they commemorated faded from people's memory, the ballads are the most elusive of printed matter. Many survive in single copies only, and many others are known only by entries in the *Stationers' Register*, and how many of them were ever printed it is quite impossible at this time of day to tell.[1] But that they formed a valuable part of the booksellers' stock is certain: not only were they readily saleable, but they drew people to the bookstalls and thus encouraged them to look around.

The publication of plays had not concerned the early printers very seriously.[2] Only twenty-seven plays appear to have been printed by 1558 (though eight of these were reprinted later), but during Elizabeth's reign there were 168 publications of plays, some of them running to two or more editions. Their popularity greatly increased in the last decade of the century, no less than 103 plays being published between 1590 and 1602. As is well known, they have survived in limited numbers—many in single and at times mutilated copies. The players were often opposed to their printing, so that what went to the press was frequently an imperfect version got together by various means, honest or dishonest, as the case may be. A good example of this is seen in the preface by John Day to his edition of *The Tragidie of Ferrex and Porrex* by T. Norton and T. Sackville [c. 1570], in which he says:

One W. G. [i.e. William Griffith] getting a copie therof at some yongmans hand that lacked a litle money and much discretion, in the last great plage. an. 1565. about v yeares past, while the said Lord was out of England and T. Norton farre out of London, and neither

---

[1] For the fullest information about the ballads and the printers, see 'An Analytical Index to the Ballad-Entries (1557–1709) in the Registers of the Company of Stationers of London', by Hyder E. Rollins, *Studies in Philology*, vol. XXI (1924), pp. 1–324. See also Louis B. Wright, *op. cit.* pp. 418–35.

[2] The magnificent work of Sir Walter Greg, *A Bibliography of the English Printed Drama to the Restoration* (4 vols. 1939–59), makes more than a token mention of the plays unnecessary.

of them both made privie, put it forth exceedingly corrupted, even as if by meanes of a broker for hire, he should have entised into his house a faire maide and done her vilainie, and after all to bescratched her face, torne her apparell, berayed and disfigured her, and then thrust her out of dores dishonested.[1]

Shakespeare's plays naturally suffered from this kind of unlawful printing, and the briefest examination of say the 'Bad Quarto' of Hamlet (1603), side by side with the 'Good Quarto' of 1604 will make clear why Shakespeare's fellows, Heminge and Condell spoke of 'stolne and surreptitious copies, maimed and deformed by the frauds and stealthes of injurious impostors that exposed them'. Whether the text was fraudulent or genuine, however, was not any easy matter for the ordinary person to determine, and the plays sold well enough to encourage the book-trade to print them, and often to reprint them. These little quartos of thirty to forty pages were sold for sixpence, and advertised by fixing on to posts in prominent places a print of the title-page,[2] which was often so worded as to attract customers, and tempt them to buy a play said to be 'Very delectable and full of mirth', or one labelled as 'the most lamentable tragedy' and so on. As an example of the kind of appeal made by these title-pages we may take the following: *The Tragedy of King Richard the Third. Containing, his treacherous Plots against his brother Clarence: the pittiefull murther of his innocent nephewes: his tyrannicall usurpation: with the whole course of his detested life, and most deserved death. As it hath beene lately acted by the Right honourable the Lord Chamberlaine his seruants.*[3]

As we have already seen, some authors, or translators, or publishers have put on record the reasons that impelled them to print, and it may be valuable at the end of this section to gather up some general impressions. Three points in particular are mentioned again and again. First, the original desire of the

---

[1] *STC* 18685, sig. A2. William Griffith published *The Tragedie of Gorboduc* in 1565. Sir Walter Greg says that the charge that the first edition was 'exceedingly corrupted' appears to be unfounded.
[2] See p. 260.   [3] *STC* 22314 (1597), see also p. 300.

writer to keep his work for the eye of a limited circle. This, of course, was not a desire confined to the writers of literary works only, since there was a widespread reluctance to have one's work hawked around to become the target of malign critics. Some of these disclaimers, as has been shown above, were not really serious, but even so, it is probable that some sonnet sequences, such as those 'to the fairest Coelia', were as the author said, 'a private matter: I was fullie determined to haue concealed my Sonnets, as things privie to my selfe'.[1] Similarly, Abraham Fraunce declares that his version of Tasso's *Amyntas* 'was first prepared for one or two, and was afterward by the meanes of a few made common to manie, and so pitifully disfigured by the barbarous handling of unskilfull pen men that his own Phillis would never have taken him for Amintas',[2] and there is no reason to believe that he is not telling the truth. There is plenty of evidence that much writing circulated in manuscript, as with Shakespeare's *Sonnets*, or the *Arcadia* of Sidney, and once they had left the author's chamber, he was most likely to have lost any control over them.

Secondly, writers were at pains to emphasize the practical, didactic and moral nature of their writings. The translator of *Amadis of Fraunce* says it is put out as a means 'whereout men may learne to be noble oratours, wise and prudent counsellors, excellent Rhetoricians, expert captains, amorous companions, fervent & honest lovers, secrete messengers...'.[3] These writers purport, it is true, to give pleasure, but at the same time to profit their readers in instructing them how to live, and how 'to purge melancholy from the minde & grosse humours from the body'.[4] In publishing *The Famous, Pleasant, and variable Historie of Palladine of England*, Munday is careful to say at the outset, romance notwithstanding, that 'heerin is no offence offered to the wise by wanton speeches, or encouragement to

---

[1] *STC* 19618, W. Percy (1594), sig. A2.
[2] *STC* 23692 (1587), sig. ¶2. It was issued 'newelie corrected' in 1588.
[3] *STC* 545 [1567], sig. ¶3ᵛ.   [4] *STC* 3714 (1602), sig. A1.

the loose by lascivious matter'.[1] To ensure this, writers who exploited the rich but dangerous sources of Italian story-tellers found it wise to give their versions a moral twist, and 'by discovering all vices in their ugly deformities, to make their mortall enemies (the sacred Vertues) to shine the clearer, being set downe by them, and compared with them'.[2]

Lastly, one cannot fail to notice the number of times either author or printer appeals to his readers as men of some education and gentlemen. 'Learned (or Courteous) Gentlemen Readers', members of the Inns of Court and of the universities are frequently addressed and asked for their support;[3] the approach of Term encourages the bookseller to get ready new work. *The Shepheardes Complaint* [1596], a poem in English hexameters, is dedicated by its author to 'all courteous Gentlemen, Readers, Scholers, and whosoever else affect the studie of Poetrie',[4] and so on. Some of this is but fashion, and is inveighed against by Dekker when he writes:

To keepe *Custome* in reparations, he must be honyed, and come-over with *Gentle Reader*, *Courteous Reader*, and *Learned Reader*, though he have no more *Gentilitie* in him than *Adam* had (that was but a gardner) no more *Civilitie* than a *Tartar*, and no more *Learning* than the most errand *Stinkard*, that (except his owne name) could never finde any thing in the Horne-booke.[5]

Nevertheless, for certain kinds of books the support of an educated and sophisticated reading public was almost a necessity, and it was but prudent of the booksellers to flatter them.

---

[1] *STC* 5541 (1588), sig. *1. Cf. the title-pages of *STC* 18268, 19161.

[2] Wright, *Middle-Class Culture in Elizabethan England*, p. 403, quoting from the translator's preface to the first English edition of Boccaccio, *The Decameron* (1620). In Appendix I of his monograph on *Robert Greene* (New York, 1915) J. C. Jordan demonstrates how persistently Greene uses this device in his tale telling.

[3] *STC* 3631, N. Breton, *The arbour of amorous devices* (1597). In a preface the printer writes: 'Your absence this long time of vacation hindered my poore Presse from publishing any pleasing Pamphlet to recreate your minds, as it was wont.... Such as are in the country God sende them a happy and speedy return to London.' Cf. *STC* 5541, sig. *4, which reminds readers that the work was promised by Easter Term. Cf. *STC* 12367, 16674.

[4] *STC* 6820, sig. A 2.   [5] *STC* 6534, *The Wonderfull yeare. 1603*, sig. A2^v.

CHAPTER VI

PRINTERS AND BOOKSELLERS

Although they have continually been mentioned in earlier chapters something more may usefully be said concerning the printers and the booksellers. Since both functions were frequently discharged by one and the same person any attempt to separate the parts played by each may easily become divorced from reality. The early printers nearly all printed and marketed their own wares, but the practice soon grew whereby booksellers who had no press of their own put out to whatever printer they chose works that they wanted to see in print. This meant that the printer had a number of courses open to him. He could print and market a book for himself, or he might limit the risk of production by joining with one or more others in putting out a book, or he might print it for someone else, in which case his liability would cease the moment his bill was paid and the printed stock handed over.

The bookseller's outlay, on the other hand, went in the purchase of a various stock with which he could make a display on his stall, or if he had sufficient capital he could order the whole or part of an edition which he could dispose of in any way he pleased. Booksellers varied in their methods of doing business: some were energetic in their search for new works; some preferred to specialize in certain kinds of books; some liked to make a quick turnover, and put their money into slender pamphlets, broadsheets or contemporary accounts of exciting happenings at home or abroad. Both printers and booksellers were eager to serve the needs of such men as were pictured by Thomas Churchyard, the old hack-poet when he wrote:

> Some readers lookes, for newes from forrayne lands,
> A custome old, that no new world can leave,
> Some buyes new bookes, that coms from writers hands,
> To see what works, the laboring wit can weave.

Some steps in hast, and leanes on Stationers stall,
To aske what stuffe, hath passed Printers Presse,
Some reades awhile, but nothing buyes at all,
For in two lines, they give a pretty gesse,
What doth the booke, contayne such schollers thinke,
To spend no pence, for paper, pen, and inke.[1]

In these verses Churchyard recalls what might have been seen daily as bookmen searched for something to read, and in particular searched for it on the stalls in London at St Paul's the heart of the book-trade. There in the Churchyard and in the street near by were congregated the shops and stalls of those engaged in the various processes of producing and supplying the public with books. Each man displayed in a prominent place his device by which his stall could be easily identified. Richard Tottell could be found 'at the sign of the Hand and Sun'; Christopher Barker 'at the sign of the Tiger's Head', or Francis Coldocke 'at the sign of the Green Dragon', and so with others. Some men were known to specialize in certain kinds of books, so that the lawyer went straight to Tottell or the searcher for the latest topical pamphlet to John Wolfe. Otherwise, customers had to go from stall to stall until they found what they wanted, or to accept the apprentice's offer to 'go see if in the Churchyard I can find them'. As they went from stall to stall men would find stuck up in conspicuous places on posts or walls the title-pages of books which set out in great detail at times the contents of the work, thus enabling the prospective reader to get some idea of what the book was about.[2] Thus *The Merchant of Venice* is enticingly summarized on its title-page which reads: *The most excellent Historie of the* 'Merchant of Venice'. *With the extreame crueltie of* 'Shylocke' *the Jewe towards the sayd Marchant, in cutting a just pound of his flesh; and the obtayning of* 'Portia' *by the choyse of three*

[1] STC 5242, *The Mirror of Man, and Manners of Men* (1594), sig. A2ᵛ.
[2] For references to the pasting of title-pages on posts see, for example, STC nos. 195, 1301.1, 16674, 24598, 25743.

chests. As it hath beene divers times acted by the Lord Chamberlaine his Servants. Written by William Shakespeare.

This practice, unfortunately, led to the wildest filling up of the title-page with overemphatic statements, calculated to catch the attention of the passer by. When these works are only ephemeral pamphlets dealing with monsters, portents, unusual happenings or startling news of one kind or another, the cheap Jack methods may perhaps be ignored, but in far too many instances works on religion, various arts and crafts, or books of instruction had unduly verbose and vociferous title-pages. Take, for instance, the title-page of Angel Day's work on letter-writing. It is called:

The English Secretorie: or plaine and direct Method for the enditing of all manner of Epistles or Letters, as well Familiar as others: the like whereof hath never hithertoo beene published. Studiouslie now corrected, refined, & amended in far more apt and better sorte than before: according to the Authors true meaning, delivered in his former edition, Togeather (also) with the second part then left out, and long since promised to be performed. Also, a declaration of all such Tropes, Figures or Schemes as either usually, or for ornament sake, are in this method required. Finally, the partes & office of a Secretorie, in like manner amplie discoursed. All which for the best & easiest direction for young learners etc. are now newlie, wholie & jointly published. By Angel Day.[1]

Titles like this obviously defeat their own ends, since they run on and on until the eye is fatigued and the imagination blunted. Although we may sympathize and understand the composer's intentions, we cannot but deplore these typographical monstrosities, however limited the bookseller found himself in means of making his wares known. Besides displaying the new title-pages in this way, the apprentices would be outside the stalls crying, 'What lack you Gentlemen? See a new Booke; new come forth Sir—but a new Booke, Sir!' At times no doubt they were fortunate in attracting custom,

---

[1] *STC* 6402 (1592). The first edition was published in 1586.

but many books must have lain on the stalls for a long time awaiting a purchaser, a condition expected by Thomas Campion who addressed his book in the following terms:

> Whether thus haste my little booke so fast?
> To Paules Churchyard. What! in those cels to stand?
> With one leafe like a riders cloke put up
> To catch a Termer? Or lye rustie there
> With rimes a terme set out, or two, before?
> Some will redeeme me—Few. Yes, reade mee too—
> Fewer. Nay, love me—Now thou dot'st I see.[1]

Authors tried to get their books known by giving lists of their works hitherto printed or soon to come into print. The most extensive of such lists known to me is that set out by John Dee in *A letter, contayning a most briefe Discourse Apologeticall* (1599). In this he notes down the titles of no less than fifty-one books and manuscripts, some of them already in print, some of the rest 'perfectly finished: and some, yet unfinished'.[2] As this list was composed towards the end of his life Dee could not have had much hope that all of it would get into print, and a more realistic list is that of Thomas Hill inserted at the end of his *The proffitable Arte of Gardening, now the third time set fourth* (1568). In this Hill lists eight titles of 'bookes and treatises, all readie Printed', followed by five others which are 'now in a readynesse to be imprinted and the most of them with the Printers'. Lastly, he describes eight others 'which remaine wyth mee fullye ended, halfe done, and part begunne of them'.[3]

---

[1] *STC* 4543, *Observations in the Art of English Poesie* (1602), sig. A 4.

[2] *STC* 6460, sigs. A 4, B 2ᵛ.

[3] *STC* 13491. The list is printed in full in Wright, *Middle-Class Culture in Elizabethan England*, pp. 566 ff. Three years later the number had risen to 23 titles (*STC* 13482, *The Contemplation of Mankinde*), grouped in three similar categories. In 1586 he published *A Briefe and pleasaunt Treatise, Entituled 'Naturall and Artificiall Conclusions'*, which he says he had promised in 1576, and he adds a list of three works, 'all of which looke for at the Printers handes so shortly as may bee'. See *STC* 13481, sig. A 1ᵛ. For other examples, see E. H. Miller, *The Professional Writer in Elizabethan England* (Cambridge, Mass., 1959), p. 212.

AT THE BOOKSELLERS

Sometimes authors promise to produce further volumes 'next Term' or 'shortly', thus warning prospective purchasers of what was to come,[1] but on the whole it must be admitted that the bookseller was very limited as to what he could do to make his wares known. Undoubtedly, then as now, his shop or stall was his most valuable outlet, so that readers browsing over his stock had to be tolerated, even if as one author averred 'many peruse them ere they be sold'. Men went from stall to stall seeking what they wanted, and they may be seen through the eyes of contemporary writers, such as Samuel Rowlands, who depicts a colloquy 'between a Gentleman and a Prentice' in the following words:

GENTLEMAN. Whats that with Nashes name to it there?
PRENTICE. Marry, Sir, tis *Pierce Penny-lesse*, sir. I am sure you know it: it hath beene abroad a great while, sir.
GENTLEMAN. Oh, thou sayest true; I know it passing well; is that it? But where's the new Booke that thou tel'st me off. Which is it?
PRENTICE. Marry, looke you sir, this is a prettie odde conceit, Of a Merrie meeting heere in London, betweene a *Wife*, a *Widdow*, and a *Mayde*.
GENTLEMAN. Merrie meeting, why, that Title is stale. Ther's a Booke called *'Tis merry when knaves meete*. And ther's a Ballad, *Tis merry when Malt-Men meete*: and besides, ther's an olde Proverbe, *The more the merrier*: And therefore I thinke sure I have seene it.
PRENTICE. You are decived, sir, Ile assure you, for I will bee deposed upon all the Bookes in my Shoppe that you have not seene it: 'tis another maner of thing then you take it to bee, sir: for I am

---

[1] See, for example, *STC* 5242, T. Churchyard, *The Mirror... and Manners of Men* (1594), where he says: 'All the other books promised comes out shortly', and *STC* 6848, L. Digges, *An Arithmeticall Militare Treatise* (1579), sig. a3ᵛ, where the Printer announces the preparation of six works 'begon by the Author, heereafter to be published. All these and others long sithens the Author had finished and published, had not the Infernall Furies, envying such his Fœlicitie, and happie Societie with his Mathematicall Muses, for many yeares so tormented him with Lawe-Brables, that he hath bene enforced to discontinue those his delectable studies.'

sure you are in Love, sir, or at least will bee with one of these three: or say you deale but with two, the *Widdow* and the *Mayde*, because the Wife is another mans commoditie: is it not a prettie thing to carry *Wife*, *Mayde* and *Widdow* in youre pocket when you may as it were conferre and heare them talk together when you will? nay and that which is a further matter, utter their mindes, chuse Husbands and censure Complections, and all this in a quiet and friendly sort betweene themselves and the pinte poyt, or the quart quantitie, without any swaggering or squabbling till the vinters pewter-bearere in a boys humour gave out the laugh of them.

GENTLEMAN. Thou say'st well. Be like thy Booke is a conjuring kinde of Booke for the Feminine Spirites, when a man may raise the three at once out of his pocket.

PRENTICE. Truely, sir, I'le assure you, you may make vertuous use of this Booke divers wayes if you have the grace to use it kindely, as for example sit alone privately in your Chamber reading of it, and peradventure the time you spend on viewing it will keepe you from Dice, Taverne, Bawdy-house, and so forth.

GENTLEMAN. Nay, if your Booke be of such excellent qualitie and rare operation wee must needes have some Traffique together. Heere take your maney, is't sixepence?

PRENTICE. I certaine: tis no lesse, sir. I thanke you, sir.[1]

How large a stock was carried it is impossible to say, but that held by Roger Ward in his shop at Shrewsbury in 1585 shows that it could be considerable. Ward was a native of Shropshire who had sought his fortune in London, and in the eighties was constantly in trouble with the authorities for unlawful printing.[2] He was also in trouble elsewhere, for in the spring of 1585 the Sheriff of Shrewsbury was ordered to make an inventory of the contents of his shop prior to their being sold to pay his debts. This valuable document reveals that he had a stock of over 2500 volumes, predominantly religious, although there were a reasonable number of classical texts and

[1] *STC* 21409, S. Rowlands, '*Tis Merrie When Gossips Meete* (1602), quoted from the edition by S. J. H. Herrtage, in *The Complete Works* (Hunterian Club, 3 vols., 1872–86), pp. 6–8. For another scene at the bookseller's stall, see J. Eliot, *Ortho-epia Gallica. Eliots fruits for the French* (1593).

[2] See pp. 71 ff.

elementary books for beginners in the Classics. Other subjects were represented by a few volumes only, but the important thing to notice is the miscellaneous nature of the stock, an indication that the bookseller's object was to be able to provide a wide range of books for his customers. The inventory included, for instance, the two parts of *Euphues*, Sir Thomas Wilson's *Discourse uppon Usury*, a little pamphlet defining the duties of Constables, as well as works on the art of grafting, or the wonders of foreign travel. Over 250 sermons were in stock, as well as hundreds of Prayer Books and Catechisms, and of course Bibles and New Testaments, both in the vernacular and in foreign tongues.[1] In the same year the stock of a Scottish bookseller, Robert Gourlaw, is comprised in an inventory which 'occupies no less than six pages...in the *Bannatyne Miscellany*, and, if it may be taken to represent the current demand, points to a wide and cultivated standard of reading. Most noticeable are school books, chiefly Latin, and small books of devotion such as psalms and books of prayers. The classics are well represented in the *Iliad* and the *Odyssey*, Ovid's *Metamorphoses*, the *Ethics* of Aristotle, Virgil, Terence, Apuleius and Silius Italicus. Erasmus is much in evidence, probably in school editions. Theology, especially of a contemplative character, is the chief element; two copies of Bradford's *Meditations* are followed impartially by three copies of "ane lytill Fortoun buik". The immense popularity of Sir David Lyndsay is easily perceived, and lighter literature is well represented in ballads and other vernacular pieces. *Piers Plowman* and *Sir John Mandeville* appear, but contemporary English literature is practically absent, and there are no plays. There are also two copies of *Gargantua* and a Hebrew grammar.'[2]

Other lists of the stock held by booksellers tell a similar tale. As might be expected, they vary in the emphasis they

[1] See 'Roger Ward's Shrewsbury Stock: an Inventory of 1585', by Alexander Rodger. *The Library*, Fifth Series, vol. XIII (1958), pp. 247–68.
[2] *Cambridge History of English Literature*, vol. IV (1909), p. 414. The stock list of another Edinburgh Bookseller, Thomas Bassandyne, who died 18 October 1577, fills nine pages of *The Bannatyne Miscellany*.

place on the kinds of books that they order, but everywhere the largest holdings are in religious works of various kinds, followed by classical texts and grammars for the instruction of the young.[1] These were often ordered in considerable quantities. For instance, Bassandyne had 625 copies of the *Familiar Colloquies* of Erasmus in stock, while a Taunton bookseller in 1578 bought from Francis Coldocke of London five dozen copies of the Catechism. In the first six months of 1585, Richard Brett of York bought from Thomas Marshe one hundred copies of the 'epitome of the Coloquies of Erasmus', and during the same period received fifty copies apiece of Aesop and Cato, together with twenty-five copies of Terence. As for ephemeral pieces such as ballads, we are told that they were ordered in hundreds by the provincial booksellers, and we find Robert Scott of Norwich on 2 September 1569 asking for four dozen broadsheets containing an account of the acts of the hated Bishop Bonner, then on his death-bed. In the following year he bought twenty-five ballads concerning the Northern Rebellion of 1569-70.

The bookbills of various provincial booksellers show them ordering books from time to time as their stock dwindled. We find the Norwich bookseller buying two copies of *The Treasure of Gladness* on 12 July 1568, ordering two more on 4 November, four more on the twentieth of the same month, and four more in December. The following May he added three more copies to his stock and eight more in December.[2]

In addition to the books sold in London and at a few big towns, some were sold by itinerant pedlars who made a tour

[1] 'The booksellers' wills probably give the best clue to the tastes of average readers. Their proportions stand in the following scale; Theology 107, Practical and general works 44, Tales etc., 33, History 21, Translations from the Classics 7.' M. A. Bald, 'Vernacular Books imported into Scotland, 1500 to 1625', *Scottish Historical Review*, vol. 23 (1926), p. 265.

[2] H. R. Plomer, 'Some Elizabethan Book Sales', *The Library*, Third Series, vol. VII (1916), p. 320. The same article records other sales, while lists of books sent to Cambridge in 1583/4 will be found in 'Letters and Book lists of Thomas Chard (or Chare) of London, 1583-4,' by Robert Jahn, *The Library*, Fourth Series, vol. IV (1924), pp. 219-37.

of fairs and markets and made available a variety of books and pamphlets not otherwise easily within the reach of those living in small towns and villages. On the whole, we may suppose that most of what they sold was only of ephemeral value and interest—news, ballads, brief treatises on matters of health, or the like. A vivid picture of the scene in many a small town is given by John Rastell when he writes—

These Mountebanks...take up their standing in Market places, or void roomes meete for the concourse of people. There they set a stoole to stand upon, or make a little scaffold for the purpose, from which they play their part.

Their Greatest Grace is in the Countenaunce and Tongue, through which they looke so saddely, and speake so eloquently that a man would sweare upon a booke for them that they thinke as they speake & speake nomore than that thay will do. Whatsoever thing they have to sel, as *Newes out of India*, or *The Original of the Turkish Empire* or *A Pouder to kill wormes*, or *Merry Tales*, or *Songes and Ballets*, or *A Preservative againste the Plague*, or *A Water to make the skynne faire and White*, or *Pinnes, Pointes, Laces and Whistles*, & other such ware, whatsoever it be, they commend it and praise it before. But they do it with such a Grace, with such a Constancie, with such a Copie of words, with such moning of Affections, that it is wonderful.... He wil make such a doe about it as though it could scarse be bought for halfe a Kinges ransome.... He wil tel his Audience that he is come to them for good wils sake, moved in him by the Fame and worthines of them and theyr Citie or Towne.[1]

The peddling for sale of substantial works was in fact forbidden and we find action being taken against those so offending in 'the lanes of the City'.

Since the bookseller's success depended on his ability to gauge what the public wanted, his job was at least as difficult as is that of his present-day successor. There was a general feeling that books were plentiful—too plentiful some thought: no man has leisure enough 'to read the infinite number of

---

[1] *STC* 20729, J. Rastell, *The Third Booke, Declaring by Examples...that it is time to Beware of M. Jewel* (1566), sig. A3.

learned and godly books that are extant',[1] says a writer in 1603, while the printers' and booksellers' shops are said to be 'cloyed and clogged with stuffe fit for waste paper',[2] or with 'amorous pamphlets', or books 'full of sin and abomination', or merely of books of 'dreames and fantacies'. All such as these are denounced, since they fill the stalls to the detriment of worthier pieces. 'I am not ignorant', writes Thomas Underdown, 'that the stationers shops are full fraughted with bookes of small price, whether you consider the quantitie or contents of them.'[3] The bad crowded out the good, some thought, as a complaint by Philip Barrough declares:

> We see it dayly; that ridiculous toyes and absurd pamphlets being put forth without anie colour, be neverlesse plausibilie and pleasinglie accepted; whereas a man moved with an honest care to profite his countrie, being willing to leave a testimonie of the same behind him... if he hath not a delectable subject, it behoveth him to shew manie grave and substantiall reasons of his doing, or else they will not yeeld their hoped for benefit, which is to be benignelie accepted and perused with humanitie.[4]

Amid this welter of opinions the bookseller had to steer the best course he could. He bought from others, or exchanged some of his own stock for that of his competitors, in an endeavour to build up a comprehensive display. In some instances, as opportunity served, booksellers bought up the 'copyrights' of a fellow bookseller, as happened in June 1591, when Thomas Orwin had 'granted to him, by the consent of Edward Marshe, these copies which did belong to Thomas Marshe deceased'. The books thus transferred amounted to over 120 titles, but Orwin does not appear to have reprinted many of them. Similarly, in May 1584, James Roberts was

---

[1] *STC* 7539, S. Egerton, *A Lecture preached...at the Blacke-friers* (1603), sig. A3ᵛ. And cf. *STC* 3086 and 7083.
[2] *STC* 847, James Aske, *Elizabetha Triumphans* (1588), sig. A3ᵛ. And cf. *STC* 21744, sig. A2ᵛ.
[3] *STC* 13043, Heliodorus, *An Æthiopian Historie* (1587).
[4] *STC* 1509, Philip Barrough, *The Method of Phisicke* (1590), sig. A4ᵛ.

OUTPUT OF BOOKS

allowed by the Company to acquire some three dozen books hitherto printed by John Charlewood, and other examples may be found of stock being transferred *en bloc*.[1]

The reprinting of previously published books, however, was not a venture to be entered on without care, for a new book quickly ousted that of yesterday. 'Buy some new book sir', was the cry of the apprentices at their stalls, and there can be no doubt that it was the new book that attracted attention. 'Be it never so good, if once the Calendar be chaunged that it beare the date of the previous year, it is never enquired after', writes Thomas Jackson, who declares that such wares are useful for waste paper only, since 'the first question at every Stationers shoppe is what new thing?'[2] This, says another writer, is a threat by readers 'to give over reading if there want variety to feede and drawe them on'.[3]

Despite all the difficulties, however, books of every description were coming off the presses every year, and in constantly increasing numbers. For every four items published during the first two decades of the reign, there were six in the last two, so that while the years 1558–79 saw the publication of some 2760 titles, this number was increased to 4370 between 1580 and 1603. Many of these, of course, were reprints, but there can be no doubt that the increased output reflects the growing demand, and the ability of the book-trade to meet it. It is also of importance to notice the nature as well as the volume of the demand. Religious literature of various kinds still predominated, so that some 40 per cent of all works published fell into this category. Literature accounted for another 25 per cent, while the remainder was fairly evenly divided among subjects such as political tracts and theory, together with works on the law (10 per cent); history, geography, travel and news (10 per cent); scientific and quasi-scientific works (8 per cent), and

---

[1] For lists of such books and other matters concerned with transfers, see Herbert, *Ames' Typographical Antiquities*, vol. II, pp. 847, 930, 1031, 1053, 1112 and 1249.

[2] *STC* 14299, T. Jackson, *Davids Pastorall Poeme* (1603), sig. ¶5ᵛ.

[3] *STC* 14977, J. King, *Lectures upon Jonas* (1599), sig. *3ᵛ.

other works, such as books on commerce, economics, education, guides to conduct, etc. (5 per cent).[1]

Much has been written of the printers who produced this output, but for the main part it has concerned itself with the technical side of their craft. The problems concerned with the evolution of the various kinds of types, or the changes in the techniques used in printing, as well as the organization and control of the members of the Stationers' Company—these and allied matters have all been dealt with in considerable detail. Our concern, however, is with such activities of the printer and his associates as were instrumental in producing the book and placing it on the market.[2]

In the first place we have to remember that the number of printers throughout this period fluctuated between 20 and 30. In May 1583 there were twenty-three printers at work: C. Barker and J. Wolfe each had five presses; J. Day and H. Denham each had four. Four other printers each had three, seven others had two, and eight others had one apiece, making a total of fifty-two presses in all. These figures, however, are not very valuable, since some men seem to have printed a few books only, while others had an output running into the hundreds. Again, some printers are known of for a few years only, while others printed for periods up to forty years. Furthermore, before we can estimate the size of any printing business we must know more concerning the nature of its output. J. Wolfe, for example, was a busy printer who published over 300 items, but we must remember that much of his trade was in the production of pamphlets and small volumes consisting of 32 to 48 pages, while on the other hand a printer who turned out one

---

[1] These percentages have been calculated from 'A subject analysis of English Imprints for every tenth year' from 1558 to 1603, compiled by Edith L. Klotz, *Huntington Library Quarterly*, vol. I (1937–8), pp. 417–19.

[2] See, for example, T. B. Reed, *A History of the Old English Letter Foundries... Revised and Enlarged by A. F. Johnson* (1952); D. B. Updike, *Printing Types, their History, Forms, and Use: a Study in Survivals*, third edition, 2 vols. (Cambridge, Mass., 1962); W. W. Greg and E. Boswell, *Records of the Court of the Stationers' Company*.

OUTPUT OF BOOKS

of the volumes of Calvin's *Sermons* was responsible for a work in a larger format which might run to over a thousand pages.

Generalizations, therefore, as usual, are not very revealing, but we are entitled to note that the total output over the whole period was impressive, and shows that the printers were constantly printing books of every description, not only in English, but in many foreign tongues, classical and modern, while a few of them could even attempt the technically difficult task of the printing of music. The fact remains, however, that the printers were underemployed. We know little of what jobbing printing was available: Dr McKerrow suggests that this may have comprised 'various announcements...programmes of various events, descriptions of ceremonial proceedings, funerals, &c., announcements of lotteries, lottery-tickets, and perhaps price-lists';[1] but, even with this uncertain extra business, few presses had work enough to keep them steadily employed throughout the year. The entries in the *Short-title Catalogue* give the following figures: between 1558 and 1560 there were printed an average of 125 books a year, and this rose to 136 in the years 1570–9. Then from 1580 to 1589 the figure rose to 202 volumes a year, falling to 180 in the last years of the reign. If we take the highest figure of 202 volumes a year, this would only average some eight books apiece for say twenty-five printers. Now when we recall that this figure includes many slender pamphlets, proclamations, and the like, it is clear that there was reason for the agitations in the seventies and eighties by 'the poore men of this Companie for their Relief', the more so since their more favoured brethren had been given patents for the publication of whole classes of books while they got nothing. It may well have been, as Christopher Barker reported to the Crown in 1582, that there was little if any profit from some of these grants, but it was difficult to persuade outsiders of this, and the release of a considerable number of volumes by some of the patentees on 8 January 1584 'for the benefit and relief of the poorer members' was a tacit admission of their contentions, although

[1] See *The Library*, Fourth Series, vol. x (1930), pp. 144–5.

a close examination of the books released and their subsequent printing history suggests that this concession was not so valuable as it seemed at first sight.[1]

The serious and chronic lack of work for the printers, coupled with a consequent lack of capital to finance new work, led some printers to seek employment from booksellers. These latter had no presses of their own, but hired printers to produce for them works that they had purchased and believed to be saleable. This certainly provided work for the printers, but they complained that it was not very profitable, since the booksellers drove such a hard bargain with them. Be this as it may, investigation shows that many printers took whatever work came their way, and were glad of it. To take a few trial instances; between 1559 and 1562 Henry Sutton's name appears as the printer of eighteen books, of which eight were for other men; between 1566 and 1589 Thomas East printed forty-three books, of which sixteen only were for himself; Henry Bynneman between 1566 and 1570 printed fifty-one books, half of them for seventeen different individuals. Later he joined forces with Ralph Newbery as an alternative method of financing his business.

This indeed was a common way of keeping going. Printers and booksellers formed little syndicates, either to promote the publication of a single book, or to make sure of work for a period. Naturally, some large works were syndicated in this way. The cost of the production of Foxe's *Book of Martyrs* (1596), 'the fift time imprinted', was split up among as many as eleven partners and an elaborate agreement was entered into the Stationers' Court Book for 7 April 1595, setting out the number of copies each was to receive, and the price per copy. Despite this, the partners fell out among themselves, and on 21 June 1596, the Master of the Company and four others were asked 'to cast up the accoumpt and determyne of it'.[2] Other large works financed by syndicates were *The common places of Peter*

---

[1] See chapter III *passim*.
[2] Greg and Boswell, *op. cit.* pp. 51, 55.

JOINT PUBLICATION

Martyr (1583), a large folio in six parts, containing nearly 2000 pages in double columns. This was financed by four men: Henry Denham, Thomas Chard, William Broome and Andrew Maunsell. As another example we may take the second and enlarged edition of Holinshed's *Chronicles* (1587) which, as we have seen, was published at the expense of five partners. This was a work of some 3000 pages printed in three folio volumes in double columns, while another bulky production was the second edition of Hakluyt's *Voyages* (1598–60) which was financed by a syndicate of three.

Such action as this was not confined to large-scale works only. Publication by two or more men was so common that it needs no detailed illustration here, but it may be useful to examine activities when they were spread over a period. We learn from a Court Order of 2 May 1586 that Edmund Bollifant, Arnold Hatfield, Ninian Newton and John Jackson had become 'partners in printing' and seem to have acquired the types, ornaments, etc., of Henry Bynneman who had died in December 1583. Three of them were printers who had served their apprenticeship with Henry Denham, but Jackson was a member of the Grocers' Company, so that it has been suggested that 'his inclusion may have been due rather to his money than his skill'.[1] Be that as it may, the four began to print in Eliot's Court, Old Bailey, where they appear to have worked in pairs, judging from the evidence of their imprints on many books. Newton dropped out of the partnership in 1586; then Jackson followed in 1596, and Bollifant died in 1602, leaving Hatfield to find another partner. Over these years the firm were printers for at least thirty other men, sometimes only one putting his name to the imprint, sometimes two.

A close investigation of their work over these years shows that they undertook every kind of printing. They printed many books in classical and modern languages as well as a number of large works such as the folio edition of Dodoen's *Herball* (1586),

---

[1] See 'The Eliot's Court Printing-House, 1584–1674', by H. R. Plomer, in *The Library*, Fourth Series, vol. II (1921), pp. 175 ff.

with its many illustrations. On the other hand, they also printed comparatively small religious treatises, sermons and pamphlets against the Spaniards. In short, like so many of their fellows, they were glad enough to print anything, whether for themselves or for others, that would help them to make ends meet. How much they were helped in this by jobbing work it is impossible to say, but unless this was substantial they must have found life difficult. In the years 1584–1602 the partnership produced less than one hundred books of all kinds, and even when we recall that Newton left in 1586, and Jackson soon after 1595, the two surviving partners only produced 48 books in the seven years before Bollifant died. Fourteen of these were for other printers or booksellers, on which the profit was limited, so that the all-over profit from these 48 books cannot have been very large.

Partnerships such as this, short or long lived, were common. Most of them were agreements entered into for some special reason, and had no expectation of being permanent. They served the needs of the moment which were brought about by such things as lack of cash, lack of printing materials, or unwillingness to take a hundred per cent risk. Booksellers, as we have seen, as well as printers, combined in this way also.[1] In short, we probably make a mistake in trying to isolate the work of the various people engaged in the printing and selling of books. It is to be remembered that they were a comparatively small body of men, well known to one another and working in close physical proximity, so that the printers lent founts of type, borrowed printer's ornaments, initial letters, and the like, and clearly worked on friendly terms in the main. Of course there were difficulties: men printed one another's copies from time to time, especially if they were held under patent;[2] some contrived to get an unfair advantage over their fellows by opening their stalls on Sundays and Feast days, or printed more than

[1] See p. 272.
[2] See Greg and Boswell, *Records of the Court of the Stationers' Company, passim.* Arber, *Transcript, passim.*

the prescribed number of copies of a book. Nevertheless, the evidence appears to show that the printers and booksellers got on reasonably well together. Although a few men such as John Day and Christopher Barker did not seek outside employment, many of their fellows did, and common sense helped to keep their relations one with another on a friendly basis.

As for the booksellers themselves, they ranged over a fairly wide field. There were those who sold mainly what they had themselves printed, and were often rather specialized in what they had to offer. Richard Tottell, for example, could confidently expect purchasers to come to his stall 'at the Hand and Star within Temple Bar' for all kinds of law books, for it was well known that he held a monopoly for the printing of such works. At the same time, however, they would find there books of classical authors, or works by Grafton, Tusser, and others of more general interest. Men like himself probably did not carry much other stock than their own together with a certain amount of foreign books. Other booksellers were often not printers themselves, but had sufficient capital to commission printers to set up works of their own choice, which they then marketed themselves or shared with other booksellers. This latter device as we have seen was adopted at times when the costs of production of a work were too heavy for one man to carry.[1]

Less well-to-do booksellers were content to sell whatever books they could collect, carrying a miscellaneous stock similar to that of modern booksellers though on a reduced scale. Presumably like other booksellers they carried some foreign books, but the problem of the foreign book-trade in England has yet to be studied.

Where did the book-trade look to for material to print? We have already seen (mainly from the point of view of the author) the reasons why men offered their wares to the printer,[2] but it would be wrong to imagine that the trade was not also much concerned in seeking manuscripts they would wish to print.

[1] See p. 272.   [2] See chapter 1, p. 10.

At this time manuscripts circulated in plenty. Often they were written for a limited audience, without any thought of publication, as when Sir Philip Sidney tells his sister that he has written the *Arcadia* 'onelie for you, onely to you'. Many prefaces speak of the work as being written for a few and while some of these are merely conventional, much is genuine.[1] Nevertheless, it was open to anyone interested to see that such works were put into print, and who could be more interested than the book-trade?

We may take it therefore that publishers and printers were always on the look-out for suitable copy. At times they would print something that had come into their hands despite the fact that the author had not released it, and was likely to be unknown to them. Authors frequently complain of this, or of unwarranted action by their friends in releasing copy without permission, which often resulted in a version full of errors and misrepresentations of the author's meaning.

Printers could not rely solely on what was brought to them, or what they were able to obtain from those who had manuscripts rightly or wrongly come by. They had to take more positive action to keep their presses running, and we therefore hear of them commissioning translations to be made, and books to be compiled by disbursing 'great summes for the copies, translations, pictures and impressions [of] as much as is written and extant in any language'.[2] Cuthbert Burby, in publishing a translation of *The sixth Booke of the Myrrour of Knighthood* by Ortuñez de Calahorra, told prospective buyers that he had incurred 'exceeding expences', and that it had 'cost more than ordinarie...to get together all the parts of this excelent Historie'. As a consequence, he warns them that 'if a quick Terme pay the expenses of a dead Vacation, I will within the month play the Conney and bring foorth another Part: but if you prove niggards to buy, what I have dearly bought to sell, I will learne of the Camell to be three yeares in bringing

---

[1] See pp. 42 ff.
[2] *STC* 24328, G. Turberville, *The noble arte of venerie* (1575), sig. A 2.

forth my next birth, though I buy the long bearing verie deare'. The response was evidently satisfactory, for he brought out the next part in the same year, while the next two parts followed in 1599 and 1601.[1]

Even the texts of well-known English authors could cause much trouble to the printer, as was fully recognized by the early printers of Chaucer, Gower and Langland, who 'ryght diligently serched...dyvers copies', and 'did not only gather together such aunciente copies as I could come by, but also consulted such men as I knew to be more exercised in the studie of antiquities than I myselfe have ben'. Neither Gower nor Langland were reprinted in Elizabeth's reign, but there was a continuing demand for Chaucer's works. The edition of *c.* 1551 was evidently exhausted by 1561 when John Kingston printed for the bookseller John Wight a new edition 'with divers addicions, whiche were never in print before'. These were supplied by John Stow, the antiquary, who took them from an hitherto unused manuscript. Unfortunately, his zeal outran his discretion, for most of the additions were not Chaucer's work at all. The point to notice, however, is that the new edition was not put out without some effort being made by the printer to improve on the work of his predecessors.

Towards the end of the century the printer Adam Islip began to make preparations for the edition which he published in 1598. This was commissioned by three booksellers and was for the most part set up from the 1561 edition. When it was three parts printed, however, 'certaine of the best in the Companie of Stationers' approached the antiquary, Thomas Speght, who had long been collecting materials concerning Chaucer, and asked for his help. It was too late for him to be able to do very much to the actual text, but he did what he could by way of revising the text of the General Prologue of the *Tales*, adding notes, a glossary, with a number of corrected readings, and gave a half promise of a new edition later. This was soon made necessary by the intervention of Francis Thynne, a son of the editor

[1] *STC* 18868–71 (1598–1601).

of the edition of 1532. In his 'Animadversions' he drew attention to many inaccuracies and mistaken readings in Speght's text, which were accepted in good part by the editor, who published a new edition in 1602 in which he declared that 'both by old written Copies, and by Ma. Francis Thynns praiseworthie labours, I have reformed the whole Worke, whereby Chaucer for the most part is restored to his owne Antiquitie'.

The Elizabethan printer and his editors come out of their Chaucerian ventures reasonably well. The *Works* made up a substantial folio, and to reprint it—still more to add to the canon—was a formidable matter, and the printers might well have not thought it necessary to do more than to reprint the earlier text. As we have seen, they did not do this, but by attention to the text, and an endeavour to extend the canon, did their best, according to their lights, to be worthy of their great author. That in so doing they bedevilled the canon of Chaucer's works for hundreds of years cannot be held to outweigh the positive good that they did in making Chaucer available from time to time throughout the century.

Other problems confronted the printer when he turned from works of the past to those of the present. The active bustling world about him also provided much potential material waiting to be exploited. The voyages to the Indies, the progress of the wars in France and the Low Countries, the latest execution or witch-hunt, or the last monstrous birth or marvel—all such events (and they were never-ending) provided the printers with profitable material which they eagerly seized upon.

Henry Bynneman, for example, gives a good account of how he got the manuscript of George Best's *True Discourse of the late voyages of discoverie, for the finding of a passage to Cathaya, by the Northweast, under the conduct of Martin Frobisher Generall (1578)*:

Forasmuch as these three voyages lately performed...appeare above all others most notable and famous, I have bin specially desirous, by all meanes possible I could, to procure the publication thereof, thinking it too great an injurie to our commonwealth to burie in oblivion so worthie attemptes of our own nation....And for that (as I understand) many trifling Pamphlets have bin secretly thrust out, not only without the consent of the Captaynes and executioners of the same, but also rather to the great disgrace of the worthy voyage than otherwise, I having intelligence of a substantiall discourse whiche was diligently written thereof, and privately dedicated to my very Honourable Master, Sir Christopher Hatton Knight, by a gentleman of his owne, who was personally present, a Captain in all the same service, I have, without making privie the Author, procured his Coppie out of the handes of a friende of mine, who had the writing and perusing therof, and have presumed to publish and imprint the same: to the ende that thereby I mighte as well satisfy thy greedy expectation by unfolding these newe and unknowen matters.[1]

This kind of thing was going on constantly. Nashe speaks of 'such gaping' amongst the printers 'for the coppy of my Lord of Essex voyage', and this and other valuable pieces were to be got if only one knew whom to approach among one or other of the many to be seen daily walking and conversing in Paul's Churchyard. These only wanted a word from the right quarter to relate their adventures, or to display their diaries, or some account sent to them by a friend. Professor Shaaber has shown in some detail how a number of printers set themselves out to specialize in the publication of such news:

Of all the news from France printed before 1600, half, roughly speaking, was published by four men—John Wolf (who published more than 60 per cent of this half), Edward Aggas, William Wright, and Richard Field; the remaining half is distributed among more than forty. It could not have been by chance that so large a part of this news came into the hands of a small number of publishers; they must have taken steps to secure it. What these steps were we can only guess, but we can be sure they did not sit idle.[2]

Nor was it only collectors of news who were active. Thomas Wight, 'who hath the interest therein', invited William Bourne

[1] *STC* 1972, sig. b 3.
[2] M. A. Shaaber, *Some Forerunners of the Newspaper in England, 1476–1622* (Philadelphia, 1929), p. 284.

to prepare a third edition of his *A Regiment for the Sea* (1596), since the second edition was printed without Bourne's knowledge, 'so that it hath not onely those faultes that were printed out of ye first written copie, but now a number of new faults more than it had in the first'.[1] In another case, John Day had a translation made, 'sparing neither laboure, diligence or charges', as he said of another work—*The Treasure of Euonymus* [1559] of Conrad Gesner, and John Wolfe did the same when Hakluyt brought him *John Huighen van Linschoten his Discours of Voyages* (1598).[2] Other printers such as Roland Hall, Lucas Harrison or George Bishop were constantly on the look-out for religious works which would further the cause they had at heart. For a similar reason, Henry Denham commissioned Thomas Rogers to retranslate *The Imitation of Christ*, purging it of all Romish doctrine as he did so.

We can see the way that such things came about by the vivid account of a meeting between Richard Eden and Richard Jugge. Eden writes:

I chaunced in the meane tyme to meete with my olde acquayntance and freend, Richard Jugge, Printer to the Queenes Majestie, who had many yeeres before, printed the Booke of Marten Curtes, of the Art of Navigation, by me translated out of the Spanyshe tongue. Whereof, having with him some conference, he declared that he woulde prynt that booke agayne yf I woulde take the paynes to devise some addition touchyng the same matter that myght be joyned thereto. At which tyme, havyng with me in the Latine tongue these bookes here folowyng printed, which I brought with me out of Fraunce, I soone agreed to his honest request to translate them into Englyshe.[3]

For a more dramatic version of the way copy was obtained, we must go to *The Second Part of the Return from Parnassus*, which is only fiction, it is true, but may be taken as not far from what sometimes happened when author and printer met to do business.

---

[1] *STC* 3428, sig. B1.   [2] See p. 27.
[3] *STC* 23659, J. Taisnier, *A very necessarie...Booke concerning Navigation* [1579?], trans. R. Eden, sig. *₊*2.

Enter Danter the Printer

INGENIOSO. *Danter* thou art deceived, wit is dearer then thou takest it to bee. I tell thee this libel of Cambridge has much salt and pepper in the nose: it will sell sheerely underhand, whenas these bookes of exhortations and Catechismes lie moulding on thy shopboard.

DANTER. It's true; but good fayth, *M. Ingenioso*, I lost by your last booke, and you knowe there is many a one that payes me largely for the printing of their inventions; but for all this you shall have 40 shillings and an odde pottle of wine.

INGENIOSO. 40 Shillings? a fit reward for one of your reumatick poets, that beslavers all the paper he comes by, and furnishes the Chaundlers with wast papers to wrap candles in: but as for me, Ile be paid deare even for the dreggs of my wit. Little knowes the worlde what belong[s] to the keeping of a good wit in waters, dietts, drinckes, Tobacco, &c. It is a daynty and costly creature, and therefore I must be payd sweetly: furnish mee with mony, that I may put my selfe in a new suite of clothes, and Ile suite thy shop with a new suite of tearmes: it's the gallantest Child my invention was ever delivered off. The title is, A Chronicle of *Cambrige* Cuckolds: here a man may see what day of the moneth such a mans commons were inclosed, and when throwne open, and when any entayled some odde crownes upon the heires of their bodies unlawfully begotten. Speake quickly, ells I am gone.

DANTER. Oh this will sell gallantly: Ile have it whatsoever it cost, will you walk on, M. *Ingenioso*, weele sit over a cup of wine and agree on it.

INGENIOSO. A cup of wine is as good a Constable as can be, to take up the quarrell betwixt us.[1]

Once the copy had been secured and the work was set up, the business of proof-correcting began. This could be done by a printer's agent called the corrector, or by the author, or sometimes by both. The author generally attended the printer's shop and corrected his copy there and then, and we have frequent excuses for errors which have 'escaped into print'

[1] *The Three Parnassus Plays*, ed. J. B. Leishman (1949), pp. 247–8.

owing to the absence of the author, occupied with other business, or away in the country, and so on.[1] This might leave many errors undetected, especially if the book contained passages in Greek or Latin, or even in French or Italian, as the large number of errata printed just before the book was issued often shows. For example, the translator of Lavater's *Of ghostes and spirites walking by nyght* (1572), in adding a list of 'Fautes escaped in the Print', writes: 'Although some of our Printers be not Homers, neyther seene in Greeke nor Latine, nor sometime exactly in Englishe, yet can they nod and take a nap, as well as any Homer. Howebeit in deede they are herein pardonable, bycause the Copie was somewhat obscurely written, as being the first originall.'[2] Worse could happen if the author did not attend when maps, text-figures, etc., were being printed. This was admitted by Anthony Ashley, whose edition of Lucas Wagenaer's *The Mariners Mirrour* [1588] consisted mainly of large maps which he was unable to oversee sufficiently owing to his duties as an officer of the Privy Council. As a result, 'the Negligent gravers' had their will.[3] Another work that suffered from the absence of the author at the press was Reginald Scot's *A perfite platforme of a Hoppe Garden* (1574), for which the printer had to apologize in a letter to the Reader: 'Forasmuch as M. Scot could not be present at the printing of this his Booke whereby I might have used his advise in the correction of the same, and especially of the Figures and Portraitures contayned therin, whereof he delivered unto me such notes as I being unskillful in the matter, could not so throughly conceyve, nor so perfectly expresse, as the expectation of him being the Author, or you being the Reader, might be in all poyntes satisfied.'[4]

As was to be expected, the printing of a list of errata afforded an opportunity for explanations and excuses to be made by

---

[1] See, for example, *STC* 3705, sig. Ddd 4; *STC* 3811, sig. ¶1ᵛ; *STC* 18044, sig. A3ᵛ; *STC* 18380, sig. A3, etc.

[2] Quoted from Simpson, *Proof-Reading in the Sixteenth, Seventeenth and Eighteenth Centuries* (London, 1935), p. 34. *STC* 15320 (1572).

[3] *STC* 24931, sig. ¶1.   [4] *STC* 21865, sig. B3.

the interested parties. In the preliminaries of *The Droomme of Doomes day* (1576), by George Gascoigne, there is a page headed

An advertisement of the Prynter to the Reader. Understand (gentle Reader) that whiles this worke was in the presse, it pleased God to visit the translatour thereof with sicknesse. So that being unable himselfe to attend the dayly proofes, he apoynted a servaunt of his to oversee the same. Who (being not so well acquainted with the matter as his maister was) there have passed some faultes much contrary unto both our meanings and desires. The which I have therefore collected into this Table. Desiring every Reader that wyll vouchsafe to peruse this booke, that he wyll firste correct those faultes and then judge acordingly.[1]

Forty-nine faults are recorded, some of them only errors of misplaced letters and the like, but several involve the omission or the addition of whole phrases, so that the passage as printed makes nonsense.

A more indignant note is struck by Edward Dering, who throws the blame on the printer for everything that is wrong. He asserts that: 'He is a simple scholer that can not write truely, and the pointing is not so difficult that it requireth any great learning', so that the printer ought not to have had much difficulty with the copy. Nevertheless, many mistakes there are, and after noting some of them Dering goes on to nag at the reader when he says: 'These and such other escapes in the printing of my boke, as well in the wordes as in the pointing, how many soever thou shalt ascribe to me, so many injuries thou shalt doe me.'[2]

A more gentle note is struck by Thomas Fortescue, both in prose and verse, when he writes: 'Suche faultes as have paste in Printyng, as ther in dede bee many, and everywhere aboundante, so of thy courtesie excuse us, whether they bee but letters, whole wordes, or otherwise, and as the sense shall leade thee,

---

[1] *STC* 11641. The quotation will be found in J. W. Cunliffe's edition of Gascoigne's *Works* (Cambridge, 1910), vol. II, p. 215.
[2] *STC* 6725, *A sparing restraint of many lavishe untruthes* [1568], sig. *1.

so amende what so thou findeste, or lackyng, or superfluous, assuryng thyself that it sometymes paste us in more perfecte wise than thou in these receivest them.' Then on the next page he breaks into verse:

> And feare not though againe,
> thy papers faultes doe fyll:
> In printyng which escaped have,
> and paste againste our will.
> Correctours hadste thou fewe,
> and Printers ofte doe misse.
> The sence and meanyng easily,
> the reader yet maie guesse.[1]

Sometimes the printer found it worth his while to lodge an author in his own house or near by while he was working for him in one capacity or another. The outstanding example of this is provided by William Fulke, Master of Pembroke Hall. While he was writing *A Defense of the sincere and true Translations of the holie Scriptures into the English tong* (1583), the bookseller George Bishop maintained him and his two men for nine months and gave him £40, free quarters and such books for the making of the treatise as he needed. In return the work became Bishop's property.[2] Something similar may have occurred some years later when Nashe asserted that Gabriel Harvey was billeted 'for some seaven and thirtie weekes space...at Wolfes coppying against mee, never stirring out of dores'.[3] If this was so, we may be pretty sure that Harvey was at work correcting the various proofs pouring out of Wolfe's workshop. When we remember that Wolfe had one of the largest shops at that time, there could have been no lack of work for him to do.

---

[1] *STC* 17849, P. Mexia, *The Foreste* (1571), trans. T. Fortescue, sig. b iv, and b 2.

[2] *STC* 11430.

[3] R. B. McKerrow, *Works of T. Nashe* (1904-10), vol. III, pp. 94, 95. Cf. W. Baldwin, *Beware the Cat* (1584), sig. A 4ᵛ, where the narrator says 'I lay often times at my freendes house.... Sometime as while my Greeke Alphabets were in printing, to see that it might be truly corrected.'

MISPRINTS

Many writers in acknowledging their misprints promise that they shall be corrected in the next edition. Not all of them, by any means, had an opportunity to carry out this promise, but many title-pages boast that the contents within have been 'newlie corrected', or 'amended in many places', or 'newly overseene and corrected'. What this could mean in exceptional cases may be seen from Grafton's 'Preface to the loving and Gentle Reader' of his *Abridgement of the Chronicles of England* (1564), where he says that 'in the first impression of thys my abridgement... partlye by miswrytinge, partlye by misentringe, & mistaking of yeres, but chiefely by misprenting, dyvers and sundry fautes were committed, which after I had well perused, I did with diligence reforme and amende the same in suche maner as I trust wyll apere in this impression to the contentacion of all those that are desyrous to understand the true notes and discourse of tymes. And herein also I have incerted diverse and sundry other worthy notes that before were omitted, which to the diligent reader wyl also appeare, praying you to accept in good part this my little labour.'[1]

By the aid of the author and the corrector many errors were discovered and put right while the sheets were going through the press, as is indicated, for example, by notes such as 'The faultes in some copies escaped', which is often found at the head of the list of errata.[2] A rather fuller statement of the same nature is made by Thomas Tymme in his translation of *The three Partes of Commentaries*, by J. de Serres (1574), when he writes, 'Note here (good Reader) that these faultes escaped in Printing, are not so escaped in al the Bokes of this impression, but in some. Least therefore they to whome those should happen, might be troubled in the reading with obscure sense, I thought it good to make a generall note of all.'[3]

When misprints were noticed at the very last minute, long after the sheet had been printed off, there was nothing for it

---
[1] *STC* 12150, sig. B4.
[2] *STC* 369, W. Allen, *An apologie* (1581), sig. Q3ᵛ.
[3] *STC* 22242, sig. Mm4.

but to make the correction by sticking on to the printed page a little slip over the incorrect reading, or an additional slip to the 'list of Fautes escaped'.[1]

Humanum est errare one printer began his apology, and there is, as we have seen, plenty of evidence of human frailty in the productions of this period. It is also evident that both author and printer regretted this, and took what steps they could to put matters right, whether by an errata list, or by taking the opportunity afforded by a new edition. Human frailty being what it is, however, the casting out of the old devils was often the signal for the entry of the new, and it must be admitted that Elizabethan books, whether first or later editions, often carry a formidable errata list. The reason for this is to be found mainly in the fact that, since the amount of type carried by the printer was limited, as soon as one sheet was ready it was printed off and the type distributed so as to be available for another sheet. Once the sheet was printed, however, mistakes could only be rectified by a list of errata and a plea to the reader to make the necessary corrections for himself. 'Take thy pen, and bestow the paynes to correct the following', the author asks, but not many seem to have done so, since an inspection of the defective pages in many volumes shows them to be uncorrected, or at best corrected for the first twenty or thirty pages only.

While it was easy for the author to blame the printer for the faults which disfigured many Elizabethan books, the printer could often reply, with some justice, that the fault was not always on his side. The copy that was delivered to him was often far from perfect. Authors will even acknowledge that their manuscript was 'verie darke and enterlined, and I loth to write it out againe'.[2] What Henry Holland called his 'ragged hand' went straight to the press without any attempt

---

[1] *STC* 1209 (1574), sig. Q4^v and *STC* 4715 (1577), sig. x4. For many further examples, see P. Simpson, *op. cit.* pp. 19–22.

[2] *STC* 18044, J. de Montemayor, *Diana* (1598), trans. B. Young, sig. A3^v.

on his part to make a fair copy,[1] while Chettle tells us that he had to transcribe Greene's work which 'was il written, as sometimes Greene's hand was none of the best'.[2] We read of copy that was 'eyther blotted or obscurely penned',[3] or 'not legible in sundrie places' so that the printer was forced to admit to faults by which the book is made 'obscure in places, or to read contrarye to the Authors meaning'.[4]

Not only the handwriting but also the subject-matter presented difficulties. These are well expressed by Henry Billingsley in the preface to his translation of Euclid, entitled *The Elements of Geometrie* (1570), where he writes:

Marvaile not (gentle reader) that faultes here following, have escaped in the correction of this booke. For, for that the matter in it contayned is straunge to our Printers here in England, not having bene accustomed to Print many, or rather any bookes contayning such matter, which causeth them to be unfurnished of a corrector skilfull in that art: I was forced, to my great travaile and paine, to correcte the whole booke my selfe. And in deede sometimes for want of *Argus* eyes, and juste consideration, notwithstanding my diligence in correcting, faultes escaped through me; sometimes also for lacke of diligence in the Printer to amend my corrections, faultes remayned uncorrected by his meanes. So that betwene us both these faultes have escaped uncorrected: which faultes yet, to say the trouth, for the most part are such, as a very young student without noting them unto him, mought easily of him selfe find and correcte. And this I dare boldly affirme, that not many bookes, if any, concerning this art in other tounges, Greke, Latine, or Italian, are with so fewe faults of importance printed, as this booke is. The triall wherof I referre to them which have red any bookes of this arte in other tounges, & shall happen hereafter to read. And as touching these faultes to be corrected, I would wishe you before you beginne to read any of the 16 bookes in this volume contained, first to amend the faultes in that booke which you will read, according as they are here signified unto

---

[1] *STC* 4374, J. Calvin, *Aphorismes* (1596), trans. H. Holland, sig. A3.
[2] *STC* 5123, H. Chettle, *Kind-Harts Dreame* [1592], sig. A4.
[3] *STC* 13067, N. Hemmingsen, *The way of lyfe* (1578), trans. N. Denham, sig. A4ᵛ.
[4] *STC* 24324, G. Turberville, *The Booke of Faulconrie* (1575), p. 374.

you.... And if you happen in reading to finde any more faultes not here mentioned, as peradventure you may, for that divers faultes were utterly so easie and light to correcte, that I would not note them, & besides that, no one man though he be never so diligent and circumspecte can espie all thinges, I trust you will therefore impute no blame either unto me or to the Printer, but gently amend and correct them, accepting our good minde, which was to have had the booke passed to your handes utterly without fault, as touching the printing.[1]

An equally compendious plea for leniency is made by author and printer of *Florio's Firste Fruites* (1578), when they write:

Gentle Reader, for such faultes which have escaped the Authors naughty pen, the Compositors wavering hande, the Correctors daseling, and the Printers presse, we desire thee courteously to amend, for surely the Author writes scarce good English, and a ragged hand with all, and the Compositor understandes no Italian. Wherefore, standing at thy courtesie, we are perswaded thou wilt lightly pardon us both.[2]

Here at least the compositor was setting from an English text, but the compositor who was setting in a tongue unknown to him had even greater difficulties to contend with, and this is constantly harped upon by recusant writers whose works were perforce being set up by foreigners. Thus a book printed in Louvain in 1600 concludes with the following plea: 'Excuse, guid reider, the erreurs committit in ye prenting. Considder the difficultie to prent our langage in a strange countrey. God Keip Zovv.'[3] Thirty-five years earlier, the difficulties had been clearly set out by the Corrector of the Antwerp edition of Thomas Harding's *An answere to Maister Juelles chalenge* (Antwerp, 1565), who writes:

Howsoever it be, I wishe oure loving countriemen to consider how harde it is for aliantes to print English truly, who nieither understand, nor can pronounce the tonge rightly. As for the correctour, where the faultes of the printers be infinite for the unskill of the language,

---

[1] *STC* 10560, sig. EEE 2ᵛ. [2] *STC* 11096, sig. ***4ᵛ.
[3] *STC* 12730, J. Hamilton, *A Facile Traictise*, sig. x6ᵛ.

DEFECTIVE PRINTING

were he as full of eyes as *Argus*, or as sharpsighted as Lynx, yet shoulde he passe over no small number unespied. Were there here an Englishman who had skill in setting a print, and knewe the right Orthographie of our speach, then mightest thou reader looke for bookes more correctly set forth: for lacke wherof we do as we maye.[1]

'We do as we may'—and as a result orthography and syntax sometimes suffer where 'straungers are the workers, compositors and correctors',[2] and where 'the noveltie of imprinting English in these partes [Leyden]... could not choose but breede errours'.[3] So well was this known, that when Richard Bristow's *A Reply to Fulke* was secretly printed at Greenstreet House, East Ham, it was given a false imprint, 'Louaine, John Lyon, 1580', and in a letter to the Reader, 'John Lyon' asks him to correct faults, 'for although I have had great care and bene very diligent in the correcting therof, yet because my Compositor was a straunger and ignorant in our English tongue and Orthographie, some faultes are passed unammended of me....'.[4]

Some defective printing, no doubt, came from pressure by the printer who wanted to get the book finished. George Baker tells us that he had begun to revise the text of a medical work (which indeed the title-page claims to be 'Newly corrected, by men skilfull in that arte') since the former edition was very erroneous, but that after he had corrected a part only, he had to call in a helper, since the printer was pressing for the complete copy.[5] Anthony Munday definitely attributes the misprints in his translation of Claude Colet's *The famous, pleasant, and variable historie of Palladine of England* (1588) to his absence from the press at a time when the printer was determined to publish the work by a certain date. He asks for forgiveness for the misprints, 'for I beeying often absent and

---

[1] *STC* 12759, sig. A3ᵛ.
[2] *STC* 20632, J. Rainolds, *A refutation* (Paris, 1583), sig. Pp. 2.
[3] *STC* 24806, Virgil, *Thee first foure bookes of Virgil his Aeneis* (1582), sig. Q1.
[4] *STC* 3802, R. Bristow, *A Reply to Fulke* (1580), sig. Eee4ᵛ.
[5] *STC* 24723, J. de Vigo, *The whole worke of...J. Vigo* (1586). See Herbert, *Ames' Typographical Antiquities*, vol. II, p. 1016.

the Printer carefull to end his worke by the appointed time have beene the cause of all these escapes'.[1]

In an introductory epistle to his *Gerileon of England* (1592) Munday is more explicit, and says that

> Since my first entring on this Historie, to translate it: I have been divers and sundrie times countermanded by her Majesties appointment in the place where I serve, to post from place to place on such affaires as were enjoyned mee, so that not having fully finished one sheete, and the Printer beginning almost as soone as my selfe, I have been greatly his hinderance, and compelled to catch hold on such little leasures, as in the morning ere I went to horse-back, or in the evening comming into mine Inne, I could compasse from companie.[2]

A matter on which we are imperfectly informed is the rate at which the Elizabethan printer was able to turn out his wares. Such slender evidence as the first eighty years of printing can provide suggests that one sheet per day per machine was the normal rate of production, that is eight quarto or sixteen octavo pages of type. It so happens that Richard Tottell produced an account of Queen Elizabeth's progress through the City on the way to her coronation which took place on 14 January 1559. This he published on 23 January of the same year. Now if we allow for the preparation of the copy and for the Sunday intervening it looks as if about five or six days would be available for the actual printing. At a sheet a day this would comfortably fill up the time, since the pamphlet ran to five quarto sheets.

In his investigation of the rate of printing of Edward Allde, who was at work throughout this period, Dr R. B. McKerrow came to the conclusion that it was reasonable to think that he

---

[1] *STC* 5541, sig. +4.
[2] I owe this reference to Miss M. St Clare Byrne's article, 'Anthony Munday and his Books', in *The Library*, Fourth Series, vol. I, p. 244. Angel Day also complains of the haste of the printer who collected the copy as soon as Day had written it, so that 'by want of sight of the mater alreadie past my hande, & forgetfulnes by much travaile and watching of that which I had delivered from me, I fell into some multiplicitie of matter'. *STC* 6403, *The English Secretorie* (1595), sig. A 3.

produced one sheet a day, and mentions that we know of three books that were put through the press in the early or middle seventeenth century which 'all points to one sheet a day as a maximum but not unreasonable rate'.[1]

Once the book was printed the last matter to be set up, as is the practice nowadays, was what are known as the preliminaries. These varied in their nature and extent, but might include the following: the title-page, followed by the dedicatory letter and the Address to the Reader. At times this is followed by commendatory verses from and to the author's friends and after that the list of contents, while if there has not been room enough for them on the last pages of the text, the list of errata follows. All these items have been touched on to some extent earlier: indeed nearly all the passages quoted come from the dedicatory letters and those written to the reader, but a few more words may usefully be said about these preliminaries.

The growing practice of cluttering up the title-page with matter which it was hoped would attract the reader has already been mentioned. The title-page was printed off and stuck upon posts and in prominent places in Paul's Churchyard and other sites, and made its appeal sometimes by the abundance of useful, pleasurable, or instructive fare that it promised was within, or sometimes by the sensational, topical or unusual material that it contained. Books were always presented in their best light: the reader is offered an 'excellent conceited comedy', or a 'Godlye and fruitefull Sermon against Idolatorie'. The buyer of *The Garden of Pleasure* is promised a work 'contayning most pleasant tales, worthy deeds, and witty sayings of noble Princes ...No less delectable than profitable'. A book, 'the like not heretofore in Englishe' is a tempting bait, as is *The Pathway to the Pulpit*: 'Contayning an excellent Method how to frame Sermons, and to interpret the Holy Scriptures according to the capacitie of the vulgar people.'

In short, the title-page had to do its best to serve the same

---

[1] See 'Edward Allde as a Typical Trade Printer', by R. B. McKerrow, in *The Library*, Fourth Series, vol. x, p. 142.

purpose as does the modern publisher's enthusiastic account of the book which he places inside the flap of the dust jacket—a much more suitable place. At the foot of the page, the printer put his name and where the book could be bought; material which in earlier days had appeared at the end in the colophon. If the book had been printed for a bookseller, then that would be stated, so that the would-be purchaser would know where to look for it, as for example, 'Imprinted at London by H. Denham for Thomas Hackett, and are to be sold at his shop in Lumbarde Streete'. If he were printing for himself, the printer advertised this by the words: 'Printed at London by Henrie Denham, dwelling in Pater Noster Rowe, at the signe of the Starre. 1582.'

The dedicatory letter and the address to the reader which followed both seem to have been written much at the same time and very shortly before the book was ready for the public. As we have seen, the letter to the patron cannot be made to fit into any one pattern. Some were sincere, some otherwise; some related personal reasons for the dedication, others admitted that the dedicatee was unknown to the writer. Flattery and sycophancy were evils not always avoided, and self-abnegation at times reached ridiculous lengths. On the other hand, some eagerly accepted the opportunity of paying tribute for previous kindnesses and assistance. And as we have also seen, nearly all protested that the position and authority of the patron would form a shield against the envious carpings of Momus and the sons of Zoilus. A book without a patron appeared to come into the world like a bastard child, lacking a protector or any guarantee of its proper station in the world.

There are, however, two classes of writers whose reasons may perhaps be looked upon with some caution. They are the 'gentlemen' as they described themselves on the title-page and elsewhere, and the growing body of professional 'men of letters' who make so striking an appearance in the last two decades of the century. Undoubtedly there was much that was written by the gentry which they meant to circulate only among their friends, and which was penned without thought of publication. It was not possible, however, in an age when printed matter was being more and more sought after, to prevent an unscrupulous printer or friend from putting into print anything that had a chance of being interesting to a wider public than its author had intended. Some gentlemen undoubtedly disliked their private thoughts becoming public, and did all they could to prevent this. Others were not so sensitive, but hesitated to act in a way that was generally considered to be incorrect by their equals. For men such as this the convention that the work of a gentleman only 'escaped into print' was a useful one, which enabled them to have the best of both worlds. But in any case, 'the stigma of print', as it has been called, only operated (in so far as it operated at all) among a limited class. Far from being ashamed of appearing in print, men welcomed the opportunity in very many cases. The translator of Calvin or Virgil; the writers of scientific or informational works; the compilers of the great histories or biographies, for example, saw little to reproach themselves with, however much the writers of 'this tedious trash', or of works that were 'idle, unpolisht and base' might feel dismayed when they surveyed their labours.

The letters to the reader on the other hand betray more of the writer's own feelings. In the first place he is eager to give his reasons for having his work printed at all, so that such things as the pressure of friends, his desire to serve his country in making knowledge available, or the improvement of faith and morals are all matters constantly put forward in justification. These pleas are as various as life itself, and suggest a wide variety of reasons for publication. They should be read with caution, but in general they may be believed.

As for the plea that it was beneath a gentleman's dignity to print what he had written, George Pettie replied with the following vigorous outburst:

Those which mislike that a Gentleman should publish the fruits of his learning, are some curious Gentlemen, who thinke it most commendable in a Gentleman, to cloake his art and skill in everie thing, and to seeme to doe all things of his owne mother wit as it were: not considering how we deserve no praise for that, which God or nature hath bestowed upon us, but onelie for that, which we purchase by our own industrie: and if you shall chance to enter into reasoning with them, they will at the second word make protestation that they are no Schollers: whereas notwithstanding they have spent all their time in studie. Why Gentlemen, is it a shame to shew to be that, which it is a shame not to bee?....Alasse you wil be but ungentle Gentlemen if you bee no schollers: you will doe your Prince but simple service; you will stand your Countrie but in slender stead, you will bring your selves but to small preferment, if you bee no schollers....

Therefore (Gentlemen) never denie your selves to bee schollers, never be ashamed to shew your learning, confesse it, professe it, imbrace it, honour it: for it is it which honoreth you....And this I hope will satisfie those which mislike that Gentlemen should publish the fruit of their studie.[1]

The sincerity or otherwise of the professional writer, on the other hand, is a matter on which it is hard to be assured. Their lot was a hard one, and they had to adopt every device that would help them to secure an audience and a demand for more of their works. In the main they were dependent on the quality and the nature of their writings, and in many cases it was sensational or unusual enough to stimulate the appetites of the readers. If he lacked this, however, the author enticed his readers by every device of cajolement, flattery, assumed humility etc., that he could compass. This attitude is laughed at by Thomas Dekker in *The Wonderfull Yeare* when he writes:

To the Reader.

And why to the *Reader?* Oh good Sir! theres as sound law to make you give good words to the *Reader*, as to a *Constable* when hee carries his watch about with him to tell how the night goes, tho (perhaps) the one (oftentimes) may be served in for a *Goose*, and the other may very fitly furnish the same messe. Yet to maintaine the scurvy fashion, and to keepe *Custome* in reparations, he must be

[1] *STC* 12423, S. Guazzo, *The civile Conversation of Stephen Guazzo* (1586), trans. by G. Pettie, sig. A5ᵛ.

honyed, and come-over with *Gentle Reader, Courteous Reader*, and *Learned Reader*, though he have no more *Gentilitie* in him than *Adam* had (that was but a gardner) no more *Civilitie* than a Tartar, and no more *Learning* than the most errand *Stinkard*, that (except his own name) could never finde anything in the Horne-booke.

How notoriously therfore do good wits dishonor, not only their *Calling*, but even their *Creation*, that worship *Glow-wormes* (in stead of the *Sun*) because of a litle false glistering? In the name of *Phoebus*, what madnesse leades them unto it? For he that dares hazard a pressing to death (thats to say, *To be a man in Print*) must make account that he shall stand (like the olde Weathercock over Powles steeple) to be beaten with all stormes. Neither the stinking Tabacco-breath of a *Sattin-gull*, the *Aconited* sting of a narrow-eyde *Critick*, the faces of a phantastick Stage-monkey, nor the *Indeede-la* of a Puritanicall Citizen, must once shake him. No, but desperately resolve (like a French Post) to ride through thick & thin: indure to see his lines torne pittifully on the rack: suffer his Muse to take the *Bastoone*, yea the very stab, & himselfe like a new stake to be a marke for every *Hagler*, and therefore (setting up all these rests) why shuld he regard what fooles bolt is shot at him? Besides, if that which he presents upon the Stage of the world be *Good*, why should he so basely cry out (with that old poeticall mad-cap in his *Amphitruo*) *Jovis summi causa clare plaudite*, beg a *Plaudite* for Godsake! If *Bad*, who (but an Asse) woulde intreate (as Players do in a cogging *Epilogue* at the end of a filthie Comedy) that, be it never such wicked stuffe, they would forbeare to hisse, or to dam it perpetually to lye on a Stationers stall. For he that can so cosen himselfe, as to pocket up praise in that silly sort, makes his braines fat with his owne folly.[1]

Not much more need be said about this topic. Each dedication or prefatory letter must be judged as best we can from our knowledge of the author and of the circumstances in which he was writing. In any case, we should remember that the writings of these 'professionals' are only a fraction of what appeared in print, but that their literary quality is often so outstanding that they are liable to distort the general picture.

---

[1] *STC* 6534, T. Dekker, *The Wonderfull yeare* (1603), sig. A2^v.

As the compositor reached the last pages of his copy he sometimes realized that there would be a number of blank pages when he had finished. Since this would mean an uneconomical use of paper, the sheet was sometimes halved, or, if this were not possible, the remaining pages were used as 'fill ups', in which improving verses, or proverbial phrases were printed. If the space allowed something more substantial was put in. For example, at the end of his *Newes out of Powles Churchyarde* (1579), Edward Hake made use of the blank pages (as he tells the reader) 'For the fillinge up of emptie pages, this letter written by the Author to his friende lying at the point of death is inserted'.[1] In this way, the remaining five leaves of the sheet were used up. A most unusual 'fill up' is to be found in Robert Persons's *A Defence of the Censure, gyven upon two bookes of William Charke and Meredith Hanmer* (1582), where the 'corrector of the prynt' wrote:

To the ende this page shoulde not goe emptye, I have presusemed [*sic*] (without the Authours knowlege) to put downe for yonge scholers the true declynynge of a Nowne Heretike: whereof we have more experience in these dayes than olde Grammarians hadde.

He declines it as follows:

The singuler number,

An Heretike
{
In the Nominative or first case (to begin withall) he is *Prowde*.
In the Genetive case he growethe *Malepert*.
In the Datyve case he becometh a *Lyar*
In the Accusative case he waxethe *Obstinate*.
In the Vocative or preaching case he is *Seditious*.
In the Ablative or endinge case hee proveeth *an Atheist* or els *a Lybertine*.
}

The plurall number,

In bothe genders, *Impudent*, throughowte all cases.[2]

[1] *STC* 12606, sig. H3. Cf. *STC* 19929, sig. K6ᵛ.
[2] *STC* 19401, sig. A4.

THE COLOPHON

Occasionally, on the contrary, the compositor found himself running out of space as he drew to the end of his sheet. To overcome this difficulty he could, as did the compositor of John Chardon's *Second Sermon* (1587), resort to a smaller type for the last 22 lines of the book, thus just squeezing it into the last page.[1]

In the earlier days of printing this would not have been acceptable, for there was always space left for the printer's device or sign, and in addition the colophon which gave the printer's name, his place of business, the year and often the date on which the work was completed. During Elizabeth's reign, however, the colophon was slowly going out of fashion; the information which it once gave going on to the title-page. Not that it ever went out of use entirely. The second edition of Holinshed's *Chronicle* (1587) bears the following colophon on the last printed leaves of volumes 2 and 3 of that great work. 'Finished in Januarie 1587, and the 29 of the Queenes Maiesties reigne, with the full continuation of the former yeares, at the expenses of John Harison, George Bishop, Rafe Newberie, Henrie Denham, and Thomas Woodcocke.' Below this is a large printer's device of H. Denham and then the following: 'At London. Printed in Aldersgate Street at the Signe of the Starre. Cum Privilegio.'[2]

Before the printer began to take off the first sheet of any book, however, an all-important decision had to be made. How many copies should he print? Even nowadays, with all the numerous ways of estimating possible sales the publisher has to admit that his printing order is something of a guess. Indeed, if it were only reasonably accurate, publishers would be more prosperous than they find themselves today. Deprived of anything except such flair and knowledge of the market as experience had given to him, the Elizabethan publisher was even more at sea, and I suspect some rule of thumb reckoning, or custom of the trade, or the like, governed his decision.

Unfortunately, firm figures are hard to come by. Our first

[1] *STC* 5003, sig. D8ᵛ. [2] *STC* 13569.

clear information comes from 'A Copie of certen orders concerning printing', made by the Stationers' Company in 1587. It was then ordered that

> no booke to be printed in numbers exceeding 1250 or 1500 in one impression except nonpareille and brevier [i.e. Bibles, etc.] and four impressions a year of the Grammar and four of the Accidence, severally in quarto and octavo, and also all Prymers and Catechisms, and that every one of these and of all books in non-pareille and brevier do not exceed 2500 or 3000 copies at the most, except statutes and proclamations.[1]

It is unlikely, as Dr R. B. McKerrow observes, that these figures bore no relation to current printing practice, and 'we may suppose the existence of some equivalent custom by that date or there would have been traces of dissent or discussion'.[2]

From the very few figures that have survived it would appear that 1250 was a normal number. Two editions of 1500 each are both accompanied with a note of restrictions which makes it look as if there is something unusual about the number.[3] On the other hand, when small editions were printed, they generally had something special about them which limited their numbers. 'Fourtie copies, or thereabouts were printed' of Richard Cosin's *An Apologie for sundrie proceedings* (1593), 'without any purpose of further publishing', since it was 'somewhat long, and had many quotations, so that it coulde not conveniently in any short time be written out truely and faire, for so many as seemed earnestly to request it. Hereupon it was then...committed to the presse, and fourtie copies, or thereabouts were printed.'[4] This was evidently an underestimate, for the book was twice reprinted. Another small edition is recorded by John Dee, whose *General and rare Memorials pertayning to the Perfect Arte of Navigation* (1577) was limited to one hundred copies 'by the warning of my Instructor'.[5] A further small edition

---

[1] Arber, *Transcript*, vol. II, p. 43. And see vol. II, p. 883, and vol. V, p. liii.
[2] McKerrow, *An Introduction to Bibliography*, p. 214 n.
[3] See Arber, *op. cit.* vol. II, pp. 307 and 401.
[4] *STC* 5821, sig. B1.   [5] *STC* 6459, sig. K4.

was printed of R. Bristow's *A Briefe Treatise of diverse plaine and sure wayes to finde out the truthe* (1574). This was printed at Antwerp, and we are told that it was hard to come by, 'partly because there were but few printed, partly because a great parte of those few fell into Heretickes handes', and from other sources we know that the number seized was 367.[1]

One last question remained to be asked before the book was displayed for sale: what price should be asked for it? This question has been so carefully considered by Professor F. R. Johnson that most of what follows comes from his article 'Notes on English Retail Book-Prices, 1550–1640'.[2] He draws attention to the primary document concerning the basis for settling the prices of Elizabethan Books which was issued by the Stationers' Company on 19 January 1598 in 'an ordinance against the excessive price of books' which reads as follows (spelling and punctuation modernized):

Forasmuch as divers abuses have been of late committed by sundry persons in enhauncing the prices of books and selling the same at too high and excessive rates and prices, for remedy thereof it is this day ordered as followeth, viz:

That all books being new copies which hereafter shall be printed, without pictures, in the pica (the Roman, the Italica) and the English letter (and the Roman and Italica to the same), and the brevier and long primer letters shall not be sold above these rates following:

Those of the pica (Roman, Italica) the English (and the Roman and Italica to the same), to be sold not above a penny for two sheets.

Those of the brevier and the long primer letters not to be sold for above a penny for one sheet and a half.[3]

Professor Johnson adds:

This order gives us definite knowledge of the price at which the Stationers' Company considered it economically feasible in 1598 to issue new books and ensure an adequate profit to the publisher. No maximum price is set for reprints, or for books which, because

---

[1] I owe this information to Southern, *Elizabethan Recusant Prose*, p. 390.
[2] *The Library*, Fifth Series, vol. v (1950), pp. 83–112.
[3] Greg and Boswell, *Records of the Court of the Stationers' Company*, p. 58.

of special illustrations or technical subject-matter, would be regarded as justifying a higher price than the average book. For the usual new book, then, the maximum was one halfpenny per sheet for those composed in pica or larger type, and two thirds of a penny for those in long primer or smaller type.[1]

From an analysis of the prices of several hundreds of books Professor Johnson concludes that there was very little change of price throughout the period, and shows that certain kinds of books such as small pamphlets, or volumes of poetry, or law books with their restricted market and difficulty of setting demanded a higher price than other kinds of books.

It was customary for a book to be sold unbound in quires, but the booksellers were often binders as well, and in any case the binders were readily at hand in the Churchyard or near by. A few pence were all it cost to bind a medium-sized octavo, while a folio such as the First Folio of Shakespeare probably did not cost more than four shillings.

When all the above problems and processes had been carried out, the book was at last ready to be put in the forefront of the bookseller's stall, where to the accompaniment of the apprentice's cry 'Buy a new Book Sir', the book-lover would find awaiting him a work such as the following with its appealing title-page:

The Lamentable and True Tragedie of M. Arden of Feversham in Kent. Who was most wickedlye murdered, by the meanes of his disloyall and wanton wyfe, who for the love she bare to one Mosbie, hyred two desperat ruffins Blackwill and Shakbag, to kill him. Wherin is shewed the great mallice and discimulation of a wicked woman, the unsatiable desire of filthie lust and the shamefull end of all murderers.

---

[1] Professor Johnson's conclusions join very neatly with those which I was able to give in my 'Notes on English Retail Book-Prices, 1480–1560', *The Library*, Fifth Series, vol. v (1951), pp. 172–8. 'For works of one to three sheets only, the price was usually one penny, while for other works the normal price for a new book in pica or a larger type appears to have been about one third of a penny per sheet. The price shift caused by the debasement of the coinage by Henry VIII took time to make itself felt, and it is only after 1560 that an upward movement is clearly to be observed.'

SELECT BIBLIOGRAPHY

The place of publication is London, unless otherwise stated.

ALLDE, E., *see* MCKERROW, R. B.
ALLISON, A. F. & ROGERS, D. M. *A Catalogue of Catholic Books in English printed abroad or secretly in England 1558–1640*, 2 parts (the Arundel Press, Bognor Regis, 1956).
ALLISON, A. F. & ROGERS, D. M. 'Elizabethan Recusant Prose 1559–1582.' *The Library*, Fifth Series, vol. VI (1951), pp. 48–57.
AMES, J., *see* HERBERT, W.
ANDERS, H. 'The Elizabethan ABC with the Catechism'. *The Library*, Fourth Series, vol. XVI (1936), pp. 32–48.
ARBER, E. *A Transcript of the Registers of the Company of Stationers of London, 1554–1640.* 5 vols. (1875–94).
BALD, M. A. 'Vernacular Books imported into Scotland: 1500 to 1625.' *Scottish Historical Review*, vol. 23 (1926), pp. 254–67.
BALDWIN, T. W. *William Shakspere's Petty School* (Urbana, 1943).
BALDWIN, T. W. *William Shakspere's Small Latine & Lesse Greeke*, 2 vols. (Urbana, 1944).
BLAGDEN, C. 'The English Stock of the Stationers' Company'. *The Library*, Fifth Series, vol. X (1955), pp. 163–85.
BOSANQUET, E. F. *English Printed Almanacks and Prognostications: A Bibliographical History to the year 1600.* The Bibliographical Society (Oxford, 1917).
BOSANQUET, E. F. 'Corrigenda and Addenda.' *The Library*, Fourth Series, vol. VIII (1928), pp. 456–77.
BRITISH MUSEUM. *Catalogue of books in the library of the British Museum printed in England, Scotland, and Ireland, and of books in English printed abroad, to the year 1640.* 3 vols. (1884).
BUXTON, J. *Sir Philip Sidney and the English Renaissance* (1954).
BYROM, H. J. 'Richard Tottell—his Life and Work.' *The Library*, Fourth Series, vol. VIII (1928), pp. 199–232.
CAMDEN, C. Jr. 'Elizabethan Almanacs and Prognostications.' *The Library*, Fourth Series, vol. XII (1932), pp. 83–108, 194–207.
CAMPBELL, L. B. *The Mirror for Magistrates* (Cambridge, 1938).
CAMPBELL, L. B. *Parts added to The Mirror for Magistrates* (Cambridge, 1946).
CAMPION, E., *see* SIMPSON, R.
COLLINS, D. C. *A Handlist of News Pamphlets 1590–1610* (1943).
CONLEY, C. H. *The First English Translators of the Classics* (New Haven, 1927).
COPEMAN, W. S. C. *Doctors and Disease in Tudor Times* (1960).
COWLEY, J. D. *A Bibliography of Abridgments, Digests, Dictionaries and Indexes of English law to . . . 1880.* Selden Society (1932).

BIBLIOGRAPHY

DARLOW, T. H. & MOULE, H. F. *Historical Catalogue of the printed editions of Holy Scripture.* 4 vols. (1903-11).

DENHAM, H., *see* PLOMER, H. R.

ELIOT'S COURT. Plomer, H. R. 'The Eliot's Court Printing House, 1584-1674'. *The Library*, Fourth Series, vol. II (1922), pp. 175-84.

ELTON, G. R. *The Tudor Constitution, Documents and Commentary* (Cambridge, 1960).

ESDAILE, A. *A List of English Tales and Prose Romances printed before 1740* (1912).

FERGUSON, F. S. 'Relations between London and Edinburgh Printers and Stationers (-1640).' *The Library*, Fourth Series, vol. VIII (1928), pp. 145-98.

GASCOIGNE, G. *The Complete Works of George Gascoigne.* Edited by J. W. Cunliffe, in 'Cambridge English Classics', 2 vols. (Cambridge, 1907-10).

GOLDING, L. T. *An Elizabethan Puritan: Arthur Golding* (New York, 1937).

GREG, W. W. 'The Decrees and Ordinances of the Stationers' Company, 1576-1602.' *The Library*, Fourth Series, vol. VIII (1928), pp. 395-425.

GREG, W. W. *A Bibliography of the English Printed Drama to the Restoration.* 4 vols. The Bibliographical Society (1939-59).

GREG, W. W. *Some Aspects and Problems of London Publishing between 1550 and 1650* (Oxford, 1956).

GREG, W. W. & BOSWELL, E. *Records of the Court of the Stationers' Company 1576 to 1602—from Register B.* The Bibliographical Society (1930).

HARRISON, G. B. 'Books and Readers, 1591-4.' *The Library*, Fourth Series, vol. VIII (1928), pp. 273-302.

HARRISON, G. B. 'Books and Readers, 1599-1603.' *The Library*, Fourth Series, vol. XIV (1934), pp. 1-33.

HERBERT, W. *Typographical Antiquities. Begun by Joseph Ames.* 3 vols. (1785-90).

HERR, A. F. *The Elizabethan Sermon: a survey and a bibliography* (Philadelphia, 1940).

HORNBEAK, K. G. *The Complete Letter Writer in English, 1568-1800.* Smith College Studies in Modern Languages, vol. XV (Northampton, Mass., 1934).

JOHNSON, F. R. *Astronomical Thought in Renaissance England* (Baltimore, 1937).

JOHNSON, F. R. 'Notes on English Retail Book-Prices, 1550-1640.' *The Library*, Fifth Series, vol. V (1950), pp. 83-112.

JORDAN, J. C. *Robert Greene* (New York, 1915).

JUDGE, C. B. *Elizabethan Book-Pirates* (Cambridge, Mass.: Harvard University Press, 1934).

KIRSCHBAUM, L. *Shakespeare and the Stationers* (Columbus, Ohio, 1955).

LAMBLEY, K. *The Teaching and Cultivation of the French Language in England during Tudor and Stuart Times* (Manchester, 1920).

LATHROP, H. B. *Translations from the Classics into English from Caxton to Chapman, 1477-1620.* University of Wisconsin Studies in Language and Literature, no. 35 (Madison, 1933).

BIBLIOGRAPHY

LEISHMAN, J. B. *The Three Parnassus Plays* (1949).
LOWERS, J. K. *Mirrors for Rebels. A Study of Polemical Literature relating to the Northern Rebellion 1569* (Berkeley, 1953).
MCKERROW, R. B. 'Edward Allde as a Typical Trade Printer.' *The Library*, Fourth Series, vol. X (1930), pp. 121–62.
MCKERROW, R. B. *An Introduction to Bibliography* (Oxford, 1927).
MERES, F. *Palladis Tamia*, ed. by D. C. Allen. University of Illinois Studies in Language and Literature, vol. XVI (Urbana, 1933).
MILLER, E. H. *The Professional Writer in Elizabethan England* (Cambridge, Mass., 1959).
MUNDAY, A., *see* ST. CLARE BYRNE, M.
NASHE, T. *The Works of Thomas Nashe*, ed. R. B. McKerrow. 5 vols. (1904–10; reprinted, 1958).
O'DELL, STERG. *A Chronological List of Prose Fiction in English...1475–1640* (Cambridge, Massachusetts Institute of Technology, 1954).
PARKS, G. B. *Richard Hakluyt and the English Voyages* (New York, American Geographical Society, 1928).
PIERCE, W. *An Historical Introduction to the Marprelate Tracts* (1908).
PIERCE, W. *The Marprelate Tracts 1588, 1589* (1911).
PIERCE, W. *John Penry: His Life, Times and Writings* (1923).
PLOMER, H. R. 'The Eliot's Court Printing House, 1584–1674.' *The Library*, Fourth Series, vol. II (1921), pp. 175–84.
PLOMER, H. R. 'Some Elizabethan Book Sales.' *The Library*, Third Series, vol. VII (1916), pp. 318–29.
PLOMER, H. R. 'Henry Denham, Printer.' *The Library*, New Series, vol. X (1909), pp. 241–50.
POLLARD, A. W. *Records of the English Bible* (Oxford 1911).
POLLARD, A. W. & REDGRAVE, G. R. et al. *A Short-title Catalogue of Books printed in England, Scotland, & Ireland and of English Books printed Abroad, 1475–1640*. The Bibliographical Society (Oxford, 1926; reprinted, 1946 and 1963).
PROUTY, C. T. *George Gascoigne, Elizabethan Courtier, Soldier, and Poet* (New York, 1942).
RAVEN, C. E. *English Naturalists from Neckam to Ray* (Cambridge, 1947).
ROBINSON, R. Richard Robinson's *Eupolemia* (1603), ed. by G. McG. Vogt. *Studies in Philology*, vol. XXI (Chicago, 1924), pp. 637 ff.
RODGER, A. 'Roger Ward's Shrewsbury Stock: an Inventory of 1585.' *The Library*, Fifth Series, vol. XIII (1958), pp. 247–68.
ROGERS, D. M., *see* ALLISON, A. F.
ROLLINS, H. E. 'An Analytical Index to the Ballad-Entries (1557–1709) in the Registers of the Company of Stationers of London.' *Studies in Philology*, vol. XXI (1924), pp. 1–324.
ROSENBERG, E. *Leicester: Patron of Letters* (New York, 1955).
ROWLANDS, S. *'Tis Merrie When Gossips Meete* (1602). Printed in the *Complete Works 1598–1628* (Hunterian Club, Glasgow, 1872–86).
ST. CLARE BYRNE, M. 'Anthony Munday and his Books.' *The Library*, Fourth Series, vol. I (1921), pp. 225–56.

BIBLIOGRAPHY

SAUNDERS, J. W. 'The Stigma of Print. A Note on the Social Bases of Tudor Poetry.' *Essays in Criticism*, vol. I (Oxford, 1951), pp. 139–64.
SAYLE, C. E. *Early English printed books in the University Library, Cambridge.* 4 vols. (Cambridge, 1900–7).
SCOTT PEARSON, A. F. *Thomas Cartwright and Elizabethan Puritanism, 1535–1603* (Cambridge, 1925).
SHAABER, M. A. *Some Forerunners of the Newspaper in England, 1476–1622* (Philadelphia, 1929).
Shakespeare's England, 2 vols. (Oxford, 1917).
SHEAVYN, PHOEBE. *The Literary Profession in the Elizabethan Age* (Manchester, 1909).
SIDNEY, SIR PHILIP. *The Complete Works of Sir Philip Sidney*, ed. A. Feuillerat. 4 vols. (Cambridge, 1912–26; reprinted, 1962).
SIMPSON, P. *Proof-reading in the Sixteenth, Seventeenth and Eighteenth Centuries* (1935).
SIMPSON, R. *Edmund Campion* (1896).
SOUTHERN, A. C. *Elizabethan Recusant Prose, 1559–1582* [1950].
STEELE, R. *A Bibliography of Royal Proclamations of the Tudor and Stuart Sovereigns, 1485–1714.* Bibliotheca Lindesiana. 2 vols. (Oxford, 1910).
STRYPE, J. *Annals of the Reformation and Establishment of Religion*, 3 vols. (1709–28).
TAYLOR, E. G. R. *The Mathematical Practitioners of Tudor and Stuart England* (Cambridge, 1954).
TAYLOR, E. G. R. *A Regiment for the Sea*, by William Bourne, edited for the Hakluyt Society. Second Series, no. CXXI (Cambridge, 1963).
THOMAS, H. 'The Palmerin Romances.' *Transactions of the Bibliographical Society of London*, vol. XIII (1916), pp. 97–144.
THOMAS, H. *Spanish and Portuguese Romances of Chivalry* (Cambridge, 1920).
THOMSON, PATRICIA. 'The Literature of Patronage, 1580–1630.' *Essays in Criticism*, vol. II (1952), pp. 267–84.
TOTTELL, R. Byrom, H. J. 'Richard Tottell—his Life and Work.' *The Library*, Fourth Series, vol. VIII (1927), pp. 199–232.
The Tudor Translations. First Series, ed. W. E. Henley (1892–1909); Second Series, ed. C. Whibley (1924–5).
VERSTEGAN, R. *The Letters and Dispatches of Richard Verstegan (c. 1550–1640)*, ed. by A. G. Petti. Catholic Record Society, vol. 52 (1959).
WARD, R., *see* Rodger, A. 'Roger Ward's Shrewsbury Stock: an Inventory of 1585.' *The Library*, Fifth Series, vol. XIII (1958), pp. 247–68.
WHITE, H. C. *The Tudor Books of Private Devotion* (Madison, 1951).
WILLIAMS, FRANKLIN B. Jr. *Index of Dedications and Commendatory Verses in English Books before 1641.* The Bibliographical Society (1962).
WILLIAMS, FRANKLIN B. Jr. 'An Index of Dedications and Commendatory Verses.' *The Library*, Fifth Series, vol. XII (1957), pp. 11–22.
WILSON, E. C. *England's Eliza* (Cambridge, Mass., 1939).
WILSON, F. P. *The Plague in Shakespeare's London* (Oxford, 1927).

BIBLIOGRAPHY

WILSON, F. P. 'Some English Mock- Prognostications.' *The Library*, Fourth Series, vol. XIX (1938), pp. 30ff.
WILSON, F. P. *The Plague Pamphlets of Thomas Dekker* (Oxford, 1925).
WOLFF, S. L. *The Greek Romances in Elizabethan Prose Fiction* (New York, 1912).
WRIGHT, L. B. *Middle-Class Culture in Elizabethan England* (Chapel Hill, N.C., 1935).
YATES, F. A. *John Florio* (Cambridge, 1934).

INDEX

Abbot, George, Archbishop of Canterbury, 211
ABC, 72, 167-9
'A. B. Cees', 130
Abridgements, legal, 159-61
'Absey book', 167
Aelianus, Claudius, 91
Aeschylus, 90, 251
Æsop, 170, 171, 266
Agazzari, Alphonso, S.J., 76
Aggas, Edward, bookseller and translator, 102, 104, 279
Agriculture, books on, 190-3
Agrippa, Henry Cornelius, 52
Albertus Magnus, 187
Albin de Valsergues, Jean d', 78
Alessio, Piemontese (Alexis of Piedmont), 93, 181, 183, 184
Alfield, Thomas, martyr, 78
Allde, Edward, printer, 290, 291, 303
Allen, William, cardinal, 75, 113, 124, 125
Allen, Sir William, Alderman of London, 43, 44
Allison, A. F. and Rogers, D. M., *A Catalogue of Catholic Books... 1558-1640*, 75, 79, 80 n. 2, 118 n. 2, 122 n. 2, 125 n. 2, 134 n. 2
Almanacs and prognostications, 204, 205, 205 n. 2
Amadis of Fraunce, 218, 257
Amiot, Jacques, translator, 103
Anders, H., 'The Elizabethan ABC with the Catechism', 169
Antwerp, printing at, 124, 288, 299
Appian, of Alexandria, 218
Arber, E., *A Transcript of the Registers of the Company of Stationers of London*, 56, 57, 59, 60, 61-3, 65-6, 69 n. 1, 73, 77 n. 1, 98, 125, 157, 167

Arcaeus, Franciscus, surgeon, 181, 186
Arden of Feversham, 300
Aristotle, 103, 174, 175
Arithmetic, books on, 197-8
Armada, the Spanish, 231, 232, 238
Arnheim, siege of, 245
Artaxerxes, King of Persia, 35
Arthington, Henry, conspirator, 228
Ascham, Roger, 13, 14, 196
Ashley, Anthony, clerk of the Privy Council, 213, 282
Astrology, works on, 201-4
Augustine, Saint, 132
Authors
  criticism of, 6-10
  mock-modesty of, 5, 6
  patriotic motives of, 18
  professional, 34, 45-51
  'unwilling', 5, 16, 17, 19
  works printed in absence, 25
Awdeley, John, printer, 201, 247
Aylmer, John, Bishop of London, 79, 119, 127

Bacon, Anne, Lady, 114
Badius, Conrad, printer at Geneva, 141
Baker, George, surgeon, 180, 185 n. 1, 188, 289
Baker, Humphrey, mathematician, 197, 198
Baldwin, T. W., *William Shakspere's Small Latine and Lesse Greeke*, 170 nn. 1, 3, 174 n. 1, 175 n. 3
Baldwin, William, *Beware the Cat*, 10-14, 284 n. 3
Bale, John, Bishop of Ossory, 6, 126
Ballads, 86, 231 n 1, 232, 239-47, 254, 255

INDEX

Bancroft, Richard, Archbishop of Canterbury, 16, 83, 155
Banister, John, surgeon, 185
Bankside, press at, 73
Baptista, Mantuanus, *see* Spagnuoli, Baptista
Barclay, Alexander, translator, 90
Barker, Christopher, Queen's Printer, 28, 65, 67, 69–71, 159, 244, 260, 270, 271, 275
Barlemont, Noel de, schoolmaster, 179
Barnes, Joseph, printer at Oxford, 178
Barrough, Philip, medical writer, 268
Bartholomew the Englishman, 190 *see* Batman, S.
Barwick, Humphrey, 196 n. 3
Bassandyne, Thomas, bookseller of Edinburgh, 265 n. 2, 266
Batman, Stephen, translator, ix, 190
Becon, Thomas, Protestant divine, 131, 138
Bedford, Earls and Countesses of, *see* Russell
Bedingfield, Thomas, translator, *Cardanus Comforte*, 17, 19
Bell, James, translator, 129
Bellewe, Richard, legal reporter, 161
Bellot, Jacques, teacher of French, 177
Bertholdus, Andrew, physician, 181
Best, George, navigator, 278
Beza, Theodore, Calvinist reformer, 44, 88, 108, 146
Bible, 140–6
   cost of printing, 67
   numbers printed, 78, 298
   sermons and commentaries on, 145, 146
   versions: 'Bishops'', 142; Douay, 78, 143, 144; 'Genevan', 142; 'Great', 142
Billingsley, Sir Henry, translator, 287
Bishop, George, printer, 26, 65, 107, 108, 110, 111, 280, 284, 297
Bishop, John, religious writer, 5
Blagden, Cyprian, bibliographer, 66

Blagrave, John, mathematician, 42, 43
Bland, Tobias, preacher, 155
Blandie, William, translator, 38
Blenerhasset, Thomas, poet, 25
Blundeville, Thomas, writer on horsemanship, 174, 194–6
Boccaccio, Giovanni, 258 n. 2
Bollifant, Edmund, printer, 273, 274
Books
   colophon in, 297
   composition, speed of, 290–1
   controversial religious, 113–29
   copy, difficulties with, 283–90
   delay in publication, 16 n. 1
   demand for, 3–5, 268–9
   devotional, 129
   distribution of, 1, 2
   editions, errors in, 277–89; new editions, 254–6; size of, 78, 169, 269
   educational, 167–79
   errata, 282–90
   'fill-ups', 296–7
   foreign printed, *see* Antwerp, Douay, Louvain, etc.
   historical, x, xii, 214–20
   homiletic, 131–7
   importation of, 75–7
   joint-publications of, 272–5
   legal, ix, 156–66
   market for, 3, 4
   medical, ix, 179–86
   misprints, 283–90
   numbers printed, 78, 169, 269, 297–9
   output of, 3–5, 269–72
   polemical, 113–29
   'preliminaries', 291
   prices, 299, 300
   private devotion, 137
   proof-sheets, 283–6
   religious, vii–viii, 112–56
   'schismatical and seditious', 83–6
   school, 2
   title-pages, 260–1, 291–2, 297
   unauthorized, 21–6, 56–86

INDEX

Booksellers, chapter VI *passim*
provincial, 264-6
Borde, Andrew, physician, 180, 183, 184
Borough, William, navigator, 199
Bosanquet, E. F., *English Printed Almanacks and Prognostications*, 204, 205, 301
Boswell, E., *see* Greg, W. W. and Boswell, E.
Botany, 186-9, 192
Botero, Giovanni, cosmographer, 211
Bourne, William, mathematician, 199, 201 n. 1, 213, 279, 280
Bracton, Henry de, judge, 166
Bradford, John, martyr, 132, 133, 138, 151, 269
Bredwell, Dr Stephen, 189
Brende, John, translator, 106
Breton, Nicholas, 40
  Arbour of Amorous Devices, 24, 258
  Bowre of Delights, 24
  Pilgrimage to Paradise, 24
Brett, Richard, bookseller of York, 266
Brewen, John, goldsmith, 233
Bridges, John, Dean of Salisbury, 82, 83
Bridges, John, Vicar of Herne, translator, 33, 34 n.
Bright, Timothy, inventor of modern shorthand, 66, 153
Brinkley, Stephen, printer, 80
Brinsley, John, schoolmaster, 170
Bristow, Richard, D.D., Roman Catholic divine, 78, 124, 125, 289, 299
Britton, John, Bishop of Hereford, 166
Broadsheets, 239-47
Bromley, Sir Thomas, Lord Chancellor, 39, 110
Brook, Sir Robert, speaker, 161
Broome, William, bookseller, 273
Browne, Francis, Roman Catholic supporter, 117
Brownists, the, 128

Brucioli, Antonio, scripture commentator, 54 n. 1, 95
Bruni, Leonardo, *The Historie of Leonard Aretine*, 105
Bull, Henry, theologian, 138
Bullein, William, physician, 184
Bullinger, Heinrich, 88, 109
Bunny, Edmund, theological writer, 130, 136
Burby, Cuthbert, bookseller, 276
Burghley, Baron, *see* Cecil, Sir William
Burton, William, preacher, 152, 155
Busche, Alexander van den, 173
Butler, Thomas, LL.D., translator, 122
Buxton, John, *Sir Philip Sidney and the English Renaissance*, 41
Bynneman, Henry, printer, 64, 68, 272, 273, 278
Byrne, M. St. Clare, 'Anthony Munday and his books', 290 n. 2

Caesar, Caius Julius, 106
Caesar, Sir Julius, Judge and Master of Requests, 48
Caius, John, physician, 185
Caley, Robert, printer, 60
Calvin, John, 88, 105, 107, 109-11, 145, 146, 148, 202, 271
Cambridge, licence to print at, 58 n. 3
Camden, Carroll, 'Elizabethan Almanacs and Prognostications', 205 n. 2, 301
Camden, William, antiquary, 214
Campbell, L. B., 'Elizabethan Historical Patterns', xiv
Campion, Edmund, Jesuit martyr, 80, 115, 116, 118, 119, 244
Campion, Thomas, poet, 262
Canterbury, Archbishop of, 58
  see Abbot, George; Barcroft, Richard; Grindal, Edmund; Parker, Matthew; Whitgift, John
Carey, Henry, I Baron Hunsdon, 39
Carlile, Christopher, divine, 124
Carter, William, printer, 78-80, 134

308

INDEX

Cartwright, Thomas, puritan, 81, 155
Catechisms, 65, 146 ff., 167 ff., 265, 298
Cato, Dionysius, 169–70, 172
Cavendish, Richard, translator, 124
Cawood, John, Queen's Printer, 64, 65
Caxton, William, printer, 30, 250
Cecil, Sir Thomas, afterwards I Earl of Exeter, 42
Cecil, Sir William, Baron Burghley, 32, 36, 37, 38, 39, 67, 76, 105, 106, 110, 188, 226
Chaderton, Laurence, Master of Emmanuel College, Cambridge, 149
'Challenge Sermon', 113–15
Chard, Thomas, bookseller, 266 n. 2, 273
Chardon, John, preacher, 297
Charke, William, puritan, 116, 117, 296
Charlewood, John, printer, 61, 62, 269
Châtillon, Gaspard de, admiral of France, 236, 239
Chaucer, Geoffrey, 250, 277, 278
Chichester, Bishop of, *see* Watson, Anthony
Chronicles, 214–18
Churchyard, Thomas, poet, 9, 47, 259, 260, 263 n. 1
Chute, Anthony, translator, 102
Chytraeus, David, religious writer, 108
Cicero, Marcus Tullius, 18, 94, 99, 148, 171, 174
Clerke, William, legal writer, 166
Clifford, Christopher, writer on horsemanship, 195
Clifford, Margaret, wife of III Earl of Cumberland, 39
Clowes, William, surgeon, 185
Cogan, Thomas, physician, 184
Coke, Sir Edward, law writer, 162
Coldocke, Francis, printer, 260, 266
Cole, Henry, Dean of St Paul's, 114

Colet, Claude, *Historie of Palladine of England*, 289
Colman, Nicholas, bookseller, 240
Colophon, the, 297
Colynet, Antony, chronicler, 219 n. 1
Commines, Philippe de, chronicler, 16, 219
Conley, C. H., *The First English Translations of the Classics*, 8, 9, 15, 102, 104 n. 2
Cooper, Margaret, 243
Cooper, Thomas, Bishop of Winchester, 54, 82, 83, 85, 215
'Cooper's Chronicle', 54, 215
Cope, Anthony, translator, 90
Cope, Michel, preacher, 145
Copeman, W. S. C., *Doctors and Disease in Tudor Times*, 182 n. 2
Copland, Robert, translator, 205
Corro, Antonio de, theologian, 178
Corte, Claudio, writer on horsemanship, 195
Cortes, Martin, navigator, 280
Cosby, Arnold, murderer, 244
Cosin, Richard, ecclesiastical writer, 298
Court of High Commission (the Star Chamber), 57, 64, 168
Coventry, secret press at, 83, 84
Cox, Leonard, schoolmaster, 173
Coxe, Francis, quack doctor, 201, 202
Crane, R. S., *The Vogue of Medieval Chivalric Romance*, 250 n. 1
Crompton, Richard, lawyer, 164
Crowley, Robert, printer, 26, 125, 151, 215
Cumberland, Earls of, *see* Clifford
Cuningham, William, cosmographer, 7 n. 3, 66, 212
Curtius, Quintus, 218

Danett, Thomas, translator of Commines, P. de, 16, 219
Daniel, Samuel, 19, 20 n. 1, 41 n. 1, 220
Danter, John, printer, 281
Dariot, Claude, astrologer, 202

INDEX

Darlow, T. H. and Moule, H. R., *Historical Catalogue of the printed editions of the Holy Scripture*, 141 n. 1, 142 n. 2, 143 n. 1
Davie, Sampson, ballad writer, 231 n. 2
Day, Angel, miscellaneous writer, 176, 261, 291 n. 2
Day, John, printer, 26, 66, 72, 111, 138, 139, 167, 168, 255, 270, 275, 280
Day, Richard, printer, 167, 168
Dedications, 5, 32-48, 292-5
  sincerity of, 35, 54, 55, 294, 295
  stereotyped nature of, 35-7
  see Patron
Dee, John, mathematician, 199, 201, 262, 298
Dekker, Thomas, dramatist and pamphleteer, 258, 294, 295
Demosthenes, 15, 91
Denham, Henry, printer, 26, 270, 273, 280, 292, 297
Derby, Earl of, *see* Stanley
Dering, Edward, puritan divine, 139, 140, 147, 283
Desainliens, Claude, teacher of French, 176, 177
Devereux, Robert, II Earl of Essex, 83
Dictionaries, 64
Digby, Everard, divine, 196 n. 4
Digges, Leonard, mathematician, 199, 200, 204, 205, 263 n. 1
Digges, Thomas, mathematician, 44, 200
Dimmock, Sir Edward, the Queen's Champion, 20 n. 1
Diodorus Siculus, 103
Dodoens, Rembert, herbalist, 188, 189, 273
Dolce, Ludovico, Italian translator, 90
Dolman, John, translator, 93, 250
Dorset, Earl of, *see* Sackville, T.
Douay, Catholic college at, 113, 124
Douay, printing at, 113, 115 n. 2, 117, 125 n. 5

Douay version of the Bible, 143, 144
Dove, John, preacher, 44
Downame, John, religious writer, 44
Drake, Sir Francis, 34
Drant, Thomas, B.D., translator, 100
Drayton, Michael, *England's Heroicall Epistles*, 47
Drury, John, S.J., 119
Dubravius, Janus, bishop, writer on husbandry, 15 n. 2
Ducket, Everard, *see* Haunce
Dudley, Ambrose, Earl of Warwick, 40 n. 2, 150
Dudley, Anne, wife of Ambrose, Earl of Warwick, 40 n. 2, 153
Dudley, Robert, Earl of Leicester, 15 n. 4, 16, 34, 37-40, 42, 44, 45, 52, 106, 109, 194, 200

East, Thomas, printer, 190, 272
East Ham, secret press at, 80, 82, 115
East Molesey, Surrey, secret press at, 82, 83
Eden, Richard, translator, 213, 280
Education, books on, 167-79
Edward III, King of England, 160
Edward VI, King of England, 138, 141, 157, 167
Egerton, Sir Thomas, Viscount Brackley, Lord Chancellor, 44, 50, 54 n. 1
Eliot's Court Printing-House, 273, 274, 303
Elizabeth I, Queen of England, 35, 38, 45, 48, 49, 57, 81, 85, 109, 129, 138, 141, 157, 167, 228-30, 290
Elyot, Sir Thomas, diplomatist and author, 182, 183
Encyclopedias, 189-90
Erasmus, Desiderius, 87, 175, 265, 266
Erra Pater, 'Doctor in astronomy and physic', 205
Essex, Earl of, *see* Devereux
Estienne, Henri, 220

310

INDEX

Euclid, 287
Euripides, 251
Evans, Lewis, controversialist, 121, 131 n. 4

Family of Love, 128
Fawsley House, Northants, secret press at, 83
Feckenham, John, Abbot of Westminster, 122, 123
Felton, John, Roman Catholic martyr, 127, 128
Fenner, Dudley, puritan divine, 120, 175
Fenton, Sir Geoffrey, translator, 92
Ferrers, George, Master of the King's pastimes, 10–12, 14
Field, John, puritan divine, 40, 81, 102
Field, Richard, printer, 279
Fioravanti, Leonardo, surgeon, 186
Fitzgerald, Frances, Countess of Kildare, 35
Fitzherbert, Sir Anthony, judge, 161, 163–5, 189–92
Fitzwilliam, Sir William, Lord Deputy of Ireland, 41
Fleetwood, William, Recorder of London, 161
Fleming, Abraham, translator, 91, 131, 176
Florio, Giovanni, 20 n. 1, 94, 104, 220, 288
Flower, Francis, patent holder, 72
Fortescue, Sir John, Lord Chief Justice, 166
Fortescue, Thomas, translator, 283, 284
Foxe, John, martyrologist, 150, 272
Frampton, John, translator, 210
Frankfort Mart, 45
Fraunce, Abraham, poet and translator, 21, 40, 173, 175, 257
French grammar, books on, 176, 177
Frobisher, Martin, navigator, 209, 278

Fulke, William, puritan divine, 123, 125, 151 n. 2, 202, 284, 289
Fulwell, Ulpian, poet, 36
Fulwood, William, translator, 18, 175

Gaebelkhover, Oswald, physician, 181
Gale, Thomas, surgeon, 180, 185, 186
Galen, Claudius, 181, 185, 186
Garcie, Pierre, writer on navigation, 205
Gardiner, Samuel, divine, 18
Gascoigne, George, poet, 22, 90, 237, 283
Geneva, printing at, 141
'Genevan Bible', 141, 142
Gentillet, Innocent, controversialist, 236
Geography, books on, 205–14
Gerard, John, herbalist, 188, 189
Gerileon of England, 290
Gesner, Conrad, zoologist, 180, 181, 280
Gibbons, Richard, S.J., translator, 135
Gibson, John, Protestant religious writer, 130
Gibson, William, ballad writer, 231 n. 2
Gifford, George, divine, 43, 153
Gilbert, Sir Humphrey, navigator, 22
Glanvill, Ranulphus de, Chief Justiciar, 166
Goeurot, Jehan, physician, 181, 182, 184
Golding, Arthur, translator, 15, 26, 90, 105–11, 145
Gomara, Lopez de, chronicler, 210
Googe, Barnaby, author and translator, 8, 15 n. 3, 121, 192
Gough, John, divine, 122, 123
Gourlaw, Robert, Edinburgh bookseller, 265
Gower, John, poet, 250, 277
Grafton, Richard, printer, 205, 216, 217, 285

INDEX

Grammar Schools, 168–75, 248
Grantham, Henry, translator, 178
Grassi, Giacomo di, writer on fencing, 196 n. 4
Gratarolus, William, physician, 18, 98 n. 2
Gray, Dionis, mathematician, 198 n. 2
Greek, translations from, 13–14, 90–2, 97, 103
'Greek Alphabets', 284 n. 3
Greene, Robert, pamphleteer and poet, 46, 47, 258 n. 2, 287
Greenstreet House Press, 80, 82, 115, 117, 289
Greenwey, Richard, translator, 90
Greg, Sir Walter W., bibliographer, 59, 64, 68, 222
  A Bibliography of the English Printed Drama to the Restoration, 255 n. 2, 256 n. 1
  London Publishing between 1550 and 1650, 60, 222, 223
Greg, Sir Walter W. and Boswell, E., *Records of the Court of the Stationers' Company, 1576 to 1602*, 58, 59, 68, 73
Griffith, William, bookseller, 255, 256 n. 1
Grindal, Edmund, Archbishop of Canterbury, 39, 110
Grisone, Federico, writer on horsemanship, 194
Guazzo, Stefano, writer on conduct, 95
Guevara, Antonio de, 17, 53, 220
Guide-books, 211, 214
Guido de Chauliac, surgeon, 181, 185, 186
Guillemeau, Jacques, surgeon, 186
Gylby, Goddred, translator, 148

Hacket, Margaret, witch, 243
Hacket, William, fanatic, 228, 232, 233
Hake, Edward, satirist, 26, 296
Hakluyt, Richard, geographer, 28, 52, 206–8, 211 n. 1, 273, 280

Hall, Arthur, translator and politician, 12–14, 42, 103
  Ten bookes of Homers Iliades, 12–14
Hall, Roland, printer, 280
Halle, Edward, chronicler, 216
Halle, John, medical writer, 186
Hanmer, Meredith, historian, 116, 117, 296
Harding, Thomas, divine, 89, 114, 115, 288
Harmar, John, translator, 42, 44
Harrison, John, bookseller, 297
Harrison, Lucas, bookseller, 26, 107, 108, 111, 280
Harrison, William, topographer, 248
Hartwell, Abraham, translator, 98
Harvey, Gabriel, 9, 284
Harvey, Richard, astrologer, 202–4
Hastings, Henry, III Earl of Huntingdon, 40
Hatfield, Arnold, printer, 273
Hatton, Sir Christopher, Lord Chancellor, 16, 37, 50, 279
Haunce, Everard, 'Popish traitor', 227, 228, 244
Hawking, books on, 28
Hayward, Sir John, historian, 220
Heliodorus, *An Æthiopian History*, 53 n. 3, 218
Hellows, Edward, translator, 17, 18, 220
Hemmingsen, Niel, 26, 88, 107
Henry IV, King of England, Year Books of, 161
Henry VIII, King of England, 138, 160, 161
Henry III, King of France, 234
Henry IV, King of France, 234, 236, 246, 247
Herbals, 187–9
Herbert, Henry, II Earl of Pembroke, 175
Herbert, Mary, wife of II Earl of Pembroke, 40

312

INDEX

Herbert, William, bibliographer, *Typographical Antiquities*, 64 n. 1, 66 n. 3, 157 n. 1, 201 n. 4, 214 n. 5, 269 n. 1, 289 n. 5
Heresbach, Conrad, 192, 193
Hermanni, Phillip, physician, 181
Herodotus, 90, 97
Herr, A. F., *The Elizabethan Sermon*, 149 n. 1
Hessen, Landgrave of, 239
Heth, Thomas, mathematician, 203
Heywood, Thomas, dramatist, 90
Hill, Robert, divine, 41
Hill, Thomas, 'Londoner', compiler and translator, 192, 193, 262
Historical literature, xi, xii, 214–20
Hoby, Thomas, translator, 15, 94
Hoccleve, Thomas, poet, 250
Hodgkins, John, printer, 84
Holdsworth, Sir William, lawyer, 160, 162, 164, 165
Holinshed, Ralph, chronicler, 217, 218, 248 n. 2, 273, 297
Holland, Henry, translator, 286
Holland, Philemon, translator, 90, 100, 103, 104
Holyband, Claude, *see* Desainliens
Homer, 12–14, 252, 265
Hopkins, Richard, translator, 89, 134, 135
Hopton, Sir Owen, Lieutenant of the Tower, 229
Horace Flaccus, Q., 100
Horn-book, 167
Hortop, Job, seaman, 208
Howard, Henry, I Earl of Northampton, 203
Howard, Lord Thomas, of Effingham, 34
Howell, Thomas, poet, 40
Howlet, William, S.J., 115, 116
Humphrey, Laurence, Professor of Divinity at Oxford, 118, 152
Hunsdon, Lord, *see* Carey
Hunting, books on, 28, 195
Huntingdon, Earl of, *see* Hastings
Husbandry, works on, 191

Hutton, John [of Cambridge?], 43

Information, books of, ix, 189–96
Injunctions of 1559, 57
'Inkhorn terms', 96, 99
Inns of Court, 15, 20, 21, 81, 102, 179, 258
Instruction, books of, ix, x, 190–6
Islip, Adam, printer, 277
Italian, books on grammar, 178
Italian, translations from, 92, 178
Ivry, battle of, 236, 246

Jackson, John, member of the Grocers' Company, 273, 274
Jackson, Thomas, Canon of Canterbury, 269
James, Thomas, translator, Fellow of New College, 54 n. 1, 95
Jewel, John, Bishop of Salisbury, 113–15
John XXI, Pope, *The Treasury of healthe*, 181, 183 n. 1
Johnson, Francis R., bibliographer, 299–300
Johnson, Robert, translator, 211
Johnson, Thomas, botanist, 189
Jones, Richard, printer, 24, 53
Jordan, John C., *Robert Greene*, 258 n. 3
Jugge, Richard, Queen's Printer, 26, 65, 280

Kepler, Jean, astronomer, 201
Kethe, William, preacher, 156
Kildare, Countess of, *see* Fitzgerald
Kingston, John, printer, 277
Kirchmeyer, Thomas, anti-catholic writer, 121
Kitchen, John, lawyer, 165
Klotz, Edith L., bibliographer, 247, 270
Knightley, Sir Richard, of Fawsley House, Northamptonshire, 83
Knollys, Sir Francis, statesman, 43

Lambard, William, historian, 164, 214

313

INDEX

Lambley, K., *Teaching...of the French Language...during Tudor and Stuart Times*, 176, 177
Laneham, Robert, 196 n. 4
Lanfranc, *Mediolanensis*, surgeon, 186
Langland, William, 250, 265, 277
Lanquet, Thomas, chronicler, 215
Lathrop, Henry B., *Translations from the Classics...1477–1620*, 89, 171, 172, 173, 251–2
Latin, teaching of, 168–72
Lavater, Ludwig, 282
Law, books on, ix, 156–66
Leland, John, antiquary, 50, 214
Lemnius, Levinus, herbalist, 181
Lentulo, Scipio, grammarian, 178
Lever, Ralph, logician, 174
Lever, Thomas, puritan divine, 133
Lewis, David, judge, 53
Leyden, printing at, 289
Lily, William, grammarian, 168, 169
Linschoten, Jan Huygen van, navigator, 27, 280
Littleton, Sir Thomas, judge, *Tenures*, 157, 162, 165
Livy, 100
Lloyd, Ludowick, poet, 6
Llwyd, Humphrey, antiquary, 214
Loarte, Gaspare, S.J., 89, 134, 137
L'Obel, Matthew de, botanist, 188
Lodge, Thomas, poet, 21, 47, 53, 135, 220
Logic and rhetoric, books on, 173–6
Louvain, printing at, 113, 288, 289
Low Countries, 234, 236, 246
  English forces in, 200, 224, 225, 245
  war in, 39, 219, 237, 239
Lucar, Cyprian, writer on ballistics, 201
Luis de Granada, O.P., 89, 134, 135
Lupton, Thomas, controversialist, 53, 120
Lydgate, John, poet, 250, 265
Lyly, John, dramatist, 85, 249, 254, 265

Lyndsay, Sir David, poet, 265
Lyon (Lion), John, fictitious printer, 115 n. 2, 289
Lyster, John, 148
Lyte, Henry, botanist and translator, 188

McKerrow, R. B., 271, 291, 298
  The Works of Thomas Nashe, 45 n. 2, 46 n. 1, 203, 284 n. 3
Malory, Thomas, romance writer, 218, 250
Manchester, secret press near, 84
Mandeville, Sir John, 'traveller', 265
Manners, Roger, V Earl of Rutland, 50
Mantuanus, Baptista, *see* Spagnuoli
Manwood, John, legal writer, 166
Marbury, Francis, translator, 101
Markham, Gervase, agricultural writer, 35, 195
Marlorat, Augustine, writer on divinity, 109, 110
'Marprelate, Martin, Gentleman', 81–6
Marprelate Press, 82–4
Marshe, Thomas, printer, 214, 215, 252, 266, 268
Martin, Gregory, biblical translator, 79, 144
Marvels, broadsheets and ballads, 239–43
Mary, Queen of England, 56, 141
Mary, Queen of Scots, 231
Mascall, Leonard, writer on agriculture, 180, 193, 195
Masterson, Thomas, mathematician, 198
Mathematics, works on, 197–200
Matthiessen, F. O., *Translation: An Elizabethan Art*, 104 n. 2
Maunsell, Andrew, bookseller, i, 147, 170, 273
Medicine, books on, ix, 92, 179–84
  foreign works on, 181
  vernacular treatises on, 180–1

314

INDEX

Men of letters, gentlemen, 292-4
 professional, 294-5
Meres, Francis, translator, 135
Mexia, Pedro, 220, 284 n. 1
Middleton, Henry, printer, 139
Mildmay, Sir Walter, Chancellor of the Exchequer, 32, 107, 110
Miller, E. H., *The Professional Writer in Elizabethan England*, 45 n. 2, 262 n. 2
Minsheu, John, lexicographer, 179
Moffett, Thomas, physician, 41
Momus, sons of, 6, 7, 10, 32, 95, 180, 292
Monardes, Nicolas, navigator, 210
Monopolies to print, 6.; 6
Monsters, 241-2
Morley, Thomas, musician, *Canzonets*, 41
Mornay, Philippe de, Calvinist reformer, 40 n. 1
Morte Darthure, 218
Morton, Thomas, of Berwick, 37
Mosse, Miles, divine, 32
Mothe, G. de la, teacher of French, 177
Mulcaster, Richard, schoolmaster, 39, 166
Munday, Anthony, translator, 102, 173, 253, 254, 257, 289, 290
Muscovy Company, 213

Nashe, Thomas, 9, 21, 46, 85, 203, 284
Nassau, William of, 239
Navarre, King of, *see* Henry IV
Navigation, books on, 212, 213
Neville, Alexander, translator, 8, 19, 20
Newbery, Ralph, Warden of the Stationers' Company and printer, 61, 65, 272, 297
New College, Oxford, 42, 54 n. 1
Newman, Humphrey, colporteur, 83, 84
News, 102, 103, 220-47, 261, 278, 279
Newton, Ninian, printer, 273, 274

Newton, Thomas, translator, *Old Age* (Cicero), 18, 19
Nichols, John, religious controversialist, 119-20, 228, 229
Nichols, Josias, religious writer, 148
Nicolls, Thomas, translator, 90
Norden, John, topographer, 140, 214
Norman, Robert, writer on the compass, 199
North, Sir Thomas, translator, 90, 103, 104, 220
Northampton, Earls of, *see* Howard
Northbrooke, John, divine, 36
Northumberland, Earl of, *see* Percy
Norton, Christopher, rebel, 127, 231
Norton, Thomas, lawyer and poet, 220, 230, 231, 255
Norton, Thomas, rebel, 127, 231
Nostradamus, Michael, 183
Nowell, Alexander, Dean of St Paul's, 147, 167
Nyndge, Alexander, 243

Ockland, Christopher, grammarian, *Anglorum Praelia*, 66
O'Dell, Sterg, bibliographer, 248
Oliffe, Richard, bookseller, 246
Ortelius, Abraham, map-maker, 22
Ortuñez de Calahorra, D., *The Mirrour of Princely deedes and Knighthood*, 62, 252, 276
Orwin, Thomas, printer, 268
Osorius, Hieronimus, Bishop of Silves, Portugal, 28, 129
Ovid, 106, 172
Oxford, Earls and Countesses of, *see* Vere
Oxford, licence to print at, 58 n. 3

Painter, William, translator, *The Palace of Pleasure*, 92
Palingenius, Marcellus, i.e. Manzolli, Pierre Ange, poet, 172
Palladine of England, 257, 289
Palmerin romances, 92, 253
Palmerin d'Oliva, 253

INDEX

Palmerin of England, 62
Pamphlets, sensational, 233, 234
Parke, Robert, translator, 210
Parker, John, murderer, 233
Parker, Matthew, Archbishop of Canterbury, 39, 114, 142
Parkinson, John, herbalist, 189
Parr, Katherine, sixth queen of Henry VIII, 138
Parry, Sir Thomas, ambassador, 43 n. 1
Parry, William, traitor, 244
Partridge, John, pamphleteer, 127
Patent-holders, 58, 64–6
Patron, chapter II *passim*
    flattery of, 35, 36
    generosity of, 44–51
    influence of, 39
    reasons for, 33, 37, 38, 41–4
    request of, 15
    rewards by, 34
    role of, 37
    vogue of, 31, 51
    see Dedications
Patronage, 5, 6, 16, chapter II *passim*
Paynell, Thomas, translator, 90
Peacham, Henry, the elder, 173
Pembroke, Earls of, *see* Herbert
Penry, John, Welsh puritan, 82
Percy, Henry, VIII Earl of Northumberland, 226
Percyvall, Richard, colonist and politician, *Bibliotheca Hispanica*, 179
Persons (Parsons), Robert, S.J., 78, 80, 115, 116, 119, 135, 136, 296
Pettie, George, translator, 92, 95, 96, 293, 294
Petty Schools, 167 ff.
Phaer, Thomas, translator, 13, 162
Phillip, William, translator, 27 n. 2
Phillips, John, puritan, 121, 122
Phillips, Roland, Vicar of Croydon, 80
Phrase-books, polyglot, 179
Pilkington, James, Bishop of Durham, 245

Plautus, 90, 252
Plays, publication of, 255, 256, 260
Pliny, 94, 103
Plomer, H. R., 'The Eliot's Court Printing-House, 1584–1674', 273, 303
Plutarch, 103, 220
Pollard, A. W., *Records of the English Bible*, 141 n. 1, 303
Ponsonby, William, bookseller, 24, 28 n. 1
Possevino, Antonio, S.J., 89
Posts, books advertised on, 256, 260
Prayer, Book of Common, 140
Predestination, 128
Printers, chapter VI *passim*
    enterprise of, 4, 276–80
    initiative of, 27, 259
    of text-books, 2
    precarious trade of, 1, 2
    rebellious, 69–73
    religious and moral motives of, 26, 27
    signs, 29, 214, 260, 292
    University, 58
    see Printing
Printing
    'Bad copy', 286–8
    Crown control of, chapter III *passim*
    foreign, 288–90
    lewd and seditious, 75
    licences for, 61–4
    monopolies, 58, 65–8
    partnerships, 273–4
    production regulated, 68
    proofs and proof-reading, 281–8
    rate of, 270
    reasons for, 29, 256–8
    secret, 82–84, 115, 117–18, 133–6
    type destroyed, 73
    unauthorized, 68–86, 115–19, 124–6, 168–9
Pritchard, Thomas, moral writer, 130
Privy Council, 57
Proclamations, 223–5

INDEX

Proctor, John, bookseller, 28, 29
Prognostications, 204, 205
Prouty, C. T., *George Gascoigne*, 237 n. 2
Purfoot, Thomas, printer, 188
Putnam, Bertha H., *Treatises...on Justices of the Peace*, 164

Queen's Printers, 64, 65, 166, 226, 228, 280
Queen's Printer, report by, 67, 68

Rabelais, François, 265
Rainolde, Richard, rhetorician, 173
Rainolds, William, Roman Catholic divine, 144
Raleigh, Sir Walter, 47, 238
Ramus, Pierre, logician, 174, 175
Rastell, John, Jesuit, 267
Rastell, William, lawyer, 160
Rastell, William, printer, 160
Read, John, surgeon, 181
Rebellion of the North (1569–70), 230, 231
Record, Robert, mathematician, 185, 197, 199
Redman, Robert, printer, 163
Religious books, vii–viii, 112–56
 Bible, 140–4
 controversial, 113–29
 catechisms, 146–8
 devotional, 129–40
 sermons, 148–56
Renwick, W. L., 25
Rheims, Bible printed at, 143
Ribaut, Jean, 210
Rich, Barnaby, author and translator, 90, 97
Rich, Robert, II Earl of Warwick, 49
Rishton, Edward, Roman Catholic divine, 125
Roberts, James, printer, 64, 268
Robinson, Richard, hack-writer, 19, 28, 43, 44, 48–51
Robinson, Robert, printer, 240, 244
Roesslin, Eucharius, 181, 182, 186

Rogers, Thomas, Protestant divine and translator, 27, 132, 155, 280
Rollins, Hyder E., *An Analytical Index to the Ballad-Entries in the S.R.*, 231 n. 1, 255 n. 1
Romances, medieval, 250
Rosenberg, Eleanor, *Leicester: Patron of Letters*, 15 n. 4, 31, 35, 38, 40 n. 1, 44 n. 1, 215 n. 4
Rouen, English books printed at, 117, 135
Rowlands, Richard, pseud. Verstegan, 77, 211
Rowlands, Samuel, miscellaneous writer, 263, 264
Russell, Bridget, wife of II Earl of Bedford, 40
Russell, Francis, II Earl of Bedford, 33, 41, 53, 56, 107
Russell, Lucy, wife of III Earl of Bedford, 39, 40
Rutland, Earls of, *see* Manners

Sabie, Francis, poetaster, 7
Sackville, Sir Thomas, I Earl of Dorset, 255
Sadler, John, translator, 15, 20 n. 1
Sallust, Caius, 90
Saluste du Bartas, W. de, 19, 55
Sandys, Edwin, Bishop of London, 81
Saunders, Nicholas, of Ewell, 220
Savile, Sir Henry, translator, 90
Saviolo, Vincentio, writer on duelling, 196 n. 4
Saxton, Christopher, topographer, 66, 214
Schilander, Cornelius, surgeon, 186
Schola Salernitana, 182
Scot, Reginald, writer on witchcraft, 41, 42, 282
Scot, Sir Thomas of Kent, 42
Scott, Robert, bookseller of Norwich, 266
Seneca, Lucius Annæus, 19–20, 90, 172

317

INDEX

Seres, William, printer, 65, 72, 107, 214, 215, 245
Sermons
  accuracy of text, 153
  augmented text, 155
  collected, 145
  controversial, 155
  delight in, 149
  mangled, 154
  number of printed, 149, 265
  reasons for printing, 149–50
  rewritten for printing, 150, 151
  taken down in longhand, 152; in shorthand, 153
  text of, 152–5
Serres, Jean de, chronicler, 219, 285
Shaaber, M. A., *Some Forerunners of the Newspaper in England, 1476–1622*, 279, 304
Shakespeare, William, 170, 256, 257, 260, 300
Sheavyn, Phoebe, *The Literary Profession in the Elizabethan Age*, 31, 51
Sherry, Richard, schoolmaster, 173 n. 2
Shorthand, 66, 153, 154
Shrewsbury, Earl of, *see* Talbot
Sidney, Sir Philip, 24, 41, 46, 52, 239, 248, 254, 257, 276
Silver, George, writer on small arms, 196 n. 4
Sims, Valentine, printer, 23
Smith, Henry, preacher, 153, 154
Smith, Sir Thomas, statesman, 166
Smythe, Sir John, military writer, 196 n. 3
Sommers, Will, jester, 4
Sophocles, 90, 251
Southampton, Henry, III Earl of, *see* Wriothesley, 39
Southern, A. C., *Elizabethan Recusant Prose*, 75 n. 1, 79 nn. 1, 3, 113 n. 1, 114, 115 n. 2, 122, 125, 134 n. 2, 144 n. 2, 299 n. 1
Spagnuoli, Baptista, poet, 172
Spanish books printed in England, 178
Spanish grammar, books on, 178, 179

Speght, Thomas, editor of Chaucer, 277, 278
Spenser, Edmund, 40
  Complaints, 24
  Faerie Queene, 24, 47
Sports, books on, 28, 195, 196
Stanford, Sir William, judge, 162
Stanley, William, VI Earl of Derby, 37, 150
Star Chamber, 57, 64, 168
Stationers' Company
  Clerk's Book, 59
  Court Book, 58, 59, 68, 73
  incorporated, 56, 59
  searchers, 72, 73, 77, 79, 82
  Wardens, 56, 62
  Wardens' Book, 59
Statutes at Large, 156, 159
Steele, R., *A Bibliography of Royal Tudor and Elizabethan Proclamations*, 224 n. 1
Stepney, William, teacher of Spanish, 178, 179
Stock lists, booksellers', 264, 265
Stocker, Thomas, translator, 41, 90
Stockwood, Thomas, translator, 102
Stonor, Dame Cecilia, 80
Stonor Park, Oxfordshire, secret press at, 117, 118
Story, John, Roman Catholic martyr, 128 n. 1
Stow, John, chronicler, 76, 215–17, 276
Strype, John, ecclesiastical historian, 81
Stubbe, Peter, sorcerer, 243
Studley, John, translator, 126
Sturtevant, Simon, 171
Surgery, books on, 185–6
Sutton, Edward, bookseller, 179
Sutton, Henry, printer, 272
Swinburne, Henry, ecclesiastical lawyer, 166
Sylvester, Joshua, translator, 19

Talbot, Gilbert, VII Earl of Shrewsbury, 19

318

INDEX

Tartaglia, Niccoló, writer on ballistics, 200
Tasso, Torquato, 21, 41, 257
Taverner, Richard, translator, 169
Taylor, E. G. R., *Mathematical Practitioners of Tudor and Stuart England*, 43 n. 1, 200 n. 1, 213 n. 2, 304
Terence, Publius, 90, 171, 171 n. 2, 252
Theloall, Simon, barrister, 162
Thomas à Kempis, 87, 132, 282
Thomas, William, Italian scholar, 177, 178
Thorius, John, translator, 178
Throckmorton, Francis, conspirator, 226, 227
Thucydides, 90, 103
Thynne, Francis, editor of Chaucer, 277, 278
Title-pages, 260, 261, 291, 292
Tofte, Robert, poetaster, 23, 24
Tomson, Laurence, translator, 122
Topcliffe, Richard, informer, 79
Tottell, Richard, printer, 64, 65, 67, 157–9, 162–3, 166, 216, 260, 275, 290
Traheron, Bartholomew, Protestant writer, 185
Traitors, trials of, 127, 128, 226, 227, 227 n. 1, 228, 232
Translators and translations, chapter IV *passim*
 art of, 99–101
 competence, 95
 encouraged, 15
 enemies, 93–8
 from Greek, 90, 103, 172, 252
 from Latin, 90, 103, 172, 251
 medical 92–3, 108
 moral value, 91, 97
 numbers of, x, 103, 104
 reasons for, 12, 13, 18, 19
 religious, 39
Travels and voyages, 27, 205–14
Treasure of Pore men, The, 182
Trevisa, John, translator, 190

Trogus, Pompeius, historian, 91, 92 n. 3, 105
Turberville, George, translator, 28, 172, 195
Turler, Jerome, traveller, 211
Turner, William, herbalist, 181, 187
Tusser, Thomas, agricultural writer, 191
Twyne, Thomas, translator, 52
Tyler, Margaret, translator, 252, 253
Tymme, Thomas, translator, 53, 139, 285
Tyrell, Anthony, preacher, 153, 154

Udall, John, puritan, 82
Udall, Nicholas, dramatist, 171
Underdown, Thomas, translator, 15, 53 n. 3, 268

Vasseus, Joannes, physician, 181
Vaughan, Edward, religious writer, 130
Vautrollier, Thomas, printer, 66 n. 1
Vegetius Renatus, Flavius, military writer, 20 n. 1
Vere, Anne, wife of Edward, XVII Earl of Oxford, 180
Vere, Edward de, XVII Earl of Oxford, 17, 39, 41, 53 n. 3, 105, 106, 108
Vermigli, Pietro Martire, Protestant theologian, 88, 272
Verstegan, Richard, *see* Rowlands, R.
Vesalius, Andreas, anatomist, 186
Vigo, Joannes de, physician, 181, 183, 185, 186
Viret, Pierre, 88
Virgil Maro, Publius, 13, 172, 252, 293
Vogt, G. McG., 'Richard Robinson's *Eupolemia*', 44 n. 1, 48–51
Voyages and expeditions, 206–14

Wagenaer, Lucas Janssen, writer on navigation, 213, 282
Waldegrave, Robert, printer, 61, 83, 254

INDEX

Walsingham, Sir Francis, statesman, 52, 206
Wandsworth, printing at, 81
Ward, Roger, printer, 71–3, 168, 264
Warde, William, translator, 93
Warrington, accident to secret press at, 84
Warwick, Earl and Countess of, *see* Dudley
Watkins, Richard, printer, 64
Watson, Anthony, Bishop of Chichester, 50, 53
Webster, Richard, printer, 25
Weever, John, antiquary, 7
West, William, lawyer, 163
Wheeler, John, secretary of Merchant Adventurers' Company, 33 n
Whetstone, George, miscellaneous writer, 220
Whibley, Charles, editor, 90, 91, 101, 104 n. 1
Whitaker, William, Regius Professor of Divinity, 118, 119
White, Edward, bookseller, 63, 244, 245
White, Helen C., *Tudor Books of Private Devotion*, 133, 137, 138, 139
Whitgift, John, Archbishop of Canterbury, 32, 39, 143, 154
Whittingham, William, translator, 141, 142
Whittinton, Robert, schoolmaster, 87
Wickham, William, Bishop of Lincoln, 143
Wight, John, bookseller, 277
Wight, Thomas, bookseller, 279
Wigston, Roger, of Wolston Priory, 84
Wilcox, Thomas, puritan divine, 81

Wilkes, Sir Thomas, patent-holder, 65
Willes, Richard, geographer, 212
Williams, Franklin B. Jr., *Index of Dedications*, 31, 304
Wilson, George, Vicar of Wratton, Norfolk, 196 n. 4
Wilson, Sir Thomas, Secretary of State, 15, 91, 99, 173, 265
Winchester, Bishop of, 75
Winchester College, 42
Windet, John, bookseller, 246
Witches, and Witchcraft, 242–4, 278
Witches, works concerning, 243 n. 4
Wither, George, poet and pamphleteer, 32
Wolfe, John, printer, 27, 63, 69–71, 102, 111, 221, 260, 270, 279, 280, 284
Wolfe, Reyner, printer, 168, 215
Wolston Priory, Warwickshire, secret press at, 84
Woodcock, Thomas, bookseller, 297
Worde, Wynkyn de, printer, 172, 190
Wright, Louis B., 27 n. 1, 192, 212, 249, 253 n. 2, 255, 258 n. 2, 262 n. 3
Wright, William, bookseller, 246, 279
Wriothesley, Henry, III Earl of Southampton, 39

Xenophon, 90, 92

Year Books, 157, 160, 161, 166
Yonge, Nicholas, musician, 23
Young, Sir John, of Bristol, 36

Zoili, the, 3, 6–10, 29, 36, 93, 95, 129, 292

For EU product safety concerns, contact us at Calle de José Abascal, 56–1°, 28003 Madrid, Spain or eugpsr@cambridge.org.

www.ingramcontent.com/pod-product-compliance
Ingram Content Group UK Ltd.
Pitfield, Milton Keynes, MK11 3LW, UK
UKHW010851060825
461487UK00012B/1053